PRICES, INCOME, AND PUBLIC POLICY

The ABC's of Economics

Prices, Income, and Public Policy
THE ABC'S OF ECONOMICS

CLARK LEE ALLEN

Professor of Economics

JAMES M. BUCHANAN

Professor of Economics

MARSHALL R. COLBERG

Professor of Economics

Florida State University

McGRAW-HILL BOOK COMPANY, INC.

New York   Toronto   London

1954

PRICES, INCOME, AND PUBLIC POLICY

Library of Congress Catalog Card Number 53-12863

C

THE MAPLE PRESS COMPANY, YORK, PA.

PREFACE

"A specter is haunting teachers of economics, the specter of bad teaching." With these words the American Economic Association's Committee on the Undergraduate Teaching of Economics and Training of Economists began its report, submitted in 1950. The committee summarized the fault with the elementary course in a single word, "indecision," and its major recommendation in four words, "make up your mind." Among its specific recommendations were those to the effect that the number of objectives and the content of the elementary course should be reduced and that the student should be given more training in the use of analytical tools.

We are in essential agreement with the committee's conclusions and recommendations, and it is hoped that this book will represent a step in the proper direction. We have eliminated much of the descriptive detail that looms so large in most textbooks. Our decision has been to concentrate on analysis and on its application to problems of public policy. The mass of descriptive and institutional material which has been omitted will appear to some instructors as the most important and interesting aspect of the subject. This book is not for them. But we do hope that those who are interested in teaching students the use of analytical tools in application to real-world situations will find this volume useful.

One point which seems to be frequently overlooked in discussions of the proper content of the elementary course is that the wholehearted interest and enthusiasm of the instructor is the first requisite for enlisting the interest and enthusiasm of the students. Economic principles can be made vital to the student only if his instructor is vitally interested in analytical economics. If the interests of the staff teaching the elementary course run to historical and institutional materials, this is probably conclusive evidence that a course embodying such material should be offered. Economists who feel that the most fruitful approach to problems of policy lies in analysis but who assume that they must teach descriptive realism to sophomores are forever doomed to frustration. We feel that economics can be made meaningful to beginning students, and, to quote the committee again, "the most abstract principle can be given the breath of life by careful selection of illustrative material and skillful class presentation."

Part A, which comprises almost one-half of the book, is devoted to the principles of price formation in competitive and monopolistic markets. The efficiency of the price system in allocating resources is the central theme developed. The competitive solution is presented as an ideal, and departures from this solution are shown to lead to an inefficient utilization of the nation's available resources. The emphasis is placed upon the formation of price in output and input markets rather than upon the behavior of firms and individuals.

Part B is concerned with the economy as a whole, and the forces which generate fluctuations in the level of economic activity are analyzed. The theory of national income is first discussed, and this is followed by a consideration of the theory of money and the price level.

Part C is devoted to the application of the analytical tools developed in Parts A and B to selected important questions of political economy. Some of these problems are, of course, highly controversial. With Lord Acton, however, we do not consider it "judicious to refrain from judging" or that objectivity and impartiality are necessarily synonomous. Hence certain value judgments are made and conclusions reached. While some may not agree with these conclusions, their quarrel will be, it is hoped, not with the analysis but rather with the underlying ethical presuppositions.

Mastery of the subject matter included in this book is, we believe, a big order for the full-year course. For this reason, we have concentrated on the essentials of analysis and have deliberately kept the wordage of the book down to a minimum. It is hoped that the reduced size of the book will make for more thorough instruction. It should also allow the instructor to utilize supplementary materials of his own choosing which could not be employed effectively with a more encyclopedic volume. One of the excellent books of problems in price theory now available should provide an appropriate supplement to Part A. Any of the several excellent books of readings which have appeared in recent years may be useful as a companion piece to Parts B and C. If supplementary materials are not used, selected portions of this book should prove useful as a one-semester text. For those departments which offer a beginning course of the institutional-survey type, this book may serve the needs of a second, analytically oriented course.

We have not omitted topics simply because they require mental effort on the part of the student. We have, however, attempted to make the book a consistent whole with the various parts closely integrated, rather than a bundle of loose ends. We have also made extensive use of concrete illustrations, drawn whenever possible from the real world, in order to make principles more understandable. In each case, we have tried to make the illustrations relate as closely to the student's everyday experience as is practicable. The book will tax the abilities of the beginning student— just as learning the ABC's taxed his abilities when he was first confronted with the alphabet in elementary school.

As the book is organized, it is suited to a two-semester course beginning with Price Theory. For a two-semester course beginning with the National Income material, the following outline may be helpful: Chapters 1 and 2, followed by Chapters 17–27. Then, Chapters 3–16, and Chapters 28–34. A one-term course may begin with either price analysis or with the national income approach.

We are indebted to many people who have lent a helping hand. We are especially grateful to our students who studied the manuscript in mimeographed form and to our colleagues, particularly Mr. Jerome W. Milliman and Miss Sadie G. Young, who pointed out weaknesses without hinting that the book was anything less than a *magnum opus*. Dr. William R. Allen of the University of California at Los Angeles read Part A, and Mr. Tilford C. Gaines of the Federal Reserve Bank of New York read Parts B and C. Their incisive comments have improved the book immeasurably. Like other critics, they lacked the veto power and cannot be held accountable for what now appears. Miss Dorothy Peddie, Mrs. Gennelle Jordan, and Miss Mary Jane Martin typed the manuscript with never a complaint beyond the suggestion that this was going to be a revised edition before it came out the first time.

C. L. ALLEN
J. M. BUCHANAN
M. R. COLBERG

CONTENTS

PART A

PRICES DIRECT OUR ECONOMIC BEHAVIOR

CHAPTER 1

CONSUMERS ARE SOVEREIGN: THE ORGANIZING PRINCIPLE

An old German fable describes a beautiful world where wants are satisfied with a minimum of effort. Some of the rivers in this fabulous land are filled with the best old wine, and others flow with fresh milk. Along the streams grow trees that bear fresh rolls daily. The fish swim on top of the water near the land; they are roasted and ready to eat, and, when called, they jump promptly into one's hands or mouth. Chickens, ducks, and turkeys sit in the trees. They, too, are ready to eat and at the slightest beckon fly slowly into one's mouth. The roasted pigs which roam the forests come equipped with knives and forks on their backs. Cheeses hang in the trees in such profusion that all the people in the world could never eat them all. The stones and the snow are sugar, and the rain is honey. One has but to shake a tree, and silver and gold, diamonds and pearls, and beautiful dresses and shoes come tumbling down. If one bathes in the water, he is cured of all sickness, and old people are made young again. A gold piece is paid for every hour that one sleeps, and the one who is the most stupid and who can sleep the longest and eat the most is made king of the country.

The stories of the Garden of Eden, Aladdin and his wonderful lamp, the travels of Marco Polo, the Big Rock-Candy Mountain, and Li'l Abner's Shmoo all recount places and circumstances where wants are satisfied with virtually no effort. Contemplation of a world where one's every desire is promptly and effortlessly satisfied is a fit subject for reverie while one is stretched out on the beach on a warm summer afternoon, and perhaps we shall be able to enjoy such a listless and useless existence when we all get to heaven. But life in the Western world in the twentieth century is not like that. All of us are confronted with the stark fact that our wants exceed our means to satisfy them. There just are not enough goods and services to satisfy all our wants. The first and fundamental economic fact that we must face is the reality of *scarcity*. We cannot satisfy all of our wants. Some may, at least temporarily, be fully satisfied, but others can be only partially satisfied, and some cannot be satisfied at all.

If the scarcity of economic goods necessitates less than the complete satisfaction of all wants, some kind of allocation of our limited resources is required. If all of our wants cannot be satisfied, some mechanism must be employed to determine which are to be satisfied first, and in what measure. A problem of choice is ever present. That is to say, we must *economize;* this is the essence of economics.

But if the economy is to satisfy our highest-ranking wants, somehow those goods which we want and are willing to pay for must be produced. Out of the hundreds of thousands of goods which our resources—men, machines, and materials—could be used to produce, it is important that the particular commodities which will satisfy those wants to which we have given top priority be produced in adequate quantities. It would be uneconomic to produce too many books at the expense of producing too few paper dolls. The question is: What determines which and how much of the countless products that might be produced actually will be produced? Which of the many combinations of factors of production which might be employed in the production of a given product actually will be so employed? Who is to receive the products which are produced? These are the central problems of economics.

The determination of what is to be produced and how it is to be produced is a problem of almost infinite complexity. Consider briefly a much simpler problem, the operation of a production assembly line in a modern automobile factory. Here there is no question as to what is to be produced, but the purely technological problem of how the thousands of parts are to be assembled into a smooth-working, long-lasting machine which will provide satisfaction to its owner is almost overwhelming. When one visits the automobile plant, he observes a maze of overhead wires which feed electric power to portable motorized tools; bodies, fenders, hoods, and motors float through the air, timed to arrive at the right spot at just the right moment; skeleton cars in various degrees of completion creep along the final assembly line, which is fed by tributary and subassembly lines; and the necessary number and kinds of parts, tools, and workers are stationed along the assembly line. One pauses in admiration for the wit of man when he realizes that the lack of even a small bolt would be sufficient cause to bring the entire complex machinery to a halt until the shortage was eliminated. Such stoppages cannot be permitted to occur.

It is clear that behind such industrial operations there must be a centralized planning agency. Detailed blueprints must have been worked out well in advance, and everything must follow a carefully considered time schedule, with each part of the organization performing its specialized function in strict coordination with the activities of all other parts. Our ability to devise and execute such plans has made possible the minute division of labor which characterizes contemporary large-scale production and which has contributed to the constantly improving standard of living that our people enjoy today.

But, it should be noted, no matter how carefully and accurately the executives, engineers, and economists of the automobile industry plan their operations, they are dependent upon their suppliers—perhaps several thousands of them—for raw materials, parts, and tools. The production of the steel which the automobile industry uses, for example, represents a scarcely less complex industrial process than the fabrication of the automobiles themselves. This means more careful planning, and not only must the several processes in steel production be coordinated with each other, but, in addition, the plans of the steel industry must intermesh with those of the automobile industry—and all other industries for which steel is a raw material. The resources of the economy must furthermore be marshaled in such a way that food, clothing, shelter, and countless other goods and services will be produced for the workers in the steel, automobile, and other industries. These resources must be used to produce goods of the appropriate kind and in sufficient amount; if we produce more lamb-chop frills than we can use and less penicillin than we need, we are guilty of waste. And if, as has frequently happened in the past, we do not use some of our resources at all, our economic sin is compounded. This is under any circumstances undesirable, and in time of national emergency it may be critical.

What, then, is the organizing principle by which a private-enterprise economy determines what is to be produced and in what amounts? How does a capitalistic society determine with which resources and in what combinations a given commodity is to be produced? And, since some wants cannot be satisfied, what determines in our economy whose wants will be left unsatisfied or only partially satisfied?

The answers to these questions indicate the prime economic difference between a private-enterprise economy such as ours and a totalitarian economy such as that of Soviet Russia. The Russian communists have attempted to solve the problem of what is to be produced, how it is to be produced, and for whom it is to be produced by setting up a central planning agency with power to regiment the economy's resources in any way which it chooses in order to produce the goods which it decides need to be produced. If the central commissariat decides that heavy industrial equipment is more important in the years just ahead than increasing consumer living standards, for example, steps will be taken to allocate productive resources to those industries with the result that less is produced for immediate consumption. Everything operates on the basis of the master plan, and the wishes of the individual as consumer and producer are subservient to those of the state.

A private-enterprise system has no central commissariat or commission or bureau or brain trust set up to tell each worker what job he must work at and to determine what goods are to be produced and how the national product is to be divided among consumers. What prevents our producing more automobiles than we are able to produce tires and gasoline for if there is no over-all production plan? There clearly must be some organizing force to prevent complete confusion and chaos, but if there is no deliberative body with power to allocate resources among various competing uses, what is the organizing principle in a private-enterprise economy?

The answer is that a private-enterprise economy uses the impersonal forces of the market to determine the allocation of its resources. Market forces are reflected in price changes, and prices determine what is to be produced, how it is to be produced, and for whom it is to be produced. Let us contrast the workings of the Russian communistic economy with that of the American capitalistic economy when both are confronted with the same type of problem. Suppose that the Russian planners have miscalculated with the result that they have produced more wheat than they had planned but less rye. It will be necessary for them to increase the ration of white bread to consumers and to reduce the ration of dark bread. That is to say, they will encourage the consumption of what is abundant and discourage the consumption of what is in short supply. As they revise their estimates for the coming year, they will plan to increase the production of what is in short supply (rye) and decrease the output of what is relatively abundant (wheat). The function of the central planning board may be put in these terms: to encourage the consumption of what is in oversupply and to discourage the consumption of what is in undersupply; to encourage the production of what is in undersupply and to discourage the production of what is in oversupply.

Suppose, now, that in the United States the wheat crop is larger than had been anticipated, whereas the rye crop is below expectations. The oversupply of wheat would be reflected in the market by a decline in the price of wheat. This would have two effects: (1) The consumption of wheat, because of its low price, would be increased. (2) The production of wheat, because of lower profits to producers, would be decreased. The undersupply of rye would cause rye prices to rise and would have the opposite effects: (1) The consumption of rye would be decreased. (2) The production of rye would be increased. The function of prices in a capitalistic economy is identical with the function of the planning commissariat in a communistic economy[1] and may be put in these terms: to encourage

---

[1] Even the Russians have found it necessary to make use of prices in rationing goods to consumers.

the consumption of what is in oversupply and to discourage the consumption of what is in undersupply; to encourage the production of what is in undersupply and to discourage the production of what is in oversupply.

The important role of profits in the allocation of resources in a private-enterprise economy should be noted. The price of a commodity in undersupply tends to increase. An increase in price increases the spread between the producing firms' revenues and costs. This added profit serves as a magnet, drawing other resources into this line of production. In this way the relative undersupply of a good tends automatically to be corrected. Conversely, if a product is in oversupply, the fall in its price reduces profits and may cause losses. These losses will drive resources away from the production of the good in oversupply. Because of the central importance of profits and losses in guiding firms into and out of various lines of production, the free-enterprise system has sometimes been described as the "profit system," although the term "profit-and-loss system" would be better.

If profits and losses were not present to direct firms into different lines of economic activity, some central directing body would be required. But as long as the price mechanism is free to operate and to utilize the profit-and-loss guide, a private-enterprise economy is able automatically to channel its available resources into those areas of production which are indicated to be desirable by the consuming public. The determination of which goods and services are to be produced is really made in the final analysis by the consumer himself. Every dollar spent for a good constitutes a vote for the production of that commodity, and the number of votes cast determines what will be produced. These dollar votes set up the consumer ranking of wants. The wants which will be satisfied are those which are most intense in a pecuniary sense, and they may be different from the most intense physical wants of the people. But the important thing is that the fundamental decisions which run the economy are made by millions of individual consumers shopping in the nation's market places. This has been referred to as the "principle of consumer sovereignty," and it is the organizing principle which in a private-enterprise economy renders a governmental planning agency unnecessary.

CHAPTER 2

EVERYTHING DEPENDS ON EVERYTHING ELSE: THE INPUT-OUTPUT TABLE

A general impression should have been gained from Chapter 1 of the role which market prices play in a private-enterprise economy and the complexity of privately determined economic relations geared to meeting the wants of his majesty, the consumer. It is useful at this point to gain a somewhat more detailed understanding of these matters.

It may be helpful to think of a private-enterprise system as a great web of economic interrelationships. Each filament hangs from at least two points. The worker depends on the employer for a job and income, but the latter depends on him for productive services. The household depends on the retailer as its source of food, but the store owner depends equally on the householder's purchases for his own income. The city depends on the country as its source of agricultural products, but the farmer relies equally on the city for his tractors, clothing, and processed foods. And the student depends on the teacher as a purveyor of knowledge, but the teacher cannot ply his chosen profession without students.

The whole complex web of private enterprise hangs together well despite the absence of central planning. In *The Wealth of Nations*, the first of the "great books" in economics, Adam Smith, writing about the time of the American Revolution, observed that each individual follows his own self-interest, mindless of the good of society; however, in so doing he also promotes the social welfare by placing his labor and property in those slots where they will be most productive.[1]

ALLOCATION OF RESOURCES BY THE PRICE SYSTEM

More specifically, how are resources allocated through the market mechanism? Consider a stretch of unused oceanside land along Miami Beach, Florida. Zoning regulations would not permit the erection of a

---

[1] Adam Smith, *The Wealth of Nations* (New York: Modern Library, Inc., 1937), p. 423.

paper mill on the beach, but—more important for the present discussion—
neither would the laws of economics. The owner of the land will readily
see that his opportunity for a maximum rental income (or selling price)
lies in awaiting an attractive offer from someone who wishes to erect a
hotel on the site. The hotel builder will be able to outbid all other potential
users of the property because the land will be productive of more income
to him than to the owner of any other sort of enterprise. It is important
to see also that this is as it should be from a social point of view. The
land will be put to the use in which it can contribute most to consumer
satisfaction. Some may object that only the wealthy consumer will derive
any satisfaction from this use of the land. Their quarrel is with the distribution of income and wealth among the American people, however,
and not with the efficiency of the market mechanism in allocating the
land to its most productive use.

To illustrate the principle of allocation further, consider the case of a
corporation president who has "come up through the ranks." He may be
a better bookkeeper than his best accountant, a better shipping clerk than
anyone in his company, and a better engineer than he can hire. Yet his
most productive activity—the one which will add most to the corporation's (and his own) income—is the making of top-level decisions. He will
refrain from spending his time on the accounts, on the shipping platform,
and on the engineering drawings, delegating these responsibilities completely to others.

Similarly, regions find it advantageous to specialize in production which
brings the maximum income, neglecting other opportunities which they
might exploit quite efficiently. For example, sugar beets could be grown
more efficiently in a technical sense in the corn belt than in Michigan or
Colorado; yet they are not grown in large quantities in such states as
Iowa and Illinois. The reason is that although sugar-beet output per acre
would be greater in Illinois than in Colorado, Illinois finds corn production more profitable (a "sweeter" business). In this case Michigan and
Colorado may be said to have a "comparative advantage" in the production of sugar beets, while Illinois and Iowa have a comparative advantage in corn. The bookkeeper, clerk, and engineer similarly can keep
their jobs because they have a comparative advantage in these pursuits
over their capable boss, because of his inability to do their work and at
the same time tend to his executive duties.

To generalize, specialization by an economic unit, whether it is as small
as the individual worker or a plot of land or as large as an entire nation,
is based on the desires of owners of resources to earn the largest possible
incomes. This means that each unit of each resource must be devoted to
the employment which that unit can *most efficiently* perform, in view of
product and resource prices, since such action will bring in maximum

personal income. Since resources are thus attracted to their most productive uses, the real income of society as a whole tends to be maximized.

It is important that the beginning student grasp the essential nature of the allocative process as it works in a private-enterprise economy; it is equally important, however, to avoid coming away with a wholly unsophisticated faith in the perfection of the process as it actually operates in the world in which we live. Much space will be devoted in subsequent chapters to an examination of these deviations. For the present it is sufficient to note that in fact there is substantial monopoly power in the hands of many businessmen and labor-union leaders, that legislation affecting economic matters is always shaped in part by lobbyists and others representing interested groups (farmers, manufacturers, labor unions, bankers, physicians, etc.), and that national emergencies may require special interference by the Federal government with the normal economic processes. And, as mentioned earlier, the proper allocation of resources is a separate problem from that of the desirable distribution of income and wealth.

THE FLOW OF MONEY, GOODS, AND SERVICES

Viewed broadly, a private-enterprise system is one in which individuals sell the productive services of their labor and property to enterprises in

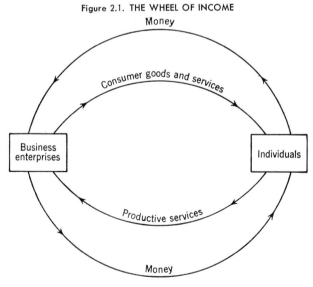

Figure 2.1. THE WHEEL OF INCOME
Money
Consumer goods and services
Business enterprises
Individuals
Productive services
Money

exchange for money income and in which enterprises sell goods to individuals in exchange for the money thus earned. This two-way traffic is continual, but its volume is, of course, greater in years of full employment and high national income than in years of depression. The circularity of the economic process can best be shown by a simple diagram.

The upper half of Figure 2.1 depicts the flow of money from individuals to business enterprises in exchange for consumer goods and services; the lower half shows the flow of money from enterprises to families in exchange for the productive services of labor and property. This figure is meant to give a general picture only. Actually many people work for Federal, state, and local governments instead of private firms. Enterprises make purchases from one another as well as from individuals, and families save a portion of the money income which they receive. The wheel may also suggest that all productive services are used to produce goods for immediate consumption, whereas actually a portion goes to producing durable items (*e.g.*, houses, factories, ships) which yield their services over a prolonged period of time.

INPUT-OUTPUT ANALYSIS: A MORE DETAILED PICTURE OF INTERDEPENDENCE

In recent years, American economists and statisticians have developed an interesting method of showing the interdependence of economic activities.[1] This type of analysis attempts to show in a somewhat detailed fashion the actual structure of the web of economic interdependence. It tries to provide meat with which the bare bones of economic principles may be enclosed. This technique is known as "interindustry" or "input-output" analysis. Both terms suggest the same basic idea, which is that the output of every industry is an input to another industry or to final consumers.[2]

An input-output table for the United States for 1947 is shown in Table 2.1. Government statisticians who compile these figures face so complex a task that several years inevitably elapse between occurrence of the transactions and publication of the data in this form. Actually, the Washington statisticians use a much more detailed classification of industries than appears in this table; fortunately, it is possible to consolidate a large table into any size which is felt to be handy. Also luckily, it is not difficult to understand the basic idea of the table, although the

---

[1] The pioneer in this field is Professor Wassily W. Leontieff of Harvard University. See *The Structure of American Economy, 1919–1939* (New York: Oxford University Press, 1951).

[2] Every baseball fan is familiar with something similar to an input-output table, namely, the league schedules which are published each spring. In order to find out when and where the home team is playing out of town one looks across the table. But if one wishes to find out when the other teams in the league are playing at the local ball park, one looks down the home-team column of the table.

meaning of some items, such as "private capital formation," cannot be easily grasped until the associated concepts have been mastered.

It will be noted that Table 2.1 contains 50 rows and 50 columns plus a column and a row for totals. The same industries are listed both horizontally and vertically, identified by the same number in each listing. All industries are both sellers and purchasers. Viewed in the vertical listing they are sellers of goods which they have produced (sellers of output). Looked at in the horizontal listing they are purchasers of materials and other input items (*e.g.*, labor) needed in their manufacturing processes.

The relation between the wheel of income of Figure 2.1 and the input-output table can be noted by observing that if the real world were as simple as that depicted by the wheel of income, all entries in the input-output table would be zero except for those in row 50 and column 50. If all inputs of firms were purchased from households, this would be reflected in row 50. And if all outputs of firms were sold to households, this would appear in column 50.

A Look across the Table

To find the yearly output of an industry, look at the column at the extreme right (labeled "total gross output") opposite the name of the industry in the vertical listing. For example, total gross output of Paper and Allied Products (row 8) was $7,899 million (about $7.9 billion) in 1947. The disposition of this output can be found by examining the figures in columns 1 through 50, opposite row 8. As would be expected, large purchases were made by the Printing and Publishing industry, the figure in row 8, column 9, being $1,081 million. Another large figure is the $2,597 million (row 8, column 8) representing intraindustry purchases—those made by organizations within this industry from other organizations within the same industrial classification. Producers of Food and Kindred Products were also large purchasers, as is shown by the $453 million entered in row 8, column 2. Unfortunately, it is necessary to show $836 million as "undistributed" (row 8, column 43), representing purchases of Paper and Allied Products by industries which cannot be given separate listings in so condensed a table.

The purchases just mentioned and the others listed in row 8, columns 1 through 45, may be thought of as "intermediate demand," since they represent purchases by producing firms from manufacturers of Paper and Allied Products; they are inputs needed in the production processes of the purchasing firms. To a smaller extent the output of Paper and Allied Products is purchased without further processing by households. It can be seen in row 8, column 50, that $344 million worth of Paper and Allied Products was bought by Households—one of the "final demand" ac-

Table 2.1. Interindustry Flow of Goods and Services by Industry of Origin and Destination, 1947
(In millions of dollars)*

PURCHASERS → (columns 46–50: FINAL DEMAND); SELLERS ↓

SELLERS	1 Agriculture & fisheries	2 Food & kindred products	3 Tobacco manufactures	4 Textile mill products	5 Apparel	6 Lumber & wood products	7 Furniture & fixtures	8 Paper & allied products	9 Printing & publishing	10 Chemicals	11 Products of petroleum & coal	12 Rubber products	13 Leather & leather products	14 Stone, clay & glass products	15 Iron & steel	16 Nonferrous metals	17 Plumbing & heating supplies	18 Fabricated structural metal products	19 Other fabricated metal products	20 Agric'l, mining & const. machinery	21 Metalworking machinery	22 Other machinery (except electric)	23 Motors & generators	24 Radios	25 Other electrical machinery	26 Motor vehicles	27 Other transportation equipment	28 Professional & scientific equipment	29 Miscellaneous manufacturing	30 Coal, gas & electric power	31 Railroad transportation	32 Ocean transportation	33 Other transportation	34 Trade	35 Communications	36 Finance & insurance	37 Rental	38 Business services	39 Personal & repair services	40 Medical, educ. & nonprofit org's.	41 Amusements	42 Scrap & miscellaneous industries	43 Undistributed	44 Eating & drinking places	45 New construction & maintenance	46 Inventory change (additions)	47 Foreign countries (exports to)	48 Government	49 Gross private capital formation	50 Households	TOTAL GROSS OUTPUT
1 AGRICULTURE & FISHERIES	10,856	15,048	783	2,079	19	192	–	9	–	1,211	–	–	49	*	–	11	–	–	–	–	–	–	–	–	–	–	–	4	4	–	5	1	8	–	2	–	–	–	–	116	–	–	250	865	92	1,008	1,276	569	21	9,785	44,263
2 FOOD & KINDRED PRODUCTS	2,378	4,910	15	60	9	*	*	30	*	685	*	–	444	2	3	*	–	–	*	–	–	*	–	–	*	–	–	5	21	1	81	6	34	71	9	–	–	–	2	251	*	9	134	3,469	2	608	1,528	728	–	22,141	37,636
3 TOBACCO MANUFACTURES	–	–	828	–	–	–	–	–	–	1	–	–	–	–	–	–	–	–	–	–	–	–	–	–	–	–	–	–	–	*	–	–	*	–	–	–	–	–	–	–	–	7	45	–	–	77	217	3	–	1,485	2,663
4 TEXTILE MILL PRODUCTS	64	2	–	1,303	3,882	3	285	43	25	13	2	444	88	33	–	–	*	*	8	2	1	18	2	9	36	147	9	47	76	8	–	8	7	27	*	–	–	*	29	4	–	15	580	–	47	61	919	101	21	1,469	9,838
5 APPAREL	44	204	–	–	1,963	–	5	20	–	30	–	–	2	3	–	–	*	–	1	*	–	2	–	*	*	100	10	2	*	*	*	*	3	15	1	–	–	–	20	16	*	12	150	21	1	214	301	193	1	9,987	13,321
6 LUMBER & WOOD PRODUCTS	148	81	18	18	2	1,094	385	267	1	45	6	–	17	17	36	28	23	5	34	15	4	67	3	10	41	46	33	5	65	60	–	5	1	28	*	–	135	1	*	1	–	17	444	5	2,330	174	170	14	36	67	6,002
7 FURNITURE & FIXTURES	–	–	–	12	–	–	7	5	–	–	–	–	–	–	–	–	*	–	–	–	–	5	–	102	1	26	20	1	–	*	–	–	*	–	*	41	78	–	–	4	–	–	199	–	198	78	35	52	569	1,459	2,892
8 PAPER & ALLIED PRODUCTS	2	453	65	78	25	5	15	2,597	1,081	331	112	20	54	179	*	*	9	5	79	2	2	39	4	17	48	33	20	75	69	4	2	–	4	568	2	1	–	2	62	26	–	145	836	57	170	44	154	59	–	344	7,899
9 PRINTING & PUBLISHING	–	39	–	2	–	–	–	–	767	16	–	–	–	–	–	–	1	–	11	2	1	5	–	1	5	–	–	2	–	*	36	4	20	98	33	213	–	2,234	27	173	13	321	585	30	–	*	72	156	89	1,491	6,447
10 CHEMICALS	830	1,451	25	800	142	26	63	183	97	2,655	213	604	126	116	99	85	21	18	88	17	5	62	10	9	178	111	22	55	167	55	32	5	20	73	3	*	–	7	198	222	2	30	1,181	42	635	305	812	186	–	1,964	14,050
11 PRODUCTS OF PETROLEUM & COAL	457	58	*	30	5	74	1	63	3	325	4,829	12	2	50	846	49	7	3	12	9	4	24	1	2	18	31	11	2	8	471	270	87	448	200	2	15	780	*	57	56	1	8	357	15	617	56	680	177	*	2,437	13,670
12 RUBBER PRODUCTS	122	9	–	13	18	9	6	9	3	1	1	41	50	8	*	*	2	2	5	75	2	53	2	2	31	496	12	5	37	1	1	–	130	63	1	7	*	–	71	4	–	5	468	4	56	94	168	21	8	709	2,825
13 LEATHER & LEATHER PRODUCTS	–	–	–	2	53	4	7	–	4	–	–	–	1,037	–	–	–	*	*	1	3	11	7	*	*	1	13	3	8	10	*	–	–	2	2	–	–	–	–	34	6	–	14	283	–	1	108	84	30	17	2,065	3,810
14 STONE, CLAY & GLASS PRODUCTS	65	253	1	1	*	14	34	28	–	258	46	7	5	430	180	33	9	6	52	7	10	57	23	7	92	192	6	26	59	17	12	1	2	37	*	–	–	–	25	6	–	3	363	59	1,741	99	205	17	15	341	4,844
15 IRON & STEEL	6	2	–	–	1	10	97	–	–	5	6	14	1	23	3,982	33	172	553	1,374	532	143	930	118	13	196	1,102	370	16	35	44	153	–	6	–	1	–	–	–	–	–	–	130	719	–	876	57	605	13	–	–	12,338
16 NONFERROUS METALS	–	–	–	–	–	2	16	–	14	189	1	*	*	13	324	2,599	94	63	272	24	23	366	40	26	654	176	62	55	170	6	45	–	2	–	*	–	–	–	–	*	–	21	524	2	315	98	167	5	–	19	6,387
17 PLUMBING & HEATING SUPPLIES	–	–	–	–	–	–	–	–	–	–	–	–	–	–	15	–	39	41	7	–	–	35	1	–	32	8	6	–	–	*	–	–	–	–	–	–	–	–	–	–	–	7	106	–	878	64	42	7	60	397	1,745
18 FABRICATED STRUCTURAL METAL PRODUCTS	–	–	–	–	–	–	5	–	–	–	–	–	–	–	7	–	19	42	18	33	1	67	*	–	9	10	31	1	–	*	7	–	1	–	–	–	–	–	–	–	–	9	248	–	1,564	15	67	4	145	13	2,316
19 OTHER FABRICATED METAL PRODUCTS	83	543	15	*	6	35	132	17	1	130	78	12	16	4	24	4	72	90	213	93	67	326	28	63	211	956	62	68	38	5	26	5	7	59	1	–	–	1	32	6	–	46	1,138	24	652	127	280	38	74	537	6,445
20 AGRIC'L, MINING & CONST. MACHINERY	59	–	–	–	–	–	–	–	–	–	–	–	–	5	15	7	–	23	–	115	20	96	–	–	–	3	14	–	–	28	3	–	*	–	–	–	–	–	57	*	–	11	261	–	116	105	566	82	1,640	66	3,292
21 METALWORKING MACHINERY	–	–	–	–	–	–	–	–	–	–	–	–	–	–	8	7	6	9	53	51	57	90	7	6	19	223	12	8	*	–	8	–	1	–	–	–	–	–	–	–	–	6	264	–	–	17	205	11	734	31	1,833
22 OTHER MACHINERY (except electric)	–	13	–	35	21	14	11	14	35	1	5	–	–	2	27	4	110	43	41	307	68	565	50	2	82	402	195	26	3	6	47	–	12	8	–	16	–	–	146	1	–	53	1,717	–	338	288	990	84	3,450	1,080	10,312
23 MOTORS & GENERATORS	–	–	–	–	–	–	–	–	–	–	–	–	–	–	–	–	34	7	1	32	29	317	17	5	52	–	51	10	–	1	5	–	4	–	–	–	–	–	3	–	–	10	257	–	3	33	85	11	128	–	1,095
24 RADIOS	–	–	–	–	–	–	–	–	–	–	–	–	–	–	–	*	1	–	13	–	–	4	8	243	95	19	15	4	–	–	–	–	–	3	1	–	–	*	23	–	–	2	74	–	–	56	113	83	296	639	1,692
25 OTHER ELECTRICAL MACHINERY	–	–	–	–	–	–	–	–	–	1	–	–	–	7	8	46	53	9	125	22	16	158	57	165	350	599	53	21	18	17	30	–	8	6	49	–	–	5	62	4	–	25	608	–	716	161	244	76	1,331	673	5,723
26 MOTOR VEHICLES	111	3	–	–	–	1	–	–	–	–	*	–	–	1	*	*	–	–	32	24	7	*	–	–	12	4,401	*	–	–	8	*	–	131	20	*	–	*	–	1,054	*	–	70	671	1	36	401	1,020	151	2,982	3,128	14,265
27 OTHER TRANSPORTATION EQUIPMENT	10	–	–	–	–	–	–	*	–	1	*	*	–	*	2	1	–	–	–	–	–	–	*	–	–	12	295	–	–	*	38	76	132	–	–	–	–	–	2	–	–	14	456	–	1	18	324	1,245	1,203	171	4,001
28 PROFESSIONAL & SCIENTIFIC EQUIPMENT	–	–	–	–	–	–	2	6	32	13	–	–	–	1	*	–	34	3	3	1	2	36	2	3	9	70	23	176	24	*	–	–	2	–	*	–	–	7	52	176	–	6	229	–	22	32	184	79	260	630	2,119
29 MISCELLANEOUS MANUFACTURING	4	11	–	4	256	1	16	15	–	29	–	*	22	9	5	*	1	1	18	*	1	45	20	30	61	22	3	26	156	2	4	5	4	10	*	–	–	149	164	46	53	112	638	21	32	43	187	85	511	1,934	4,756
30 COAL, GAS & ELECTRIC POWER	61	193	4	105	36	24	18	123	29	188	556	37	15	204	242	104	13	15	52	23	14	68	8	6	39	62	28	10	25	1,272	443	4	91	493	10	63	3,016	5	307	163	54	–	23	219	30	27	355	195	–	133	9,205
31 RAILROAD TRANSPORTATION	440	548	21	94	60	143	54	224	68	287	270	36	36	145	423	100	19	37	77	44	12	100	11	13	50	228	37	14	31	151	410	3	58	75	5	6	422	27	29	52	2	10	798	253	706	74	590	332	266	2,061	9,952
32 OCEAN TRANSPORTATION	73	126	3	13	11	9	*	16	*	44	94	*	1	14	30	52	*	*	*	*	*	*	–	*	*	1	*	2	10	*	–	218	–	–	–	–	–	–	–	–	–	5	2	–	–	–	1,340	126	–	102	2,292
33 OTHER TRANSPORTATION	553	367	16	79	25	138	40	117	25	95	470	7	21	70	140	19	6	5	17	10	3	29	3	8	19	67	13	5	14	35	195	35	253	311	3	4	125	29	14	190	2	6	1,102	97	572	38	314	186	103	3,860	9,855
34 TRADE	1,360	418	38	228	369	60	60	176	31	173	19	55	57	52	216	140	36	54	110	51	22	183	18	34	83	56	74	39	48	40	30	6	423	202	7	43	747	135	386	292	7	80	808	1,061	2,506	149	987	45	2,336	27,107	41,657
35 COMMUNICATIONS	2	41	1	9	19	10	6	8	39	23	15	6	5	10	16	6	3	6	13	6	4	23	3	4	13	16	10	6	9	18	18	2	42	326	66	85	62	429	123	66	11	–	83	11	44	–	38	148	–	1,269	3,173
36 FINANCE & INSURANCE	238	145	1	20	24	77	18	18	23	18	125	7	7	46	44	14	6	14	19	11	7	32	7	9	23	22	21	6	18	48	24	120	298	1,002	5	1,851	555	22	118	93	26	–	–	72	400	–	135	32	–	6,993	12,814
37 RENTAL	2,393	91	2	25	96	19	17	26	61	34	–	10	19	18	36	21	4	10	20	6	6	32	2	9	19	21	20	11	35	46	24	7	147	1,961	52	211	208	58	710	402	180	–	–	386	84	–	–	223	804	20,289	28,855
38 BUSINESS SERVICES	8	533	98	71	97	19	57	22	58	424	42	21	49	11	25	5	16	10	25	12	11	64	3	25	32	76	10	51	57	9	22	2	33	1,706	86	143	37	64	121	17	95	–	421	55	134	–	3	38	–	179	5,097
39 PERSONAL & REPAIR SERVICES	368	119	*	3	3	42	4	4	20	11	13	1	1	31	3	3	1	4	3	2	1	5	*	*	1	3	2	1	4	16	11	5	264	1,415	16	113	25	68	559	76	22	30	2,294	228	819	–	–	83	271	7,333	14,301
40 MEDICAL, EDUC. & NONPROFIT ORG'S.	–	–	–	–	–	–	–	–	–	–	–	–	–	–	–	–	–	–	–	–	–	–	–	–	–	–	–	–	–	–	–	*	*	–	–	16	–	–	–	85	–	–	350	–	–	–	–	5,078	–	7,856	13,385
41 AMUSEMENTS	–	–	–	–	–	–	–	–	–	–	–	–	–	–	–	–	–	–	–	–	–	–	–	–	–	–	–	–	–	–	–	–	–	–	–	–	–	–	–	7	392	–	14	–	–	–	128	–	–	2,403	2,944
42 SCRAP & MISCELLANEOUS INDUSTRIES	–	–	–	24	–	–	–	250	–	110	–	7	–	13	650	456	8	4	3	9	6	38	1	*	3	–	–	1	–	–	–	–	35	386	10	106	34	20	1	1	13	–	12	–	1	–	30	1	–	–	2,233
43 UNDISTRIBUTED	–	2,059	132	438	1,310	880	329	201	610	1,740	788	329	323	570	287	101	211	172	1,000	356	250	1,463	45	204	822	490	406	227	1,049	356	61	214	73	2,320	88	617	547	575	1,303	960	269	–	–	536	–	–	–	–	–	–	24,711
44 EATING & DRINKING PLACES	–	–	–	–	–	–	–	–	2	–	–	–	–	–	–	–	–	–	–	–	–	–	–	–	–	–	–	–	–	–	–	–	11	–	–	–	–	–	–	152	–	–	1,030	–	–	–	–	–	–	12,075	13,270
45 NEW CONSTRUCTION & MAINTENANCE	199	117	1	39	16	12	7	42	15	36	26	12	19	34	81	20	5	5	24	16	6	28	2	7	16	44	23	7	18	265	1,118	1	134	182	178	32	4,084	3	56	342	25	–	–	73	7	–	–	5,464	15,709	154	28,704
46 INVENTORY CHANGE (depletions)	2,660	402	1	120	185	*	14	87	26	140	8	3	33	2	3	102	–	*	3	*	*	4	–	*	2	7	8	47	157	*	–	–	–	–	–	–	–	–	–	–	–	851	–	–	–	–	22	–	–	–	4,887
47 FOREIGN COUNTRIES (imports from)	690	2,001	104	208	279	183	6	621	8	594	258	2	35	143	43	573	*	1	6	35	1	16	1	1	2	15	11	54	141	7	41	302	33	–	33	105	–	–	–	–	3	69	12	–	–	–	–	1,313	–	1,325	9,275
48 GOVERNMENT	813	1,134	104	639	376	338	112	497	335	762	780	114	136	323	573	245	86	113	277	167	86	514	64	62	274	656	120	134	191	1,142	1,075	256	766	3,750	344	1,111	3,997	212	503	170	318	74	2,176	1,410	470	73	831	3,458	216	31,308	63,685
49 GROSS PRIVATE CAPITAL FORMATION	DEPRECIATION AND OTHER CAPITAL CONSUMPTION ALLOWANCES ARE INCLUDED IN HOUSEHOLD ROW																–	–	–	–	–	–	–	–	–	–	–	–	–	–	–	–	–	–	–	–	–	–	–	–	–	–	–	–	–	–	–	–	–	–	–
50 HOUSEHOLDS	19,166	6,262	387	3,286	4,013	2,564	1,063	2,161	3,034	3,431	4,907	1,024	1,140	2,255	3,945	1,519	624	943	2,335	1,178	930	4,339	534	595	2,092	3,303	1,880	856	1,989	5,066	5,675	914	6,205	26,240	2,165	8,015	14,003	1,044	7,951	9,199	1,456	–	1,801	4,254	11,492	–	847	30,058	218	2,116	220,474
TOTAL GROSS OUTLAYS	44,263	37,636	2,663	9,838	13,321	6,002	2,892	7,899	6,447	14,050	13,670	2,825	3,810	4,844	12,338	6,387	1,745	2,316	6,445	3,292	1,833	10,312	1,095	1,692	5,723	14,265	4,001	2,119	4,756	9,205	9,952	2,292	9,855	41,657	3,173	12,814	28,855	5,097	14,301	13,385	2,944	2,233	24,711	13,270	28,704	4,802	17,320	51,060	33,514	191,625	769,248

*Asterisk denotes entry of less than $0.5 million. The data are from Division of Interindustry Economics, U.S. Bureau of Labor Statistics, and are as shown in W. D. Evans and M. Hoffenberg, "The Interindustry Relations Study for 1947," *The Review of Economics and Statistics*, May, 1952. Reproduced by permission of the editors of *The Review of Economics and Statistics*.

counts.[1] Exports to foreign countries constitute a further final disposition of output, amounting to $154 million (the figure in row 8, column 47). Governmental bodies within the United States purchased $59 million of Paper and Allied Products (row 8, column 48), while $44 million worth of the output was added to inventories.[2]

A Look down the Table

Suppose one wishes to investigate the opposite question, namely, from what sources did a particular industry purchase the materials, components, labor, machinery, and other input items which it needed during the same year? If we are interested in the motor-vehicle industry we look at the entries in column 26. The bottom figure in the column is $14,265 million, which was the total gross outlay for the inputs needed in the manufacture of automobiles, trucks, and other motor vehicles in 1947. Inspection of the column shows that this important industry made such purchases as $496 million worth of Rubber Products (row 12), $1,102 million worth of Iron and Steel (row 15), $599 million worth of Electrical Machinery (row 25), and $228 million worth of Railroad Transportation (row 31). The industry bought over $4.4 billion worth of inputs from itself, as shown in column 26, row 26. Procedures adopted by the Federal statisticians are such that this large intraindustry item includes many transfers between different plants (factories) belonging to the same company (*e.g.*, General Motors), although "purchase" in a strict sense may not take place.

Near the bottom of the Motor Vehicles column is an entry of $656 million in payments to Government (row 48). This represents taxes paid by the industry. Governments—Federal, state, and local—are large producers of a great variety of goods and services (including input-output tables themselves) in our country and must consequently be included in the table. Unlike other entries in the column, these payments do not represent direct expenditures on inputs by the Motor Vehicles industry. As will be explained in Part C, taxes paid by individuals and firms are not generally based on benefits received from governmental bodies. Instead, taxation and government expenditures are the principal means by which income is redistributed in our society.

The large entry, $3,303 million, in the Household row (50) in column 26 represents inputs purchased by the motor-vehicle manufacturers from

---

[1] The amount actually spent on these products by households exceeded $344 million, since wholesale and retail margins are included in the $27,107 million shown in row 34, column 50, as households' purchases from "trade."

[2] The *net* change in inventories of Paper and Allied Products firms was a $43-million reduction, however. It can be seen in row 46, column 8, that $87 million of inventories was used up by the industry in its manufacturing process.

individuals. It consists mainly of labor services purchased by the industry but also includes the input of the services of capital (property). This is properly an entry in the Household row, since individuals, mainly through their ownership of shares of stock (*e.g.*, in the Chrysler Corporation), are actually the providers of the services rendered by buildings, machinery, etc., used by the motor-vehicle industry.

As was seen earlier, Households enter the table as purchasers of output as well as sellers of productive services. As buyers, Households must be viewed in column 50. Households are, of course, large purchasers of both original products of Agriculture and Fisheries (row 1) and of Food and Kindred Products (row 2). Hence almost $10 billion of the $44.3 billion output of farms and fisheries was bought directly by Households, and over $22 billion of the $37.6 billion output of Food and Kindred Products was purchased by Households. It can be noted in column 44, row 1 plus row 2, that $4,334 million worth of these products was bought by Eating and Drinking Places for slightly less direct input into the digestive processes of householders. A rough impression of the value of housewives' services can be gained from the difference between the cost of food purchased by Eating and Drinking Places ($4,334 million) and the $12,075 million of purchases by Households from these establishments (as seen in row 44, column 50).

Imports into the United States from foreign countries are listed vertically (row 47) since, like items made in this country, they are available for purchase by our industries and households. Exports from the United States are shown in the horizontal listing (column 47) because they are a means of disposing of American output. It will be noted that total exports ($17,320 million) greatly exceeded total imports ($9,275 million) as would be expected, since in 1947 this country was providing much material assistance to the war-torn countries of Europe and Asia.

It should be noted in concluding this brief examination of the input-output table that "total gross output" for each industry is equal to "total gross outlay." This may seem peculiar, since it appears to imply that industries made no profits, that is, that value of products was no greater than cost of production. This is due to inclusion of profits in gross outlays so that the table really shows value of output to be equal to the sum of costs plus profits—a fairly obvious matter since profit or loss in any business equals value of sales minus cost.

The student of economics is seldom required to memorize any substantial number of statistics. He may be expected to keep in mind a few figures like the approximate magnitude of the Federal debt or the approximate size of the yearly national income, but not much more than that. Useful impressions can, however, be gained through looking at a statistical compilation such as an input-output table.

INTERDEPENDENCE OF ECONOMIC ACTIVITIES

From an inspection of the input-output table the student should gain a feeling of the high degree of dependence of different types of activities upon each other. A change in any one of the entries would generate other changes throughout the table. It is quite obvious that a government order stopping automobile production in wartime would quickly affect the steel, rubber, textile, and other industries which sell input items to the automobile makers. It would also have an immediate effect on the auto workers, probably reducing their incomes during a period of shifting of their labor to tank plants, airplane factories, or other expanding industries.

This temporary drop in auto workers' incomes would affect their purchases of amusements, clothing, liquor, and other items, and this would have ramifications on entertainers, motion-picture-theater owners, New York City garmentmakers, tavern keepers, and farmers, to name only a few. These in turn would alter their purchases, and the effects would spread with decreasing force to other segments of the economy (as ripples caused by a leaping fish spread to all parts of the pond).

Strikes in some rather basic industries have become familiar occurrences in recent years. An input-output table in fuller detail than the one shown in Table 2.1 can indicate quickly the manner in which the effects of a shutdown in one industry are spread to other segments of the economy.[1] A strike in the steel industry, for example, would soon be reflected in reduced inputs for the metal-fabricating, machinery, motor-vehicle, and construction industries. On the other hand, industries such as agriculture, printing, and lumber would be relatively little affected in the short run by the strike. The steel industry depends for its own inputs upon such activities as mining of iron ore and coal, scrap metals, transportation, and labor. A strike in the steel plants is immediately felt in reduced sales to the steel industry including, of course, a cessation of sale of labor services by the striking workers.

Civilian-defense and Mobilization Implications

The input-output table should convey some important lessons in civilian defense. Although Table 2.1 does not show how the output of one region is used in other regions, it suggests the great reliance which every section of the country must place on every other section, not only for direct-consumption goods but also for industrial materials of tremendous variety. Should an atomic bomb fall on any populated place in the nation its economic repercussions would quickly be felt over the rest of the country in shortages of input items which that locality furnished. Any larger-

---

[1] A 500-row, 500-column compilation is in process. A single table of this detail would be one hundred times as large in area as Table 2.1.

scale atomic attack might deprive many parts of the country not directly hit of such necessities as food, fuel, and electric power. "We are all in the same boat," or, we might say, "We are all caught in the same input-output web."

An important use of the input-output table for mobilization purposes is its ability to indicate precisely the points in the economy where strategic "bottlenecks" are likely to arise. If, for example, a more detailed input-output table should show that a great number of essential industries are dependent upon one particular metal which is being imported, steps could be taken to stock-pile that metal or to encourage the utilization of substitutes. The Munitions Board has been charged with the responsibility for stock-piling a long list of relatively critical materials. It has been forced to make its main calculations with little aid from input-output analysis, however, because of the newness of this analytical tool.

Other Levels of Economic Interdependence

Economic interdependence can be measured at many levels other than the national level reflected in the interindustry table which we have examined. Statistical economists are engaged in the difficult job of compiling such data on both broader and narrower bases. For example, an international input-output table could be compiled showing countries, or groups of countries, in the horizontal and vertical listings. Then the table would show from which countries each nation imported and to which each exported goods and services. (As in Table 2.1, there would necessarily be "capital items" which would balance the table.) The United States, for example, depends heavily on foreign countries for such important materials as copper, tin, natural rubber, manganese, and asbestos. To an increasing extent we are becoming dependent on South America and Canada for iron ore. Friendly foreign nations rely heavily on the United States for such commodities as wheat, cotton, steel, automobiles, and munitions.

On a narrower basis, each region of the United States depends heavily upon input items furnished by other regions. To give only a few examples, the South depends on the North for motor vehicles, books and magazines, flour, and fullbacks, while both regions depend on the West for plywood, salmon, moving pictures, and divorces. The North relies on the South for lumber, cotton, sulfur, turpentine, textiles, and winter sunshine.

It should be recognized that the interdependence of various segments of the economy is limited by the extent of the market area. For the products traded internationally, the market area is the whole world or large portions of it. For the basic industrial products, the market area is usually the entire nation. But for most trades and services, the market area is much more limited. Doctors in a particular town depend upon the local barbers for haircuts and shaves. In turn, the barbers depend largely on the local doctors and hospitals for medical care.

The varieties of economic interdependence which have been mentioned in this chapter are all traceable to the advantages of specialization perceived by Adam Smith nearly two centuries ago. Maximum aggregate production of goods and services can be secured if each individual, each unit of land and other capital, each enterprise, each region, and each nation is permitted to specialize in providing the commodities and services for which it is best suited. This requires that all other desired goods and services be obtained through trade with other specialists. In short, the best way to "produce" an article is often to produce something else and then trade it for the article wanted.

CHAPTER 3

DEMAND ORIGINATES WITH THE CONSUMER

Everyone has heard that prices are set by "the law of supply and demand," and, because economists concern themselves to such a degree with the study of prices, it has been suggested by the more cynical that if one could teach a parrot to answer "supply and demand" to any question, the parrot would have been transformed into an economist. Since, as we saw in Chapter 1, prices play such an important part in the allocation of both final products and productive factors, and since the complexities of the private-enterprise system described in Chapter 2 are welded into a relatively efficient operating machine through the workings of the price system, it is not surprising that the study of price formation should occupy a considerable part of the study of economics.

Even if the supply-and-demand answer of the parrot were true, it would not be worth much. Any answer that can be stretched to fit all situations is entirely too general to be of significant value. Upon closer examination, it can be seen that "supply" and "demand" must be taken very broadly if the answer is to be true at all. If supply and demand are merely used as convenient terms to indicate separate categories of forces determining price, the parrot might be correct, but his statement would be relatively useless. In a more specific sense, supply and demand do not always determine prices. It is the purpose of this chapter to discuss more fully the specific meaning which the economist attaches to "demand."

THE NATURE OF CONSUMER DEMAND

Demand implies, in the first place, a desire for a good or service. No demand exists for those things which possess no utility, *i.e.*, capacity to render satisfaction. But demand implies in addition to this an ability and a willingness to pay for the good or service. If one of these elements—desire, ability to pay, willingness to pay—is lacking, it may be said that "potential" demand exists. Such institutions as advertising, salesmanship, and installment credit attempt to convert potential into "effective" demand.

Many things other than price affect the desire, ability, and willingness to purchase a good or service. The major determinants of an individual's ability to buy are, quite obviously, his wealth and income. The latter includes not only current income but also expected income. Further, the prices of closely related goods and services have a great deal to do with one's willingness to purchase a particular commodity. The price of pork is a major factor in shaping a consumer's decision about buying beef. Estimates of future price trends also affect consumer behavior. If potential buyers of television receivers anticipate a substantial increase in prices, they may buy new sets sooner than they otherwise would.

The Law of Demand

But the current price of the good or service itself must be of primary importance in determining the amount that will be bought. As was pointed out in Chapter 1, this is one of the major functions of price. In order to isolate the relation between the price and the amount of the good that a consumer will be willing to purchase during any given period, we must assume that all other things affecting demand remain unchanged. It is clear that, other things being equal, the higher the price of a commodity, the fewer units of it will be demanded by any given consumer. That is to say, there is an inverse relation between price and quantity demanded: the higher the price, the smaller the quantity demanded; the lower the price, the greater the quantity demanded. If the price is sufficiently high, consumers will try to find a substitute for the commodity. The substitute may be a second choice, but, if the price differential between the first and second choice is sufficiently great, consumers will purchase the second choice. One may assume, for example, that if the price of butter and margarine were the same or nearly so most consumers would buy butter, but if butter is priced at 80 cents and margarine at 20 cents per pound, many who prefer butter will switch entirely or in part to margarine.

The inverse relationship between price and quantity demanded may be called the fundamental law of demand. The nature of this relationship may be illustrated in either of two ways: (1) arithmetically, by the use of a "demand schedule," or (2) geometrically, by the use of a "demand curve." There may be a few exceptions to this law, but its application is so nearly universal that they may be disregarded. Table 3.1 represents a hypothetical consumer's demand schedule for milk.

The demand schedule is read as follows: *If* the price of milk is 35 cents per quart, Mr. A will demand 4 quarts per week; *if* the price is 30 cents, the quantity demanded will be 6; *if* the price is 25 cents, the quantity demanded will be 7; and so on. This is not to suggest that Mr. A has actually gone to the trouble of determining what quantities of milk he would buy at all prices between 10 cents and 35 cents per quart. If the price, in fact, is in the neighborhood of 25 cents, it is only necessary for him to determine what he will buy at the current price. But if, in the morning, the milkman leaves a note indicating that after the first of the month the price will be 30 cents a quart, Mr. A will have to determine whether he will reduce his milk consumption. To determine the number of quarts which he would buy at 10 cents a quart would be a purely academic question and one not likely to occupy much of Mr. A's time.

Figure 3.1. MR. A'S DEMAND FOR MILK

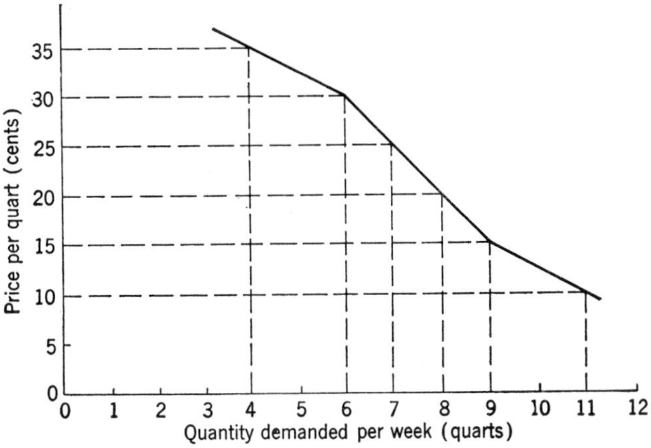

We may assume, however, that for Mr. A and for every other milk consumer in the market there is a demand schedule which indicates for all prices the quantities of milk which would be demanded.

Table 3.1. Mr. A's Demand for Milk

Price per quart, cents	Quantity demanded, quarts per week
35	4
30	6
25	7
20	8
15	9
10	11

For many purposes it is more convenient to represent the demand for milk as a graph rather than as a schedule. Figure 3.1 represents graphically Mr. A's demand for milk and is referred to as a demand curve. The various quantities demanded at the several prices indicated in Mr. A's schedule have been plotted, with price per quart indicated on the vertical, or y, axis and the quantity demanded measured on the horizontal, or x, axis. A line has been drawn to join the several points plotted on the assumption that, if the price were, for example, between 20 and 25 cents, the quantity demanded would be between 8 quarts and 7 quarts per week. The demand curve is read in the same way as the demand schedule: *If* the price of milk is 35 cents per quart, Mr. A will demand 4 quarts per week; *if* the price is 25 cents, the quantity demanded will be 7; and so on.[1]

It is important to note that a consumer's demand curve describes the situation as of a particular moment. The arrival of a baby in Mr. A's household might cause him to increase the quantity of milk he would take at any price; in that event his demand curve would shift to the right. This is one of those forces other than price which influence willingness to purchase. If, on the other hand, Mr. A's twin sons left home to play football at the state university, his demand curve would shift to the left— that is, at any price he would be willing to buy fewer quarts of milk than before. For some commodities, the demand curve may shift forward and backward with considerable rapidity. A consumer's demand curve, accordingly, represents a sort of instantaneous photograph; it describes a situation as of a given instant of time.

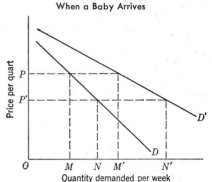

Figure 3.2. MR. A'S DEMAND FOR MILK INCREASES—

When a Baby Arrives

The nature of the shifting of demand curves is illustrated in Figure 3.2. D represents the original demand curve. At price OP the quantity demanded would be OM; at a price of OP' the quantity demanded would be ON. Suppose now that for some reason the demand increases, and the consumer's new demand is represented by the curve D'. At price OP the consumer would now take OM' units, and at price OP' he would take ON'. At any price on the new curve D' the consumer would demand more units than he would have taken at that price when his demand was represented by curve D.

It is not accurate to speak of an "increase in demand" unless at any price more units will be demanded than before, that is, unless the demand curve has shifted upward and to the right. Suppose that the price is originally at OP and the quantity demanded is OM. Now, if the price falls to OP', the quantity demanded will be ON. This does not represent an increase in demand; demand is still represented by the curve D. The quantity demanded has increased, but the demand has remained unchanged. Demand does not change unless the curve shifts. A change from D' to D— that is, a shift to the left—would, of course, represent a decrease in demand.

[1] See Section 1, Appendix B.

A change in any one or several of the underlying forces other than price affecting a consumer's desire, willingness, or ability to purchase is said to change *demand*. A change in price causes a change in *quantity demanded*. It is necessary to make this distinction quite clear in order that the influence of price may be analyzed separately from that of such determinants of demand as taste and income.

Market demand is simply the summation of the individual demands of the consumers who comprise the market, and the market demand schedule or market demand curve may be determined by adding together the schedules or curves of all the individuals in the market. Suppose that we illustrate the problem by assuming that the market consists of five consumers of milk such as Mr. A. (If there were 5,000 or 5,000,000 the principle would be the same.) If the price is 20 cents per quart, we have seen that Mr. A would demand 8 quarts per week. Suppose that at this price Mr. B would take 15 quarts, Mr. C 6 quarts, Mr. D 20 quarts, and Mr. E 3 quarts. The market demand for milk at a price of 20 cents would then be 8 + 15 + 6 + 20 + 3, or a total of 52 quarts per week. Similarly, the quantity demanded at all other prices could be determined, and a market demand schedule or a market demand curve could be prepared.

We have seen that, other things remaining the same, almost without exception a greater quantity will be demanded at a lower than at a higher price. Consumer demand curves and consequently market demand curves slope downward from left to right. The demand curve may be a straight line, it may be concave or convex, or it may look like descending stairsteps; but, regardless of its general shape, it must have a negative slope over most of its range. The fundamental law of demand tells us this, but it tells us nothing concerning the degree of responsiveness of quantity demanded to price changes. We must take notice of the important fact that the same drop in price for two commodities may cause the quantity demanded of one to increase much more than the quantity demanded of the other. This is illustrated in Figure 3.3. The curve D_m may be assumed to represent the market demand for milk and the curve D_b to represent the market demand for beer. The curves are drawn so that they intersect at price OP. At that price the quantity demanded is the same for each

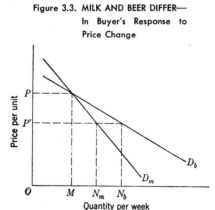

Figure 3.3. MILK AND BEER DIFFER—In Buyer's Response to Price Change

commodity; if the price of milk is OP, the market will take OM units of milk, and if the price of beer is OP, the market will take OM units of beer. Now suppose that the price of each commodity falls to price OP'. Since the price has fallen, the quantity of each demanded will increase. But the market will increase its purchases of milk only from OM to ON_m, whereas its purchases of beer will increase from OM to ON_b. The quantity of beer demanded is more responsive to a change in price than is the quantity of milk.

ELASTICITY OF DEMAND

We were able to compare the demands for milk and beer in Figure 3.3 only because these two commodities are measured in similar units and may be sold at roughly comparable prices. But suppose that one desired to compare the demands for oranges and baby carriages, or even to compare the demands for dozens of oranges and crates of oranges. No such simple comparison would be possible. In this case, if comparisons are to be made, it is necessary to introduce the idea of the *relative* rather than the absolute responsiveness of quantity demanded to a price change. This concept, known as "elasticity of demand," was developed by the famous English economist, Alfred Marshall, writing about 1890.[1] Marshall's innovation consisted in concentrating attention on the *percentage* change in amount demanded in relation to the *percentage* change in price which causes the response. He termed the ratio of these two percentages the "elasticity of demand."

If a very small change in price, say 1 per cent, calls forth an equal percentage change in quantity demanded, the elasticity of demand between those prices is said to be unity, or 1. If a very small change in price causes an even smaller percentage change in quantity demanded, the elasticity of demand between those prices is said to be less than 1. If a very small change in price results in a greater percentage change in quantity demanded, the elasticity of demand between those prices is said to be greater than 1. A somewhat crude but very useful rule of thumb for determining the elasticity of demand may be derived from Table 3.2.

This table consists of a demand schedule with a total expenditure column added. If the price is $10 per unit, the table indicates that no units will be demanded, and, accordingly, consumer expenditure on the commodity at that price will be zero. If the price is $9, one unit will be bought, and total consumer expenditure will be $9, and so on.

It will be observed that as the price falls total expenditure increases for a time, reaches a maximum, and then decreases. Why does this hap-

---

[1] Alfred Marshall, *Principles of Economics* (London: Macmillan & Co., Ltd., 1938), 8th ed., pp. 103–104.

Table 3.2. Demand and Total Expenditure Schedule

Price	Quantity demanded	Total expenditure
$10	0	$ 0
9	1	9
8	2	16
7	3	21
6	4	24
5	5	25
4	6	24
3	7	21
2	8	16
1	9	9
0	10	0

pen? Since the total expenditure column is the product of two terms, price and quantity demanded, and since each time we reduce one term we increase the other by an equal amount, why does not the product remain constant? It will be noted that the sum of price and quantity demanded does remain constant at 10.

The explanation for the behavior of the total expenditure column is to be found in the fact that, percentagewise, the subtraction of one unit from price is quite a different thing from the addition of one unit to the quantity demanded. Consider the drop in price from $9 to $8. The decrease in price of $1 represents a relatively small percentage change—a little over 11 per cent. But the corresponding change in quantity demanded from one to two represents a 100 per cent increase. That is to say, a relatively small percentage change in price has resulted in a very large percentage change in quantity demanded, and the demand between prices $9 and $8, therefore, has an elasticity greater than 1.

Consider now the effect of a drop in price from $2 to $1. This 50 per cent reduction in price has resulted in a much less than 50 per cent increase in quantity demanded, and between these prices, accordingly, the demand has an elasticity of less than 1. One may generalize by saying that as long as total expenditure increases as price decreases, elasticity of demand is greater than 1; if total expenditure decreases as price decreases, elasticity of demand is less than 1; and if total expenditure remains constant as price changes, elasticity of demand is equal to 1.

This relationship of elasticity to total expenditure is illustrated graphically in Figure 3.4. Total expenditure may be represented by the area of a rectangle drawn within the triangle limited by the demand curve and the price and quantity axes, since total expenditure is price multiplied by the quantity taken. If the demand curve is a straight line it will have an elasticity of 1 at its mid-point, an elasticity of greater than 1 in its upper half, and an elasticity of less than 1 in its lower half.[1] Elasticity continually falls as price is lowered. In spite of the fact that the actual shape of a demand curve may not be linear, this conclusion holds good in a great many cases; for most commodities, the elasticity of demand will probably be greater at higher than at lower prices.

Let us consider the famous mineral-spring illustration used by Cournot, a French mathematician and economist, in 1838. An owner of such a spring, which costs him nothing to operate, is concerned with the appropriate price to be placed on the mineral water, which is in great demand for its healing powers. He wants to set the price which will provide the greatest possible total revenue; he will, then,

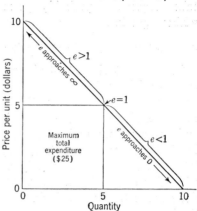

Figure 3.4. CONSUMERS SPEND MOST—
Where Elasticity Is Unitary

try to establish the price where the elasticity of demand is unitary. He will try neither to charge the highest possible price nor to sell the largest possible quantity, since either of these policies would result in a lower total revenue for him.[2]

[1] It can easily be seen from the figure that at high prices a tall and narrow rectangle represents total expenditure and that as price is lowered the area of this rectangle increases. The largest possible rectangle is one whose sides cut each side of the triangle in half. At prices below this the rectangle becomes low and wide but is reduced in area. See Section 3, Appendix B.

[2] For many purposes the relationship between total expenditure and price provides a measure of elasticity which is sufficient. Frequently, however, we wish to know more precisely what the elasticity of demand is. In Fig. 3.4, we know that the elasticity of demand at any price above $5 is greater than 1. But how much greater? Is it 1.1 or 10 or 100? If we know that two demand curves have an elasticity greater than 1 at a given price, how are we to determine which of the demands is the more elastic? To answer these questions a more precise measure of elasticity is required.

Price elasticity may be defined as percentage change in quantity demanded divided by the percentage change in price. This formula becomes the following when broken down into its component parts:

$$\frac{\text{Change in quantity}}{\text{Original quantity}} \text{ divided by } \frac{\text{change in price}}{\text{original price}}$$

This definition may be put more precisely in algebraic form as follows:

$$e = \frac{dq/q}{dp/p} \quad \text{or} \quad \frac{dq}{dp}\frac{p}{q}$$

where e represents elasticity, dq an infinitesimally small change in quantity demanded, q the quantity demanded at the original price, dp an infinitesimally small change in

By saying that the demand for a commodity is elastic, we are also saying that there are other commodities which are good substitutes for this one in the mind of the consumer. For example, the demand for one particular brand of gasoline is probably highly elastic, since other brands are close substitutes. On the other hand, the demand for gasoline of all makes taken together is probably inelastic, since automobiles can hardly run without gasoline.

Applications of the Elasticity Concept

The concept of elasticity is extremely useful in analyzing many problems faced in real-world situations. In spite of the paucity of data concerning the actual forms of the demand functions, and thus of accurate measures of elasticity, price decisions must be made by business firms and organizations and by certain governmental agencies. For example, in Florida, a large marketing cooperative has substantial power to regulate the amount of oranges shipped out of the state each season. A knowledge of the elasticity of demand for oranges is essential for sound policy decisions on the part of this agency. If the cooperative wants to maximize the income of the citrus growers in a bumper-crop year, it should try to impose enough restrictions on the shipment of oranges to move the price up to the point where the elasticity of demand is unitary, *i.e.*, where total expenditure by consumers on oranges is maximized. If, under existing regulations, the elasticity of demand is greater than 1 at the established market price, the shipping regulations should be relaxed.

Public commissions charged with the responsibility for determining the appropriateness of rates for such enterprises as railroads and public utilities (since competition is a poor regulator of their prices) often must take into consideration the elasticity of demand for the product. This has been especially true of the Interstate Commerce Commission in its decisions relating to railroad freight rates. Because of the overbuilding of railroads during the nineteenth century and the rapid development of competitive carriers (especially trucks and pipelines), the American railroads have often been in a difficult financial position. In order to obtain more operating revenue, railroad management has frequently sought ICC approval for either general rate increases or boosts in particular rates. On such

---

price, and p the original price. If a fall in price is just offset by a proportionate increase in quantity demanded, elasticity of demand is unitary. If a fall in price is more than proportionately offset by a quantity increase, demand is elastic, and if it is not proportionately offset by a quantity increase, demand is inelastic. Suppose a 1 per cent change in price results in a 1 per cent change in quantity demanded. In our formula dq/q is equal to $\frac{1}{100}$ and dp/p is equal to $\frac{1}{100}$, and applying the formula elasticity is found to be 1. By using the formula we can determine the exact numerical value of the elasticity of demand. A geometric technique for determining elasticity of demand is demonstrated in Section 3, Appendix B.

occasions the Commission must weigh all available evidence in order to determine whether a rate increase will actually increase or decrease railroad revenues.

If the ICC decides that elasticity of demand for railroad services is greater than unity, it will probably deny the request for higher rates on the grounds that a rate increase would decrease railroad income. In this case (unlike that of Cournot's mineral spring), the lower cost of rendering a lower volume of railroading services would have some beneficial effect, but the Commission would pay more attention to the demand side, since total costs of railroading are not very responsive to small changes in the volume of freight hauled.

A final example of the use of elasticity may be helpful. Once an athletic stadium is built, the institutional or private owners generally try to take in as much money as possible at the gate. This means that they should attempt to establish admission prices at approximately the point of unitary elasticity of demand. It is probable that many stadiums could actually increase gate receipts by lowering prices if owners were not afraid to experiment with price. If they place the price of admission below the point of unitary elasticity and are disappointed at the fans' response, they may encounter particular resistance if they then raise price again.

The demand schedules and demand curves have so far been discussed as if they could be statistically estimated. It is perhaps important here to mention the difficult problems that are encountered in any attempt to compute statistically the demand schedule for a particular commodity during a particular period of time. Demand schedules and demand curves for such commodities do exist, but it is often almost impossible to sift out the data necessary for deriving them. The major difficulty to be somehow surmounted is that the underlying determinants of demand seldom if ever remain constant. And the demand curve can only be derived when such things as income, tastes, prices of other commodities, etc., do remain unchanged. Statistical procedures may be used to remove certain changes, but these are frequently unreliable. In spite of these problems, attempts are constantly being made to compute actual demand curves. The nature of demand affects the policy decisions of business firms and government officials, and the more information they have available the more probable it is that the proper decisions will be reached.

For our purposes, however, the demand schedules and curves may be considered as analytical tools to be used in the building up of the body of economic analysis. We know that such schedules and curves exist, so we shall proceed to use them regardless of the difficulties that might be encountered in the actual attempts to construct them.

CHAPTER 4

PRICE IS DETERMINED BY SUPPLY AND DEMAND

In Chapter 3 we considered at some length the relationship between price and quantity demanded which obtains for all economic goods. The amount of a good or service which a consumer, or all consumers taken together, will demand depends upon the price of the commodity, assuming that all the other forces affecting demand remain unchanged. The fact that, in general, at higher prices consumers will buy less than at lower prices suggests one of the main functions of price in a private-enterprise economy. Price is essentially the institutional device which the economy employs to parcel out the available goods and services, which are scarce, among the many consumers, whose wants are virtually unlimited. Prices are, in brief, *the rationing devices* of a free-enterprise economy. All economic goods are scarce; that is, there is less of each commodity than people would consume if there were no restraints imposed upon their consumption. If this were not true, the good would not be an economic good at all but would be classified as a free good.

THE RATIONING FUNCTION OF PRICE

The manner in which prices ration economic goods is not difficult to understand. If goods are in short supply at the prevailing prices and sellers find their shelves becoming empty and reordering difficult, they may for a time post signs saying, "One to a customer"; but before long they will see that it is more satisfactory—and more profitable—to raise prices. At higher prices, the quantities consumers are willing to buy will diminish—some buyers will reduce their purchases, and others will discontinue completely the purchase of some goods. The limited supply is, accordingly, rationed among consumers who are most willing and able to pay the higher prices. Goods are rationed to those whose dollar demand is strongest and not necessarily to those whose real or physical needs are greatest.

Similarly, if store managers note that the turnover of goods is slow and shelves are filled with unsold merchandise, they will find it necessary to lower prices in order to stimulate consumption. Close-out sales, end-of-the-month sales, bargain basements, and special price reductions are all outward indications of prices serving their normal rationing function. Even a society whose food supply consisted exclusively of manna from heaven and which carried on no food production at all would find it convenient, if not necessary, to utilize prices if the manna were not sufficient to provide everyone with all he wanted. If no one produced food, and manna fell to the earth every Wednesday morning at ten o'clock but in a quantity not quite sufficient to keep everyone fully satisfied, it is likely that prices would be employed to prevent the waste of manna.

The Fixed-supply Case

In order to isolate the rationing function of price, let us consider a commodity in absolutely fixed supply; we may suppose that there is just so much of the commodity available and that there is no way, at least in the short run, to increase the amount which consumers may buy. In such an event, price changes must result from each change in demand. If the demand should increase—that is, if the demand curve should shift to the right—the price would rise; if the demand should decrease, the price would fall. This is essentially the manna-from-heaven case, and for certain problems in the real world supplies of goods can be best considered as relatively fixed and demand forces to be the primary determinants of price. This is especially true if the period under consideration is very short, because, as we shall soon see, supply can change significantly only over rather long time periods.

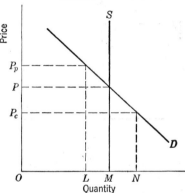

Figure 4.1. THE FIXED-SUPPLY CASE— Price Is Determined by Demand

The case of the commodity in fixed supply is represented graphically in Figure 4.1. Quantity demanded and quantity supplied are measured along the x axis, and price is measured along the y axis. D represents the demand curve for the commodity in question. Since it slopes downward from left to right, it indicates that the higher the price, the less will be demanded. For example, at price OP_c, the quantity demanded would be ON units, but at a higher price such as OP_p, only OL units would be taken. The curve S represents the supply curve. Since it is assumed in this case that the supply is fixed, the curve is drawn as a vertical line; OM units are available to consumers at any price.[1] If the price is OP_c, the quantity supplied is OM; if the price is OP_p, the quantity supplied is still OM.

If we take the demand and supply curves as given in Figure 4.1, the market price will be OP, and the quantity bought and sold will, of course, be OM. That the intersection of the supply and demand curves determines the equilibrium price can be demonstrated as follows. If the price were higher than OP, such as OP_p, the quantity demanded at that price, OL, would be less than the quantity supplied OM. If the price remained at OP_p, the difference between OM and OL, which is LM, would be wasted. But since suppliers of the commodity are willing, if necessary, to accept a lower price than OP_p, and since, if they are to get rid of their entire stock,

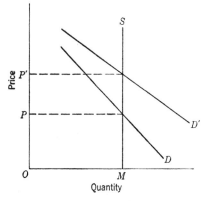

Figure 4.2. DEMAND INCREASES WITH FIXED SUPPLY—

The Same Amount Is Sold at a Higher Price

they must sell at a lower price, the price cannot remain at that level or at any price above OP. Similarly, if the price is less than OP, for example, OP_c, the quantity which consumers want to buy will be greater than the total amount available; specifically at price OP_c the quantity demanded will be ON, which exceeds the amount available by MN units. Since sellers in the fixed-supply case wish to realize as high a price as will permit them to dispose of their entire stock, they will raise the price until the quantity demanded just equals the quantity supplied, which, in this case, means a price of OP. This is called an "equilibrium price," because if the price is set at OP, it will tend to remain there unless either the demand or the supply curve shifts. At equilibrium, the quantity demanded will just equal the quantity supplied.

Suppose now that for some reason, for example an increase in the income of the community, demand increases. This is represented in Figure 4.2 by a shift of the demand curve to the right. On curve D' the quantity demanded at any price is greater than on curve D at the same price, and if demand shifts from D to D' it is proper to say that demand has increased. When demand is D, equilibrium price is OP. When demand is D', price is

[1] At low prices a seller may prefer not to sell all of his stock of a commodity. He may then be considered to "demand" the commodity himself, the amount which he demands being greater the lower the price of the good. This demand of the seller for his own product is sometimes called his "reservation demand," and this is included in the market demand curve.

OP'. In both cases the quantity exchanged is OM. The cause of the increase in price from OP to OP' is the increase in demand from D to D'. This is the meaning of the statement made earlier that, in the case of absolutely fixed supply, demand is the determinant of price.

The fixed-supply case corresponds reasonably closely with a number of real-world situations. Let us suppose that the government has on hand 1,000 unused C-47 airplanes which have been declared obsolete for military purposes. No more planes of this type will be built, and the government plans to dispose of those on hand for whatever price they will bring. Domestic airlines, South American governments, and wealthy playboys may be interested in the purchase of the planes. The number that can be sold will vary inversely with the price that is charged. We may assume that the curve D in Figure 4.2 represents the demand for C-47 planes. OM in the figure is 1,000, and the supply curve is S. The price which the government is able to realize for each plane will then be OP, say $25,000. If the demand were greater than D, say D', the price would be higher, in this case OP', say $40,000.

The problem of wartime rent control also fits the fixed-supply case reasonably well. We may assume that because of restrictions on residential construction the total quantity of housing units must remain essentially fixed. We may assume that curve S in Figure 4.1 represents the supply of residential units of a given type in a given community. If the demand for housing of this type is represented by curve D, the equilibrium price (rent) would be OP. If the government decides that OP would be too high and that such rents would exploit tenants, it may establish maximum (ceiling) rents at level OP_c. As a consequence, the number of residential units demanded at the ceiling price would exceed the number of units supplied, MN units being demanded in excess of the quantity available. The effect of the governmental regulation of price would be to alter the allocation of scarce housing among the members of the community. If prices had been permitted to rise to their equilibrium level, some people would have had to give up their dwellings because they could not have afforded to pay the rent. Under rent control, people are provided with housing on a first-come-first-served basis. Those who have housing under rent control get it at a lower cost, but others willing and able to pay ceiling prices or even more are unable to find residential units available. One may say that with free market prices housing units are scarce, whereas with rent control the housing market is characterized by shortages.

The farm-price-support program of the Federal government also illustrates the fixed-supply situation. Referring again to Figure 4.1, we may assume that D represents the demand for butter, and at the moment the supply of butter is represented by S. The equilibrium price is OP. But we may suppose that the government has decided that this price represents too small a return to the dairy farmers, and it has set a floor on the price of butter at the "parity" level OP_p. At price OP consumers would take the entire stock of butter available, but at price OP_p the quantity demanded falls short of the quantity supplied by LM units. Presumably it will be necessary for the government to buy the LM units of butter and destroy them, store them, divert them to other uses, or otherwise dispose of them. Just as in the case of rent control, where price ceilings result in a problem of shortages, the setting of a price above the equilibrium level results in a problem of surplus disposal. Only at the equilibrium or free market price is there no rationing or surplus-disposal problem. It would be premature at this point to conclude that price ceilings and price-support programs are good, bad, or indifferent, but it is clear that any interference with the operation of free market prices creates problems which in the absence of such interference are nonexistent. The price-control and price-support programs will be examined more fully in Part C.

THE PRODUCTION-MOTIVATING FUNCTION OF PRICE

In addition to the rationing function, prices also serve the extremely important function of calling forth, or motivating, supply. As the time period under consideration becomes longer, this function tends to overshadow the rationing function in significance.

Although the supply of almost any commodity or service is virtually fixed at any given instant of time, the quantity offered on the market may be varied if producers are given time to change the rate of production. If the prospect is for prices to rise, producers will expect production to be profitable, and the quantity supplied will increase as the price rises. The time required to change the rate of output varies significantly from commodity to commodity, but certain generalizations may be made which are applicable to almost all commodities and services. Given sufficient time to change the rate of output, more will be supplied at a higher price than at a lower price, other things remaining the same. In graphic terms, the supply curve, which indicates the relationship between price and quantity supplied, slopes upward from left to right in the typical case. The degree of response of quantity supplied to a change in price depends largely upon the length of the time period taken into account.[1] In extremely short time periods, approaching the instantaneous, the amount supplied can vary only slightly regardless of price. Businessmen can add to their inventories if they want to cut down on the quantity supplied, or they can deplete their inventories if they want to increase the amount supplied, but production cannot be greatly altered. Given a little time, however, produc-

[1] This is another way of saying that the elasticity of supply is less when very short time periods are considered than for longer periods. For a discussion of elasticity of supply see Section 3, Appendix B.

tion can in most cases be stepped up or cut back. If a firm desires to increase the rate of output during the next month, for example, a few additional men may be hired, an extra shift may be introduced, or more hand tools may be utilized. If a cut in output is indicated, workers may be laid off, machines allowed to remain idle, and so on. If long-run considerations are taken into account, the amount supplied can vary almost without limit in response to price change. If the price is established at a level which indicates that production in the industry should be expanded, plans may be made for new firms to enter the industry, or old firms may decide to build new and larger plants. On the other hand, if the prevailing and anticipated prices indicate that production should be cut down significantly, plans may be made by firms to allow old plants to wear out without being replaced.

Producers are confronted constantly with three different problems related to supply and price: (1) what prices should be asked for goods already on hand; (2) at what rate existing plant capacity should be utilized in the production of additional goods; and (3) what should be done with respect to increasing or decreasing firm capacity. These are frequently designated as "market," "short-run," and "long-run" problems, because of the difference in time required to effectuate each type of decision. Decisions made regarding prices to charge in order to move existing inventories are quickly reflected in sales volume. Short-run decisions take a little longer to become effective; for example, if the rate of output is to be stepped up 20 per cent, the product will not actually come off the production lines at the augmented rate until all necessary "inputs" have been increased appropriately—which may take weeks or months. A long-run decision now made to increase the size of the firm will probably require a considerably longer time to effectuate, since new financing, construction, and staffing will be required.

Decisions facing wholesalers and retailers, who distribute but do not manufacture goods, may usefully be viewed in a like manner. There is always the market, or very short-run, problem of what prices to charge for existing stocks of goods. There is also the frequently recurring problem of what merchandise to order from suppliers. And finally, there is the problem of what changes, if any, to make in size and number of stores or other outlets. The last (long-run) problem is not likely to figure in the distributor's calculations so frequently as the other two, but it is often the most important element in determining the eventual success or failure of the enterprise.[1]

[1] In some kinds of business it is sufficient to distinguish only two types of problems rather than three. The operator of a motor court, for example, has only two important decisions related to supply and price: (1) what rates to charge in order to maximize income from existing accommodations and (2) whether to build additional cabins or reduce the number he keeps ready for tourists.

The distinction between the market situation, the short-run situation, and the long-run situation may be further illustrated by reference to the sale of strawberries. Farmer Jones, we may assume, raises strawberries and sells them at a roadside stand. On a given Saturday afternoon he has 150 quarts of strawberries to sell. He believes that it is important that he sell all of them that day, since they are perishable and he considers it wasteful to allow any to spoil. The price which will just move all the berries will be determined by the demand for strawberries, and Farmer Jones in arriving at an asking price will attempt to estimate what the "equilibrium" price will be; that is, at what price will the demand-for-strawberries curve in his market intersect the highly inelastic supply curve? If the next week Farmer Jones again has 150 quarts of strawberries for sale but demand has increased, he will be able to get a higher price. But the higher price will not result in an increase in the quantity supplied —the supply is virtually fixed by the yield of his strawberry patch and cannot be increased in response to daily or weekly fluctuations in the demand for strawberries.

If, however, high prices for strawberries are anticipated for the next year or so, Farmer Jones may attempt to increase his yield by more careful cultivation and greater use of fertilizers, with the result that the antici-pated higher prices may call forth a somewhat greater output in the short run. If, furthermore, high prices are expected to prevail as far ahead as the eye can see, Farmer Jones may increase his acreage in strawberries, and his neighbors may begin to set out strawberry plants, with the result that in a year or two, after the new plants begin to bear, the supply of straw-berries may be substantially increased. This represents a long-run in-crease in the amount supplied resulting from anticipated high prices. In this way prices serve the production-motivation function. If the supply is small in relation to the demand, prices will be high, and this will en-courage an increase in output. Conversely, if prices are low, this will re-sult in a reduction of output.

We have so far in this chapter described the two major functions of prices: the rationing function and the production-motivating function. To separate these functions for purposes of analysis, we began by assuming that supply was fixed, or perfectly inelastic, and we observed in this case that changes in demand resulted in changes in price, and the intersection of the supply and demand curves established the highest price at which all of the supply would be bought. This price was described as an equi-librium price, since, in a free market, any price established above or below that level will be temporary, and price will tend to move toward equilib-rium. In the short run, the rationing function is the chief function per-formed by prices. In the long run, production motivation becomes the primary function of price. If prices remain relatively high, profits will be large, new plants will be built, new firms will enter the industry, and output will be expanded. If prices are relatively low, equipment will be permitted to wear out and replacements will not be made, some plants may be abandoned, and some firms may go bankrupt with the result that production is diminished. In this way the economy produces more or less of a commodity depending upon consumer preferences as reflected through price changes.

SHIFTS IN DEMAND AND SUPPLY

It is appropriate now to consider in somewhat greater detail the effects on price of shifts in demand or supply. The demand for a given com-

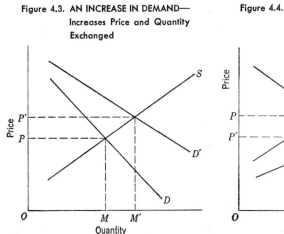

Figure 4.3. AN INCREASE IN DEMAND— Increases Price and Quantity Exchanged

Figure 4.4. AN INCREASE IN SUPPLY— Lowers Price and Increases Quantity Exchanged

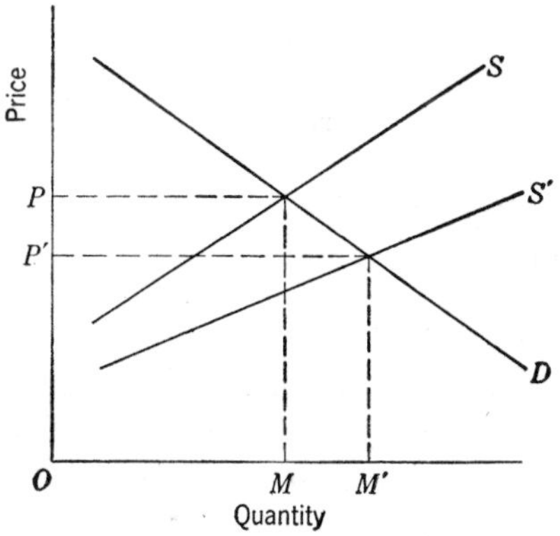

modity may increase, for example, if the income of the community increases, if the prices of other commodities increase and the given commodity is substituted for them, or if there is a change in tastes which makes the commodity more desirable to consumers. If the supply curve is upsloping and does not shift, and if the demand increases, *i.e.*, if the demand curve shifts to the right, both the price and the quantity exchanged will increase. If in Figure 4.3 we assume that the original demand is D, price will be OP, and the quantity exchanged will be OM. If now for some reason demand increases from D to D', the price will rise from OP to OP', and the quantity bought and sold will increase from OM to OM'. Conversely, if we assume that the original demand curve was D' and shifts to D, that is, if the demand decreases, the price will fall from OP' to OP, and the quantity exchanged will decrease from OM' to OM.

If now we assume that the supply increases with no change in demand, because of a bumper-crop yield, for example, or a new and cheaper method of production, price will fall and the quantity exchanged will increase.

This is illustrated in Figure 4.4. If the original demand and supply are indicated by curves D and S, the original price will be OP, and the quantity exchanged will be OM. As a result of the increase in supply to S', price will fall to OP', and the amount bought and sold will increase to OM'.[1]

THE MEANING OF EQUILIBRIUM PRICE

A final word concerning the idea of an equilibrium price is in order. The concept of equilibrium price should never be taken for more than it actually is. It is not a real price in a real market. It represents that price which would tend to be established in a particular market during a given time period provided that everything affecting the supply and demand schedules remained unchanged. The fact is that the underlying forces of demand and supply do not remain fixed, particularly as the time period under consideration increases in length. The concept of an equilibrium price is, nevertheless, extremely useful for purposes of economic analysis. It makes for a much clearer understanding of the forces which do determine real prices than would otherwise be possible.

In this context it is not difficult to appreciate the virtual impossibility of predicting accurately the level of the actual price of a particular commodity at a specific time. The prognosticator not only would need to know the actual shapes of the demand and supply curves but would also have to predict how much and when these functions would shift relative to each other. So many of these underlying forces are so dependent on unpredictable factors, such as the personal whims of consumers, business executives, and government officials, that accurate prediction is impossible. But businessmen, public officials, and consumers must make some predictions, and the study of economics can help by providing a mechanism by which the various price-determining factors can be sorted out, classified, and separately analyzed. The economist cannot accurately forecast the price of beef in Kansas City on next July 1, but he can say that the price will be high enough to prevent an apparent shortage and low enough to prevent an apparent surplus if markets are free. No one will want beef and be willing and able to pay the market price for it and be unable to find it. No butcher will be unable to sell his beef at the going price. The recognition of the simple fact that prices in free markets tend to be established at levels which will clear the market should go far toward separating the sense from the nonsense in much popular discussion of economic matters.

---

[1] If it is assumed that both supply and demand increase, the quantity exchanged will increase, but the price may be higher, lower, or unchanged, depending on the relative magnitude of the increases. Similarly, if both supply and demand decrease, the quantity exchanged will decrease, but price may be higher, lower, or unchanged.

CHAPTER 5

COST AFFECTS PRICE THROUGH SUPPLY

The fact that economic goods and services are scarce was emphasized in Chapter 1. In saying that goods are scarce we are also saying that they cost something. Cost in its everyday usage means a certain sum of money that must be given up in order to acquire a particular commodity. If it takes $10 to acquire possession of a new hat, we say that the new hat costs $10. Upon closer examination, however, the idea of cost is a much more fundamental one than merely that of the money given up to acquire a unit of a commodity. What is really given up when $10 is paid out for the new hat? The purchaser of the hat is sacrificing $10 worth of something else which could have been purchased with the $10. The real cost of the hat is the pair of shoes which could have been purchased instead for the same $10 but which now will never be worn. Cost is fundamentally the alternative good or service sacrificed in the process of acquiring another good or service. The concept may be extended to the whole economy as well as to the single purchaser. While the buyer in our example forgoes the purchase of a new pair of shoes to be able to buy the new hat, the whole economy also forgoes something in order to get the hat produced. The real cost to society consists in the alternative goods and services which could have been produced with the resources which went into the production of the hat. If we are talking about a woolen hat, perhaps the wool could have been used instead to make a pair of gloves. Or the labor might have been used to produce milk shakes, and the machinery to produce toy soldiers. Whatever the productive resources (inputs) which went into the production of the hat could otherwise have produced may be considered as the real cost of the hat.

So much for the general meaning of cost. But why is it necessary to introduce the idea of cost in order to explain the workings of the price system? We saw in Chapter 4 that prices were normally set by supply-and-demand forces. In order to look behind the supply curve it is necessary to examine cost of production from the business firm's point of view. Cost of production affects price through its effect on supply; it is the obstacle which must be overcome in adding to the supply of any economic good. We study costs, therefore, in order to gain a fuller understanding of supply. An examination of the forces of supply thus involves a look at the behavior of business firms.

The business firm transforms productive resources into consumer goods and services. In this production process, the firm must purchase inputs (productive services) and sell the outputs (goods and services). Production gives rise to revenue when goods are sold, but also to costs when resources or services are purchased. Productive services cost something in money terms to business firms precisely because the same resources could produce alternative products elsewhere in the economy. In order to be able to purchase inputs for the production of any commodity, the firm has to compete with other potential users of the inputs, and this competition sets input prices. Thus a firm's costs really derive from the alternative production possibilities of the inputs which it uses.

ECONOMICS OF THE FIRM

In this chapter for the first time, therefore, we are concerned with the economics of the firm. Each industry consists of a number of firms, *i.e.*, the business units which carry on production activity, and each firm operates one or more plants. The Great Atlantic and Pacific Tea Company, for example, is a firm in the grocery industry, and each retail outlet is a plant. Many of the decisions affecting the utilization of society's economic resources are made by the management of firms. In response to anticipated consumer demand the managers of firms decide what goods should be produced, whether output should be expanded or contracted, and whether more or fewer factors of production should be employed. Business managers are presumed to be attempting to maximize profits, and their success is measured by the magnitude of the firms' profits.

Profits are, of course, closely tied to prices; other things being equal, an increase in demand with the resultant rise in price will make production more profitable. The profits of firms are not, however, determined exclusively by the prices of the products which they offer for sale. Firms are buyers as well as sellers, and the prices of the input factors[1] which they buy are quite as important in determining their profit positions as the prices of their products. Profits are, in fact, the difference between total revenue and total cost. Before the behavior of firms can be analyzed

---

[1] The term "factor," "factors of production," or "productive services" is used to refer to those things which the firm buys; the term "product" refers to those things which the firm sells. The product of one firm may, of course, be a factor of another firm. Sheet steel, for example, is a product of the steel industry and a factor of the automobile industry. See the input-output table in Chap. 2.

effectively, accordingly, it is necessary to understand some more detailed aspects of costs.

The total costs of a firm represent the payments made by the firm to owners of factors of production. These include, among others, payments in the form of wages to laborers of various kinds and skills; purchases of raw materials and power; rent on land and buildings; salaries to the company executives; interest on borrowed funds; advertising and selling costs; and depreciation of tools, machines, and other physical equipment. The several cost elements must be classified for purposes of analysis. The kind of classification employed depends upon the purposes of the analysis. All costs are classified by the economist into two broad categories: fixed costs and variable costs.[1] Fixed costs are those which do not change in total as output changes; these are the costs which the firm would have to bear even if the plant were completely closed down for a time. Variable costs, on the other hand, are those which do vary as output changes. Rent and the salary of the corporation president are illustrations of fixed costs. Rent must be paid to the landlord whether nothing, little, or much is produced, and the amount of rent paid will not usually be affected by the size of the output. Variable costs are illustrated by wages paid to laborers and the cost of raw materials. If a shoe factory produces 200,000 pairs of shoes in a month, the cost of the leather used will be greater than if the monthly output is only 100,000 pairs. By definition, the total fixed cost remains constant as output increases, but total variable cost increases with an increase in output.

Total Cost and Total Revenue

The nature of total costs is illustrated graphically in Figure 5.1. The *TC* curve represents the total costs of a firm for the various outputs as measured on the x axis. If the output is *OL*, for example, total cost will be *LA*; if output is greater, say *OM*, total cost will be greater, in this case, *MB*. It will be noted that when output is zero, total cost is *OF*. This, then, is total fixed cost. When output is *OM*, the total cost of *MB* consists of a fixed cost of *MH* (which equals *OF*) and variable costs of *HB*. The vertical distance between the *FF'* line and the *TC* curve measures total variable cost at any output.

The curve *TR* in Figure 5.1 represents the firm's total revenue. As output increases, it is assumed that the firm's revenue increases proportionally. At an output of *OL*, the total revenue is *LA*, and at an output of *OM*, the total revenue is *MJ*. It will be noted that in the figure total cost and total revenue are equal at outputs *OL* and *ON*. These points are known as

---

[1] The classification of costs employed by the accountant is somewhat different. See Appendix A for an elaboration of this point.

"break-even" points.[1] The firm depicted in Figure 5.1 must be able to sell at least *OL* units of its product; otherwise it will incur losses. For outputs between *OL* and *ON*, total costs are less than total revenue; that is, the firm can operate within this range and make a profit. For outputs greater than *ON*, the firm would again incur losses. On the assumption that the management wishes to maximize profits, the firm must operate somewhere between output *OL* and output *ON*. The particular output where profits are greatest will be where the vertical distance between the

Figure 5.1. BREAK-EVEN CHART

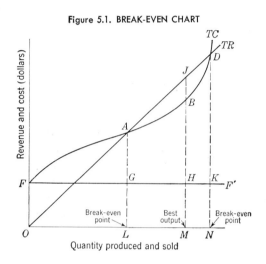

TR and the *TC* curves is greatest. In this figure this is at output *OM*, where total cost is *MB*, total revenue is *MJ*, and profit is *BJ*.

It is clear that, if a firm actually had sufficient data to draw its total cost and total revenue curves, it would be a simple matter to determine the output at which profits would be maximized. In practice they do not, of course, have precise data of this sort. We may assume, however, that the firm's officers are actually attempting to make as accurate estimates as possible concerning costs and revenues. To a considerable extent the firm's policy makers are required to make "educated guesses," but the break-even chart indicates what they are guessing at, and such charts are becoming increasingly popular with managers of firms.

---

[1] In some situations there is only one break-even point. It is taken as a rule of thumb, for example, that it requires 100 performances for a Broadway play to make expenses; there will be no second break-even point as long as the performance draws a good house. When businessmen refer to *the* break-even point, they refer, of course, to the first one.

Average and Marginal Costs

It is frequently helpful to think in terms of average costs rather than total costs; this allows costs to be directly related to prices. Corresponding to the concepts of total cost, total variable cost, and total fixed cost, we have average total cost, average variable cost, and average fixed cost, *i.e.*, the total, variable, and fixed cost per unit of output. The average total cost is the sum of the average variable and the average fixed cost. The relationship between total and average costs is indicated in Table 5.1. The

Table 5.1. Production Costs of a Hypothetical Firm

(1)	(2)	(3)	(4)	(5)	(6)	(7)	(8)
Output	Total fixed cost	Total variable cost	Total cost	Average fixed cost	Average variable cost	Average total cost	Marginal cost
1	$50	$ 20	$ 70	$50.00	$20.00	$70.00	$20
2	50	39	89	25.00	19.50	44.50	19
3	50	57	107	16.67	19.00	35.67	18
4	50	74	124	12.50	18.50	31.00	17
5	50	90	140	10.00	18.00	28.00	16
6	50	105	155	8.33	17.50	25.83	15
7	50	120	170	7.14	17.14	24.29	15
8	50	136	186	6.25	17.00	23.25	16
9	50	154	204	5.56	17.11	22.67	18
10	50	174	224	5.00	17.40	22.40	20
11	50	196	246	4.55	17.82	22.36	22
12	50	220	270	4.17	18.33	22.50	24
13	50	246	296	3.85	18.92	22.77	26
14	50	274	324	3.57	19.57	23.14	28
15	50	304	354	3.33	20.27	23.60	30
16	50	336	386	3.12	21.00	24.12	32
17	50	370	420	2.94	21.76	24.70	34
18	50	406	456	2.78	22.56	25.33	36
19	50	444	494	2.63	23.37	26.00	38
20	50	484	534	2.50	24.20	26.70	40

output, fixed cost, and total variable cost columns are assumed to be given. Column 4, total cost, is simply the sum of the total fixed cost and the total variable cost for each output. Column 5 indicates the average fixed cost and is derived by dividing total fixed cost by output. Average variable cost, column 6, is the variable cost per unit of output, and it is determined by dividing total variable cost by output. Column 7 is the total cost per unit of output, and it may be derived either by dividing total cost by output or by adding average fixed cost and average variable cost. Marginal cost, column 8, is neither a total nor an average cost. It represents the *additional* cost incurred as a result of producing an additional unit of output. The total cost of producing 10 units of output, for example, is $224. If output is increased to 11 units, the total cost will be $246. The additional cost incurred as a result of producing the eleventh unit is, accordingly, the difference between $246 and $224, or $22, which is the marginal cost at that output.[1] Marginal cost, as we shall soon see, is a very important concept in economic analysis, and we shall also meet other marginal concepts which are important devices in the economist's kit of tools.

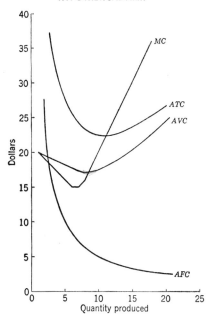

Figure 5.2. SHORT-RUN COST CURVES OF HYPOTHETICAL FIRM

The same relationship illustrated in Table 5.1 may be shown graphically in Figure 5.2. The way in which average fixed cost, average variable cost, average total cost, and marginal cost vary as output changes is shown in the four fundamental cost curves.

The average fixed cost curve shows that fixed costs per unit decrease continuously as output increases. Since it is derived by dividing the total fixed cost of $50 by the output, the fixed cost per unit of output will become smaller and smaller as the output increases. If output were 10 units, for example, average fixed cost would be $5. If the output were increased to 100, the fixed cost per unit would be 50 cents; if 1,000 units were produced, the average fixed cost would be 5 cents. As output increases, the average fixed cost approaches but never reaches zero. The decline in average fixed cost is a matter of particular significance in those industries where fixed costs are relatively high. If a die for the right rear fender of a Chevrolet, for example, costs $1,000,000, the die cost per automobile will be $1,000 if only 1,000 Chevrolets are produced, but it will be only $1 per unit if 1,000,000 cars are produced. Businessmen recognize the relation-

---

[1] Since variable costs are the only costs which change as output changes, marginal cost is also the difference between successive total variable costs. When output is 10, for example, total variable cost is $174, and when output is 11, total variable cost is $196. The difference, $22, is marginal cost.

ship between output and average fixed cost by the use of such terms as "spreading the overhead."

It will be noted that the average variable cost curve indicates that variable cost per unit of output decreases, then reaches a minimum value, and thereafter increases. The initial decline in average variable cost is due to the fact that, within limits, more units of the variable factors are needed to utilize the fixed equipment effectively. For example, the efficiency of a garbage truck may be more than doubled by the addition of a second man. This is the same as saying that the variable costs per ton of garbage collected decrease as the amount collected per truck increases over this range. But it is also likely that the efficiency of the garbage truck will not be proportionately increased by the addition of a third man. In other words, average variable costs begin to increase with the third man, and continue to increase as more men are added. In graphic terms, the average variable cost curve is of a general U shape.

The average total cost curve is the summation of the other two. It is also seen to be U-shaped, with its minimum value appearing at a greater output than that at which average variable costs are at their lowest level. For very small outputs both average fixed costs and average variable costs are decreasing as output increases, and the sum of the two is, accordingly, decreasing. As output increases, the average fixed cost becomes a smaller and smaller part of average total cost, and the increase in average variable costs ultimately more than offsets the decrease in average fixed cost, with the result that average total costs begin to increase as output increases.

The marginal or incremental cost curve indicates the rate of change in total costs as output increases. It will be noted that the marginal cost curve declines, reaches a minimum, and then rises. The shape of the marginal cost curve reflects the fact, illustrated in Figure 5.1, that total cost at first increases at a decreasing rate and then increases at an increasing rate. It can be seen that the marginal cost curve intersects both the average variable and the average total cost curves at their lowest points. As long as average variable cost is decreasing as output is increasing, the additional cost of producing an additional unit must be less than the average in order to bring the average down. If average variable cost is unchanged as output increases, marginal cost must equal average variable cost. And if average variable cost increases as output increases, marginal cost must be greater than average variable cost in order to bring up the average. Similarly, the marginal cost is less than average total cost as long as average total costs are decreasing with an increase in output, equal to average total cost when average total costs are constant, and greater than average total costs when they are increasing. The marginal cost curve will, accordingly, lie below the average variable cost curve as long as the average variable cost is decreasing, intersect it at its minimum value, and lie above when it is increasing; the marginal cost curve will also lie below the average total cost curve as long as the average total cost curve is decreasing, intersect it at its minimum value, and lie above it when it is increasing as output increases.[1] These relationships are so important to an understanding of the economics of the firm that a careful study of Figure 5.2 and Table 5.1 is prerequisite to an understanding of the following chapters in this section.

LONG-RUN COST

So far we have been considering the short-run aspects of costs. We have assumed that a plant of given size is employed and that the firm is able to use the fixed input factors in combination with various quantities of variable input factors, varying output by making changes in the number of workers employed, the quantities of raw materials used, and so on. If, however, we take into account long-run considerations, the problem is somewhat different. The long run refers to a time period sufficiently great to allow for an increase in the scale of operations, which means investment in new fixed input factors. In the long run, accordingly, even the amount of fixed factors is subject to variation, and it is appropriate to say that in the long run all costs are variable and none are fixed. This, in fact, is what the economist means by "long run"—the period in which all costs are variable.

We are concerned here with problems of scale. We seek an answer to the following questions: How do costs change as the whole scale of the firm's operations changes? Will operation on a larger scale necessarily lead to more efficient production? Or is there an optimum or most efficient size for a business firm? An important distinction must be made clear before these questions may be answered. The single-plant firm must be distinguished from the multiple-plant firm; a firm may operate one plant or any number of plants. Let us consider the single-plant firm first.

---

[1] A common-sense notion of the relation between average and marginal concepts may be gained from the consideration of a baseball player's batting average. Suppose that after the July 1 game a player's average for the season is .252, but after the July 2 game his average has fallen to .250. It is clear that during the July 2 game he must have batted less than .250—he probably went hitless—since the last or "marginal" game has brought the average down. Suppose that after the July 3 game his season's average remains at .250. It is clear that he batted .250 on July 3—probably one hit in four trips to the plate; i.e., when the average did not change, marginal must have equaled average. After the July 4 double-header, our hero had boosted his season's average to .255. In this case marginal must have been greater than average to have brought the average up.

For a fuller discussion of the relationships between total, average, and marginal quantities, see Section 2, Appendix B.

It seems evident that firms operating very small plants are likely to be inefficient, *i.e.*, high-cost, in almost any line of production. The production unit is too small to take full advantage of the use of specialized labor and equipment. A good example of inefficient single-plant firms is provided by the case of very small farms. They have been proved inefficient relative to larger farms because they are not large enough to utilize mechanized equipment effectively. It would hardly pay a wheat farmer with a 10-acre plot to purchase the combine that the farmer with a 1,000-acre plot would use. But it seems equally clear that firms operating very large plants are also likely to be inefficient in almost any line of production. The production unit simply gets too large for the job to be accomplished properly. For example, an ocean-going freighter would be inefficient if used as a shrimp boat, and an auditorium is of little use as a classroom. We can conclude, therefore, that average total costs for the single-plant firm fall for a range as the plant size is increased, reach a minimum, and then begin to increase as the plant gets larger.

The efficiency or inefficiency stemming from the size of the technical production unit, the plant, need not be the main consideration determining the appropriate scale of operations for the multi-plant firm. A firm may own many plants, all technically of the most efficient size. The question now becomes: Is there any general relationship between the size of the firm (regardless of the number of plants operated) and the average costs of production? It seems probable that the same sort of answer as was made in the case of the single-plant firm may be reached here, although in a somewhat modified form. Extremely small firms operating only one plant, even should this plant be of the optimum size, are in many instances less efficient than firms operating several plants. An example may be provided by the movie-theater industry. The single-theater firm seems clearly less efficient than the many-theater firm, as evidenced by the predominance of the latter type of firm in the industry. The advantages of scale here are perhaps largely those of booking and scheduling. Other examples are provided by the emergence of the grocery chains, where the advantages of centralized purchasing and distribution are the important considerations. For many industries, it seems probable that the number of plants that a firm operates has little effect on its efficiency over a rather wide range. In the fishing-industry example discussed in Chapter 6, it is pointed out that the firm operating several boats has little, if any, cost advantage over the firm operating a single boat (plant). It is clear, however, that once a firm operates a great many plants, even should they all be technically efficient, the problems of coordinating the firm's activities begin to loom large. It has been noted, for example, that as universities become larger the administrative costs become a larger proportion of the total budget. So, just as in the case of the single-plant firm, the multiple-plant firm becomes inefficient once it gets too large. Some idea of the causes of inefficiency in a multi-plant firm may be gained from a comparison of the paper work involved in a cash purchase from an independent hardware retailer and from a retail outlet of a large manufacturing firm, say of paint. Every sale of the retail outlet must be recorded in triplicate, one copy to be sent to the home office, one to go to the district sales manager, and one to be kept in the local store. These are necessary for the operations of the multi-plant firm to be coordinated properly, but they increase the cost of goods and services.

Figure 5.3. LONG-RUN AVERAGE COST

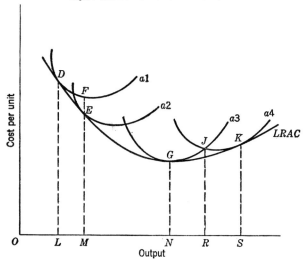

In summary, we may say that, for both the single-plant firm and the multi-plant firm, average total costs tend to decrease over a certain range as the scale of operations is increased, then reach a minimum, and then increase as the scale of operations becomes too large. Since the same conclusions apply to the two types of firm, we will find it useful to concentrate on the single-plant firm in the more detailed discussion which follows.

The nature of the long-run cost concept may be understood more easily by a study of Figure 5.3. Curves a_1, a_2, a_3, and a_4 represent short-run average total cost curves for plants of alternative sizes, a_1 representing the plant with smallest capacity and a_4 representing the largest of the four plants. If the firm is considering the construction of a new plant— a long-run consideration—it must determine what size plant to build. If it is anticipated that demand conditions will justify only a small output, such as OL, the a_1 plant will be the appropriate size. If, however, it is anticipated that the plant will need to produce an output of OM, that output can be produced at a lower cost with plant a_2 than with a_1. Plant

a_3 represents the "optimum"-sized plant; any smaller size fails to take full advantage of the economies of large-scale production, and larger plants suffer from "diseconomies" of too large size. If output ON is produced with plant a_3, the optimum output is being produced by the optimum-sized plant; the average total cost is then NG, and this is less than the amount for which any other output can be produced. If, however, an output greater than OR is to be produced, it can be produced at a lower cost with plant a_4 than with a_3. The envelope curve $LRAC$, which is tangent to each of the short-run average total cost curves, is the long-run average cost, or "planning," curve; *it indicates the lowest cost at which any output can be produced on the assumption that sufficient time is allowed to permit the construction of the appropriate-sized plant* and, further, that a plant of any size can be constructed. Considerations of this sort are important when firms are contemplating the building of new plants. The construction of a plant which in relation to the market demand is either too large or too small will result in reduced profits and may bring financial failure. For long-range planning there are no fixed costs; the amount invested in "fixed" input factors will vary depending upon what size of plant is to be built. Once the appropriate size has been decided upon and the plant is constructed, however, the decisions of the firm's management become short-run decisions, and fixed costs are clearly distinct from variable costs. The day-to-day decisions of management are short-run decisions; but periodically, when the construction of a new plant or the abandonment of the old plant is contemplated, important long-run decisions must be made.

An illustration may be useful in showing the difference between long-run and short-run cost considerations. Suppose a veteran of the Korean War wishes to go into the business of producing concrete blocks (which was a popular field for veterans of World War II). He can erect a plant which can turn out anywhere from 1,000 to 20,000 or more blocks a day, depending on the number and size of the block-making machines. The average cost per block is somewhat higher in the smallest plants. If he can raise enough capital, he will probably erect a plant which can turn out 5,000 or 10,000 blocks a day rather than 1,000 or 2,000 a day. If he acquires a plant capable of turning out 50,000 blocks a day, however, his average cost may again go up. Such a plant requires highly skilled supervision, accurate planning of receipts and shipments, and skillful handling of inventory.

Suppose he settles this long-run problem and erects a plant to turn out blocks on the most economical scale, say 10,000 per day. His short-run average cost curve could be represented by a_3 of Figure 5.3. An output of 10,000 a day would be the quantity ON. At this output he would be minimizing both long-run and short-run costs; the former would have been achieved by selecting the best-sized plant and the latter by operating it at the most efficient rate. At a daily output of 8,000 or 12,000 blocks, for example, his short-run average costs would be somewhat higher than at the optimum rate of 10,000 per day. The veteran might or might not make a change in the size of his plant at a later date. He would, however, constantly be faced with the short-run problem of deciding upon the exact daily output.

SUMMARY

In summary, it should be noted that the long-run average cost curves of both the *plant* and the *firm* are U-shaped. As the firm expands in size, by increasing the capacity and/or the number of plants, it encounters both economies and diseconomies of large-scale production. Among the economies which tend to reduce unit costs as the size of the firm is increased are the following: improved ability to borrow capital funds and at lower costs, higher degree of division of labor among workers and capital equipment, greater resources for research and selling activities, ability to buy factors at discounted prices, and greater diversification of products. If, however, the firm becomes too big, administrative costs are likely to increase at a disproportionate rate with the result that unit costs after a point are likely to increase. What constitutes the optimum size of firm varies greatly from industry to industry; in the cotton-textile industry it appears that the optimum-sized firm is relatively small, whereas in the steel industry it is quite large. The shape of the firm's long-run average cost curve is also subject to a wide degree of variation; for some industries the curve may be relatively flat on both sides of the minimum point, while for others the decreasing-cost segments of the curve may be quite steep. The important thing to observe is that there is an optimum size for both plant and firm, and goods are produced at the lowest possible cost only when the optimum-sized firm is operating its optimum-sized plants at optimum outputs. As will be seen in the next chapter, this represents the equilibrium situation in a perfectly competitive industry.

CHAPTER 6

COMPETITION KEEPS PRICES DOWN

In Chapter 4 it was shown that prices are determined by supply and demand, and in Chapter 5 the point was made that the laws of supply are based on the behavior of business firms in attempting to maximize profits. Output decisions were shown to depend essentially on the relation between revenues and costs. The nature of the cost relations was explored in some detail.

It should be understood that the simple demand and supply schedules and curves used in Chapter 4, if considered rigorously, assume certain conditions to be present on both sides of the market, the buying side and the selling side. Specifically, competition among both buyers and sellers is assumed to be present. In the real world, however, these conditions may or may not exist. It is necessary, accordingly, to outline carefully the meaning of these assumptions.

THE CONCEPT OF COMPETITION

Competition among Buyers

The fundamental requirement for competition in the economic sense is that there be both many buyers and many sellers in a market. On the buying side, there must be a sufficient number of buyers so that no single one exerts an appreciable influence on the price which he must pay. This may be stated in terms of demand and supply curves in the following way. The supply curve facing the individual buyer (consumer) must be horizontal at the market price. The consumer must be able to purchase as much or as little of the commodity as he desires without causing price to change. This may be illustrated in Figure 6.1. The amount demanded at the market price *OP* will be determined by the intersection of the consumer's demand curve with the horizontal supply curve. This situation is typical of most markets for final products and services. There are some opportunities for quantity discounts and purchases of large "economy" sizes, but for the most part the consumer has little or no control over the

price he pays. This may be stated in another way: Pure competition on
the buying side of the market for final products and services is the rule
rather than the exception.

Figure 6.1. SUPPLY CURVE FACING THE
            BUYER—
            Is Horizontal in Pure Competition

Figure 6.2. DEMAND CURVE FACING THE
            SELLER—
            Is Horizontal in Pure Competition

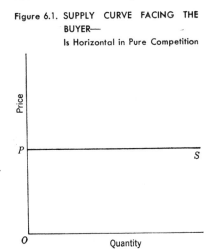

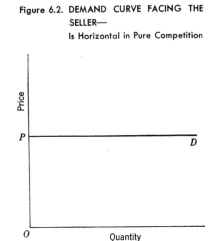

Competition among Sellers

The same is not true, however, for the selling side of the market. Here,
pure competition is the exception. Most sellers have some control over
price; prices paid by consumers are generally "set" by sellers. The principal exceptions are sellers of certain agricultural and fishery products and
sellers of securities and commodities in organized exchanges. A farmer
has no control over the price at which he sells his cotton; he cannot affect
price at all by withholding a portion of his crop from the market. The
price at which he must sell is set for him by either the impersonal forces
of the market, the organized buyers, or, more likely, the government. He
can sell as much or as little as he wants to at the going price (provided,
of course, that there are no quota limitations). The same kind of situation
is faced by the small-scale seller of securities in the New York stock
exchanges. Sales are made at the prevailing market price, and prices
are not set by the seller.

Pure competition on the selling side can be described graphically by
saying that the seller is faced with a horizontal demand curve at the
ruling price. This is illustrated in Figure 6.2. In order for pure competition to be present among sellers there must be a large enough number
of them so that no one can influence price by the withholding of supply.
As mentioned above, this is a rather exceptional case, since in most instances sellers do control price to some degree. The means by which they
can exercise control is the withholding of a portion of their potential

supply from the market, which tends to increase price. If this ability to raise price by restricting supply rests with a seller, some degree of monopoly power is present. The degree of monopoly can vary greatly. Some sellers such as the corner grocer may vary prices only within narrow limits; with any appreciable increase in his prices, sales would fall off a great deal. Concerns possessing patent rights to the exclusive manufacture of certain commodities, on the other hand, may be able to vary price within rather broad limits without the loss of so large a proportion of sales. In these cases, the demand curve facing the seller is downsloping, as illustrated in Figure 6.3. The particular problems faced by sellers in such imperfectly competitive markets and

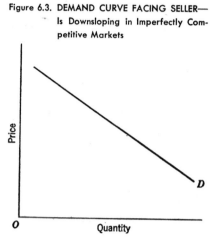

Figure 6.3. DEMAND CURVE FACING SELLER—Is Downsloping in Imperfectly Competitive Markets

the social implications of monopoly will be discussed in some detail in the following chapter. The present chapter will examine the case of the perfectly competitive market for output more thoroughly.

Significance of the Competitive Assumption

Firms selling under conditions of pure competition do represent exceptional cases. Descriptively, therefore, the analysis of their behavior is not very important. But such analysis remains extremely significant. Economic analysis must always be kept separate and distinct from description. Economic principles are designed to provide the student with a set of tools with which he can understand the workings of the free-enterprise system. To do this, he needs more than factual descriptions. In spite of the fact that sellers do exercise some control over prices, one of the most valuable tools in all of economics would be lost if we dismissed the case of fully competitive markets as unimportant. This analysis is necessary for several reasons. First, competitive markets represent, in one sense, a normative ideal; it is well for the student to master an understanding of how the free-enterprise system would work if there were no monopoly elements present, since proper public policy must generally imply an attempt to make the system tend more toward, rather than away from, this position. Second, many real problems simply cannot be solved within any analytical framework other than that of purely competitive markets. Even where industries are composed of imperfectly competitive firms, many problems affecting the whole industry can best be solved if the departures from pure competition are ignored. Third, a thorough knowledge of the theory of price formation in competitive markets will greatly facilitate the understanding of the theory of noncompetitive behavior.

ECONOMICS OF THE COMPETITIVE FIRM

All firms must make three basic decisions: (1) what to produce, (2) how to produce, and (3) how much to produce. These are the only decisions which must be made by the firm selling in competition; it does not have the additional decision, what price to charge. Once having decided what to produce and how input units shall be combined to produce it, the firm adjusts its output to a given market price. As the market price changes, it will try to change its output so as to move toward a position in which profits are greatest.

As was observed in Chapter 5, profits are greatest when output is such that total revenue exceeds total cost by the largest possible amount. *This maximum-profit output may be reached by expanding output as long as the addition to revenue resulting from the sale of the additional output is greater than the addition to cost caused by producing the extra output.* If a firm is selling its output competitively, the addition to revenue as a result of putting one more unit of output on the market is always equal to the price of a unit. The firm can, by the definition of pure competition, sell as much or as little as it wishes without causing the price at which it sells to shift. The addition to cost as a result of changing output is the marginal cost. Therefore, another way of defining the maximum-profit output for the purely competitive firm is to say it is that output for which *price equals marginal cost.*

A firm will, therefore, tend to adjust output to the point at which marginal cost equals price.[1] But reaching this equality does not imply that the firm always makes a profit. Whether or not profit appears depends on the relation between total cost and total revenue or between average total cost and price. The equality between price and marginal cost guarantees that a position of maximum profit or minimum loss has been attained, but it does not provide any information concerning the absolute profit or loss position. If a firm has made the basic decisions concerning what to produce and has constructed a single plant to embody a certain quantity of physical resources, its ability to change output is limited. It can change the inputs of its variable factors and thus

---

[1] Even this statement must be qualified. It is true only if marginal costs are rising. The equality of price and marginal cost will not represent the position of maximum profit or minimum loss if perchance marginal cost is falling. For then it would be possible to improve the firm's position by expanding output further, since price would exceed added cost.

adjust output somewhat, but it cannot change the over-all scale of its operations, since that would require changing fixed as well as variable factors. The marginal cost function represents the rate of change in total cost as output is changed within the limits of a given scale of plant. Since, for the individual seller in pure competition, price does not change as his output varies, the equation of price and marginal cost is reached by an output, rather than a price, adjustment. Thus, the marginal cost function becomes the supply function for the competitive firm in the short run. It represents the quantities which will be supplied at all possible prices. This is illustrated in Figure 6.4. At a price OP_3, the firm will supply an amount OM_3, at OP_2 an amount OM_2, at OP_1 an amount OM_1.

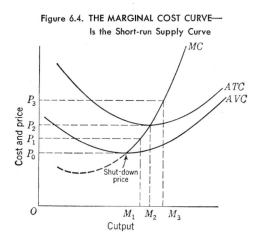

Figure 6.4. THE MARGINAL COST CURVE—
Is the Short-run Supply Curve

Some qualification must be made here, however; the marginal cost function represents the supply function of the firm only above a certain minimum price. If a firm cannot cover its *variable* costs, it should shut down even if it must abandon its equipment completely. No firm should sensibly supply any amount at a price below that which would bring in enough revenue to cover variable costs. This can be shown in Figure 6.4. If AVC represents the average variable cost curve of the firm, then no quantity would be supplied at any price below OP_o. If price fell below this point, the firm would close down; therefore, OP_o can conveniently be labeled the "shut-down price." Thus, the marginal cost curve becomes the supply curve at all prices above OP_o. As long as price is above OP_o, the firm will continue to operate even if it is not covering total costs. For at prices above this level, it will be more than covering variable costs; *i.e.*, it will be making some return on its fixed investment, whereas it would lose the entire amount of its fixed costs if it did not operate at all.

If we include an average total cost function, ATC in Figure 6.4, it can be seen that, between prices OP_o and OP_2, losses would be incurred, since price is less than average cost and total revenue is less than total costs. At price OP_2, the firm would be breaking even, and at prices above this level, it would make positive profit.

ECONOMICS OF A COMPETITIVE INDUSTRY

The supply curve for a whole industry of competitive sellers in the short run is derived by the summation of that part of all the firms' marginal cost curves which lies above the minimum points on their average variable cost curves. If a hypothetical competitive industry consists of 100 identical single-plant firms, one of which is pictured in Figure 6.4, the industry would supply an amount equal to 100 OM_1 at a price OP_1, 100 OM_2 at a price OP_2, etc. This industry supply function and the market demand function would determine, by their intersection, the competitive price in the short run.

Pure competition requires that there be a large number of sellers, but it also requires that there be freedom of entry. New firms must be able to enter the industry without any restrictions, and old firms must be able to leave the industry when they desire. It can readily be seen that there will be an incentive for firms entering the industry to build plants of the optimum size. Firms which build high-cost plants of either too small or too large size will be squeezed out by new competitors who enter the industry with plants of optimum size. Similarly, firms must also be of optimum size. Competition tends to ensure "survival of the fittest." This is one of the major advantages of competitive markets; competition will tend to ensure that plants and firms are established for a high degree of efficiency. The optimum size, of course, need not be the same, even for firms within a single industry; but operating efficiency cannot for long be different among different firms.

Long-run Adjustments

The fact that a considerable degree of competition does exist in the American economy tends to support the hypothesis concerning long-run average costs advanced in Chapter 5. Firms or plants do not continue indefinitely to become more and more efficient as they get larger and larger. If this were the case, the larger firms could always drive the smaller ones completely out of business by producing and selling at lower costs. The existence of a substantial degree of competition requires that the optimum-sized firm be reached at a relatively small fraction of industry output.

With freedom of entry into and egress from an industry there will be a tendency for enough firms to be in the industry so that each firm will be making only a normal return on invested capital.[1] If, in addition, profits are made, this will attract capital investment in new firms, and the movement will continue until only an average rate of return on investment is present. On the other hand, if less than an average return is being obtained on investment, plants will not be replaced as they wear out, and the number of firms in the industry will be reduced. Thus, while adjustments in the short run are made as a result of individual firms varying their outputs, the long-run adjustments are effected largely by firms entering and leaving the industry.

The long-run supply curve of the industry cannot be arrived at by adding up cost curves of firms. It can easily be seen that if time for new firms to enter is taken into account, the possibilities of expansion or contraction of industry output become almost unlimited. The quantity supplied becomes more and more responsive to changes in price as the time period is lengthened. This was discussed in Chapter 4. If new firms can come into the industry and thus expand total industry output, without causing the prices of the productive factors which the industry employs to be increased, the long-run supply curve is horizontal. Price of output will tend to move toward this level; if it is temporarily above this long-run normal level, new firms will come in and increase output sufficiently to bring price back down to this equilibrium again. This case is descriptively applicable only to a fairly small industry whose demand for inputs is not sufficiently great to affect the price of any productive factor which it employs.

For most industries of substantial size, the entry of new firms will tend to cause the prices of the productive factors used by the industry to be increased. The new firms will, for example, try to hire away the executives and skilled workmen from the older firms and will be willing to pay higher prices for the best raw-material sources. In this case, an expansion in the industry is accompanied by a general increase in the average cost of production. The long-run supply curve of the industry is upsloping to some degree, the amount of the slope depending on the rate of increase in the minimum average cost of each firm as the industry expands.

In any case, if there is pure competition among sellers, the major long-run expansion or contraction in industry output as a result of changes in demand forces will come about by the entry or egress of firms. Price will tend to move toward and fluctuate around a level which will just allow each firm in the industry to cover average costs of production, including

---

[1] This return is included in total costs. In everyday usage, the entire return on the capital invested in a firm by its owners is termed "profit." Economists, however, usually restrict the meaning of profit to returns which are in excess of normal interest on the capital employed by an enterprise. In the latter sense, profits tend to be eliminated by the entrance of new competitors.

a normal rate of return on invested capital. As was pointed out in Chapter 4, the supply side is a much more important determinant of price than the demand side in the long-run case. Firms will tend to be of the most efficient size, and prices will tend to be equal to average as well as to marginal cost of production.

The long-run equilibrium position for an individual firm in a competitive industry is represented in Figure 6.5. Price is equal to marginal cost so that in the short run profits are maximized. Marginal cost equals short-run average cost, since the firm is operating at the most efficient output. Short-run and long-run average costs are equal at the lowest cost point, since the firm is of the most efficient size. Price is equal to average cost,

Figure 6.5. LONG-RUN EQUILIBRIUM—
Of the Competitive Firm

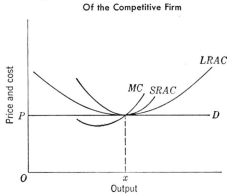

since the firm is just covering its cost of production, including the approximate rate of return on capital which it could earn elsewhere; it has, therefore, no incentive to contract or to expand. New firms have no incentive to enter the industry since there is no abnormal return being made to attract them. Although the position represented is purely an imaginary one toward which the market forces tend to push the individual firms, it is extremely useful as a starting point in the analysis of particular problems. It may be helpful to take a highly competitive industry and trace through the changes resulting from the required movement from one such long-run equilibrium position to another.

THE FISHING INDUSTRY: AN EXAMPLE OF COMPETITIVE ADJUSTMENT

We have for this purpose selected commercial fishing which, as it is practiced along the South Atlantic and Gulf Coasts, is probably one of the best examples of pure competition (on the selling side) in the United States today. In some cases even this industry is dominated by a few large companies or characterized by organization of the fishermen. But for the most part it corresponds very closely to the economist's conception of pure competition as far as the catching and initial sale of fish are concerned.[1] (The processes of distribution are usually less completely competitive.)

The plant (boat, nets, and other gear) is small for operations near the shore where fishing is carried on. This is conducive to small-sized "firms," which often consist of two-man partnerships. A small firm is large enough to own one efficient plant, which is quite different from the situation in an industry like steelmaking, where a plant of economical size is so large that a steel company must be large to own even one plant. Further, the fishing industry is not normally characterized by important advantages of multi-plant ownership such as exist in the food-retailing business, where the economies of large-scale buying and advertising have created the chain stores, each chain operating a large number of fairly small retailing "plants." Firms owning only a single satisfactory fishing vessel are normally at no disadvantage compared with those owning several. The firm of optimum size, represented in Figure 6.5, is relatively small. It is quite possible that fishing firms ranging quite widely in size are of equal efficiency. The $LRAC$ curve of Figure 6.5 would then be horizontal over this range. If the firm is very small, however (*e.g.*, only large enough to own a rowboat), it is clear that efficiency will be reduced. Above a certain size, efficiency of the firm may be diminished by a lessening of managerial skill in the coordination of activities of a large fleet.

The fishing industry also satisfies the further requisite of pure competition that firms may enter and leave at will. Only small capital and moderate skill are required to set oneself up in the fishing business along many of our shores. Indeed, entry is so easy that a successful sports fisherman can usually sell to a shore dealer any part of his salt-water catch which he wishes to dispose of.

It is also necessary that there be many buyers as well as many sellers in order to render competition fully effective. Generally this condition is also met. In most localities, fishermen have a considerable choice of shore dealers to whom they may sell their catch. This is a result of the simplicity of the dealer's business and the rather small capital investment necessary for the erection of suitable landing piers and sheltering structures.

When a fisherman lands his boat at the shore dealer's docks he finds posted a single price per pound for each variety of fish normally caught in

[1] The fishing industry was used by Alfred Marshall in his *Principles of Economics*, (London: Macmillan & Co., Ltd., 1938), 8th ed., Book V, Chap. V, to illustrate short-run and long-run competitive price. The need to use this industry as illustrative of pure competition is more pressing today than in Marshall's time, especially because of the triumph of trade-marks and advertising.

those waters. He can sell as much as he has caught at that price but can sell none at a higher price. This is the meaning of the horizontal demand curve for the product of the perfectly competitive firm. The price is established by the shore dealer in accord with the over-all supply-demand situation for each variety of fish and is changed frequently as these conditions change. No fisherman feels it necessary to advertise. The boats do not carry signs to the effect that one should "Buy Mac's Mackerel," "Purchase Pete's Pompano," or "Try Tony's Trout."

Each fishing firm is unable to affect price; all it can do is adjust its own operations to the prevailing market prices. When prices are favorable, fishermen generally work longer and harder in order to take advantage of this situation. To some extent it is possible for them to consider relative prices of fish, modifying gear and tactics in such a way as to increase the proportionate catch of the kinds of fish which have become more worth while. In the main, however, fishing by net is unselective, and the principal short-run response to price changes consists in altering the number of hours of work. During World War II, when fish prices were high, it was common for fishermen to work seven days a week.

"Long-run" adjustments take place much more quickly in commercial fishing than in most other types of production. The number of plants utilized can be increased rapidly by simply pressing certain types of pleasure boats into this use or by bringing fishing boats from other territories where conditions are less favorable.

Suppose the commercial fishing industry of a coastal region is in a position of long-run equilibrium in the sense that the number and size of fishing enterprises are appropriately adjusted to the prevailing demand and cost conditions. Fishermen will be receiving normal wage rates for labor in their skill category, and capital invested in boats and gear will be earning a normal net return. On the left side of Figure 6.6, the industry is first assumed to be fully adjusted in both size and rate of operation to demand D_1; consequently, the short-run supply curve and the demand curve intersect at a price which is equal to long-run supply price OP_1. (The long-run supply curve has been assumed to be horizontal because the fishing industry does not purchase large quantities of any factor which is likely to change permanently in price because of either larger or smaller purchases by fishermen.) Equilibrium output for the industry is OA.

A single firm in the same industry is represented on the right side of Figure 6.6. At the market price OP_1, determined by the over-all supply-demand conditions pictured, the firm can sell all that it produces. Its best rate of operation is Oa, where marginal cost equals price. The firm which is pictured is of the most efficient size as indicated by its operation at the point of lowest average cost in this industry equilibrium situation. The industry is assumed to be made up of 1,000 such firms, requiring that the scale in which quantity is measured be thousands of pounds for the industry and pounds for the single enterprise.

Suppose a decrease in the demand by consumers for fish now occurs, caused, for example, by a substantial fall in the price of beef. This results quickly in a lowered demand by shore dealers, represented by D_2 in the industry diagram, and the dealers will lower the price which they will pay for fish. The disappointed fishermen will quickly respond by working less, reducing output of the typical firm to Ob, at which output marginal cost is again equated to price. The sum of these actions will be similarly reflected in the industry diagram at the left where total output will be reduced from OA to OB, determined by the intersection of curves S and D_2.

Figure 6.6. DECLINE IN DEMAND FOR FISH—
Causes Short-run and Long-run
Adjustments

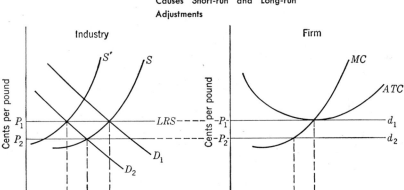

Fishing boats and gear will now be used less intensively, and the return to capital and labor will fall off. This decline in the attractiveness of fishing will cause some firms to leave the industry. The egress will take some time but, as already mentioned, much less time than a comparable adjustment would require in most industries. The ultimate effect of the decline in demand will be a reduction in the number of firms in the business of catching fish, but the size of remaining organizations should be no smaller than before. The rate of catching fish will be diminished by this exit of firms, that is, the industry supply curve will shift to the left, and price will respond by gradually rising again to the previous level OP_1. As firms leave the industry, the typical remaining firm will gradually increase its rate of operations back to Oa. Thus its own position will eventually be the same as before the decline in demand. The industry will be smaller than before; hence the new industry supply curve S' (on the left-hand side) will meet demand curve D_2, rather than D_1, at the original price OP_1. The industry short-run supply curve has moved to the left because fewer than 1,000 firms are now in the industry.

The foregoing discussion of a movement from one long-run equilibrium position to another has assumed that sufficient labor and capital will leave an industry when rates of return fall below those which can be earned in alternative employment; that is, it has assumed some degree of mobility of productive factors. To the extent that lack of knowledge or inertia prevents such a shift, the number of firms may not decline in the manner indicated in response to a decrease in demand. In that event, the price of fish would be permanently lowered by the reduced demand, since supply would not be contracted sufficiently. The entire analysis is further dependent on the assumption that prices of all input items (*e.g.*, gasoline) remain constant throughout the period required for full adjustment to the new demand conditions.

SUMMARY

We have in this chapter examined the workings of purely competitive markets. It has been shown that competition among sellers tends to keep output prices in some relation to costs of production. Output prices always tend to be equal to marginal costs of production in fully competitive industries. This equality between price and marginal cost means that the consumer is required to pay for a product an amount equivalent to the additional cost incurred in producing an additional unit of that product. This cost represents the amount which could have been produced elsewhere in the economy by the resources that are used up in the production process. Output prices in the short run may be above, equal to, or below average costs of production. Competition ensures that firms in expanding industries enjoy abnormal profits and that firms in declining industries incur losses. This forces firms to move to those areas of production indicated as desirable by consumer demand.

In the long run, prices tend to equal average costs of production. Furthermore, average costs of production tend to be forced to the minimum level by the pressure upon firms to operate at the most efficient scale. In this way competition makes for the optimum allocation of resources and the production of goods at the lowest possible costs. Alternately, it can be stated that competition tends to secure for the economy as a whole the maximum real income which is attainable with the available resources.

CHAPTER 7

MONOPOLY INCREASES OUTPUT PRICES

Competition is vital to the efficient operation of a private-enterprise economy, but everyone who has anything to sell prefers to be a monopolist. Paradoxically, the most vocal supporters of the private-enterprise system are among the worst offenders in this respect. The reason for the universal desire to monopolize is not difficult to understand. Competition from other sellers always tends to hold down the price which can be secured for a given commodity or service, thus reducing the profitableness of the sale that could otherwise be enjoyed by a single seller (monopolist). Ordinarily, we think in terms of sellers of physical items of merchandise—food, clothing, shoes, cars, etc. We should not, however, overlook those who sell services (*e.g.*, radio repairmen, lawyers, doctors, and landlords). Further, everyone who works for someone else is a seller of labor services, while such institutions as banks, building and loan associations, and finance companies are in business to sell credit to borrowers. All of these sellers prefer to have substantial monopoly power, and frequently they take all possible steps to secure this advantage.

This should immediately make clear an important role of government when the economic system is organized on a private-enterprise basis. The central government, with the aid of state and local governments, should act as a referee in the great game of business to try to keep the players within the rules, that is, competitive. This is the basic idea behind the antitrust laws, which have had a measure of success in breaking up some large monopolies and in inhibiting the growth of others. Other Federal and state laws, however, have frequently had the opposite effect—that of *promoting* monopoly—as will be shown in some detail in Part C.

THE STRENGTH OF COMPETITIVE FORCES

Fortunately for the health of our economic system, competition has great force despite the constant efforts of sellers to move in the direction of monopoly. Every seller has competition from others who are selling more or less similar products or services. For example, a single power company generally has an exclusive franchise to sell electricity in a given locality. Although possessing a great deal of monopoly power (which has led to the regulation of rates by publicly appointed commissions), even the power company has competition from sellers of gas, coal, and oil, which may be substituted for electricity in cooking and heating. Less directly, electricity must compete with all other commodities for the consumer's dollar. (The family which splurges on *filet mignon* one night may be more careful about turning off unneeded lights after supper.)

Usually the competition facing a monopolistic seller is much more immediate than in the case just cited. Strictly speaking, each seller of a product or service which is different in any way from the product or service of other sellers is a monopolist. Thus Esso gasoline is not precisely the same commodity as Texaco, Shell, Sinclair, or Amoco gasoline, so the seller of each brand can properly be designated a "monopolist." Yet there is strong competition for sales among the makers and distributors of these and many additional brands of motor fuel. Hundreds of other commodities are sold under brand names, such as magazines, chocolate bars, aspirin, breakfast foods, and life-insurance policies. Some economists have been led to designate this type of situation as "monopolistic competition"—the competition among many producers of quite similar products each of which is differentiated from others at least in name. This terminology, while usefully suggestive of the interplay of both monopolistic and competitive forces in our country, is not really necessary. The term "monopoly" is sufficient, since there is a difference in degree, but not in kind, between the competition faced by a power company and the competition among sellers of different brands of gasoline, tooth paste, or cosmetics. Substitutes may be quite remote or very close, but there are always some substitutes, and hence there is always some degree of competition.

ECONOMICS OF THE MONOPOLISTIC FIRM

Geometrically speaking, the monopolist is not confronted by the horizontal demand curve which faces the purely competitive seller (*e.g.*, the small commercial fisherman) but by a negatively inclined demand curve. He can increase the physical volume of his sales only by lowering his selling price and, unlike the perfectly competitive firm, he can raise price without losing all of his customers. This situation is directly traceable to the lack of perfect substitutes (in the opinion of some buyers).

In order to understand the way in which the monopolist determines price, it is necessary to introduce another in the economist's arsenal of "marginal" concepts, namely, marginal revenue. Suppose the demand for a product of a monopolist is represented by the simple schedule in

Table 7.1, which was used earlier (Table 3.2) to illustrate the concept of elasticity of demand.[1] As before, the third column, total revenue, is found simply by multiplying each related price and quantity. Thus the column shows what the dollar sales of the monopolist would be at each of the alternative prices which he might choose. The marginal revenue column is then derived from the total revenue column; since "marginal revenue"

Table 7.1. Derivation of Marginal Revenue

Price per unit	Quantity demanded	Total revenue	Marginal revenue
$10	0	$ 0	$ —
9	1	9	9
8	2	16	7
7	3	21	5
6	4	24	3
5	5	25	1
4	6	24	−1
3	7	21	−3
2	8	16	−5
1	9	9	−7
0	10	0	−9

means *additional* revenue, it is only necessary to record the difference in total revenue at each quantity. Thus a quantity of 2 units will sell for $8 per unit, yielding a total revenue of $16. At the next higher quantity (3 units), total revenue is $21; the addition to the monopolist's revenue would therefore be $5 if he increased sales from 2 to 3 units by cutting price from $8 to $7. Similarly, an increase in sales from 5 to 6 units would reduce his total revenue from $25 to $24; hence marginal revenue corresponding to a quantity of 6 is −$1 (a one-dollar reduction in revenue).

It should be noted that, except at the very top of the demand schedule where the two are equal, marginal revenue is always less than price. Why is this so? Suppose the monopolist is selling 2 units at the price of $8 per unit. In order to sell the third unit he must price *all* 3 units at $7. Thus he gains $7 in revenue by the sale of the third unit, but he takes in $1 less on each of the first 2 units (since he now sells each at $7 instead of $8). His marginal revenue, therefore, is $5 ($7 − $2). To the perfectly competitive firm, marginal revenue and price are identical because selling additional units does not affect price; to the monopolist, marginal

[1] For a more complete discussion of the marginal-revenue concept, see Section 2, Appendix B.

revenue is below price because selling more units does depress the price of all units which could otherwise have been sold at a higher price.[1]

It should be easy to see from a combination of the foregoing and the earlier study of elasticity of demand that the monopolist seeking to maximize profit should never sell at a price which falls along the inelastic portion of his demand curve. Marginal revenue is negative whenever demand is inelastic; total revenue then falls as price goes down, and negative marginal revenue reflects this fact. If the monopolist, through error in judgment, sudden change in demand conditions, or kindness of heart, is selling at a price for which marginal revenue is negative, he can increase his profit by raising price. This will usually help in two ways: (1) total revenue will be greater at the higher price, and (2) total cost normally will be lower because fewer units will be produced for sale.

Figure 7.1. OPTIMUM MONOPOLY PRICE— When Marginal Cost Is Zero

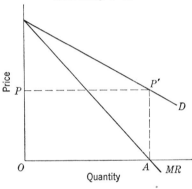

There may be some cases, like that of the mineral spring mentioned in Chapter 3, where cost of production is zero (assuming that the drinkers bring their own cups, do not trample on the grass, do not litter the spring, and pay their bills without being watched). In this no-cost case, the monopolist has only to decide at what output the dollar value of his product will be greatest. In Figure 7.1, optimum price lies on the demand curve directly above the point of zero marginal revenue and exactly at the point of unitary elasticity of demand. Marginal revenue at this "best" output is zero. Sale of any additional units would reduce the seller's income, since marginal revenue would be negative.

Normally production is not costless, of course, and the monopolistic producer is faced with a more difficult problem than that of merely selecting the output at which the dollar value of sales is greatest. He must now give active consideration to the cost side as well as the revenue side.

Solution of the problem of optimum output under monopoly is most clearly demonstrated through use of the concepts of marginal revenue and marginal cost. As already stated, marginal revenue is *additional* income resulting from the sale of a small additional quantity of a good. And, as shown in the two preceding chapters, marginal cost is *additional*

---

[1] We are assuming that the monopolist follows a policy of selling to all buyers at a single price. Frequently, however, he practices "price discrimination," charging different buyers different prices. This more complicated case will be examined in Chapter 9.

cost incurred in producing a small additional quantity of a good. It is quite obvious that it is advantageous to produce any unit which will add more to revenue than it adds to cost, *i.e.*, any unit for which marginal revenue exceeds marginal cost. It should be equally clear that it is *not* advantageous to produce any unit for which marginal cost exceeds marginal revenue. Therefore, the monopolist who is striving to maximize profit should try to carry on production at exactly the rate at which marginal revenue and marginal cost are equal. This optimum behavior can be viewed geometrically in Figure 7.2. Optimum output is OA, determined by the intersection of MC and MR. Optimum price AP is the highest price at which this quantity can be sold as shown by the demand curve.

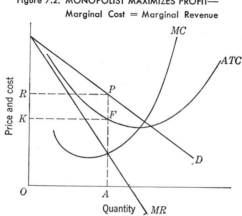

Figure 7.2. MONOPOLIST MAXIMIZES PROFIT—
Marginal Cost = Marginal Revenue

Profit per unit is FP, determined by the difference between price and average cost of output OA. This is not the largest profit *per unit* which could be earned, but the area $KRPF$ shows the largest *total profit* which can be secured.

A Practical Example

The principle just described may be readily illustrated by the pricing of movie tickets in many small towns in the United States where there is only one theater or where all the theaters are owned by the same distribution company. In the determination of the "best" price to charge movie fans, the company will probably give considerably more attention to demand than to cost. This is because a large share of the costs of film exhibition are fixed or "sunk" in the short run (in rental charges for buildings, costs of projection equipment, fire-insurance payments, etc.). The marginal (additional) costs of taking care of additional customers (up to the limits of seating capacity) are relatively low. These would be made up only of such items as the increased cost of usher and janitorial services and additional wear on seats and carpets. Geometrically, the situation might look like the hypothetical one shown in Figure 7.3.

In this situation, the optimum price will be only slightly above the price at which elasticity of demand is unitary, and the number of movie tickets sold will be only slightly less than the quantity Oz which would yield the maximum total revenue. The case is not very different from Cournot's no-cost mineral spring, because marginal costs are low. If the

Figure 7.3. MONOPOLISTIC DETERMINATION OF PRICE OF MOVIE TICKETS

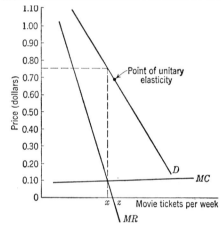

marginal cost curve were higher in relation to the demand curve, optimum price for the monopolist would exceed the maximum-expenditure price to a greater degree.

Long-run Monopoly Adjustments

In both the geometrical description and the practical example given above, we have been concerned exclusively with the short-run pricing and output decisions of the monopolistic firm. The ATC curve in Figure 7.2 was assumed to be the short-run average total cost curve for the firm depicted, and the motion-picture-theater firm in our practical example was assumed to be fixed in size. We now turn to the long-run adjustments which the monopolist will make. It will be found that these are somewhat different from those made in the competitive case.

The monopolist, like the competitive firm, has a U-shaped long-run average cost curve; that is, if the firm is either too small or too large, its production cost per unit will be higher than if it is of optimum size. The size to which the firm will actually be built will depend on the anticipated demand for its output. This size may happen to be that for which cost per unit is at a minimum, but it is more likely that the firm will be either too large or too small to minimize cost. The latter case is especially likely to occur if monopoly exists because the market is too small to support more than one firm (for example, a general store in an isolated town with a population of 200 persons).

When the monopolistic firm is too *large* to be of maximum efficiency, it is probable that the market for its product is sufficiently large to support several, or possibly a great many, competing firms. In this case it would be socially desirable to have competition rather than monopoly. Competition would tend to force firms to be of the most efficient size in order to survive. This force is lacking to the extent that competition is absent.

The long-run considerations which have been discussed pertain to the *firm* rather than to *plants*. In general, there is no reason why a monopolistic firm of substantial size (*e.g.,* a motion-picture-theater company which owns all five theaters in a small city) cannot have plants (theaters) of optimum size. There is more likelihood, however, that it will have plants which are either smaller or larger than optimum than would be the case under pure competition, since the monopolist is under less compulsion to achieve operational efficiency.

In so far as new firms, attracted by monopoly profits, are able to produce close substitute products, the long-run adjustments in monopoly tend to be similar to those in competition. For example, a firm possessing a monopoly in the sale of a particular brand of lawn mower could not long remain in production at an inefficient (high-cost) scale of operations. Other firms, producing at lower costs and consequently selling their mowers at lower prices, would be able to drive the inefficient firm out of business. On the other hand, an inefficient gas company with an exclusive franchise to serve a city might be able to remain in business indefinitely, but the owners might have some incentive to increase efficiency in order to increase profits. We may conclude, therefore, that the same sort of pressures toward efficiency are present in monopoly as in competition. The difference is primarily one of degree rather than kind. All monopolists are faced with some competition, and the degree of efficiency of monopolistic enterprises is closely related to the degree of competition which exists.

THE SOURCE OF MONOPOLY POWER

One route to monopoly is through the merger of firms in the same general line of business. For several years following the financial panic of 1897, a great wave of mergers swept the country. Such companies as U.S. Steel, Standard Oil, and American Tobacco attained tremendous size and much monopoly power. An allied monopolistic movement of the nineteenth century was built on a form of organization known as a "trust." This form is looser than the merger, since cooperating corporations maintain their identities but delegate to a "trustee" power to determine policy for the group. Since the trustee controls all the corporations, he will see that none of them is hurt by competition within the group. The antitrust laws as originally passed by Congress were directed particularly against this form of monopoly.

Patents and copyrights confer on their holders exclusive rights to processes and products—monopoly power which our government deems appropriate as a means of encouraging inventive initiative. Also, the ignorance and inertia of consumers operate to reduce their readiness to substitute the product of one seller for that of another and hence confer a measure of monopoly power on sellers. Locational advantage is another extremely common source of monopoly power. The owner of a delicatessen located on the ground floor of a large apartment building in a neighborhood where other stores are excluded by zoning laws will clearly derive some power to raise his prices without losing all of his customers. Similarly, vendors of refreshments on trains and in athletic stadiums have locational monopoly power which they almost invariably use to raise prices above those charged on the outside.

The most common origin of monopoly power, however, is that already mentioned—the differentiation of products by means of brand names. Most consumers' goods, apart from most fresh vegetables, fruits, sea food, and meats, are sold under such names, and sellers miss few opportunities between skywriting and subway ads to impress their trade-marks on the public mind. Brand names are of less importance for industrial goods (metals, building materials, machine tools, etc.) but are nevertheless quite common here, too. The aim of sellers is always to reduce competition by creating the impression that substitutes are not "just as good." Usually there are some physical differences in products sold by different firms, but even where the commodities are identical, as in the cases of different brands of aspirin or cornstarch, sellers attempt to differentiate their wares by means of highly publicized trade-marks and persistent advertising.

SELLING COSTS

As was pointed out in Chapter 6, the purely competitive seller does not have to advertise, since he can sell as much as he wishes at the prevailing market price. The monopolistic seller, however, generally does not merely accept demand as it is but attempts to influence it in his favor by means of advertising. His efforts may be quite passive, as when a grocer paints his store front red and puts up a sign bearing his name, or extremely active, as when a large firm broadcasts a "commercial" on television or buys a huge electric display on Broadway.

Analytically, selling costs are difficult to portray simply. When production costs alone are considered, it is possible to assume that the demand curve is not affected by the cost incurred. Selling costs, however, affect the demand curve directly, preventing a demonstration merely of the adjustment of output and determination of price in a stable demand-cost situation. The effects of selling outlays on the market position of a monopolist may perhaps best be shown by Figure 7.4. Let us assume him to be the same movie distributor considered earlier. The curves D_b and MR_b represent the demand and marginal revenue curves of the monopolist before he has undertaken any advertising outlay. The demand curve

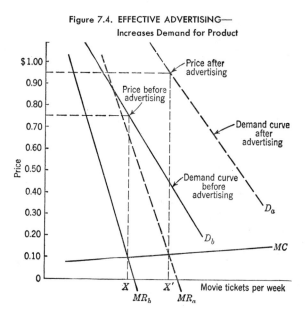

Figure 7.4. EFFECTIVE ADVERTISING—
Increases Demand for Product

thus represents the various quantities of tickets which will be purchased at various prices for a given attraction which has only been announced in the newspaper. No sexy spreads have been placed in local newspapers and no lurid signs placed outside the theater. Now assume that a half-page advertisement is placed in the Sunday paper and that billboards outside the theater and elsewhere in town are used in ballyhooing this particular attraction. The major economic effect of this action is represented by a shifting of the demand curve to the right. In Figure 7.4, D_a represents the demand curve after selling outlay has been made, and MR_a the corresponding marginal revenue curve.

If the selling outlay was made as a fixed sum and is not dependent on the number of units sold, marginal costs are unaffected. So now, instead of 75 cents proving to be the optimum price and OX the number of tickets sold, the price will be set at 95 cents and an amount OX' of tickets sold. The monopolist is thus able to sell more tickets at a higher price because of the shift in demand caused by the advertising outlay. He may not have made more profit, however, for the advertising outlay is a cost. The monopolist is able to increase his profit only if the additional revenue secured as a result of the selling outlay is greater than the additional selling and production cost involved. In our example, if the original quantity sold per week were 1,000 (OX = 1,000), then the initial total revenue was $750 (1,000 × $0.75). After the advertising outlay, the total revenue (if OX' is 1,500) is $1,425 (1,500 × $0.95). The additional revenue as a result of the selling campaign is thus $675 ($1,425 − $750). The additional production cost of securing the additional customers is approximately $50 ($0.10 × 500) in our example.[1] It can now be calculated that the advertising campaign is a success only if it cost less than $625 ($675 − $50).

Although treated as a fixed cost in our simple example above, selling outlays need not be fixed but may vary as output varies. When advertising campaigns and budgets are rigidly determined for considerable periods into the future, it seems more realistic to think of such costs as fixed. But when day-to-day advertising plans are connected closely with changing sales volumes, it seems better to treat costs as variable outlays. If, for example, a large part of a firm's selling costs consists of salesmen's commissions, these clearly depend on sales volume and are variable costs. In considering selling costs as variable, it is perhaps useful to think of them as being necessary to create the demand required for the profitable sale of output. Thus production costs are necessary to create supply and selling costs to create demand for the products of a typical monopolistic firm.

MONOPOLY AND PROFITS

It should not be assumed that monopoly power ensures profits automatically, although abnormal profits are always the motivation for attempts to secure a monopolistic market position. Many patented items are never produced because demand-cost conditions would not permit profitable production in the opinion of businessmen. Even if original demand-cost conditions are satisfactory, profits made by early firms may be reduced or wiped out by the appearance of other enterprises which sell close substitutes. The first man to recognize the profit potential of a new site for a gasoline station, for example, may earn a good income only until others erect stations in the vicinity. It is quite possible that his enterprise and the others will then all earn for their proprietors even less than they could make by working elsewhere. The attraction of being at

[1] This neglects the slight increase in marginal cost between OX and OX'.

once president, vice-president, general manager, etc., of a firm, as well as the hope that conditions will improve, induces many small enterprisers to continue in business long after the more rational course would be to give up. There is a strong tendency for businesses which require little capital and experience to be overcrowded and chronically unprofitable for most firms. Examples are filling stations, gift shops, concrete-block plants, and small grocery stores. Ease of entry is a necessary condition to the existence of pure competition, but the entry of new firms producing close substitutes is often effective also in reducing the profits of firms which sell differentiated products. Where entry is extremely difficult, as it is in the automobile industry because of the large investment needed, profits tend to be much more dependable as long as national income is high. The monopoly power which firms in such industries possess is sometimes defended by economists as socially desirable to the extent that the attraction of abnormal profits is required to induce the large investment necessary for entry into the field. If entry of new firms is impossible because a monopolist is protected by an exclusive patent or franchise, he may be able to secure substantial profits over a period of many years.

Profits serve, therefore, the same function in monopolistic industries as in competitive ones. Profits tend to attract new firms, and the subsequent entry of new firms tends to eliminate the profits. The major difference between monopoly and competition in this respect is the rate at which new firms can take away the abnormal or excessive profits of existing firms.

THE SOCIAL IMPACT OF MONOPOLY

From a social point of view, monopoly, with few exceptions, is objectionable. A given sum spent on a monopolistically produced good gives the consumer command over a smaller "bundle" of productive services than if the sum had been spent on a competitively produced good. This is because price under pure competition tends to equal marginal cost of production, whereas price under monopoly exceeds marginal cost. Under competition, the buyer is paying for the productive services which enter into the product; under monopoly, he is paying for these services and in addition is paying a markup above these costs.

Selling costs (especially advertising) are often excessive, particularly when monopoly power is due to product differentiation. Advertising is often annoying (singing commercials and billboards), misleading (most patent medicines), meaningless (breakfast foods endorsed by athletic heroes), or in questionable taste (some movie advertisements). Most advertisements (and high-pressure salesmanship) give little actual information about the product or its price, being designed merely to keep the product in the public mind. The problem is quite intangible, but it is apparent that a substantial waste of resources is involved in the excessive advertising with which Americans are constantly bombarded.

Stated more generally, monopoly is objectionable because it distorts the utilization of our resources in such a way as to reduce the national real income, and it acts to distribute income in a way which most people consider unsatisfactory.

The only exception to this generalization is that in some industries the economies of a large firm are so great that monopoly is both natural and desirable. Examples are such "public utilities" as streetcar and telephone companies. In such cases it is socially desirable to permit monopoly and regulate rates through publicly appointed commissions or, alternatively, to have direct government ownership (local, state, or Federal) of such enterprises. This special case will be explored more fully in Part C.

CHAPTER 8

OLIGOPOLIES AND CARTELS ALSO
KEEP PRICES HIGH

Broadly speaking, any firm which departs from the purely competitive ideal in the sale of output may be termed a monopoly. It is important, however, to distinguish three quite different situations which may confront such an imperfectly competitive firm: (1) the firm may find it feasible to set output and price without regard to the reactions of other enterprisers; (2) the firm may find it important to take such reactions into account; or (3) the firm may surrender its price-setting power to an industry-wide association, or cartel.

In the preceding chapter, the first of these situations was assumed to exist. The demand for the monopolist's product was considered as being unaffected by his own profit-seeking actions (apart from his own sales-promotion efforts). This assumption is justified either if substitutes are remote or if the firm in question is not sufficiently important to cause sellers of close substitutes to alter their policies. An electric-power company is an example of a monopolist with only remote substitutes for its product. A lipstick producer may exemplify the second situation; each brand of lipstick is quite a close substitute for the others, but a firm may set its price on the assumption that its price policies will not affect the policies of other firms in the industry, since it supplies such a small part of the total market. In both cases the monopoly analysis of the last chapter is applicable.

OLIGOPOLY PRICE POLICY

In a great many industries, however, the number of firms is sufficiently small relative to the total market to make each highly sensitive to the actions of the others.[1] To distinguish this situation, economists have

[1] "Industry" can be defined as narrowly or as broadly as desired by the analyst, and for different purposes different definitions are useful. Generally, the commodities grouped together are fairly close substitutes—*e.g.*, the "rayon industry,"—but often are much more heterogeneous—*e.g.*, the "chemical industry."

coined the term "oligopoly," meaning a market including only a few sellers. The oligopolists may be selling either exactly the same commodity, for example, industrial materials such as steel, copper, sulfur, lime, pig iron, or cast-iron pipe, or differentiated products such as trucks, refrigerators, motel accommodations, or theatrical productions.

Oligopoly is frequently the ultimate outcome of a situation in which the optimum-sized firm is large relative to the market served. In terms of the long-run average cost curve explained in Chapter 5 (Figure 5.3), the lowest cost outputs often can be attained only by relatively large firms. In cities such as Nashville or Des Moines there are likely to be only two, three, or four major department stores. The market area served is not large enough to support more department stores of the size necessary to secure the full advantages of modern retail distribution such as a large variety of merchandise, delivery service, credit facilities, and advertising.

Demand Curve of the Oligopolist

Whatever its historical origin, oligopoly must be viewed analytically as a separate case from monopoly. The possible outcome of the rivalry between oligopolists is so unpredictable that it is not worth while to make such extensive use of geometrical analysis as was made for pure competition and for monopoly. Neither is the concept of equilibrium very useful in the oligopoly case. The basic situation in which an oligopolist is likely to find himself may, however, be made clear with a diagram.

We may assume that the oligopolist of Figure 8.1 is selling OA units at price OP_1. He may feel that by reducing price and increasing the quantity sold he might be able to increase his total profits. Since he is one of a few sellers in the market, before he attempts a price reduction he is almost certain to ask himself the question, "If I cut my price, what will other sellers in the market do?" Suppose, first, that he decides that his rivals are not likely to cut prices even if he does. In that event he will assume that a price reduction will make it possible for him to increase sales substantially, since he not only will be able to sell more units to his own customers but should in addition be able to take customers away from his rivals. He will then visualize his demand curve as having the general shape of D_1; if he cut price to OP_2, his sales would increase to OC.

If, on the other hand, the oligopolist assumes that if he reduces his price his rivals will either reduce their prices or increase promotional efforts or both, he will visualize his demand curve as sloping down more steeply to assume the general form of D_2. In this event, he would expect a reduction in price to OP_2 to increase sales only to OB.

Suppose that the oligopolist mistakenly believes that he can lower price without having his rivals follow suit. He expects to sell OC units at price

OP_2. But if his rivals in fact also cut their prices, he will find that his sales are only OB, and this he may find less profitable than selling OA units at price OP_1. If he now attempts to increase price back to OP_1, he may find that his rivals do not follow his lead in raising prices, and he will, accordingly, now be unable to sell as many as OA units at the original price; his demand curve now assumes the form of D_3. Since the oligopolist can never be sure what his rivals' reactions to price cutting will be, and since if he misjudges them he may be in a worse position as a result of lowering his price, he is likely to feel that the conservative policy is to make no efforts in the direction of price competition. The result is that

Figure 8.1. DEMAND FACING OLIGOPOLIST—
Depends on Rivals' Reactions

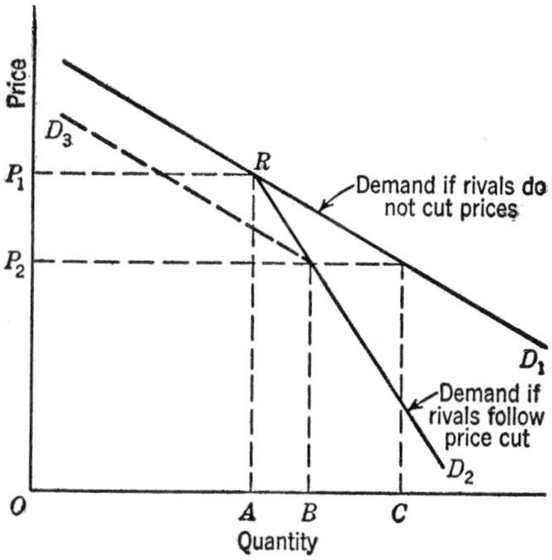

in oligopolistic markets, even when there is no collusion among sellers, price changes are likely to be infrequent.

Oligopolistic Strategy

The pricing problems facing firms in this sort of situation become similar to those facing opposing generals in war or opposing players in a poker game. Action taken depends to a large degree upon a subjective estimate of what other sellers will do as a result of such action. The demand curve which is important for the decision making of the firm is derived from specific assumptions concerning rivals' behavior. It may be assumed to be like D_1 if no reactions are expected; it may be supposed that it is like D_2 if immediate reactions are expected. Or it may be assumed to be of many other shapes. The essential point is that the oligopolist's demand curve is not based solely or even primarily on the objective market facts but rather on his subjective estimates of his rivals' behavior; these estimates may or may not be accurate. Actual behavior depends in such cases in part on the types of personalities making the decisions. One predominant characteristic of oligopolistic markets is that the whole pricing structure can be significantly affected by individual business leaders. The pricing policies of the automobile industry and of the automobile-tire industry were for many years strongly influenced by Henry Ford and Harvey Firestone.

From time to time, competition among oligopolists results in "price wars" in which rivals continue to undercut one another until prices are driven far below usual levels. A warring oligopolist may even cut price temporarily below average variable cost if he is attempting to ruin one or more competitors to his own ultimate gain. In an all-out price war, the survivors are likely to be the firms with the most reserves, in the form, for example, of highly liquid assets and good sources of credit. Price warfare, or "cutthroat competition," is likely to occur only when productive capacity is large in relation to demand. Rate wars were chronic among the overbuilt American railroads during the last century. Similarly, cutthroat competition frequently breaks out in cities, especially during a depression, in such fields as dry cleaning and gasoline distribution.

In periods of general prosperity, oligopolistic rivals are not likely to engage in strenuous competition on a price basis. Instead, they are likely to reach explicit or tacit understandings regarding prices and to brand as a "price chiseler" any seller who fails to fall in line. There are various ways of causing a "chiseler" to change his policies—e.g., by threat of a price war or through pressure on his suppliers. Where oligopolists are strongly organized and firmly led, price may be approximately the same as that which a monopolist would set if he were in control of the entire productive capacity of the industry. This situation is especially likely if the various firms all produce identical or very similar commodities (e.g., cigarettes) and if costs are nearly the same. To the extent that products and costs differ, the rivals will prefer different prices, and if a single price is maintained through collusion it is apt to be a compromise which may not maximize profit for any particular firm.

The trade association is an extremely common device for securing collusive action regarding price. Such associations perform certain desirable services for their members and the public, such as setting quality standards, standardizing specifications, and dispensing information regarding raw-material prices. It is probably fair to say, however, that their real importance rests in keeping member firms in continual contact with each other, thus permitting ample opportunity for agreements regarding price.[1]

---

[1] Adam Smith observed in 1776: "People of the same trade seldom meet together, even for merriment and diversion, but the conversation ends in a conspiracy against the public, or in some contrivance to raise prices." *The Wealth of Nations* (New York: Modern Library, Inc., 1937), p. 128.

These agreements are far more likely to be in the form of a cocktail conspiracy than to take a written (traceable) form.

Price Leadership

When one firm in an industry is substantially larger than any other firm—a common situation, existing, for example, in the production of steel, "tin" cans, and corn products—the dominant firm is likely to be the price leader. This means that the company is usually the first to announce a price change, either with or without prior consultation with other firms, and that rivals quickly match the leader's move. Such a price leader generally makes a move in full anticipation of being followed; he can maximize his own profit by equating marginal cost with marginal revenue as related to the demand which will exist after followers have made the appropriate price and output adjustments. His task of choosing a profitable price is made far easier by the virtual certainty of being followed—a situation that does not exist in ordinary noncollusive rivalry among oligopolists.

To the extent that the price leader is acting not only in his own interest but in the interest of the industry as a whole (probably doing so under pressure from the others), he may purposely set the price at a level which is not the optimum for his own firm but which is a good compromise from the point of view of all the firms. This situation is more likely when no one firm is substantially larger than other firms in the industry. Usually a price leader is of substantial size, however, and possessed of particularly aggressive management. Like outright price agreement among oligopolists, price leadership is more common when the rival firms produce the same or quite similar commodities. When a company views its own product as distinctive (as in the case of patent medicines), monopoly pricing tends to prevail.

The Pressure for Secret Price Cuts and Non-price Concessions

Whenever oligopolists maintain identical, or nearly identical, prices as a matter of policy—whether by outright collusion or through following the leader—there may be a strong tendency for individual firms to undercut the published price in subtle ways in order to increase their shares of the market. The tendency for the individual firm to cut the agreed-on price is especially strong in periods of slack demand. In such cases individual firms are likely to find that through adherence to the agreed-on price they are not maximizing profits. Such a situation is depicted in Figure 8.2.

The oligopolist is confronted by the demand curve D as long as his rivals adhere strictly to the agreed price OP_2. His marginal revenue is then represented by MR and his marginal costs by MC. The optimum price for this firm would, under these conditions, be OP_1, but he has agreed to maintain price OP_2. He would like to lower price but cannot do so without incurring the anger of managers of other firms and probably causing a reduction in the demand for his own product as a result of retaliatory price cuts.

When this sort of difference exists between agreed-on and optimum price, the firm has an incentive to make hidden price cuts in order to secure additional sales without unduly disturbing rival companies. A very large number of practices which amount to secret price cutting are available to businessmen. These include rebates, favorable credit terms, "money-back" guarantees, engineering services, repair and maintenance work, liberal trade-in allowances, and lavish entertainment of the buyers. To the extent that such practices are followed (wisely) by a firm such as the one whose cost and revenue data are pictured in Figure 8.2, sales can be increased toward the optimum OB. Rivals may, however, engage similarly in such concessions; this would reduce the demand (curve D) of the firm in question. Oligopolistic firms, especially the price leaders, frequently tire of the increasing concessions made by rivals and overtly lower the dollar price in order to prevent a further creeping encroachment on their own sales. Completely effective collusion within an industry thus requires agreement not only as to the basic price but also

Figure 8.2. DIVERGENCE BETWEEN AGREED AND OPTIMUM PRICE—
May Lead to Secret Price-reducing Arrangements

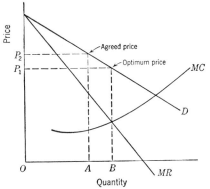

with respect to a very large number of ancillary matters pertaining to the terms of sale. It is easy to see that effective collusion becomes increasingly difficult as the number of firms involved increases.

The term "nonprice competition" is frequently used by economists to cover the multitude of practices used in oligopolistic industries to attract sales when it is the industry practice not to engage in outright price cutting. These include advertising and other sales-promotion efforts in addition to the nonprice concessions mentioned above. Actually, it is frequently difficult to classify a particular practice as either a price reduction or a nonprice action to gain sales. For example, more liberal credit terms may involve a lower interest rate which actually reduces price to the installment purchaser. But alternatively, the credit arrangement can be considered as a separate commodity purchased by the buyer;

in that light the easier credit terms can be viewed as a nonprice concession with respect to the commodity bought on terms. Similarly, a higher trade-in allowance can either be considered as a reduction of price of the new article or as a nonprice concession to the buyer.

In the cigarette industry, competition among the big three—Camel, Chesterfield, and Lucky Strike—is mainly on a nonprice basis. Normally, instead of competing in price, the sellers of these cigarettes advertise very heavily, each striving to increase its share of the market and, less directly, to build up the total market for cigarettes. Probably sales of any one of these brands would fall off substantially if its producer stopped advertising while the others continued their heavy selling outlays.

The risk which oligopolists may run by maintaining price and engaging instead in nonprice competition was forcibly shown during the severe depression of the 1930's when cigarette buyers were of necessity more price conscious. Starting with almost negligible sales in 1931, makers of "10-cent brands" increased their volumes until they accounted for over 20 per cent of domestic cigarette sales for a few months in the fall of 1932.[1] This caused the big three to cut their prices in January, 1933, to the neighborhood of 10 cents a pack, and their sales responded quickly at the expense of the regular 10-cent brands. In periods of higher national income, however, the practice of nonprice competition may serve the interest of the large cigarette producers well.

The Economic Significance of Oligopoly

The social losses resulting from collusive practices of oligopolists are quite similar to those set forth in connection with monopoly. Output in such industries tends to be restricted, prices are maintained at high levels, and too few resources are employed relative to the more competitive areas of the economy. It should be recognized, however, that oligopoly itself is not necessarily contrary to the social interest in all cases, since it may be based on actual economies of large-sized firms. These economies may be so great relative to the market served that they leave room only for a very limited number of firms in an industry. When, however, oligopoly results from the exclusion of new, potentially efficient firms by such means as patent holdings, withholding of needed materials, or collusion with investment bankers (who market new securities), the situation is clearly contrary to the public interest. Even where the small number of sellers is traceable to the economies of scale, this efficiency does the public little good if real price competition is not present to assure prices consistent with the efficiency.

[1] As described in Neil H. Borden, *The Economic Effects of Advertising* (Chicago: Richard D. Irwin, Inc., 1942), Chap. 8.

For consumers' goods, at least, nonprice competition by oligopolists probably results in a wasteful employment of resources in advertising and other selling activities, much of which does more to misinform than to educate the public. Also, the buyer is likely to be wooed by means of added services, coupons, premiums, and eye-catching gadgets, many of which he would prefer to do without if, instead, price were reduced by the full amount of the cost of these extras. Looked at broadly, this again means that society is forced to devote resources to the production of such extras in excessive amounts, reducing the real income of the nation.

PRICE POLICY OF CARTELS

We have examined the tendency of oligopolistic firms to engage in collusive practices in order to prevent competition on a price basis. The understanding which is reached is frequently extremely informal, constituting nothing more than a gentleman's agreement to maintain price or to follow any change made by the leader. In other cases, oligopolists may systematically surrender their price-determining power to a central agency which may also be given additional powers such as the authority to allot exclusive sales territories among the cooperating firms. The firms may then be said to belong to a "cartel."

Cartels are perhaps even more common in industries where the number of firms is large and where a substantial degree of competition could otherwise exist. This situation is due especially to the direct governmental support of cartel arrangements in many areas of the economy. Milk boards, for example, are governmentally sponsored agencies which have the authority to set minimum retail prices on milk in a great many localities, effectively cartelizing the sale of this highly essential commodity. In other cases, cartel arrangements may be effectuated by private organizations such as marketing cooperatives or professional societies (*e.g.*, bar associations). In the discussion which follows, we shall be concerned with the operation of cartels in situations where the number of sellers is large rather than with cartels in oligopolistic situations.

A Practical Example

The principle of cartel price determination may be illustrated by the pricing of barbershop services, since these prices are fixed by such agreements in most American cities and towns. The individual barbershops surrender to the association, or "union," the power to determine price. The association officials must evaluate the total conditions of demand for barbershop services in the area as well as the cost conditions and estimate the "best" price from the point of view of the barbers and barbershop operators.

The determination of the price of haircuts may be depicted as in Figure 8.3. Curve *D* represents the total demand for haircuts in a particular town and *MR* the corresponding marginal revenue curve. It should be emphasized that these are "industry" demand and revenue curves and do not represent the curves which would face any individual barbershop. The curve *MC* represents the industry marginal cost curve. It is drawn so that marginal costs change slowly as quantity changes, reflecting that many firms are included, and, therefore, a substantial change in the total number of haircuts sold in the city may take place without any one shop being overworked,

Figure 8.3. CARTEL DETERMINATION OF PRICE OF HAIRCUTS

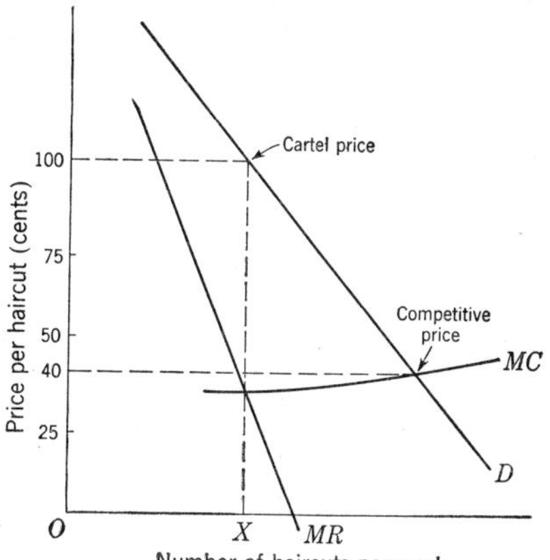

i.e., being placed in a high-cost operating situation. It may be seen from a glance at Figure 8.3 that the profit-maximizing price will be $1 and the number of haircuts *OX*.

For the individual barbershop proprietor, however, this may not be a wholly satisfactory solution. He may recognize that his best interest lies in going along with the dictates of the association, but he will be strongly tempted to make price cuts and to offer nonprice concessions (*e.g.*, free scalp massages). His position would then be similar to that described for the oligopolistic firm depicted in Figure 8.2. The individual barbershop could increase its profits (or decrease its losses) by cutting its prices, provided that it could be sure that the other barbershops in town did not do the same. If all other barbershops did cut price and if the price-setting power of the "union" were to vanish, the situation would approximate that of pure competition, with price falling to about 40 cents in Figure 8.3. (The particular prices shown have no special significance but have been chosen arbitrarily to illustrate the principle.) This pressure for price cuts makes cartel agreements always difficult to maintain unless severe disciplinary measures may be taken against violators.

Difficulties of Restricting Entry

In Figure 8.3, the cartel- or association-set price is substantially higher than the price which would prevail under competition. It is possible, however, that the industry might be made up of either more or fewer firms than would be operating in the competitive case. One of the major difficulties faced by such associations is their frequent inability to restrict entry into the industrial, occupational, or professional group. If, in our example, entry could be limited (with state and municipal support) by means of restrictive licensing, the number of barbers might be kept down and sizable monopoly profits retained by association members.[1] If, however, the association or cartel possesses the power to set price but does not have the power to restrict entry of firms into the industry, individual firms will gain little in the long run. For, attracted by apparent high earnings to be secured through the high price, many new firms will enter the industry. As new firms come in, old firms must share the market with them and hence lose sales. This movement may well continue until no firm in the industry is making more than a competitive rate of return on its investment. But each firm will be operating at far less than its lowest-cost output. Our barbershop example is a good one to illustrate this point. It seems likely that few barbershops, if any, make abnormally high profits. Yet most of them tend to operate at far less than the lowest-cost capacity. The position of a single firm (barbershop) may be illustrated in Figure 8.4. The firm would like to operate "at capacity," or sell OB haircuts per week, since at this sales volume the firm's marginal cost equals the cartel price. But there are so many barbershops in town that each one must operate at far less than its most desirable output. And since new barbershops can normally be opened without difficulty, the final position for a single firm is shown at output OA. At this position, average costs (including a normal rate of return on fixed investment and normal wages of management) are just covered, and no abnormal profits are present.

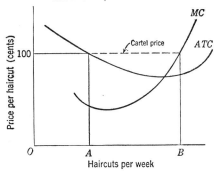

Figure 8.4. SINGLE BARBERSHOP OPERATES AT HIGH COST, LOW OUTPUT

The social loss due to the cartel type of agreement is twofold: first, prices are higher than they would be under competition, and, second, the many resources which are devoted to the production of the cartelized good or service are underutilized. This problem of excess capacity is especially prevalent in those areas of the economy in which firms can be set up without too much initial capital investment, e.g., small retail establishments. With such excess capacity present, once the cartel-like price agreements are broken, price wars are likely to ensue. A good

---

[1] Certain professional groups, such as medical doctors, actuaries, and public accountants, have been notably successful in restricting entry.

example is provided by the gasoline price wars so often found among filling stations when a cartel-like arrangement somehow breaks down.

The Economic Significance of Cartel Agreements

The word "cartel" has been deliberately employed to define this type of market situation, although it generally connotes a European rather than an American type of monopolistic restriction. It is true that open price agreements of the cartel sort among large industrial firms have occurred largely on the continent of Europe, particularly among German firms. The antitrust laws have fairly effectively prevented this sort of agreement among large firms in the United States.[1] It is, however, precisely in situations like that described by the barbershop example that the cartel restrictions are most serious in this country, and these have too often been overlooked in considerations of the over-all monopoly problem.

The importance of such local monopolistic restrictions should not be underestimated. In 1946, the nation's bill for barbershop services exceeded the aggregate amount spent for refrigerators, washing machines, and sewing machines, despite the postwar boom in household-appliance sales. In that same year, considerably more than one-half of personal-consumption expenditures in the United States were devoted to such items as rents, laundry, dry cleaning, locally produced foods, recreation, barbershop and beauty-parlor services, local transportation services, medical expenses, death expenses, and automobile repairs.[2] All these industries are outside the jurisdiction of the Federal antitrust laws, since these apply only to firms operating in interstate commerce. And in nearly all of these service types of industries, some sorts of cartel agreements are likely to be found. In many cases state and municipal governments actively support this type of monopolistic agreement through official price-setting commissions and boards. The Federal government also supports cartel-like agreements, especially among sellers of agricultural commodities. Competitive forces are allowed little or no influence in the setting of fluid-milk prices, for example. These are set by milk-marketing boards largely composed of representatives from both the producers and the distributors of milk.

The so-called "fair-trade" laws, allowing manufacturers to set minimum resale prices, have the effect of cartelizing large portions of the retailing industry. These and other governmental supports for monopolistic restriction will be discussed more fully in Part C.

[1] American firms, however, have frequently entered into cartel agreements with firms in other countries. See Chap. 33.

[2] J. W. Markham, "The Effectiveness of Federal Anti-trust Laws: Comment," *American Economic Review*, Vol. 40, p. 169 (March, 1950).

CHAPTER 9

MOST FIRMS SELL MANY PRODUCTS

So far our discussion has been based on the assumption that each firm and each industry produce but a single commodity—sometimes defined broadly, however, to include rather dissimilar goods which are fairly close substitutes (*e.g.*, Chevrolets and Cadillacs). It has been further assumed that enterprisers charge but a single price at any one time. These conditions are sometimes met: a cotton farmer may sell nothing but cotton and at a single price; a doughnut shop may vend only doughnuts at a definite price per dozen; and a taxicab company may sell only rides and at the same rate per mile to each customer.

MULTIPLE OUTPUTS

More commonly, however, manufacturers, transportation agencies, wholesalers, and retailers handle a large number—sometimes thousands—of commodities. Often the same plant facilities are used for many or all of the different goods sold by a particular firm. The same commodity is sometimes sold at different prices to different buyers; this is known as "price discrimination." The very same kind of cornstarch or baking soda, for example, is sometimes sold by the same firm under different labels at different prices. More frequently, however, a firm which wishes to increase profits by means of price discrimination produces two or more similar but somewhat different commodities (*e.g.*, the plain funeral and the de luxe job) and charges prices which are out of line with the difference in costs of production. Buyers who wish to pay considerably more for small differences in quality are generally given the opportunity to do so.

While the desire to engage in price discrimination is one motive behind the production of multiple products, it is probably not the most important one. It is sometimes necessary for a firm to produce a multiplicity of commodities in order to obtain the lowest average cost for any one commodity. This is clearly the case when one good is subject to a seasonal demand; it is then likely that firms will handle another commodity with an opposite seasonal-demand pattern. Not long ago, it was common for coal distributors to handle ice during the summer months in order to make more even use of their labor, trucks, and other equipment. (The decline in the ice business consequently raised problems in the coal business.) A freight train usually has to carry numerous varieties of cargo simultaneously in order to maximize profit. A retail food store clearly must handle many items in order to operate at maximum efficiency. Butcher shops are becoming quite rare in this country; apparently it is usually more efficient to sell groceries and meat under one roof.

Another important reason for the prevalence of multiple products is the degree of protection which it provides against a sudden drop in the demand for a particular commodity. A firm which is producing numerous commodities is hurt less if the bottom drops out of the market for one of them. Convertibility of productive capacity from one good to another is a similar sort of insurance. Neither multiplicity of products nor convertibility is of great help, however, when demand *in general* declines sharply.

The advantages of large-scale operation which can be secured only through multiple outputs are likely to be especially important to firms possessing some degree of monopoly in the sale of one or more products. The equilibrium output of the monopolist, it will be recalled, is determined by the equality of marginal revenue and marginal cost. This output may be reached at a point where excess capacity is present, particularly where price is determined by a cartel arrangement, as was shown in Chapter 8. Added output would, under these conditions, lower average cost per unit, but it will obviously not pay the monopolist to reduce the price of the monopolized good in order to take advantage of the excess capacity. If he can produce another commodity with the existing capacity, however, he will be able to make better use of his plant. If the additional revenue which can be secured from the second commodity more than covers the additional costs incurred in its production, it will be profitable to produce the second product. (We are assuming the demand for the first product to be unaffected by sale of the second.) The price of the second product might remain well below the price which would cover average total cost of production if the same good were turned out by a single-product firm. A monopolist in one line of output may be selling in a highly competitive situation for other lines of output.[1]

Profit margins on multiple outputs are likely to differ from product to product. A firm may secure high profit margins on products for which it is in a monopolistic position and low margins on those which it sells more competitively. For example, the Goodyear Rubber Company is a monopolistic seller of Goodyear tires, or an oligopolistic seller of tires, since there

---

[1] See Eli W. Clemens, "Price Discrimination and the Multiple-product Firm," *The Review of Economic Studies*, Vol. 19, pp. 1–11 (1951), for a more rigorous analysis.

are only a few major tire producers. On the other hand, Goodyear sells rubber washers in a highly competitive market. On this account, the relative profit margin on tires probably exceeds that on rubber washers.

It can usually be said that, when multiple products are handled by a firm, short-run profits are maximized (or losses minimized) when marginal revenue from each good is equal to the marginal cost of that good. The rule is consequently similar to that which holds for the single-product firm. The difference between price and marginal revenue will depend on the degree of monopoly power. Since marginal revenue is equal to marginal cost at the optimum output, it can alternately be said that price will exceed marginal cost in varying degrees depending on the extent of competition in each market. In the example just given, the price of tires is probably above marginal cost, while that of rubber washers is probably about equal to their marginal cost.

Joint Products

The measurement of cost for purposes of guiding price policy or for controlling efficiency is complicated by the production of multiple rather than single products. It is likely to be especially difficult to allocate the *fixed* costs which are common to two or more commodities. In some cases it is impossible even to allocate *variable* costs among commodities. This is true when the same production process yields two or more commodities in fixed proportions. The commodities are then known as "joint products" and their costs as "joint costs."

Many commodities which are popularly designated as "by-products" are produced under conditions of joint costs. This is particularly true in the short run, since it is often necessary to alter equipment and processes in order to vary the proportions in which goods are turned out. Joint products are extremely common in the chemical industry, even as a long-run matter. As an extremely simple illustration of this tendency, the decomposition of water yields hydrogen and oxygen in fixed proportions. In the refining of petroleum, such products as gasoline, kerosene, paraffin, oil, and gas are obtained. While the proportions of these products can be varied considerably in the long run, there is little short-run variability. Joint products are common in the meat-packing industry; there is an almost complete short-run fixity of proportions between mutton and sheepskin, for example. Joint products appear also in the processing of frozen orange concentrate, where molasses and peel (used in cattle feed) are obtained along with the juice concentrate.

A great deal of research and advertising effort go constantly into the attempt to convert nonsalable by-products into marketable ones. The discovery of the usefulness of orange peel as a food for cattle turned what was formerly a bothersome waste product into a valuable income producer. Gasoline was once considered a by-product of the production of kerosene, but the position is now reversed. Today's by-product may be tomorrow's main product.

The existence of joint costs makes it necessary to analyze the determination of price and output somewhat differently. Analysis of the production and pricing of joint products is greatly facilitated if only two commodities are considered, although in reality a larger number frequently result from a single productive process. Let us consider the production of cottonseed and cotton fiber which appear in a weight ratio of approximately two to one. The ginning of 1 pound of raw cotton, therefore, yields $\frac{2}{3}$ pound of cottonseed and $\frac{1}{3}$ pound of fiber.

Figure 9.1. JOINT COSTS AND COMPETITION—

One Supply Curve for Two Goods

Suppose the cotton-ginning industry is purely competitive. It is necessary to draw only one short-run industry supply curve for cottonseed and cotton fiber, since the production of one more unit of cottonseed ($\frac{2}{3}$ pound) is necessarily accompanied by production of one more unit of fiber ($\frac{1}{3}$ pound). Separate demands will exist for each commodity, however, and these are designated in Figure 9.1 as D_s and D_f, respectively. It will be recalled from Chapter 6 that the short-run supply

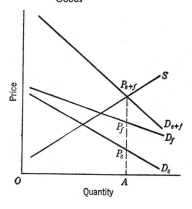

curve for a purely competitive industry is derived by the horizontal summation of the marginal cost curves of all firms (counting only those portions which lie above minimum average variable cost).

Curve D_{s+f} has been derived by the *vertical* addition of demand curves D_s and D_f. The short-run equilibrium output for the industry is that at which the joint supply curve S cuts curve D_{s+f}. The output of each product is then OA, and the prices are, respectively, AP_s and AP_f, since these are the highest prices at which the quantity of each which is produced may be sold.

Suppose an increase in the demand for cottonseed now occurs (for example, as a result of an increased demand for oleomargarine), no change taking place in the demand for cotton fiber. Geometrically, D_s will move upward and to the right. This will necessarily move D_{s+f} upward, so that the industry will find it desirable to turn out more than OA units of each good. (The intersection of D_{s+f} and S will lie farther to the right.) Since D_f has not changed, the price of cotton fiber will decline below AP_f. The price of cottonseed, for which demand has increased, will rise above AP_s.

A general proposition regarding the competitive production and sale of joint products may be stated as follows: An increase in the demand for one of two joint products will raise the price of that product and lower the price of the other; a decrease in the demand for one joint product will lower its price and raise the price of the other. This will happen because, in order to take advantage of a stronger demand for one joint product, firms will necessarily also increase the supply of the other joint product, while a cutback in output of one joint product in response to a decrease in its demand will necessarily diminish the supply of the other.

Competitive sellers will normally dispose of their entire output of joint products. Some of the products may not be worth selling, however; they may have a price of zero and find their way only to the scrap pile. It may even be necessary for firms to incur further costs in order to dispose of unsalable by-products. An extreme example of a by-product with a large negative value is found in the radioactive water which must be safely disposed of by atomic installations.

A monopolist, however, may find it profitable not to sell his entire output of one joint product, even when a positive price could be secured if all units were sold. This is only likely, however, if the demand for one good is substantially weaker than for the others. In this situation the monopolist may withhold from the market—and perhaps destroy—a portion of his output of one good in order to be able to keep its price at a revenue-maximizing level. He will not sell any quantity for which marginal revenue is negative, since this would diminish his profit.

PRICE DISCRIMINATION

As has been indicated, production of multiple products is often motivated by the desire to engage in price discrimination. Sometimes the goods are distinguished only by their packages and brand names; usually the difference is more substantial but not sufficient to justify the price differential. In other cases the good sold to different buyers is clearly the same despite the difference in price. For example, a rich man's appendectomy is likely to be surgically identical with that of a poor man, but it is likely to cost a great deal more. (Moral: when you visit your doctor wear your oldest clothes.)

It is necessary for an imperfectly competitive seller to be able to classify customers and thus to separate the market for the product into segments in order to be able to engage in discriminatory pricing. Many bases of classification may be employed: apparent income or wealth, time of day, size of the buyer, outlook for future sales to the same buyer, reciprocal economic or political favor, etc. Not only must he be able to partition the market, but he must also be able to keep the segments separated.

That is, no resale must be possible since, if it were, customers purchasing the good or service at the lower price could resell to persons who would otherwise be required to pay higher prices. The possibility of resale is the main factor limiting the application of price-discrimination policies.[1]

To the extent that price differentials among customers result from actual differences in the cost of supplying different types of buyers, price discrimination should not be said to be present. A large jobber, for example, may buy materials for resale and/or further processing in carload lots, while a small jobber uses more costly l.c.l. (less-than-carload lot) shipments. A correspondingly lower delivered price to the larger firm does not constitute price discrimination. If, however, the large jobber is given a price which is lower by more than the cost saving effected by his large-scale purchases, the smaller jobber is being subjected to discriminatory pricing. This type of discrimination in interstate commerce is illegal under the Robinson-Patman Act of 1936 if it tends to promote monopoly, but it is always hard to prove a monopoly effect, since both cost allocation and the degree of monopoly are inherently difficult and debatable matters.

Price discrimination in purely intrastate commerce, like local monopoly, largely escapes legal intervention. The case of discrimination by surgeons has been mentioned. Much room for such discrimination also exists in repair work on nonhuman machines of many kinds where the exact service rendered is often concealed by mechanical intricacy. The man who drives a large car often pays more for an identical act of servicing than does the small-car owner. The average customer is at the mercy of the television and radio-repair shop once he leaves his ailing set. Similarly, the influential citizen whose presence is expected to improve a neighborhood often receives a lower price when buying real estate from a developer than does the more ordinary customer.

Basing-point Pricing

A form of price discrimination which depends on the geographical location of customers is known as the "basing-point" system of pricing. Under this scheme of pricing, all rival sellers agree to maintain the same *delivered* price in any given locality regardless of the place of origin of the shipment. Under a single basing-point system, such as the famous "Pittsburgh-plus" system used by the steel industry prior to 1924, the delivered price of steel at any destination was the price at the Pittsburgh steel mills plus the freight cost by railroad from Pittsburgh to the destination. For example, steel shipped to Washington, D.C., from nearby

---

[1] Personal services obviously cannot be resold; hence the prevalence of price discrimination in such markets. A poor family cannot resell the obstetrician's services costing $50 to a rich family who may be charged $500 for the same service.

Baltimore was priced as if it had come all the way from Pittsburgh. The various steel companies were able to compete for sales in every locality but could not compete with one another on a price basis.

Beginning in 1924, the steel industry utilized a "multiple-basing-point" system in place of the Pittsburgh-plus system which was abandoned as a result of a Federal Trade Commission cease and desist order. Under this version, delivered prices of a commodity in any locality are again the same regardless of the place of origin of the shipment. The delivered price is the mill price at the nearest city which has been designated as a basing point plus freight cost from that city. Under this system, the aggregate amount of fictitious, or "phantom," freight paid by buyers is not so great as under a single-basing-point system, since the multiplicity of basing points means that a larger number of buyers actually purchase from a mill from which freight is computed. Nevertheless, there is a phantom freight charge to many buyers unless *every* source of a material is designated as a basing point. (In that event, the system would approximate the more natural "f.o.b. mill" method of pricing, in which freight is charged from the actual plant of origin to the destination.)

There are several economic objections to both single- and multiple-basing-point pricing systems. First, it is one highly effective method of price collusion. The firms' officials within an industry must necessarily meet together to work out details of the system, including mill prices at the basing points. This makes it virtually certain that mill prices will be set well above marginal cost of production in line with principles of cartel pricing.

Second, a system of basing-point pricing distorts the pattern of location of plants utilizing the material which is priced in this manner. Industrial plants are most economically located when the sum of production costs and transportation costs (on raw materials and finished products) is minimized. This frequently means that location near the source of a basic material (*e.g.*, steel) is advantageous as a factor in reducing the total cost of getting a good produced and to market. Under a basing-point system, there is no advantage in being near a material source, however, if freight on the material is not computed from that source but from some more remote basing point. Location of plants near basing points, rather than near all sources of the material, is promoted.

It was pointed out in Chapter 8 that the cartel form of pricing is much more profitable to the cooperating firms if new firms (which are attracted by the profits being made) can be prevented from entering the field. A multiple-basing-point system offers the cartel a useful weapon against potential new competitors. Suppose that some industrialists propose to erect a new plant in Los Angeles to produce a commodity subject to basing-point pricing. Suppose further that the nearest existing basing point is San Francisco. The cooperating firms can quickly make, or threaten to make, Los Angeles a basing point, which will mean that delivered prices in that city and its environs will be lowered. This will diminish the profitability of a new firm in Los Angeles, since such a firm could no longer enjoy its full natural locational advantage on sales in its immediate vicinity. Threatening to establish a new basing point may be enough to prevent the new firm from starting. Its exclusion would then have been accomplished without lowering delivered prices at all.

Basing-point pricing has been used in a number of important industries producing relatively standardized commodities such as steel, portland cement, corn products, cast-iron soil pipe, lead, sugar, and lumber. As will be described in Part C, basing-point systems have recently been abandoned in the corn-products, cement, and steel industries as a result of Federal Trade Commission action and Supreme Court decisions.

Price discrimination in transactions between firms, whether employed on a geographical basis (as when basing points are used) or on some other basis, distorts the pattern of resource allocation in an uneconomical way. Some firms secure an advantage over other firms which is not traceable to their efficiency in using resources. "Survival of the favored" partly replaces the more desirable "survival of the fittest." Also, unnecessarily large amounts of resources are devoted to transportation, to the extent that improper location of economic activity is fostered by geographic price discrimination.

Discriminatory pricing when applied to individuals (*e.g.*, the rich man with the inflamed appendix) may appear less reprehensible. It can plausibly be argued, however, that private sellers should not take it upon themselves to effect a redistribution of real income by charging "what the traffic will bear." Income redistribution is more appropriately a function of government. To the extent, however, that such professional persons as surgeons can afford or will be willing to handle some cases on a charity or near-charity basis only by charging high prices to those most able to pay, the case against price discrimination is less convincing.

CHAPTER 10

THE DEMAND FOR PRODUCTIVE SERVICES

In Chapter 2, the wheel of income was employed to provide a broad, general, and simplified view of interdependence in the economy. This wheel of income is reproduced in Figure 10.1. As was indicated in Chapter 2, the private-enterprise economy is essentially a two-market system. The first market comprises the activities of private individuals or families as purchasers and business enterprises (firms) as sellers. This is some-

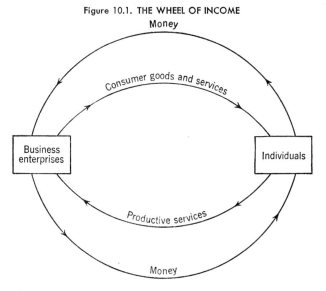

Figure 10.1. THE WHEEL OF INCOME

times called the market for final products and services, and it is shown as the upper half of the income wheel. The preceding chapters have been almost exclusively devoted to an analysis of the forces determining the prices of these products and services, which represent outputs of business units and inputs to private households. In order for the income wheel to be brought to full circle, there remains the important task of analyzing the forces which determine the prices of services for which the roles of buyers and sellers are reversed. The lower half of the income wheel depicts the second market, one in which private individuals are the sellers and business firms are the purchasers. For the most part, private individuals sell services to business firms, by far the most important of which are labor services in their various forms. Labor services are not the only services sold by individuals, however; the services of capital goods of various types—land, buildings, machinery, etc.—are also sold. Individuals may, of course, either sell the services of a capital good to a firm, as is done when a building is leased annually, or sell the capital good directly, as is done when the building is purchased outright by the firm. Even in the latter case, the amount which the firm is willing to pay for the building will be based on its estimate of the value of the services which the building will render in the future.

The major distinction between labor and the other types of productive factors, which may all be grouped together and called "capital," is that the outright purchase alternative does not exist in the case of labor. A firm can only hire labor services; it cannot purchase a laborer outright. It could do this only if slavery were legal.[1]

The services or resources sold by individuals to firms constitute inputs to the firms and outputs of private households. This wheel-of-income approach is oversimplified, however, and account must be taken of the fact that not all inputs of firms are purchased from private individuals. A significant portion of the total inputs of firms are at the same time outputs of other firms. This is the essence of the input-output approach presented in Chapter 2. The products which are not outputs of the household sector but which do serve as inputs of firms may be called "intermediate" products. The behavior of firms selling this type of product is not essentially different from that of firms supplying products and services directly to final consumers. The behavior of firms purchasing intermediate products is no different from that of firms purchasing productive inputs from private individuals. Hence, there is no need for separate discussion of the determination of intermediate-product prices.

While not all inputs of firms are outputs of private individuals, neither are all outputs of private individuals inputs for firms. Many individuals, for example, medical doctors, lawyers, dentists, and baby sitters, sell productive services directly to other private individuals. The demand for such services is in all respects similar to the demand for final consumer goods sold by firms. The supply of these services sold directly is of the

---

[1] There are some exceptions in which laborers are actually purchased in an economic sense. The example that conveniently comes to mind is that of professional baseball players. Under the famous and much debated reserve clause, players' contracts are freely purchased and sold among the various clubs. Even here, however, the athlete cannot be forced to play (although failure to do so may end his baseball career).

same nature as that of labor services sold to firms, which will be discussed in Chapter 11. For our purposes, therefore, we can analyze the input market *as if* all inputs to firms were outputs of individuals, and *as if* all outputs of individuals were inputs to firms.

It will be found that the prices of inputs are determined by the forces of demand and supply, just as are the prices of outputs. The reversed roles of the demanders and suppliers, however, create some fundamental differences in the analysis and make a special examination of input markets necessary. This analysis of input or productive-service prices has sometimes been called "distribution theory," since the forces which determine the prices of productive services at the same time determine the distribution of income in a free-enterprise economy. Again a glance at the wheel of income is useful in showing that the payments made by firms to the owners of productive services are the personal incomes of the owners of these inputs. The income that any individual can earn in a free-enterprise economy is determined by the *amount* of productive services (inputs) which he has to sell to firms and by the *prices* at which he can sell these services. As a matter of fact, by far the most important price to almost any individual is the price at which he can sell his productive capacity, and, for most individuals, this means his labor services. This single price outweighs in significance to him any price which he pays as a buyer in any final product market.

The prices for input units may be determined by the interplay of competition among firms for inputs on the buying side and by competition among individual sellers of inputs on the selling side. To the extent that we have concerned ourselves in previous chapters with the firm's attempt to maximize profits, we find that we have already analyzed to some degree the firm's behavior in buying inputs. As a matter of fact, the behavior of a firm can always be analyzed in two separate ways. The first is by concentrating on output units, the second by concentrating on input units.[1]

In one sense, the output decisions of firms may be considered as primary and the input decisions as derivative. For consumers' choices in final product markets determine which outputs will yield profits and which losses. Consumers' choices guide the firms in their decisions concerning what is to be produced. This is the working out of the principle of consumers' sovereignty discussed in Chapter 1. Firms' demand for input units is derived from their decisions concerning what to produce, how to produce, and how much to produce. The demand for productive services may, therefore, be called a *derived* demand, since it stems from the final consumers' demand for the product which that input will help

---

[1] See Appendix C for an integrated discussion of the firm's behavior in input and output markets.

to produce. There exists a demand for coal miners because there is a demand for coal; as the demand for coal increases, so does the demand for miners. A demand for shoemaking machinery exists because of the demand for shoes. If everyone suddenly started going barefoot, the demand for shoemaking machinery would vanish. When beaver hats went out of style, the demand for beaver hunters was reduced, and the total income of those engaged in beaver hunting was depressed.

In analyzing the pricing of inputs or productive services, we shall find that a distinction must be made between the competitive and the monopoly cases, just as in the pricing of final products. This chapter and the next will discuss the formation of prices for input units when the buying and selling sides of the market are both fully competitive. This requires that there be sufficient numbers of both buyers and sellers for no one to exert control over the price. Firms, as buyers, must accept market-determined supply prices; individuals, as sellers, must accept market-determined demand prices.

Before firms' demand for inputs can be thoroughly examined, the nature of the production process itself must be recalled. All firms perform the task of transforming input units into output units. In accomplishing this transformation they attempt to secure a profit. The process of transformation involves the combining of several types of input in varying amounts in such a way as to produce one or several types of outputs. Thus, a laundry combines water, soap, starch, machines, labor, buildings, paper, and a bundle of dirty clothes and transforms them into a nicely starched bundle of clean clothes. A delivery concern combines labor, trucks, gasoline, oil, street surface, and packages in downtown locations and transforms these into packages on your doorstep.

Almost without exception, the individual firm is faced with alternative ways of combining inputs to produce the same output. The problem of choice is present, since one input unit may be substituted for another. The firm is faced with two basic decisions: (1) how to combine input units to produce any output at the lowest possible cost and (2) how much output to produce. The answers to both of those questions will clearly depend, in part, upon the prices of the various productive services which serve as inputs to firms.

THE DEMAND FOR LABOR

The Law of Diminishing Returns

Just as we did in discussing costs of production, we shall find it helpful to take certain inputs as fixed. Let us suppose that a firm has made certain currently irrevocable decisions concerning how much of all types of inputs to employ except one. We shall call these "fixed factors," and the payment for them represents "fixed costs," discussed in Chapter 5. The one input which may be varied we shall call the "variable factor." It should be emphasized that this may be any of the various types of input. For the sake of convenience, we shall call it "labor" and call the fixed input "capital." If the fixed capital is in the form of land, our assumption could imply that we have a given amount of land, say 10 acres, and we may cultivate the plot of land with 1, 2, 3, 10, 100, or n workers. The proportions between land and labor are variable. As we add successive units of the variable factor to the fixed factor, the total output, or product, will perhaps increase at an increasing rate for a while, but soon it will start increasing at a decreasing rate and will ultimately reach a maximum. This may be stated differently as follows: The *additional* product resulting from the use of additional units of the variable factor may for a time increase, but soon the additional product resulting from the use of an additional unit of the variable factor will begin to diminish and will become successively smaller as more units are added. This principle is called the law of variable proportions or the law of diminishing returns. It is a physical law, not an economic one, although it is extremely important for economic analysis. Although no fully satisfactory proof of the law has been devised, it appears to be universally true. Partially satisfactory proofs have been provided, based both on empirical evidence and on deductive logic. It has been observed, for example, that food concentrates may be used to increase the output of milk from a dairy cow, but after a point the additional output resulting from additional units of concentrate diminishes.

Once having stated the law of variable proportions, or diminishing returns, we need to make use of it in deriving a firm's demand curve for units of a given type of input. Perhaps the best approach will be to take as an example a wheat farmer of classical Greece, where the monetary unit was wheat. Given a plot of land fixed in size, how many units of the

Table 10.1. Production Function of a Grecian Farm

Number of laborers applied to a given amount of land	Total product per year, bushels	Marginal product, bushels
0	0	
1	700	700
2	1,050	350
3	1,250	200
4	1,350	100
5	1,400	50

variable factor, labor, would this Grecian farmer desire to purchase at all possible prices? Suppose the production function (the relation of output to input) were that shown in Table 10.1.

If the wheat farmer were a competitive purchaser of labor, as is assumed in this chapter, he would have no control over the wage rate. Labor would be available to him at a given wage, and he could hire as much or as little as he desired. It can easily be seen from the production function of Table 10.1 that if the wage rate were more than 350 bushels per year, but below 700, only one worker would be employed. The addition of a second worker adds only 350 bushels to total product, and, unless this amount were greater than the wage, it would not pay to hire a second man. At any wage less than 350 but more than 200, two workers would be hired, and so on. These results may be found most directly by referring to the column showing marginal product. Similar to all marginal concepts in economics, the marginal product is defined as the addition to the total product as an additional unit of variable factor is added. The marginal product schedule becomes the farmer's demand schedule for labor. This is illustrated geometrically in Figure 10.2.

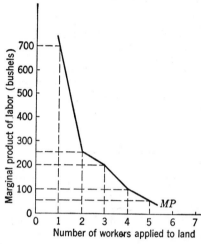

Figure 10.2. THE DEMAND FOR LABOR—
Is Based on Its Marginal
Productivity

The demand curve for the variable input factor is found to slope down to the right, just as did the demand curve for a final product. The inverse relation between quantity demanded and price still holds. There is a fundamental difference, however, between this and the downsloping demand curve for a consumer's good. There the downslope was based on a consumer's desire for the good, which diminished in intensity as more of the good was purchased. Here the downslope is based upon a much less subjective phenomenon—the objective physical law of declining marginal product, or diminishing returns.

The Marginal Revenue Product

The wheat farmer of classical Greece was employed in our example because wheat, the output produced, was also money in that civilization. To make the example more realistic and up to date, but unfortunately somewhat more complex, we must introduce money into the picture. A modern wheat farmer does not pay wages in wheat money; rather he sells his wheat for a money return and purchases the labor which he employs for a money wage. The curve of declining marginal physical product derived by adding more units of the variable factor to the fixed factor no longer constitutes a demand curve. The additional physical output of successive workers must be translated into money terms. If the wheat farmer is also selling in competition, as is usually the case, he can sell any amount of wheat at a given price per bushel. If the production function were identical with that of the Grecian farmer, and the market price of wheat were $2 per bushel, the demand schedule for labor could then be derived by combining the marginal physical product and the price. This is shown in Table 10.2.

Table 10.2. Derivation of Marginal Revenue Product

Number of laborers applied to a given amount of land	Total product per year, bushels	Marginal product, bushels	Marginal revenue, price	Marginal revenue product
1	700	700	$2	$1,400
2	1,050	350	2	700
3	1,250	200	2	400
4	1,350	100	2	200
5	1,400	50	2	100

If the farmer employs one worker, his total revenue is $1,400. The addition of a second worker would add 350 bushels to total product; this 350 bushels could be sold at $2 per bushel. Therefore, the addition of the second worker would add $700 to the farmer's revenue. At any wage above $700 it will not pay to hire the second man; at any wage below $700 it will pay to hire him.

In this case, the demand curve is derived from both the law of diminishing returns and the price of the product. The multiplication of marginal physical product by marginal revenue per unit (which is the same as price per unit, since output is sold competitively) gives "marginal revenue product." It represents the addition to the farmer's revenue resulting from the addition of an input unit.

The marginal revenue product curve derived from the schedule in Table 10.2 is shown in Figure 10.3. Although this curve is based on a combination of both the marginal physical product of the input and the price of the output, its downslope is due solely to the law of diminishing returns, just as before. This is because the price at which the output may be sold remains fixed, since we assumed that the wheat farmer was selling his product in a competitive market.

If, however, the firm purchasing inputs should be a monopolist on the output side, the corresponding marginal revenue product curve would have a downward slope for an additional reason. Suppose, for example, that the wheat grown by this farmer has certain unique curative properties. Not only would the law of diminishing returns be operative, but, in addition, the demand price at which output could be sold would decline as more output units were put on the market. This may be illustrated in Table 10.3. The production function is identical with that in the two earlier schedules. But now instead of being able to sell as much wheat as he desires at a fixed market price per bushel, the farmer finds that the more he wishes to sell the lower the price he must accept. He can market the first 700 bushels for $4 per bushel but must lower the price to $3.50 in order to sell 1,050 bushels, to $3.20 to sell 1,250 bushels, to $3 to sell 1,350 bushels, and to $2.75 to sell 1,400 bushels.

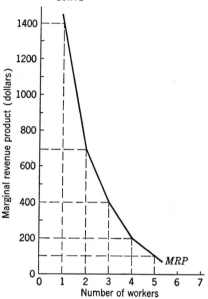

Figure 10.3. **THE MARGINAL REVENUE PRODUCT CURVE**

Table 10.3. **Marginal Revenue Product for a Monopolist**

Number of laborers applied to a given amount of land	Total product per year, bushels	Marginal product, bushels	Price per bushel	Total revenue	Marginal revenue product
1	700	700	$4.00	$2,800	$2,800
2	1,050	350	3.50	3,675	875
3	1,250	200	3.20	4,000	325
4	1,350	100	3.00	4,050	50
5	1,400	50	2.75	3,850	−200

The marginal revenue product has the same meaning as before. It is the addition to total revenue which results from employing an additional input unit. It constitutes the demand curve for the variable factor, as in the earlier example. Algebraically, however, it is no longer equal to the marginal physical product multiplied by the price of output. From a glance at the schedule in Table 10.3, it is apparent that the marginal physical product resulting from the addition of the second man multiplied by the price at which the output produced by two men could be sold would be 350 × $3.50, or $1,225. This figure is sometimes referred to as the value of the marginal product. But the employment of the second worker would not increase the monopolistic firm's total revenue by $1,225, but by only $875. This is because, for the extra 350 units to be sold, a price 50 cents lower per unit must be accepted on the first 700 units. So the actual addition to total revenue is

$$(350 \times \$3.50) - (700 \times \$0.50) = \$875.$$

INPUT ANALYSIS FOR THE FIRM

A firm which seeks to maximize profits and which is buying inputs competitively will purchase input units up to the point where the added income due to hiring another input unit is equal to the price of the input.

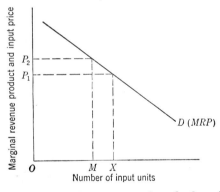

Figure 10.4. FIRM USES FEWER INPUT UNITS—
When Input Price Increases

The equilibrium position in terms of the purchase of input is, therefore, represented by the equality of the marginal revenue product and the price of the input. This may be shown geometrically in Figure 10.4, where D represents the marginal revenue product curve of the variable input to the firm. If the input price is OP_1 regardless of the number of units hired, as is the case when input is bought competitively, OX units of input will be employed. If less than OX units were employed, the addition to revenue caused by adding another input unit would exceed the cost of employing that unit. If employment were expanded beyond OX, the addition to revenue would be less than the cost of employing the additional unit. Consequently, the proper input is OX.

The curve D may also be used to show how the firm's employment of input units will vary as input price varies. If this price increases from OP_1 to OP_2, the firm's employment of this particular type of input will drop to OM. The marginal revenue product curve is the short-run demand curve of the firm for the productive factor which is considered as variable. Employment will fall to OM at price OP_2 only if the other factors of production *remain fixed*. And, as we observed in Chapter 5, there are no fixed factors of production in the long run. Given sufficient time to make all adjustments, the firm may be motivated by the input price increase to shift both the scale and the method of its operations.

This point may be illustrated by a simple example. Suppose the firm depicted in Figure 10.4 is a large 10-cent store. When renting the building and purchasing the inventory stock, the firm's management was required to make a rough prediction about the average level of wages which the firm would have to pay its prospective employees—clerks, janitors, etc. Let us assume that the prediction was made that the average wage rate for clerks would be that shown by OP_1. The size of the inventory stock, the number of departments, the number of items to be stocked, the opening and closing hours, and numerous other variables were originally set on the assumption that clerks' wages would remain at OP_1. The firm considered itself to have attained the "least-cost combination" of inputs for its expected market situation. Now let us suppose that these wage rates go up to that represented by OP_2. This may have happened for several reasons; for example, an atomic-energy plant may have been constructed in a nearby town, increasing all wage rates in the surrounding territory. With the increase in clerks' wages to OP_2, employment will be reduced from OX to OM within a reasonably short period of time after the wage increase. Clerks who are retained may be required to take care of a larger average number of sales counters. The goldfish clerk may now also have to sell parakeets and parasols.

Since the number of departments, capital equipment, etc., were all originally determined on the assumption that the wage rate OP_1 would remain unchanged, new plans will be made now that the wage rate has risen. Until it makes the necessary adjustments, the firm will not have reestablished the least-cost combination of inputs. First of all, labor-saving devices may be introduced. Self-service may be allowed to replace some clerks through installation of machines which vend soft drinks, for example. Second, the scale of operations may be varied; some departments may be dropped altogether, and those which continue to be operated may include fewer items of merchandise. The goldfish department is a likely casualty. Opening hours may be moved from 8 to 9 A.M., and the store may be open only one night rather than two nights a week. Given sufficient time for the management to shop around, it may even be that a smaller building will be rented. After all these adjustments are made, it appears most likely that the employment of clerks will be reduced even more than it was in the short run. Given time for full long-run adjustment, employment will probably fall below OM in Figure 10.4. The firm's demand curve for this type of labor is likely to be more elastic in the long run than in the short run. This conclusion applies generally to all input factors; the demand curve is more elastic in the long run than in the short run.

A change in the price of the variable input is not, of course, the only thing that would cause a firm to modify its employment of the other factors of production. The price of any of these other factors may change, and this would encourage the firm to purchase more or less of such factors. And this, in turn, would independently change the demand curve for the factor initially considered as variable.

Let us make this point clearer by reference to our 10-cent-store case. Let us assume that the firm is operating initially as before with OX clerks employed and that the wage rate is OP_1. Figure 10.5 shows this situation. Now let us suppose that the firm has a chance to rent a larger, air-conditioned building on a more centrally located street in the town for the same monthly payments now being made for the building currently occupied. After the move to the new quarters is complete, the marginal revenue productivity of clerks shifts upward. The new demand curve is shown by D' in Figure 10.5. If the wage rate for clerks remains at OP_1, employment will be increased from OX to ON. The increase in the value of the cooperating factors, in this case represented by a larger and better building and a more efficient location, has served to increase the demand for labor.

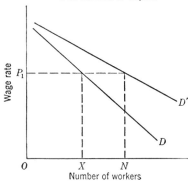

Figure 10.5. DEMAND FOR LABOR IN-
CREASES—

With Increase in Capital

MARKET DEMAND FOR PRODUCTIVE SERVICES

We have shown how the individual firm's demand curve for an input factor is derived. This is all that is required as a basis for the next step, that of deriving the market demand curve. In the case of consumer goods, we found that the market demand curve for any product was derived by the addition of the demand curves of all individual consumers. The same process is necessary for productive services. The preceding analysis has been concerned with the demand curve of an individual firm in a competitive buying position. To arrive at the total market demand curve for any given input factor it is necessary to add up the demand curves, *i.e.*, marginal revenue product curves, of all individual firms purchasing that input.[1]

[1] A logical difficulty arises, however, when this is attempted. For in deriving the marginal revenue product curve for an individual firm that sells its output in competition, the price of output is held constant. But if all firms in a competitive industry

The position of the market demand curve for a productive service depends on the total amount of cooperating factors present, just as does the demand curve for the individual firm. The greater the amount of cooperating resources in the economy, the higher will be the demand curve for a productive factor. This is the same as saying that the "productivity" of the factor is higher, the greater the amount of other factors present. The simple recognition of this fact goes a long way toward explaining the differential rates of return in separate geographical areas. For example, the productivity of labor (taking the whole labor force in this simple case) is higher in the North than in the South primarily because the average amount of capital equipment per worker is much greater in the North. The primary explanation for the continually increasing productivity of the American labor force is found in the continued additions to the country's capital stock, *i.e.*, in net capital formation.

ELASTICITY OF DEMAND FOR INPUTS

Just as in the case of outputs, we need to know more about the demand curve for inputs than the mere fact that it is downsloping. Under certain conditions, the market demand curve for inputs may be highly elastic over normal price ranges; under other conditions, it may be highly inelastic. An examination of the principal factors determining the elasticity of demand for inputs seems in order.

Since the demand for inputs, or productive services, is derived from the demand for final products, or outputs, the first determinant of the elasticity of demand for inputs is obvious. If the elasticity of demand for a final product is high, the elasticities of demand for all the inputs combining to produce that product are likely to be higher than they would be if the elasticity of demand for outputs were low. For example, the elasticity of demand for gravediggers is likely to be extremely low, because the elasticity of demand for dug graves is low (superstition and tradition prevent utilization of adequate substitutes). On the other hand, the elasticity of demand for basket weavers is likely to be high, since the elasticity of demand for woven baskets is high (wooden boxes, paper boxes, paper bags, cloth bags, metal pails, etc., are all adequate substitutes in most uses).

---

expand by hiring more units of the variable factor, then industry output expands, and the price of the output falls. While the price of output would not fall as a result of one firm's expansion, it will fall as the whole industry expands. It suffices here to point up this difficulty; little more could be added by a more extensive discussion. If there are monopoly output sellers among the competitive input purchasers, there arises no difficulty in adding their marginal revenue product curves. This is because the variations in output price as input changes are already taken into account in the marginal revenue product curves.

A second important determinant of the elasticity of demand for inputs is in the degree of substitutability that is possible among inputs. If two types of input may be readily substituted for each other in production, the elasticity of demand for each will be greater than would be the case if such substitutions were not possible. Thus, while the elasticity of demand for gravediggers in general might be very low, the elasticity of demand for mechanical gravediggers may be quite high, since labor and machines may be easily substituted for each other. A slight price change might cause a substantial change in the quantity demanded. If the possibilities for substitution among inputs in production are severely limited, the elasticity of demand is likely to be low. Thus, the elasticity of demand for truck drivers is probably very nearly equal to the elasticity of demand for trucking services, since there is a relatively rigid ratio between labor and capital equipment required to perform the trucking services. It is evident that the process of technological innovation which allows for new types of machines to be substituted for manual labor tends to increase the elasticity of demand for various types of labor. For example, the elasticity of demand for human cotton pickers is now much greater than it was before the invention and utilization of the mechanical cotton pickers.

As mentioned earlier, the demand for inputs is likely to be more elastic in the long run than in the short run, because of the workings of this substitution factor. A firm may have installed capital equipment which requires a relatively fixed number of workers; therefore, a wage increase may cause only a slight decrease in the number of workers employed in the short run. In the long run, however, when the firm has a chance to replace the existing equipment, it is probable that it will consider introducing labor-saving machinery. This dependency of the elasticity of demand for inputs upon the possibilities of substitution among inputs has long been recognized, by labor groups especially, and attempts have been made to prevent such substitution. A great many of the rigid restrictions and requirements imposed by labor organizations concerning methods of production, such as the "building codes" in various cities, are designed primarily to prevent freedom of choice in substituting capital equipment and machine processes for hand labor.

CHAPTER 11

COMPETITIVE DETERMINATION
OF WAGE RATES

The prices of productive services, like other prices, are determined by the interactions of the forces of demand and supply. In Chapter 10, we discussed the demand side when purchasers are in competition for inputs. Account must now be taken of the supply side of the picture in the situation where the suppliers of productive services sell competitively. In dealing with the demand side, we were concerned with the behavior of firms which, we may assume, seek to maximize profits. On the supply side, however, we must examine the behavior of individuals, and here it often is not clear just what they are trying to maximize. Since labor services are by all odds the most important input supplied to firms by individuals, we shall first consider the behavior of individuals in putting labor services on the market.

SUPPLY OF LABOR SERVICES IN THE SHORT RUN

Once we know the market demand schedule or curve for labor services of a given type, we need to derive a functional relationship between quantity supplied and price, i.e., a supply schedule or curve, if we are to determine the price of this service. However, no clearly defined relationship of this sort exists. In the first place, custom, tradition, and legal and institutional restrictions largely set the number of hours of work for most individuals. Even if desires to work more or less were present, these could not be readily fulfilled. A relatively small proportion of the total labor force is able to change substantially the number of hours worked in response to an increase in the wage rate. If there is no possibility of response, the supply curve of labor services for an individual is represented by a vertical line at the traditional number of hours, say a 40-hour week. This is illustrated in Figure 11.1.

In the second place, even if individuals are free to vary the amount of work done in response to changes of the wage rate, and everyone does possess such freedom in some degree through his power of determining how often he will be absent, "sick," etc., it is not clear just what the nature of the response will be. An increase in the hourly wage rate enables an individual to earn the same income with fewer hours of work, and, if he enjoys leisure (or dislikes work), he may well decide to work less as a result of a wage increase. On the other hand, each hour's leisure will cost him more in terms of sacrificed income. Leisure will be more expensive than before the wage increase, so the worker who wants to secure the advantages of higher income may work more. The direction of the response will vary from worker to worker, and it will depend in each case

Figure 11.1. SUPPLY CURVE FOR LABOR SERVICES—
May Be Vertical for an Individual

Figure 11.2. THE BACK-BENDING SUPPLY CURVE—
High Wages May Call Forth Less Labor

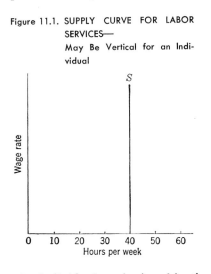

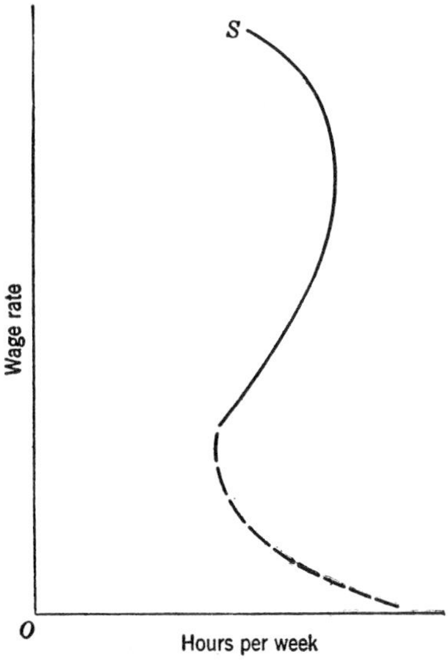

on the individual worker's subjective evaluation of leisure and money income. For many individuals who do possess considerable freedom to work as few or as many hours as they please, the wage rate they are able to earn will have little or no influence on their decision. This is especially true of those people who work in the more agreeable jobs, those who "live to work" rather than "work to live." This group includes many of the professional classes.

One rather peculiar type of response is perhaps worthy of mention here. There is some evidence to indicate that, for some groups, more labor services will be offered at higher wage rates than in the low wage ranges, but once the wage rate rises above a certain level, further increases will cause less rather than more work to be offered. This is graphically depicted in the famous "back-bending curve" shown in Figure 11.2. This has been proved to be empirically correct for several primitive communities, and may be generally applicable among most groups of manual workers.[1] (It has also been observed that in some low-income groups, the number of women workers decreases as the wage rate earned by their husbands increases.)

Since no universally applicable relationship exists between the amount of labor services supplied and the wage rate, the best representation of a short-run supply curve is probably the vertical line which we have used in the fixed-supply case. For most problems which economic analysis is called on to answer, this extremely rough approximation is sufficient. As of a given moment, there is a relatively fixed number of workers in the total labor force. The approximation becomes more acceptable and useful when particular occupational and geographical segments of the labor force are studied. There is a fixed number of plumbers in a particular town at any given date, for example, and the quantity of plumbing services supplied does not change greatly in a short time period, even should wage rates change.

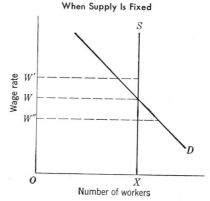

Figure 11.3. DEMAND DETERMINES WAGE RATE—
When Supply Is Fixed

If the assumption of fixed supply is accepted, the short-run determinant of the price of labor (the wage rate) is the demand for labor (marginal revenue productivity). The equilibrium wage rate for any kind of labor is established at the point where the total market demand curve for that type of labor intersects the supply curve. This is shown graphically in Figure 11.3.

OW represents the equilibrium wage rate which will tend to be established in the market when there are OX workers of this occupational category. That is, OW represents the equilibrium wage rate provided that the market for this type of labor service is competitive on both the buying and selling sides. It is the equilibrium wage rate, because this is the only rate which will cause all the workers to be employed and at the same time allow business firms to be purchasing as much of this type of labor as they desire at the going wage. In other words, OW is the only wage rate which clears the market, or makes the quantity demanded equal to the quantity supplied. It may be seen that at any wage rate above OW, say OW', the amount of labor demanded by the market would be less

---

[1] It seems quite possible that at very low wage rates another back-bending portion of the supply curve appears; mere subsistence requires a longer work week at low wage rates. This is shown by the broken portion of the curve in Fig. 11.2.

than the amount offered. Therefore, those workers who would remain unemployed would offer to work for less than OW', and wages would fall. On the other hand, if the wage rate were below OW, say OW'', there would be more workers demanded than would be available. Business firms would find it advantageous under these circumstances to increase wage rates, and as a result the wage rate would tend to increase to OW.

If the supply of labor of the type depicted increased, this would be represented by a shifting to the right of the fixed supply curve, and if conditions of demand did not also change, this would cause a reduction in the equilibrium wage rate. Conversely, if supply were reduced without a change in demand, the equilibrium wage rate would go up.

THE LONG-RUN SUPPLY OF LABOR

Although the assumption of a fixed supply is perhaps most appropriate for short-run analysis, whether applied to the whole labor force or only to a particular segment, this assumption is clearly not appropriate when longer period considerations are taken into account. The size of the labor force, as well as the occupational and geographical groupings within that force, is continually changing. We must now examine the relationship between the long-run changes in the size of the labor force and the level of wages and salaries.

The Classical Theory

The classical economists of the early nineteenth century developed a famous theory concerning the long-run supply of labor. They reasoned in the following way: If the wage rate for common labor should rise much beyond the level which allows laborers barely to subsist, there would be a tremendous increase in the number of children, and thus in the long run the size of the labor force would be increased enough to bring wages down to subsistence levels again. On the other hand, if wages should fall temporarily below the level required for the common laborer to live and support his family, famine and pestilence would be widespread, and the number of laborers would be reduced sufficiently to bring wages again to the subsistence level. This is the familiar theory of population promulgated by Thomas Malthus. It is graphically depicted in Figure 11.4.

The Malthusian theory of the long-run supply of labor has been fairly well discredited by this time, at least as applied to the world of Western civilization although it may still be substantially correct for certain other areas of the world. There are occasional references to the doctrine, and some neo-Malthusians still are found, but, for the most part, the direct dependence of the total supply of labor upon the level of wages has been refuted, both empirically and deductively. Economists in recent years have generally left the theory of population to the sociologists, because of the fact that noneconomic forces are more important in determining the rate of increase in population than those factors which are purely economic in nature. Economic forces, however, are still important and should not be overlooked, although the relationships are sometimes remote and difficult to trace. A recent example to indicate that economic forces still loom large in affecting the rate of change in population is the temporary decline in the rate of population increase in the 1930's, which must be largely attributed to the great depression. The sharp increase in the United States birth rate during and after World War II is probably traceable in part to the favorable employment opportunities and prospects.

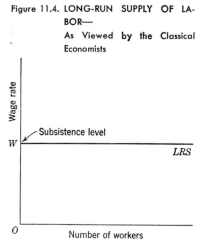

Figure 11.4. LONG-RUN SUPPLY OF LABOR—

As Viewed by the Classical Economists

Long-run Supply for Single Occupations

Although little can be said about the relationship between the long-run rate of increase in total population, and thus the size of the over-all labor force, and the level of wages, this is not true for different occupational categories. There are distinct relationships between the size of a particular segment of the labor force and the wage or salary rate in that occupation relative to other occupations. For example, if the wages of bricklayers increase relative to those of plasterers, there will not be much shifting between the two occupations in the short run. But given a sufficient time period, the increased wages of the bricklayers will (in the absence of restrictions) attract more apprentices to that trade relative to the other, and the supply offered will increase. Thus, the supply curve for bricklayers in the long run may be represented as being relatively flat in the neighborhood of the wage rate offered for jobs requiring similar degrees of skill and of about the same nature. This will be true, of course, only if workers may freely enter and leave occupational groups. Figure 11.5 represents this sort of supply curve.

If the wage for bricklayers fell below OW, there would be no workers willing to work in this business if a long enough time were considered. Of course, there would be workers willing to work for less than OW for a considerable period—those who had been trained in this occupation, especially if they had worked in it for a long time. But as new workers offered themselves for employment, none would become bricklayers, and ultimately no one would be willing to work for less than the wage OW, since he could earn more in similar work elsewhere.

A decrease in the demand for bricklayers, due perhaps to the increased utilization of concrete block, would have the effect in the short run of reducing bricklayers' wage rates. But in the long run, as bricklayers shifted to other occupations and no new apprentices entered the trade, the wage rate would rise again to a level comparable to that of other generally similar occupations such as pipe fitters, plasterers, and carpenters. Both the short- and long-run adjustments may be illustrated in Figure 11.6.

Figure 11.5. LONG-RUN SUPPLY OF BRICK-
LAYERS—
Depends on Wages in Alterna-
tive Occupations

Figure 11.6. SHORT-RUN AND LONG-RUN
ADJUSTMENTS IN WAGE
RATES

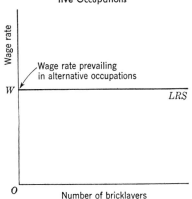

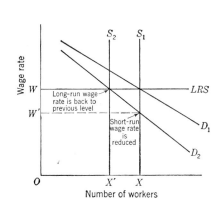

Suppose OW is the wage rate and OX the initial number of workers, while D_1 is the market demand curve for bricklayers. A reduction in demand, represented by the leftward shift of demand to D_2, then occurs. Since the supply in the short run is fixed at OX, the wage will have to fall to OW' if all the workers are to remain employed. But if other occupational groups have not been affected by the same forces which caused this change in demand, the supply curve for bricklayers will shift to the left as workers leave the occupation and as new workers fail to replace those who retire. As the short-run supply curve shifts to the left, the equilibrium wage rate will tend to increase and will continue to do so until it is again approximately OW. The new final equilibrium will be reached when the number of bricklayers is represented by OX' and the wage rate is OW, which is equivalent to that earned in similar occupations. The long-run supply curve is represented by a horizontal line at the original wage—the line LRS in Figure 11.6. Just as we observed in analyzing price formation in competitive product markets (Chapter 6), we find that demand is the primary determinant of price in the short run and supply is the primary determinant in the long run. In Chapter 6, we noted that the price of fish was temporarily depressed by a decline in demand but that price returned to its previous level as fishermen left the industry. The adjustments in competitively determined wage rates are similar in nature.

Occupational Differences in Wages

If all types of jobs were alike in terms of the agreeableness or disagreeableness of the work, and if all workers were freely able to choose among all possible occupational categories, the only wage differences among occupations would be short-run ones arising from shifts in demand. Wage differences would all tend to be eliminated under these conditions by the shifting of workers and the entry of new workers into the jobs offering the highest rewards. Obviously, however, neither of these two conditions is approximated in the real world. Some types of employment are clearly more desirable than others. Each type carries with it some nonpecuniary attributes, all of which may be summed up in terms of agreeableness or disagreeableness. Some men prefer farming because they like the open air and the freedom from supervision which it offers. Others become schoolteachers because they enjoy hearing themselves talk and enjoy long summer vacations. Others may prefer a more routine job; they can put in their eight hours and forget about it. Few men choose to become racing-car drivers, because of the personal dangers involved. In some jobs, the length of the earning period is longer, making those jobs more attractive than others. All these factors operate to make for permanent differences in wage or salary rates among occupational groups.

Even if the second condition, that workers can freely choose among all occupational categories, were fulfilled, permanent differences among occupational groups would tend to arise. Under these circumstances, the jobs which people generally deemed to be the most agreeable would be the lowest paid; jobs which people deemed to be least desirable would be the highest paid. If, for example, the wages of schoolteachers and garbage collectors were equal, and if all garbage collectors could become schoolteachers, which is the condition assumed, then all (or at least a substantial proportion of) garbage collectors would become schoolteachers. School boards would find that they could lower teachers' salaries, since the supply had increased, and garbage companies or sanitary commissions would find it necessary to increase the wages of garbage collectors, since the supply had decreased. Under these conditions, schoolteachers would permanently receive lower wages than garbage collectors because people prefer schoolteaching as an occupation to garbage collecting. This type of permanent difference is called an "equalizing difference" in wages. It is a difference in money income or wages which is necessary to equalize the total advantages (pecuniary plus nonpecuniary) to be gained in each of the various occupations. Although this is a far-fetched example, it goes a long way toward explaining the relatively low salaries of schoolteachers. Such salaries are not low primarily because of the fact that schoolteachers in most states are unorganized or that they are employed by a public agency. They are low primarily because schoolteaching is a relatively desirable profession, because entry into the occupation is relatively easy, and because enough people are willing to accept salaries lower than those paid in comparable occupations.

But, of course, the second condition assumed in our example above is not present either. Not all workers are free to choose among all occupational categories. Garbage collectors cannot often become schoolteachers even if they desire to, because they do not have the educational training to enter that profession. The long-run adjustments in supply, therefore, can take place only within occupational groupings in which shifting is possible. For example, in spite of the short earning period, professional baseball playing is considered a highly desirable occupation by most young men. If all men at the age of eighteen could become professional baseball players if they desired, there would probably be so many entering the business that wages would be notoriously low (as they are in the Class D leagues). But the fact is that only a small proportion of men are able to become top-notch professional baseball players; only this group could enter the profession if they tried. This becomes a "noncompeting" group in the sense that those outside the group cannot compete with those in the group in spite of differentials between the total advantages of this occupation over those of other occupations which might otherwise make long-run supply shifts come about.

The relative importance of differences in natural abilities and differences in acquired or environmental characteristics has long been a much-debated question. Plato argued that the division of labor was mainly attributable to differences in the natural abilities of men. Adam Smith, on the other hand, remarked that the difference between the "philosopher and a common street porter . . . seems to arise not so much from nature as from habit, custom, and education."[1] We do not need, however, to resolve this debate here. Whether because of differences in natural ability or because of environmental differences, men cannot freely enter all occupations. Those occupational groups for which the supply is limited relative to the demand will tend to receive higher wage rates than will those occupations which are open to almost anyone. The fact that garbage col-

[1] Adam Smith, *The Wealth of Nations* (New York: Modern Library, Inc., 1937), p. 15.

lectors' wages are not high despite the disagreeableness of garbage collecting can be explained by the fact that almost any able-bodied worker can become a garbage collector. There are no educational qualifications necessary and no particular skill is required.

A century ago, the average wage rates of white-collar or clerical workers were considerably higher than those of manual workers. This was true in spite of the fact that for most people white-collar work was more desirable. But educational requirements prevented more than a small fraction of the total labor force from competing for white-collar jobs, whereas there were few literacy requirements for manual work. The advent of public education, however, has served to break down the restrictive barrier between these two major occupational groups. A larger and larger fraction of the labor force has been able to enter the clerical group, with the result that white-collar wage rates have continually fallen relative to those of manual workers. The breakdown of the educational barriers formerly separating the groups has allowed the "equalizing" differences to begin to work themselves out. Manual workers now in many instances receive higher wages than white-collar workers. This differential is sometimes fallaciously attributed wholly to the fact that more of the manual workers are organized. This argument overlooks the fact that white-collar work is considered to be more agreeable by many people who are willing, accordingly, to accept lower wages in order to do that type of work.[1]

A fundamental goal of a free society must be that of equalizing opportunity among individuals. One of the major means by which this goal is achieved is by making it possible for individuals to enter the occupations of their choice. If competition prevails in labor markets and if public action to equalize opportunity continues, differences other than the equalizing differences will tend to be gradually reduced. They will not be entirely eliminated, because of the special physical or mental qualifications required in some occupations. As we shall see in Chapter 13, however, the major deterrent to interoccupational adjustments in long-run supply lies in monopoly restrictions on entry imposed by certain occupational groups in an effort to protect their income positions.

Geographical Adjustments in Long-run Supply of Labor

Another important type of adjustment which takes place in the labor force is geographical, and much of what has been pointed out in regard to occupational groups applies geographically as well. If the demand for a particular type of labor increases in a certain area but does not change elsewhere, there will be a migration of labor to the high-wage area. This

[1] For a general discussion of interoccupational differences in wages see Milton Friedman and Simon Kuznets, *Income from Independent Professional Practice* (New York: National Bureau of Economic Research, Inc., 1945).

migration will continue until wage rates are roughly equalized for similar types of jobs. This, of course, is one of the major explanations of the continuing migration of workers from the South to the North. Workers realize that they can earn higher rates of pay in Northern industrial communities than they can on Southern farms. As they migrate North, the average wage rates there are lowered below what they would have been in the absence of migration. As the workers leave the South, Southern wage rates tend to increase above what they otherwise would have been. Thus, the migration tends to promote a long-run equalization of wage rates for similar jobs among geographical regions. This type of long-run adjustment may be illustrated in the diagrams of Figure 11.7.

Figure 11.7. NORTH-SOUTH WAGE DIFFERENTIAL—
Is Reduced by Northward Migration

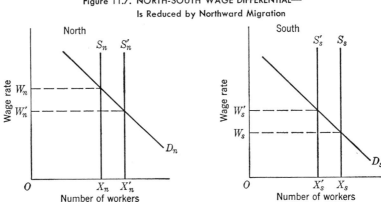

In Figure 11.7, D_n represents the demand for labor in the North, and S_n the supply of labor initially available in that area. The average Northern wage rate is OW_n. On the right-hand side, D_s, S_s, and OW_s represent the demand, supply, and average wage rate in the South. As long as OW_n is substantially greater than OW_s, workers will continue to migrate from the Southern region to the North. This will tend to shift the supply curve for Northern labor to the right, shown by S'_n, and the supply curve of Southern labor to the left, shown by S'_s. This migration will tend to lower Northern wage rates and increase Southern wage rates, bringing the two more nearly into an equality with one another. Of course, it should never be overlooked that in analyzing problems of this nature we are still employing our helpmate, *ceteris paribus*. Here we have had to assume that the demand curves for labor in the two regions remained unchanged. Actually the demand (productivity) curve of labor is continually shifting upward in both regions because of increased capital investment and improved technology. With this recognized, it is highly likely that Northern wage rates in general are never actually reduced by in-migration of Southern workers. They continue to increase, but they increase at a slower rate than they would were the South made a separate country and immigration prohibited.

Money wage rates for similar jobs may never be fully equalized in all geographical areas even in the same economy and even if all the adjustments are allowed to take place. Equalizing differences may be present in this sense, also. If Southern workers, on the average, prefer the smell of the sweet magnolias to the hustle and bustle of urban Northern life, they may well decide that life in the South is more agreeable. There will be a nonpecuniary advantage to work in the South. Thus, wage rates in the North might be permanently higher for similar jobs, the difference being necessary to make Northern jobs equally attractive on all counts with Southern jobs. There is no clear evidence, however, that this sort of equalizing difference does explain any or all of the present differences in wage rates in the two areas. The differences which do exist may be more readily explained by the fact that the long-run resource adjustments have not been carried out.

CHAPTER 12

ECONOMIC RENT AND INTEREST

The inputs of firms consist not only of the labor services of persons whom they employ but also of the services of material goods which they either buy or hire. To the extent that inputs consist of materials which are used up within a short period of time (*e.g.*, flour in the production of bread), the material is generally purchased outright by the using firm. When the required input consists instead of the services of a durable good, it is necessary for the firm either to buy the capital good—perhaps with funds raised by selling securities—or to rent it. In the latter case, title remains with the owner, but the services of the good belong for a specified period to the renter. Examples are numerous, *e.g.*, the renting of office space by a lawyer, the renting of punch-card machines by a government agency, or the renting of vacant property by the operator of a parking lot. Rental prices for the services of particular capital goods are determined by the forces of supply and demand in much the same way as is the price of labor inputs.

THE CONCEPT OF ECONOMIC RENT

So far we have used the terms "rent" and "rental" to denote the price paid for the use of a capital good. These terms should be distinguished from "economic rent," which, in economic analysis, has been given a different definition. To the economist, economic rent is the income received by any sort of productive factor *over and above what it could earn in the next best use*. The rental income received by the owner of a capital good is likely to consist of economic rent to a considerable degree, since capital goods are often highly specialized to a particular use. In the extreme short run, all capital goods are, of course, specialized. In considering the concept of economic rent we are, therefore, concerned with specialization over a period sufficiently long to allow resources to be shifted from one use to another. For example, sandy soil in an area may be permanently suitable only for growing pine trees. The entire earnings of the owner of such land are economic rent, because the land has only one use. On the other hand, a fertile plot of land near a large city would command a high rental but might yield little or no economic rent to its owner because of its adaptability to a large number of agricultural and commercial uses, the best of which may be virtually no better than the next best. These two situations, which are limiting cases, are represented on the two sides of Figure 12.1.

In each case the demand is the marginal revenue product of that type of productive service in its best employment. On the left side of the diagram, the supply of the input to the particular use pictured is drawn as perfectly elastic. This shows that the owner of the input will make none available to this use at any price below that which it could secure in another use; this other use, it is assumed, would hire the entire input at

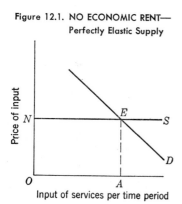

Figure 12.1. NO ECONOMIC RENT—
Perfectly Elastic Supply

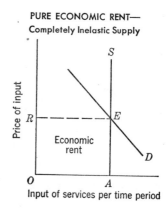

PURE ECONOMIC RENT—
Completely Inelastic Supply

a price per unit of *ON*. (The principle is similar to that of the adjustment of labor among comparable occupations, which was discussed in Chapter 11.) As a consequence, the factor of production (*e.g.*, the well-located and fertile plot of land) receives no economic rent. Its income is determined entirely by the competition among alternative uses rather than by any one best use.

On the right side of Figure 12.1, the supply of input services is shown as perfectly *inelastic* to the particular use. This indicates that the factor has no alternative employment. Its income is determined entirely by the demand in the particular industry to which it is suited; this income is called "pure economic rent." The sandy-soil example illustrates this case. Its rental or sales value is determined entirely by the demand for pine lumber and turpentine.

Many types of skilled labor and capital goods are better adapted to one particular use than to any other but are capable of doing two or more jobs. In this event, the remuneration received is a combination of economic rent and competitively determined income. Tool-and-die makers, for example, are highly specialized to that activity. If demand for their services in that line falls off, they will suffer a sharp cut in wages. If we assume that their only alternative employment is as unskilled labor, the income received in tool-and-die making over and above that which could be earned in common labor would be called economic rent. This sort of situation is pictured in Figure 12.2.

The wage rate which could be earned in an alternative occupation is assumed to be OC. It is further assumed that all of the OA skilled workers (*e.g.*, tool-and-die makers) could secure employment in this alternative occupation. This means that they will not be willing to accept less than OC in the employment being considered but will, of course, accept as much more as they can get. Supply becomes perfectly inelastic above wage rate OC at the input OA. The actual wage rate obtained will be OW, and total income to these workers will be $OWEA$, of which $CWER$ is economic rent. In this example, we have assumed that there are no "equalizing differences" which would cause workers to consider any factors other than relative money wage rates in choosing between occupations.

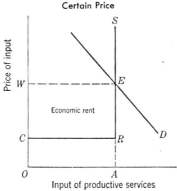

Figure 12.2. SOME ECONOMIC RENT—Inelastic Supply above a Certain Price

Similarly, most capital goods are not completely specialized to one use. A truck, for example, can usually be employed to haul any of a large variety of commodities; a building constructed to house a hardware store and a dentist's suite of offices may be shifted, if necessary, to use by a grocery store and a physician. An ordinary plot of land may be used to produce several different crops, or, alternatively, rented out for use as a fairground. In all of these cases, the supply of the capital good to any particular use is made less than perfectly inelastic by its alternative use possibilities. This is true despite the fixity in the total existing quantity of such goods on hand at any time. Like the tool-and-die makers, such semi-specialized capital goods receive income which is in part economic rent.

The moral to be drawn from the theory of economic rent is quite clear. Any worker or capital good which is highly specialized to a single occupation is in a vulnerable position. As long as demand is strong in that particular industry, the worker or capital good will receive a favorable return for its services. If the demand in that industry falls off, however, this will occasion a sharp cut in remuneration, since satisfactory alternative employments are not available. On the other hand, a capital good which is adaptable to several uses, without any changes in form or with only minor modification, receives little of its income in the form of economic rent, and the owner will be in a stronger position in the event of shifts in the demand for its services. It is generally desirable for a worker to have two or more skills rather than just one. (It is usually not wise to attempt to become a Jack-of-all-trades, however, since this may involve mastery of none.) In the case of a college student, premature professional specialization may leave him with few alternative occupational possibilities and therefore highly dependent on the demand for his special training.

Long-run Adjustments in Economic Rent

We have mentioned the vulnerability of the recipient of economic rent to a decline in demand for his specialized services. If, on the other hand, the demand for such services increases, the economic rent will increase sharply because of the short-run inelasticity of supply. Suppose, for example, that there is an increase in the demand for air-conditioned office buildings in a particular city. The rental price (and the economic rent) on those buildings which are already air-conditioned will increase. Some adjustments in supply may be forthcoming in the form of conversion of suitable non-air-conditioned buildings into air-conditioned ones, but after this has occurred rentals will probably still be very favorable to those who were wise enough, or fortunate enough, to invest in this field. Rentals may be much greater than the amount necessary to pay all operating expenses, including depreciation and a normal return on the capital invested in construction.

These extra profits will normally attract new investment in the construction of air-conditioned buildings, but the acquiring of new building sites and accomplishment of the construction are likely to occupy several years. (Expansion of the air-conditioning industry itself may occasion delay.) During this period, above-normal profits will continue to accrue to the owners of buildings already air-conditioned. Eventually, however, the construction of new air-conditioned office buildings will bring rentals down to a level where only ordinary returns are made on investment in that field. "Windfall" profits, which were due to the luck or wisdom of early investors in the field, will disappear.

If, on the other hand, the demand for some specialized capital good declines, causing earnings to be less than normal, a reverse sort of adjustment will take place. Suppose the demand for hotel accommodations in a city declines because of the erection of new motels. New hotels will not be built, and existing ones are likely to be undermaintained. Hotel owners will gradually withdraw part of their capital from this field. They may reinvest the funds so withdrawn in completely different capital goods— for example, in cattle. In a long-run sense, capital is not specialized in form and consequently does not receive economic rent. Instead, it earns a competitively determined return.

Similarly, an individual who has specialized training and experience in a particular occupation may be able to retrain himself for another type of work if a change in vocation appears desirable. In a long-run sense, workers are not so highly specialized and hence receive less economic rent than in the short run. The working life of the individual is not sufficiently long to permit very many complete switches in occupation, however.

THE CAPITALIZATION PRINCIPLE

We have discussed the payments for the services of capital goods. What is the relationship between the value of these services and the value of capital goods themselves? It is not correct to say simply that the value of a capital asset is the aggregate income which it can bring to its owner over its useful life. It is necessary to *discount* all returns which will be received in the future in order to find their value today.

The process of discounting is just the opposite of computing compound interest. A sum kept in a savings account will be increased periodically by the amount of interest earned, calculated at the rate announced by the bank, and if the interest is left on deposit the owner of the account receives further interest on this interest. In discounting, however, we start with a future payment or a schedule of future payments and calculate the capital sum which will yield this income at a given rate of interest.

Suppose that, under the terms of a will, Joe Jones will receive the sum of $1,000 payable on his twenty-first birthday, which will occur in exactly two years. What is this future income worth today? (The question might be a practical one, since it would probably be possible for Jones to sell his claim to the $1,000 to someone who would look upon the transaction as a suitable investment.) The value of $1,000 to be received in two years would be found by "discounting" this sum at a suitable rate of interest. If 5 per cent were an appropriate interest rate, the present value C would be found from the formula $C = \dfrac{\$1,000}{(1 + 0.05)^2}$. This capital value works out to be $907.03. This is equivalent to saying that if one invests $907.03 currently at an interest rate of 5 per cent compounded annually, its value would grow to $1,000 in two years' time. Similarly, the present value of the future payment of $1,000 which will not be secured until six years from today would be found by dividing by one-plus-the-interest rate raised to the sixth power.

In the above example, only one payment is due the beneficiary of the will. Suppose instead that the payments will continue to be received for an indefinitely long period into the future, as is likely to be the case with urban land, for example, which may be rented out for a very long period for use as a building site or other purpose. The capitalization formula then simplifies to the following: $C = I/r$, where C is capital value, I is annual income, and r is the annual interest rate. This, then, is the formula for finding the capital value of a perpetual income; simply divide the expected annual income by an appropriate rate of interest. Suppose, for example, it is believed that an urban lot will bring a net rental (after property taxes and upkeep) of $1,000 a year for as long into the future as one can see. At an interest rate of 5 per cent it is worth $20,000. This is the obverse side of the process which indicates that an asset worth $20,000 will provide an annual income of $1,000 if the return is 5 per cent.

In the case of a capital good which depreciates with use (*e.g.*, a power shovel), the capitalization formula $C = I/r$ may still be used if I is defined as net yearly income after allowance for depreciation. When proper allowance is made each year for depreciation, the annual net income can be considered to be a perpetual income. It is made perpetual through purchase of a new capital good whenever the old one wears out.

The discussion of the capitalization formula immediately raises the problem: What interest rate should be used in capitalizing any particular asset? Actually, this presents a difficult problem in any real case of capitalization. The individual making the calculation must select an interest rate which appears to represent the rate of return being received on newly produced capital goods of the same general sort. This interest rate will be higher in more risky employments than in those where the chance of failing to collect the interest or of losing the principal is small. An interest rate of 25 per cent might be appropriate, for example, in finding the capital value of an American-owned oil well in a Central American republic with an unstable government. On the other hand, a low interest rate (perhaps 4 per cent) might be appropriate in figuring the value of land rented on a 99-year lease to a well-established utility company in this country. Since the capitalized value of an asset varies inversely with the rate of interest, the high interest rate used would serve to keep down the estimated value of the oil well, while the low interest rate used would enhance the calculated value of the land leased to the utility company.

When buyers and sellers of capital assets argue about an appropriate sales price, they may be considered really to be bargaining with respect to what the annual income from the asset will be and as to what constitutes an appropriate interest rate on such an investment. The seller tries to make the expected annual income appear as large as he can and the appropriate interest rate as low as possible. The shrewd prospective buyer will point to a probable low income from the good and to the uncertainty of the return as justifying a low selling price.

THE RATE OF INTEREST

We have just seen how the interest rate enters into the evaluation of capital goods through the capitalization process. There remains the question as to how the interest rate itself is determined. This is one of the most complex problems in economics.

The Productivity of Capital

Interest is based on the productivity of capital goods, or, speaking more broadly, of "capital"—which is the aggregate of all goods (including land) in existence at any time. The productivity of capital makes it worth while for firms generally to pay the owners of capital goods rentals which will not only cover depreciation of these assets but also provide a further return. Competition among firms for capital makes the payment of such an interest return not only worth while but necessary. Not all capital-goods owners, however, receive such a net return over their cost of production; rentals may be sufficient only to cover depreciation or may fail even to do that. But to the extent that resources are properly allocated, the current output of capital goods will consist of items which can actually earn a return over their lifetime above cost of production. This is true whether the new capital goods are replacements for existing ones or additions to the total stock of capital.

A useful way of viewing the determination of the rate of interest, in the long run under pure competition, is the following:

Interest rate = X dollars per year net income (above depreciation)
÷ cost of producing a capital good yielding X dollars per year net income

This formula is not quite correct,[1] but it is sufficiently close to be instructive. It shows the interest rate under competition to depend on the net productivity of new capital goods and on their cost of production. Thus if $50 per year net income can be secured by producing a capital good which costs $1,000 (or $50,000 secured by producing a good which costs $1 million), the rate of return is 5 per cent. The interest rate tends to be equal for all capital goods in the same risk category, since otherwise resources will be shifted from the production of items yielding smaller returns to those yielding more net income.

The rate of interest obtained by new buyers of *old* capital goods tends to be equated to the interest rate yielded by *new* capital goods through

---

[1] The inexactness of the formula results from the fact that interest is involved in the cost of production of any capital good; hence the interest rate actually appears on both sides of the equation. This has been pointed out by Professor Frank H. Knight. A more correct (but formidable) formulation has been given by him in several articles, including "Capital, Time and the Interest Rate," *Economica*, N.S. I (1934), pp. 257–286.

adjustment in the selling prices of old capital goods in accord with the capitalization principle. This must be so because no one with funds to invest will rationally buy an old capital good (*e.g.*, a ten-year-old apartment building) unless he can get it at a price which will yield him at least as high a rate of interest on his investment as he could secure from a new asset of a similar nature (*e.g.*, a new apartment building). Similarly, the owner of an old capital good will not normally have to sell it for a price so low that it will yield a new buyer a higher rate of return than he could secure by buying a new capital good, since prospective investors are in competition with one another.

Thus new buyers of both new and old capital goods of any given sort tend to receive the same rate of interest on their investments when there is competition on both the buying and selling sides. For example, when the United States Treasury early in 1953 began selling a new issue of long-term bonds yielding $3\frac{1}{4}$ per cent, the price of already existing long-term bonds immediately fell because of the higher rate on the new issues. Old owners of old capital goods may, however, receive much higher or much lower returns on amounts which they have invested, since their returns are affected strongly by shifts in the demand for the specialized services of their capital goods (in the manner described for air-conditioned office buildings).

Interest as the Price of Borrowed Money

The rate of interest may also be thought of as the price of the use of money. Whenever a loan is made, some sort of I O U passes from borrower to lender as evidence of the loan, and the I O U specifies the rate of interest to be paid as well as conditions of repayment of the principal. The I O U's may take many forms: for example, a businessman's note given to his bank, a bankbook given to a depositor (who has loaned the use of his savings to the bank), a corporation bond which shows that the holder has loaned money to the company, or a government bond which evidences borrowing on the part of a public agency.

While the interest rate can be considered to be the price paid for the use of someone's money (the view which will be examined in Part B), it is more basic to consider it the return on capital, as has been done in the present chapter. Money is completely unspecialized purchasing power made available to borrowers who then generally use it to buy materials, equipment, or other assets of a more or less specialized nature. Because money is completely unspecialized to any one use, the return to a lender contains no economic rent. "Money capital" may be said to be in perfectly elastic supply to any given use at the going or market rate of interest. This is indicated in Figure 12.3 by the supply line *RS*. Demand for money capital in the use pictured is represented by curve *D*. The amount OA will be borrowed, and total interest payments on the associated I O U's will be $OREA$ per time period. No economic rent is involved, because there is no difference between the rate of return which money earns in this use and in the next best alternative use.

The demand for money capital (D in the diagram) is based on the expected marginal revenue product of capital goods which the borrower can acquire with the money capital. Therefore, the borrower will tend to borrow until this expected marginal return to him is equal to the interest rate he has to pay to borrow money. The interest paid on borrowed money thus reflects the expected productivity of capital goods, the use of which

Figure 12.3. SUPPLY OF MONEY CAPITAL TO A BORROWER—
Is Perfectly Elastic at Prevailing Interest Rate

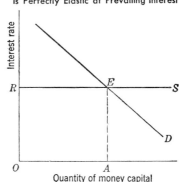

can be acquired by the borrower. Once the capital goods have been bought or leased, the actual return which they will yield may turn out to be greater or smaller than was anticipated, making the decision to borrow either a good one or a poor one. Normally, this does not affect the lender of money, however, since the I O U's which he has received carry a definite interest rate which must be paid.

Whether one is considering interest as the net return on investment in capital goods or as the payment to holders of I O U's, it should be recognized that the return varies greatly according to the risk of loss of principal and interest. Pure interest is received only on capital goods or I O U's of great safety (such as on a plot of land rented on a 99-year lease to a large utility company, on a government-insured savings account, or on a short-term United States government bond).[1] All less safe capital goods

[1] The risk in holding a bond which will mature (repay the principal) at a more distant date is greater than the risk in holding a bond of near-term maturity, because the market value of the former will drop more sharply if there is a general rise in interest rates. Not even United States government bonds are completely safe with respect to the principal sum unless one holds the bond until the maturity date, or unless one buys savings bonds which carry a definite redemption schedule.

and I O U's frequently earn a return above pure interest which is a premium for the greater risk involved.

The Interest Rate Rations Money Capital

The interest rate under competitive conditions can clearly be said to perform a rationing function with respect to money capital. In order to be able to afford to pay interest on a loan and ultimately to repay the principal, a firm must put the borrowed funds to good use. This tends to exclude the less productive employments and thus to ration new savings to firms better able to use them. In terms of Figure 12.3, the demand curve for some uses of new capital will be higher than for other uses, and this difference will cause more money capital to flow into employments where the demand is stronger. Other possible users of new capital will have demands which will not be effective at all except at interest rates below the going rate. These uses will receive none of the new capital, and this is as it should be, since the prospective productivity of capital is too low in such fields to justify the use of new capital there.

The rationing, or allocation, function of the interest rate is so important that even a completely communistic society, in which individuals receive no interest income, must account for interest or suffer the consequences in terms of lower production efficiency. Entries for interest must be made on the books of a completely planned economy in order to secure a reasonably correct allocation of scarce capital among the various industries. If one industry uses ten times as much capital as another but both use the same amount of labor, the total cost of production is much greater in the first industry, but this would not be evident if interest were disregarded. The planning authorities could not make any proper comparison of utility of output and cost of input if they failed to account for interest. Their inherently difficult job of planning would become virtually an impossible one.

The "production-motivation" function of the interest rate in a private-enterprise economy is less clear than the capital-rationing function. Capital in any economy is built up through the allocation of a sufficient quantity of resources to uses other than current consumption. Under conditions of full employment of resources, an increase in the production of capital goods is brought about by an increase in saving and investment which causes input units to be transferred out of consumption-goods production and into capital-goods production. Increased saving decreases the demand for consumption goods; increased investment increases the demand for capital goods.[1] Under conditions of less than full employment,

[1] Backward economies, such as those of some Asiatic nations, generally have such large populations in relation to resources and technological knowledge that they find it necessary to devote practically all of their resources to the production of food and

it may be possible to increase the output of capital goods without reducing the output of other goods by putting idle resources to work. Means whereby this can be done will be discussed in Parts B and C.

The production-motivation function of the interest rate is traceable in part to its effect on the rate of saving.[1] This effect is not clear. Some (probably most) families and firms pay little or no attention to interest rates when they make their decisions regarding saving. Some who calculate more closely find the prospect of higher interest rates an incentive to increase their savings. Others who are aiming at accumulating a certain sum by a particular date find that they need to save *less* if interest rates are higher, since interest will do more for them in reaching their goal. This inverse relationship between saving and the interest rate is especially important with respect to savings which are placed in endowment and annuity policies sold by insurance companies. The lower the interest rate which insurance companies can earn on such savings, the higher the premiums they will charge on the contracts. Consequently, a large number of families find it necessary to save more as interest rates go down. On balance, the volume of new savings in any time period appears not to be affected greatly by the rate of interest. For this reason, and for others to be developed in Part B, the effect of the interest rate on capital accumulation is not so clear as its capital-rationing function.

---

other nondurable goods. They consequently are able to accumulate little capital without outside help. They are poor because they have limited capital, and they are unable to accumulate capital because they are poor.

[1] The interest rate also affects capital formation through its effect on the rate of investment—*i.e.*, its effect on the total purchases of capital goods. This effect is being neglected in Part A but will be considered in Part B.

CHAPTER 13

MONOPOLY INCREASES INPUT PRICES

In the last few chapters, we have discussed the formation of input prices when both the buying and the selling sides of the input markets are competitive. Just as is true in the output markets, however, monopoly elements are often present in the markets for inputs, both among buyers and among sellers. Firms as buyers obviously prefer to be monopolistic in their purchases of inputs; that is, they prefer to be strong enough to enforce, within limits, their own purchase prices on sellers. Individuals, on the other hand, desire to sell their productive services at the highest possible prices and will attempt in any way possible to avoid submitting to the impersonal forces of the market. This chapter will discuss the effects of monopoly influence on input markets both in buying and in selling.

MONOPOLY ON THE BUYING SIDE

It was noted in the discussion of output markets that monopoly elements are largely confined to the selling side. As was mentioned in Chapter 6, perfectly competitive behavior is normal on the buying side for final products. In the case of input markets, however, we must consider the possibilities of monopolistic influences on the part of both buyers and sellers. In order to distinguish it clearly from sellers' monopoly, economists define the buyers' domination of the market as "monopsony." Firms possessing significant control over the prices which they pay for input units are called "monopsonists."[1] Such control arises when buyers are few or when they act in collusion, just as control over output prices arises when sellers are few or when they are organized. If there is a significant number of buyers, so that no one purchases more than a small proportion of the total market supply of the input type under consideration, no one buyer could exert control over the price which he pays. The single buyer would be faced with a market-determined supply price, and

[1] More detailed analysis would require that we distinguish "monopsonists" and "oligopsonists," just as we distinguish "monopolists" and "oligopolists" on the output side. This is not necessary here; any degree of buyer control over price may be placed in the inclusive category, monopsony.

he could purchase as much or as little as he desired without himself appreciably affecting the price. He would be faced with a horizontal supply curve at the ruling price, just as are competitive buyers of final products, as was illustrated in Figure 6.1.

The monopsonistic buyer, on the other hand, does exert control over price; by changing the amount of his purchases he is able to change the price that he pays. He is faced with an upsloping rather than a horizontal supply curve. As he purchases more, the price which he must pay will increase. By lowering the input price he will not lose his whole source of supply. For example, a textile firm operating a mill in a small town may find that it can hire 100 workers at an average hourly wage of 75 cents. These workers include those who live in the town, many of whom may have lived there for a long time and may prefer almost any work in this town to employment on surrounding farms or in other cities. If, however, the firm decides to hire 200 workers, it may find it necessary to pay more than 75 cents, perhaps 85 cents an hour. Some of the second 100 workers will have to be convinced that working in the mill is preferable to working on farms, and some may have to commute from surrounding towns or actually move from other areas.

Figure 13.1. SUPPLY CURVE FACING MONOPSONISTIC BUYER

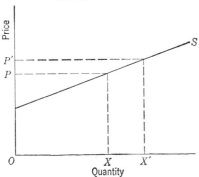

In order to secure more than 200 workers, still higher wages might have to be paid. The supply curve for workers facing the textile firm is upsloping; as more units of input are purchased, the price of inputs increases. This general situation may be depicted in Figure 13.1.

In order to understand the manner in which buyer control over input price affects allocation of productive services among alternative uses, it is now necessary to examine the behavior of a firm faced with an input supply curve such as the one depicted in Figure 13.1. It will be recalled that the firm buying in a competitive market will tend to extend its purchases of input units up to the point where the marginal revenue product of the input is equal to the market price of the input. This was shown in Figures 10.4 and 12.3. But the monopsonist will not do this. For the additional cost of purchasing additional input units will, for such a buyer, be greater than the price which must be paid. And the monopsonist will purchase inputs only up to the point at which the *additional revenue* secured by the employment of the input is equal to the *additional cost* incurred by its employment.

This may be shown more clearly in Figure 13.2, which represents the textile-mill example used above. The additional cost of hiring the second 100 workers will not be only 85 cents per man-hour, or $85 per hour for the group, since the first 100 will also have to be paid 85 cents per hour when the second group is hired. They will be unwilling to work for a lower wage while doing the same work.[1] So the total additional cost of hiring 100 more workers is 85 cents × 100 + 10 cents × 100, or $95 per hour. The firm will hire the second 100 men, accordingly, only if it considers them to be worth (i.e., their marginal revenue product to be more than) $95 per hour of work. If the marginal revenue product curve is that

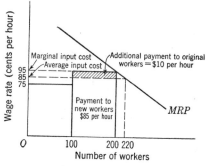

Figure 13.2. MARGINAL REVENUE PRODUCT EXCEEDS WAGE—

For Monopsonistic Buyer of Labor Services

pictured, the second 100 will be employed. The firm will continue to employ inputs until the marginal input cost is equal to the marginal revenue product. The two are equal at 95 cents per hour in the figure. (But the firm will be paying only 85 cents per hour.) Thus the average input cost (price) is less than the marginal revenue product.[2]

[1] Monopsonists as well as monopolists may engage in price discrimination. In order to do so, however, the monopsonist must separate sellers into distinct categories. In the textile-mill case, worker morale might suffer seriously if workers were paid different wages for similar work.

[2] A more general view of the monopsonist's most profitable input may be represented by Fig. 13.3. Profits will be maximized if the firm buys inputs to the point

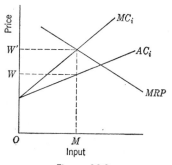

Figure 13.3.

where marginal input cost equals marginal revenue product. This is OM in the figure. These inputs can be purchased at a price of OW each, as is indicated by the average input cost curve.

The net results of monopsony control over input price are very similar to those of monopoly control over output price. The buyer's control causes him to restrict the number of inputs he will purchase, since he secures a smaller number at a lower price, just as restriction of output enables the monopolist to secure a higher price. In Figure 13.2, it can be seen that if the buyer's control over price were eliminated and a uniform supply price of 85 cents existed instead, he would purchase the services of about 220 workers rather than 200. If the textile mill were opened in a large rather than a small town and 85 cents were the established wage rate, no workers could be hired for less. The single buyer's control over price would be removed, and as a result more input units would be purchased rather than less. Monopsony also tends to keep wage rates below the competitively determined levels. If, in the above example, there were only 200 workers in the market area and enough buyers were in the labor market to bring wages up to the marginal revenue product, the wage rate would tend to be 95 cents rather than 85 cents per hour.

Monopsony distorts the allocation of economic resources in much the same way that monopoly does. Monopsony power gives the buyer an incentive to restrict the number of inputs purchased, and this restriction decreases output, making output prices higher than they would otherwise be. This is true whether the firms in question are selling outputs competitively or monopolistically. The allocation of resources could be improved by a shifting of productive factors toward the monopsonistic firms and away from the more competitive markets. Resources are more productive in the monopsonistic firms' employ than they are elsewhere. For example, in Figure 13.2, the marginal revenue product of an hour's labor is actually 95 cents, but labor receives only 85 cents. In employments where buyers are competitive, a wage rate of 85 cents would represent the full marginal revenue product of an hour's labor. Clearly, the allocation of resources could be improved by a shifting of resources into the area where labor is worth 95 cents an hour and away from those employments where it is actually worth only 85 cents.

Our specific example has been in terms of monopsonistic control over a particular labor market. The degree to which such monopsony control is present in our economy is a much-debated question. There are likely to be many cases in which firms do exert some control over prices paid to workers;[1] the extent of the control is probably slight in most situations, especially in the long run. Significant monopsony power in labor markets may well exist only in short-run situations. In the short run, labor is substantially immobile, and a certain share of any labor force will be willing to accept lower wage rates rather than change employment. Even in the

[1] We are assuming throughout this section that competition prevails on the selling side of the input market.

short run, however, there are some workers who are willing to move in response to wage differences.

Monopsony power in labor markets in the long run is likely to be present only in cases where no alternatives, or inferior alternatives, are open to workers. This type of monopsony power is much more likely to be present among buyers of the more highly skilled and better-paid types of labor than among the less highly skilled. This is because the alternative employment opportunities open to these more highly specialized types of workers are much more severely limited than are the opportunities open to common or unskilled labor. Buyers of highly specialized labor are fewer, the necessary condition for substantial monopsony control. For unskilled labor, there are normally several potential buyers available, and, therefore, no one buyer is likely to be able to influence significantly the wage rate. Even here, however, switching among jobs might require a degree of geographical mobility; if mobility is insufficient, employers may enjoy monopsony power. For example, the wage rate for common labor might temporarily differ in adjacent towns but would not long remain unequal.

Monopsony control over price is not limited to labor markets. It may be present in varying degrees in many markets. It is perhaps relatively common in the purchase of intermediate goods where the processing buyers are large monopolistic or oligopolistic concerns. The market for leaf tobacco provides an example. The fewness and the size of buyers, the large tobacco companies, are such that substantial control over the buying price for tobacco is probably exerted.

Many large buyers may find it advantageous to encourage and promote the establishment of small sellers in order to be able to exert monopsony control over buying price. The large grocery chains and mail-order houses are often accused of buying from small and exclusive suppliers at lower than competitive prices. Once a small firm has invested substantial amounts in specialized equipment designed to turn out a product to the specifications of a large buyer, it is difficult for it to refuse any bid which will cover variable cost, if the buyer chooses to exert such a "monopsonistic squeeze."

MONOPOLY IN THE SALE OF PRODUCTIVE SERVICES

Sellers of inputs, or productive services, like all sellers, will prefer a monopolistic position to a competitive one. The selling side of the productive-service markets is perhaps more saturated with monopoly elements than any other sector of the economy at the present time. It is important, therefore, that the effects of this type of monopoly control be examined. For the most part, this involves a consideration of monopoly in the selling of the most important type of input, namely, labor services.

Monopoly is defined in the same way as before; it is the power of a seller or sellers to influence the selling price. Viewed in this fashion, it is clear that few single sellers of labor services are in a position to act as monopolists in the sale of their services. This position could be attained only in those cases where a person possesses some extremely unique and valuable ability or skill which is found in few other persons. For example, there is only one Bing Crosby, and, in the minds of his admirers, there are no close substitutes. In the sale of his services, Bing is able to act as a monopolistic seller. He does have the power of influencing the price which he can secure for his services.

In the usual situation, however, an individual offering his labor services independently is forced to accept a given wage, determined either by the market, if the market consists of many buyers, or by the single buyer or few buyers, if the market is monopsonistically controlled. This lack of control by the individual seller of labor services over his wage (which, after all, determines his income position in society) provides an important part of the historical explanation for the growth of labor organizations. The individual worker was felt to be helpless before the impersonal forces of the market, particularly before monopsonistic buyers. But the consumer is also helpless before the impersonal forces of the product market, particularly before monopolistic sellers of output. Yet this consumer helplessness has provided no rationale for consumer association and organization to any degree comparable with that behind modern labor organization. The main explanation for this difference in the two cases lies in the underlying feeling that the consumer always is faced with alternative choices in buying but that in many cases individual workers are faced with no choice at all. Also, it is difficult to organize consumers, because they frequently have directly opposite interests in their roles as producers and consumers. (The auto worker would like to see the price of cars low, as a buyer, but is more interested in high wages.) It was felt before labor organizations were established that individual workers must either accept the wage rate offered by a single concern or starve. This was true to a degree; monopsony elements were and are present in many sectors of the labor market. Although it can easily be overemphasized, it is true as a general rule that workers are faced with relatively few alternative occupational choices, and choosing among them may involve geographical mobility. Labor has long been recognized as characteristically immobile; the inertia connected with home, family, and community life tends to tie men to given localities for long periods.[1] But it should also be recognized that

---

[1] Adam Smith recognized this when he said that "a man is of all sorts of luggage the most difficult to be transported." *The Wealth of Nations* (New York: Modern Library, Inc., 1937), p. 75.

the appropriate wage adjustments may be secured by the movement of only a fraction of the labor force in any particular occupation.

In order to combat the "inequality in bargaining power," as the helplessness of the individual worker has been called, labor organizations have been established among large groups of workers. With the development of labor unions, instead of an individual worker's selling his services directly to employers and negotiating with them concerning terms of the working agreement, the services of whole groups of workers are sold by a central organization to which all the employees belong. The union negotiates with the employer concerning the wage rate, hours of work, and other conditions of employment. It should be noted that this type of organization is almost precisely equivalent to that discussed as the cartel case in Chapter 8. The individual worker surrenders his price (wage) negotiation power to the union.[1]

It must be recognized from the outset that labor organizations are essentially monopolistic in their economic nature. One of the primary functions of labor organizations, and the main economic function, is to exert some control over wage rates.[2] If this power exists, such organizations must be classified as monopolistic sellers in input markets.

A significant difference exists, however, between such institutional sellers of labor services and monopolistic sellers of final products. The sellers of output, firms or associations of firms, attempt to maximize profits, or net revenue. This is not universally true, but it is a general enough motivation of business firms to allow economic analysis to be based on the assumption that profit maximization is the rule rather than the exception. For labor unions, no such simple motivating force may be assumed. In the first place, profit, in the sense applicable to a firm, cannot be calculated for a union since the cost to the individual workers of providing labor services is essentially subjective. The real cost of providing labor services is, of course, the alternatives sacrificed. These may comprise leisure hours, cultural pursuits, further training, etc. Obviously, the real cost of laboring varies from worker to worker. The revenue side in terms of the total wage bill might be estimated, but profit in the sense of total revenue minus total cost cannot be the magnitude which the labor union seeks to maximize.

---

[1] In a popular advanced textbook, the analysis of unions and cartels has been included in a single chapter in order to emphasize their basic similarity. See George J. Stigler, *The Theory of Price* (New York: The Macmillan Company, 1952), rev. ed., Chap. 14.

[2] It should be emphasized that we are neglecting the non-economic aspects of labor organization. This is not to deny, or even to assess, the relative importance of the non-economic functions and activities of labor organizations.

Possible Goals of Labor Unions

A possible goal of a labor union might be to maximize the total wage bill. In this case the labor organization would attempt to set a wage rate at the point where the elasticity of demand for labor is unitary. This is similar to the mineral-spring case discussed in Chapters 3 and 7. This wage rate is indicated by OW in Figure 13.4, where D represents the demand for labor. The union would attempt to establish the wage rate OW, and OX would represent the number of workers employed. The total wage bill will be maximized by this policy. If, however, the number of union members happens to be greater than the number which employers are willing to hire at this income-maximizing wage, the union is not likely

Figure 13.4. POSSIBLE GOALS OF UNION WAGE POLICY

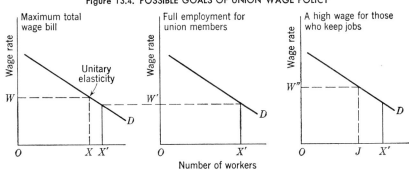

to follow this policy rigorously. It might still be the desirable policy for all the workers if those who remained employed at this wage could be convinced that they should contribute toward the support of the unemployed members. But the accomplishment of this feat might require considerably more internal discipline among members than is present in most unions. For example, in reference to the left-hand diagram of Figure 13.4, if the total union membership is represented by OX', the enforcement of a wage rate of OW would cause XX' members of the union to remain unemployed. But the total wage bill would still be greater at a wage OW than at the wage rate at which all the members can find employment. The maximum income per member could therefore be attained by enforcing the wage rate OW for OX workers and then collecting sufficient dues from the OX workers to subsidize the XX' unemployed members.

A second, and more probable, goal of labor unions is to secure the highest wage rate consistent with full employment for approximately all of the union members. Referring to Figure 13.4, middle diagram, suppose that there are OX' workers of a particular type, say plasterers. If all these workers belong to the union and the union attempts to avoid unemploy-ment among its members, it will not bargain toughly but will agree to a wage rate OW'. This wage rate will be the same as would exist in the short run in the absence of unionization. To the extent that the union has been able to restrict membership, however, the wage rate OW' will be above the long-run wage which would result under pure competition. This explains why most unions are anxious to hold down their membership by such means as the closed shop, long apprenticeships, high initiation fees, and similar restrictions.

A third possible goal of union activity is to secure a high wage rate for workers who remain employed, without much consideration either of possible unemployment among union members or of the effect on the total wage bill. This appears to be a common policy in the large industrial unions such as those in the automobile, steel, and electrical industries. Under this policy, the wage rate may be established higher than OW, say OW'' of the right-hand diagram, even if there are OX' union mem-bers. It is frequently difficult for union leaders to estimate the employ-ment effects of any particular wage increase which the union is striving to secure. The union is then likely to be willing to take a chance that employment will be nearly as large at the higher wage. An additional reason for the adoption of this wage policy is found in the fact that unions are typically controlled by older members who because of seniority rights would be less likely to be laid off as a result of wage increases.

The over-all effects of labor monopoly are much the same as those of output monopoly. The allocation of resources could be improved by a shifting of workers from the unorganized sectors to the organized sectors. Labor monopoly tends to restrict the inputs in the organized sectors of the labor market. This restriction of input necessarily means a restriction of the output of firms hiring union labor and, consequently, higher prices for final products. Also, a redistribution of income is probably effected in favor of unionized workers compared with the nonunionized labor force.

We have been assuming in our analysis that the demand for labor re-mains roughly constant while the supply forces are allowed to shift. De-mand is among the "other things" assumed to remain the same. If, how-ever, demand does shift, the same general conclusions are forthcoming. The fact that unions have been able to increase wage rates significantly without large-scale cutbacks in employment in the war and postwar periods is largely explained by the continuing upward shifting of demand. With an upward shift in firms' demand for output, induced by inflation, firms will seek to expand input. They will try to hire more workers at the established wage. But if all or most of the union members are already working at the old wage, the union will find that it is able to secure higher wages and still keep most of its members employed. It is likely to consider this policy preferable to one which would retain the old wage rate and allow many new workers to join the union or nonunion workers to come on the job. Workers on the inside looking out are not likely to be greatly concerned about the plight of workers on the outside looking in.

Although the most significant elements of monopoly in input markets are found among institutional sellers of labor services, monopolistic and oligopolistic restraints on the sale of capital goods and the lending of money capital should not be overlooked. The effects on resource allocation are similar to those of restrictive labor monopoly. For example, collusion among mortgage-lending firms which increases interest rates to prospective borrowers tends to restrict the amount of residential construction below that which would be socially desirable.

Buyers' Monopsony and Sellers' Monopoly

In considering the noncompetitive aspects of input markets, we have thus far discussed two cases: (1) buyer control over purchase price, monopsony, while assuming competition on the selling side; and (2) sellers' monopoly, which assumed competition on the buying side. The next step is the obvious one of examining the markets in which buyers are monopsonists and sellers are monopolists. This is sometimes called "bilateral monopoly," since it involves elements of monopoly on both the demand and supply sides of the market.

Descriptively, this case is of some significance. It is represented in those instances where a single union bargains with a firm which is a large purchaser of labor in a local labor market. Some price-setting power rests with each of the two bargaining parties. As might be expected, the final price and the amount of input employed are indeterminate. The final position depends to a large degree on the relative strengths of the two opposing forces. This is the only case in which "bargaining" in a true sense actually takes place. If the monopolistic seller of productive services is in a strong position relative to the monopsonistic buyer, a higher input price can be secured than if the seller's position is weak relative to that of the buyer. For example, a single independent local union bargaining with a single local firm will be unable to secure as favorable terms on wages and other working conditions as will that same union if it is backed by financial and other resources of a national labor organization.

It is in this area of bilateral monopoly that the most damaging effects of bargaining are present in the forms of strikes and shutdowns. In the area where large national unions bargain with an association of large firms, the attempts made by each side to enforce favorable settlements are likely to impose serious hardships on the public at large. When a national union of steelworkers bargains with a closely knit group of steel firms, led by one major concern and operating together on matters of labor policy, a true case of bilateral monopoly is present. As a result, each bargaining period is accompanied by threats and fears that the whole nation's productive capacity will be damaged by a shutdown of the steel industry.

This may be contrasted with the case in which strong unions sell labor services to many competitive sellers; the terms are frequently arrived at without serious productive losses through strikes, although the usual effects of monopoly are present. This is the normal case in many of the craft unions, such as the building-trades unions. Local and sporadic strikes may occur, but the substantial number of buyers prevents significant national effects.

Bilateral monopoly in labor markets has been encouraged by the developments of the last two decades. With the formation of industry-wide unions as bargaining agents on the selling side, firms purchasing labor services are encouraged to get together and agree on labor policy and thus act as if the buying side were made up of a single buyer. Bilateral monopoly perhaps best describes the setting of wage rates in such industries as coal, steel, aluminum, transportation, and communications, and it is present to a considerable degree in wage negotiations in such industries as automobiles, meat packing, and farm implements.

CHAPTER 14

EXCHANGE RATES AND THE
BALANCE OF PAYMENTS

We have assumed until this point that the economy has no commercial intercourse with other nations; that is to say, we have been concerned with what is sometimes referred to as a "closed" economy. The fact is, of course, that both consumers and domestic firms often purchase inputs from abroad, and many producers sell a part of their outputs in foreign markets. It is appropriate that we consider the effects of international trade, not only because in the real world trade across international frontiers does exist but because, in addition, international trade changes the whole pattern of economic life and enables wants to be better satisfied than they could be in a state of isolation. If international trade is a significant factor affecting the allocation of an economy's resources, it is important that it not be left out of account.

In embarking upon the study of international trade, the student should keep in mind that the essential principles which underlie this branch of economics are not fundamentally different from those which apply to the domestic economy. Trade between nations is similar in most respects to trade between regions within a country, *e.g.*, the East and the West, and, like internal trade, it is a natural application of the principle of specialization. Any exchange of commodities or services between individuals can usefully be considered a means whereby each individual *indirectly* produces the commodity which he receives in trade. Usually it is more economical for the individual, region, or nation to specialize in producing a limited number of goods, or even a fractional part of one good, and to secure other needed goods by means of trade. The economic unit can, by specialization and trade, usually produce directly and indirectly a larger volume of goods than would be possible if it attempted complete self-sufficiency.

From the point of view of the producer, international trade appears to be advantageous in that it expands his market and, at least in the short run, increases his profits. If the demand of the foreign market is added to the demand in a producer's domestic market, the firm's profits are likely to be increased in much the same way that an increase in domestic demand resulting from an advertising campaign might increase the firm's profits. And it may be that the foreign sales can be added at considerably less expense than would be required to effect a comparable increase in domestic demand. For firms in which decreasing costs are important— that is, when unit costs decrease as output increases—export sales may be particularly profitable; indeed, they may be necessary if the firm is to avoid losses. For example, an industry characterized by high fixed costs, such as the steel industry, in which the optimum-sized firm is very large, could not operate in the Grand Duchy of Luxembourg unless it could sell in export markets.

The increase in profits to the firm resulting from adding foreign markets is sufficient explanation of why firms sell goods for export. If international trade did not increase profits, it may be presumed that firms would not engage in the export business. But why do consumers buy from foreigners? The answer to this question is somewhat more involved than the other; the reasons are varied, and the analysis becomes somewhat more subtle.

Some commodities are imported because they cannot be produced domestically, and, if they are to be consumed, they must be imported. The United States, for example, imports all of its supply of crude rubber, tin, coffee, raw silk, carpet wool, jute fibers and burlap, diamonds, cacao (used in chocolate), bananas, tea, spices, manila fiber, crude chicle (used in chewing gum), quebracho (used in leather tanning), and cobalt (used in cutting tools and paint). Ninety per cent or more of our supply of the following commodities has in recent years been imported: nickel, tung oil (used in quick-drying varnishes), high-grade manganese ore (used in steel alloys and batteries), asbestos, and chromite (used in stainless steel and heat-resistant wire). The list of commodities for which domestic production is insufficient to satisfy domestic requirements is extensive. Even the United States, which, as compared with other nations, is relatively self-sufficient, depends upon the rest of the world for many of the commodities which we consider to be a part of the "American way of life." For a number of other countries, it is a matter of "import or die."

In addition to the commodities which are imported because they cannot be produced domestically, there are many goods which are imported because for one reason or another they are not produced domestically, even though technical conditions would permit their production. In some cases the quality of the imported commodities is considered by consumers to be superior to that of the domestic products. A number of years ago, when ownership of a Stutz Bearcat was the dream of all American boys— and many of their fathers—the United States was a leader in the production of sports cars. Then, until recently, for reasons which are not clear, if an American wanted a sports car he had to buy a British MG or Jaguar, a French Simca, or an Italian Ferrari. Other commodities such as English woolens, Scotch whiskies, French laces, and Italian wines are often considered by American consumers to be superior in quality to comparable domestic products, and they are imported even though there may be a considerable price differential between the domestic and the imported goods.

Probably even more important than either of the reasons just given for the purchase of foreign goods is that imported goods can often be bought at a lower price than similar domestic goods. If an American-made watch is priced at $75 and a Swiss watch of comparable quality is available at $60, many American consumers will prefer the Swiss watch. It is because some goods can be produced abroad and sold more cheaply in domestic markets than they can be produced and sold at home that domestic producers often demand from the government "protection" from foreign competition, usually in the form of a protective tariff. If, for example, a tax of $20 is levied on the importation of the $60 Swiss watch, the American watch will be less expensive to American purchasers.

THE RATE OF EXCHANGE

The price of $60 for the Swiss watch represents, of course, the price in the American currency. The costs to the Swiss firm which produced the watch, however, were incurred in terms of Swiss francs—payments made for labor, materials, and interest on capital. We may suppose that the cost to the Swiss watchmaker of producing the watch, including his profit, was 120 Swiss francs. If the watch was shipped to this country on a Swedish freighter, we may assume that transportation and insurance costs were 25 kronor. We may assume that the markups of the American middlemen and the retailer totaled $25, and we have assumed that the tariff was $20. Then it appears that

$$120 \text{ Swiss francs} + 25 \text{ kronor} + \$25 + \$20 = \$80.$$

It is clear that francs and kronor and dollars cannot, in fact, be added without being converted to some common denominator. This is effected by use of the rate of exchange, which may be defined as the price of one currency in terms of another. Let us suppose that the Swiss franc is worth 25 cents and that the krona is worth 20 cents in the foreign-exchange markets. The cost of the $80 watch may then be broken down as follows:

Cost of production to the Swiss firm (120 francs)	$30
Transportation and insurance (25 kronor)	5
American dealers' markup	25
American tariff	20
Total	$80

As long as this price remains unchanged, the American consumer is likely to buy the $75 American watch rather than the $80 Swiss watch. But now suppose that the exchange rate for Swiss francs falls from 25 cents to 20 cents. The 120 francs, which is the cost of production of the watch in Switzerland, is now the equivalent of $24 instead of $30, and, if the other prices and the tariff remain unchanged, the watch will be sold in the American market for $74 instead of $80; it is now less expensive than the American watch in spite of the "protection" of the American tariff.

In comparing domestic and foreign prices, three prices rather than two must be taken into account: (1) the price of the domestic commodity in terms of the domestic currency, (2) the price of the foreign commodity in terms of the foreign currency, and (3) the price of the foreign currency in terms of the domestic currency. The prices of the domestic and foreign commodities in terms of their own currencies are determined in accordance with the principles developed earlier in this book. There remains the problem of how the price of one currency is determined in terms of another currency, *i.e.*, how the exchange rate is established.

In the absence of government intervention which has been common in recent years, the rate of exchange is established in a highly competitive market. There are many buyers and sellers, and no one of them is sufficiently important to affect the rate of exchange. Importers, tourists traveling in foreign countries, and American investors in securities of foreign companies are typical of the American demanders of foreign exchange. Exporters, foreign tourists traveling in this country, and foreign investors in American securities represent suppliers of foreign exchange. The demand curve for foreign exchange, like other demand curves, slopes downward from left to right. If British woolens were priced in England at one pound sterling (£1) per yard, for example, and if the price of the pound were $3, the price of woolens to an American buyer would be $3 per yard. If the rate of exchange fell to $2.80, however, the price of woolens to an American buyer would fall to $2.80 per yard. At the lower dollar price Americans would buy more woolens, and therefore would buy more pounds sterling. As the price of British pounds falls, the quantity demanded increases. Similarly, the supply curve for foreign exchange may be assumed to slope upward from left to right. The supply of foreign exchange arises from payments made to Americans by foreigners for American exports. Since the amount of purchases of American goods by foreigners will increase as the price of foreign currencies increases (*i.e.*, as the dollar becomes cheaper), the amount of foreign currencies offered for dollars in international money markets will increase as the rate of exchange rises. The rate of exchange is determined by the intersection of the demand and supply curves; in Figure 14.1, the "exchange rate on

London," *i.e.*, the price of pounds in terms of dollars, is $3, and the number of pounds sterling bought and sold per period is OM.

Suppose now that the American demand for British goods increases without a corresponding increase in the British demand for American goods. In Figure 14.2, assume that the original demand of Americans for a particular British good is represented by D and the supply of the good by S; the price of the good is $3 (£1) and the quantity exchanged is 18 units. Now assume that the demand increases from D to D'. The number of units of the British good now demanded by American buyers (and supplied by British exporters) is 30 instead of 18. In order to pay for the greater quantity of imports from England, American buyers will have to acquire more pounds sterling, *i.e.*, the demand for pounds will increase,

Figure 14.1. EXCHANGE RATE ON LONDON— Determined by Supply of and Demand for Pounds

Figure 14.2. INCREASE IN UNITED STATES DEMAND FOR A BRITISH GOOD— Raises Its Price to American Consumers

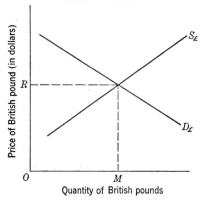

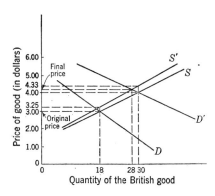

resulting in a rise in the price of the pound, from $3 to $3.25. But the rise in the rate of exchange has the effect of increasing the cost of the British goods to Americans. This is represented in Figure 14.2 by a shift of S to S'. Originally, 18 units of the British good would have been supplied by a British producer for £1, which was $3 in the American currency, and 30 units would have been supplied for £1⅓, which was $4. Since we have assumed that the rate of exchange has risen to $3.25, the 18 units, which are still supplied by the British seller for £1, would now cost the American buyer $3.25 per unit, and 30 units would cost $4.33 each. The new supply curve S' passes through the points 18 units-$3.25 and 30 units-$4.33.

The intersection of the new American-demand-for-British-goods curve D' and the new supply-of-British-goods curve S' indicates that Americans will now buy only 28 units instead of 30, and, as a result, the price of the

British good will be somewhat less than $4.33 and the demand for pounds will decrease, causing the exchange rate to be somewhat less than $3.25. (This slight further adjustment in the exchange rate is not reflected in the chart.)

In addition, the effect of the change in the rate of exchange from $3 to $3.25 (which from the British point of view is a *fall* in the exchange rate, *i.e.*, dollars are now cheaper in terms of pounds) is to make it possible for Englishmen to get $3.25 worth of American goods for their pounds instead of only $3 worth. This will make American goods cheaper to British importers than they were before and, quite possibly, cheaper than similar British goods. The increased purchases of American goods by British buyers which would result could be represented graphically by a shift of the supply-of-pounds curve in Figure 14.1 to the right, and this would also tend to lower (from the American point of view) the rate of exchange below the $3.25 level. The new equilibrium rate would be established somewhere between $3 and $3.25.

This analysis indicates that an increase in the American demand for foreign goods will normally raise the dollar price of the foreign goods in essentially the same way in which an increase in domestic demand raises the price of domestic goods. When the transaction involves two currencies, the process is somewhat more complex because of the interjection of the exchange rate, but basically the prices of foreign goods expressed in terms of the domestic currency respond to changes in demand in the same way that the prices of domestic goods react to demand changes.

Arbitrage

When exchange rates are free to fluctuate without intervention by government, the rates are likely to change several times a day, and, when trading is brisk, the changes may come so fast that it is with difficulty that traders in foreign exchange keep up with them. This gives opportunity to speculators to ply their trade, and fortunes have been won and lost in this way. One aspect of speculation in foreign exchange which deserves special mention is known as "arbitrage." Arbitrage consists of buying and selling a commodity in two different markets at the same time in order to take advantage of a momentary price differential in the two markets. Suppose that in New York the price of pounds sterling is $3 and in London the rate is $2.99. The arbitrager can make a profit by simultaneously selling pounds for dollars in New York and buying pounds for dollars in London. He may contract to sell £100,000 in New York for $300,000, and simultaneously buy the £100,000 to "cover" the transaction in London for $299,000. The $1,000 difference between the selling price and the buying price represents the arbitrager's gross profit (see Table 14.1).

Table 14.1. Arbitrage Transaction Illustrated

New York	*London*
£ = $3.00	£ = $2.99
Sell £100,000 for $300,000	Buy £100,000 for $299,000
The $300,000 covers the London transaction with a gross profit of $1,000	The £100,000 covers the New York transaction

The effect of the sales of pounds by arbitragers in New York will be to cause the rate to fall to something less than $3; the effect of the purchase of pounds in the London foreign-exchange market will be to raise the price of pounds to something more than $2.99. In a very short time— a matter of a few minutes—the discrepancy in the prices in the two markets will have been eliminated, the rate in both countries probably settling in the neighborhood of $2.99½. The economic effect of arbitrage is, accordingly, to eliminate discrepancies in exchange rates in markets throughout the world.

Exchange Controls

During the last two decades, exchange rates have been subject to a considerable degree of control by many foreign governments and have not, in most countries, been determined by the forces of supply and demand in free markets. The purpose of exchange control has been in general to "peg" the domestic currency at a rate higher than that which would obtain in free markets. The higher value of the domestic currency in terms of foreign currencies has the effect of increasing the volume of goods which can be purchased from abroad with a given quantity of the domestic currency. Conversely, by making the domestic currency expensive in terms of foreign currencies, the artificially high value of the domestic currency discourages the foreign purchase of domestic goods.

Although the governmental pegging of exchange rates clearly serves certain political objectives, such as stock-piling critical imports in anticipation of war or speeding up reconstruction following a war, it should be observed that this sort of interference by governments destroys much of the normal rationing function of price which characterizes free markets. The pegging of the value of the domestic currency at a high rate will have the effect of making the quantity of the domestic currency demanded less than the amount supplied at the pegged rate, or, what is the same thing, it will make the amount of foreign currencies demanded greater than the amount supplied at the legal rate. The setting of the price of foreign currencies below equilibrium levels creates a rationing problem and makes necessary some direct allocation of the scarce currencies among prospective users. This has given rise to what is commonly called the "dollar shortage"; the interference by foreign governments with the free market for foreign exchange has had the expected result of converting the normal scarcity of dollars into a problem of dollar shortage. (This is the same type of effect as was noted in Chapter 4 in relation to rent control.) Exchange-control policy is given further attention in Part C.

BALANCE OF INTERNATIONAL PAYMENTS

The U.S. Department of Commerce publishes annually what is known as the United States balance of international payments. This is a list by main categories of transactions which have given rise during the year to (1) payments by foreigners to Americans and (2) payments by Americans to foreigners. An understanding of the balance of payments and its implications will serve as the basis for an evaluation of policies which would have the effect of restricting international trade, a topic which will be explored more fully in Part C. Receipts from foreigners for "exports" are referred to as "credits" in the balance of payments, and payments to foreigners for "imports" are known as "debits." It is important, first, to understand why each item in the balance of payments is listed as a credit or a debit.

The principal items comprising the balance of international payments are indicated in Table 14.2. Most of the entries are probably self-explana-

Table 14.2. Principal Items in the American Balance of Payments

Receipts from foreigners for "exports" (credits)	Payments to foreigners for "imports" (debits)
1. Value of merchandise exports sold to foreigners	1. Value of merchandise imports bought from foreigners
2. Value of freight and shipping services sold to foreigners	2. Value of freight and shipping services bought from foreigners
3. Value of foreign tourists' expenditures in U.S.	3. Value of American tourists' expenditures abroad
4. Gifts made by foreigners to Americans	4. Gifts made by Americans to foreigners
5. Interest and dividend payments made by foreigners to Americans	5. Interest and dividend payments made by Americans to foreigners
6. Value of American gold and silver exports	6. Value of American gold and silver imports
7. Amount borrowed by Americans from foreigners	7. Amount loaned by Americans to foreigners
8. Amount of repayment to Americans of sums previously borrowed by foreigners	8. Amount of repayment to foreigners of sums previously borrowed by Americans

tory. It seems reasonable enough in view of the definitions given above, for example, to list the payments made to Americans for exports sold to foreigners as a credit and the value of interest payments made by Americans to foreigners as a debit. But why is the amount borrowed by Americans from foreigners a *credit?* And why are American gold imports a *debit?*

As a rule of thumb, we may observe that *any transaction which gives rise to a demand for American dollars is listed in the United States balance of payments as a credit; any transaction which gives rise to a demand for a foreign currency is a debit.*[1] To test the rule, let us see what happens when Americans export merchandise to foreigners, a transaction which is clearly a credit item in the balance of payments. Suppose that an American exporter has shipped cigarettes to a British importer. The exporter wants payment in dollars, but the importer makes payment in pounds sterling. The foreign-exchange transaction, therefore, involves a supply of pounds and a demand for dollars. This classifies the merchandise export as a credit from the American point of view.

If we can imagine a mythical "International Money Market" located in the middle of the Atlantic Ocean, where the currency of one country is

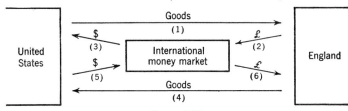

Figure 14.3.

exchanged for that of another, and if we can determine whether for each transaction there is a demand for dollars or a demand for a foreign currency, we shall be able to classify the transaction as a credit or a debit.

Suppose that an American has exported wheat to England (step 1 in Figure 14.3). The British importer takes pounds to the International Money Market (step 2) and *demands dollars* in order to pay the American importer (step 3). Since the foreign-exchange transaction involves a supply of pounds and a demand for dollars, the export of merchandise is a credit in the American balance of payments.

If, on the other hand, an American imports goods from England (step 4 in Figure 14.3), he must take dollars to the IMM (step 5) and *demand pounds* to make payment for the merchandise received (step 6). The foreign-exchange transaction this time represents a supply of dollars and a demand for pounds, and this classifies the American import as a debit item in the balance of payments.

[1] The rule may be stated more generally as follows: Any transaction which gives rise to a demand for dollars or a supply of a foreign currency is a credit item in the United States balance of payments; any transaction which gives rise to a demand for a foreign currency or a supply of dollars is a debit. This is true since a demand for dollars implies a supply of a foreign currency, and a demand for a foreign currency implies a supply of dollars. It follows, accordingly, that an increase in a credit item in the balance of payments tends to cause the rate of exchange (the dollar price of foreign currencies) to fall; an increase in a debit item tends to cause the exchange rate to rise.

In similar fashion, each of the items in Table 14.2 can be analyzed to determine whether it is a credit or a debit. If a foreigner buys shipping services from an American firm, he must take his currency to the International Money Market and demand dollars. If a foreigner travels in this country, he must take his currency to the IMM and demand dollars to spend here. If a foreigner wishes to make a gift of money to an American, he will take his currency to the IMM and demand dollars. If an American receives a dividend check from a foreign corporation, he will take it to the IMM and demand dollars. If a foreigner wishes to buy American gold, he will take his currency to the IMM and demand dollars in the same way that he would in order to pay for any other American commodity. If an American firm wishes to borrow money from foreigners, it will probably do it by selling bonds to foreign buyers. The foreign buyer will take his currency to the IMM and demand dollars with which to buy the American bonds. If a foreign firm wishes to repay an old debt to Americans, it will take its currency to the IMM and demand dollars with which to make payment. All these transactions are credit items in the American balance of payments since they represent a demand for dollars, *i.e.*, payments to Americans. In similar fashion, each of the debit items in Table 14.2 could be shown to represent a demand for foreign currencies.

Balance of Payments Must Balance

The next point to be made is that the balance of payments must always balance. The balance of payments is not to be confused with the balance of trade. The value of American merchandise exports may be more or less than the value of merchandise imports during any time period. The value of *merchandise* exports minus the value of *merchandise* imports is called the balance of trade, and it may be plus, minus, or zero. A plus balance is usually referred to as a "favorable" balance of trade, and a minus balance is called "unfavorable," although there is nothing necessarily favorable about a "favorable" balance or unfavorable about an "unfavorable" balance of trade. But taking into account the entire balance of *payments*, "invisible" as well as "visible" items, the total credits must equal total debits. This is rather curious, since decisions as to what and how much to import and how much to export, and how much to borrow and how much to lend, are made by millions of different individuals, and it would appear to be sheer coincidence if the total debits happened to equal total credits. But the totals must be equal, and a simple illustration will make the reason clear.

Suppose that in a given year Americans have exported $1,000 worth of merchandise to foreigners, and no other item appears on the credit side of the balance of payments statement. We may suppose that during the year Americans have imported $600 worth of merchandise. Americans have a "favorable" balance of trade of $400, and the partial balance of payments would take the form of Table 14.3. We know that this is only

Table 14.3. Partial Balance of Payments

Credits	Debits
Merchandise exports............ $1,000	Merchandise imports............. $600

a partial balance of payments statement, since this is a list of *payments;* the credit item of $1,000 would not have been included if the goods had not been paid for. We know that foreigners paid for $600 worth of the Americans' exports by shipping goods of that value, but Table 14.3 leaves $400 of the payment unaccounted for; there must be $400 worth of debits not yet included.

Suppose that during the year Americans bought $100 worth of shipping services from foreigners and American tourists spent $200 traveling abroad. This provided foreigners an additional $300 with which to pay for their imports from the United States, but we are still $100 short in accounting for the means of payment for the full $1,000 worth of merchandise which they actually received and paid for. We may suppose that the last $100 worth was paid for with money which foreigners borrowed from Americans. The balance of payments would then take the form of Table 14.4.

Table 14.4. Balance of Payments

Credits	Debits	
Merchandise exports............ $1,000	Merchandise imports........... $	600
	Shipping services..............	100
	Travel expenditures...........	200
	Loans by U.S.................	100
Total...................... $1,000	Total......................	$1,000

The debit side of the balance of payments may be looked upon as the source of the dollars which foreigners used to pay for the goods received by them from this country. And since the dollars paid by foreigners to Americans must equal the dollars received by Americans from foreigners, the total of the credit items must equal the total of the debits.

Balance of Payments Analysis

We are now ready to analyze the balance of payments statement and determine what insight into international commercial policy may be obtained through its study. Table 14.5 is a hypothetical American balance of payments statement for a given year.[1] The balance of trade (item 1 minus item 7) is seen to be +$5,300 million, and the balance of payments balances at $16,300 million.

[1] The Department of Commerce does not publish the actual balance of payments data in a form which is adaptable to the simple type of table used in this chapter.

Table 14.5. Representative United States Balance of International Payments
(In millions of dollars)

Credits		Debits	
1. Merchandise exports........	$12,400	7. Merchandise imports......	$ 7,100
2. Freight and shipping services sold to foreigners...........	1,100	8. Freight and shipping services bought from foreigners	1,000
3. Foreigners' travel expenditures in U.S..............	300	9. American tourist expenditures abroad.............	700
4. Interest payments to Americans by foreigners.........	1,300	10. Interest payments made by Americans to foreigners....	300
5. Amount borrowed from abroad..................	400	11. Amount loaned by Americans to foreigners.........	5,000
6. Repayment of old debts to Americans by foreigners.....	800	12. Repayment of old debts to foreigners by Americans...	2,200
Total.......................	$16,300	Total......................	$16,300

Suppose now that we are interested only in net figures. We have seen that merchandise transactions were on balance a net credit of $5,300 million. Similarly, freight and shipping services show a net credit balance of $100 million (item 2 minus item 8), and interest payments are on balance a credit of $1,000 million (item 4 minus item 10). All the other accounts show net debit balances. It will be noted in Table 14.6 that, just as the original balance of payments balanced, so does the balance of payments when stated in net terms only.

Table 14.6. Consolidated Balance of Payments
(Net figures, in millions of dollars)

Credits		Debits	
1. Merchandise...............	$5,300	4. Travel.....................	$ 400
2. Freight and shipping........	100	5. Loans.....................	4,600
3. Interest...................	1,000	6. Repayment of loans.........	1,400
Total.......................	$6,400	Total.......................	$6,400

It is possible to take the consolidation one step further. Suppose that we combine in one entry all goods and services items and in another all capital and interest items. The goods and services items are 1, 2, and 4 in Table 14.6; items 3, 5, and 6 may be classed as capital and interest items. Item 1 plus item 2 minus item 4 shows a net credit balance of $5,000 million; item 3 subtracted from item 5 plus item 6 shows a net debit balance of $5,000 million. This is indicated in Table 14.7.

Table 14.7. Condensed Balance of Payments
(Net figures, in millions of dollars)

Credits		Debits	
Goods and services............	$5,000	Capital and interest...........	$5,000

Since in Table 14.7 goods and services are a credit entry, capital and interest must be a debit; if there are only two items in the balance of payments statement, one must of necessity be a credit and the other must be a debit since, as we have seen, the two sides must balance. There are at least two conditions under which goods and services might be a credit item: (1) If large-scale loans were made by Americans to foreigners during the year so that the amount of the loans was greater than the amount of the interest paid by foreigners to Americans during the year, capital and interest items would be a net debit, and goods and services would, therefore, be a credit. (2) If Americans were paying large sums of interest to foreigners or paying off old debts to foreigners, capital and interest items might be on balance a debit, with goods and services a net credit.

In recent years the United States has maintained a favorable balance of trade largely as a result of situation 1 above. Lend-lease and other public and private loans to foreigners have been very large, and this has made possible the net export of American goods to foreigners; fundamentally, Americans have been making loans of goods to foreigners. But the more money that is loaned to foreigners in one year, the greater will be the interest payments in subsequent years, and if a favorable balance of trade is maintained by making loans, eventually the interest payments, to say nothing of the repayment of old loans, will represent a bigger payment to Americans than the amount of the annual loans by Americans to foreigners. When that happens, the capital and interest items will on balance be a credit from the American point of view, and goods and services must, therefore, be a debit. That is to say, if foreigners are to pay Americans the interest which they owe and eventually repay the principal sums borrowed, the United States must have an unfavorable balance of trade. But American commercial policy in the past has called for payment by foreigners of their debts to us while at the same time we have attempted to maintain a favorable balance of trade. Such a policy is inherently inconsistent and impossible of accomplishment. Either we must have a net debit balance for goods and services items, or we must expect foreigners to default on their obligations to us.

Americans could, indeed, export more than they import without restriction if the exports were to be given away. If the sole object of American foreign-trade policy were to maintain full employment at home, the production of goods and giving them to foreigners might be defended on the grounds that it would create jobs. But it should be noted that producing goods and dumping them in the Atlantic Ocean would have the same effect. Since we cannot produce as many goods in the aggregate as Americans would like to consume, the gift of goods to foreigners or the destruction of goods to maintain employment cannot be defended as a long-run policy. More economic solutions to the problem of unemployment will be suggested in Part B, and the effect of trade restrictions on American standards of living will be discussed in Part C.

CHAPTER 15

MUTUAL GAINS FROM TRADE:
COMPARATIVE ADVANTAGE

We have seen that from the point of view of consumers and producers there are significant reasons for engaging in international trade. The question remains as to the nature of the "gains" to the country as a whole which result from participating in foreign trade. The problem is many-sided, and it has received attention from writers on economic matters ever since the time of the mercantilists, who dominated economic thinking and policy in Europe and America during the three centuries from Christopher Columbus to George Washington. The mercantilists failed to grasp the idea of mutual gains from trade and felt that what one nation gains from trade another nation must lose. The classical economists were able to demonstrate the fallacy in the mercantilist position and to show that the real basis for trade, either international or domestic, is the mutual advantage which can be secured. Ideas are long-lived, however, and mercantilist fallacies still pervade much popular thinking on matters of international economic policy. To refute such fallacies, a demonstration of the mutual gains which may arise from trade seems to be in order. This chapter will be devoted, therefore, to a consideration of the effects on the domestic economy of engaging in international trade.

TRADE AS A SUBSTITUTE FOR FACTOR MOBILITY

If there were no restraints on the free movement of productive factors from one region to another, or from one nation to another, the total world production of goods and services would be maximized when the marginal products (in value terms) of similar units of each productive factor were equal in all uses and in all places. If the marginal revenue product of labor, for example, were less in sheep raising than in wheat growing, total production would be increased by taking some units out of sheep raising, where the losses would be relatively small, and adding them to wheat production, where the gain would be relatively great. Within a single

economic system, the payment to owners of resources in accordance with
marginal revenue productivity tends to ensure that such movements do,
in fact, take place. If similar workers produced more in wheat farming
than in sheepherding in the United States, for example, wage rates on
the wheat farms would tend to be above those on sheep ranches, and
workers would be attracted to wheat farming and away from sheepherding. The same sort of allocative process tends to take place among different geographical areas within the same economy. Resources are attracted
to areas where they are most productive, and total output of goods and
services is maximized when similar units of resources produce marginal

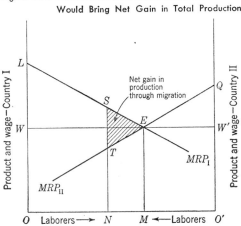

Figure 15.1. INTERNATIONAL FACTOR MOBILITY—
Would Bring Net Gain in Total Production

products of equal value in all regions. From this it is easy to see that if
the whole world were considered as the economic unit, and the maximization of world production were accepted as the appropriate policy goal,
the same principles would apply. This means, of course, that the total
world production of goods and services could be increased by a migration
of coolie laborers from East Asia to the United States. Clearly the marginal product of such labor would be greater in this country than in the
Orient. Even from a "one-world" outlook, however, the maximization of
world output resulting from the free movement of labor might not prove
an acceptable goal, since the drastic redistribution of income that would
take place might generate disruptive social, political, and cultural
problems.

The fact that the international mobility of productive factors would
serve to increase total production of goods and services (if we ignore the
possible indirect effects on production resulting from such mobility) may
be illustrated geometrically in Figure 15.1. Let us assume a two-country

world, Country I and Country II. Let us further assume that labor is the only mobile productive factor. The x axis for Country I is read in the conventional way, but the x axis for Country II is read from right to left. MRP_I is the marginal revenue product curve for labor in Country I, and MRP_{II} is labor's marginal revenue product curve in Country II. It is assumed that perfect competition prevails in both countries, that all workers are alike, and that the countries have a common currency. The total number of workers in both countries is equal to OO', ON being situated in Country I and $O'N$ being situated in Country II. Under these circumstances, the wage rate in Country I will be NS, and in Country II it will be NT, since the wage rate will tend to equal the marginal product of labor under competitive conditions. The total value of the product in Country I, *i.e.*, the area under the MRP_I curve, is $OLSN$, and the total value of the product in Country II is $NTQO'$.[1] If MN workers migrated from Country II, where wages are lower, to Country I, where wages are higher, the marginal revenue product of labor ME would be equal in both countries. The value of the total product in Country I would be increased by an amount equal to $NSEM$, while the value of the product in Country II would be diminished by $NTEM$. Since the gain from the migration is greater than the loss, the aggregate output of the two countries would be increased, in this instance by an amount equal to TSE. The combined total product of the two countries would now be $OLEQO'$, and this total could not be increased by further migration.

Even if there were perfect mobility of productive factors, trade between nations would take place because of climatic or other natural advantages for certain types of production in particular regions. In addition, even if no such natural advantages were present, countries would perhaps find it economical to specialize to some extent in particular lines of production and to trade with other countries in order to secure the cost savings which are often inherent in large-scale production. In this way all countries would produce more than if no international trade were to take place.

In the real world, however, productive factors do not move readily across international boundaries. This applies especially to labor; immigration restrictions often prevent the movement of laborers into and out of a country. Capital does tend to move much more freely, although it too has been subjected to restrictions in recent years. The immobility of productive factors among nations has been one of the features which distinguish the study of international trade from that of domestic trade. The distinction is not so sharp, however, as it might at first appear. Even within the same country, mobility is far from perfect. Laborers often do

---

[1] The area under any "marginal" curve is the total for the variable under consideration. For example, the area under a marginal physical product curve is total physical product, while the area under a marginal cost curve is total variable cost.

not move rapidly from low-wage regions to high-wage regions because of inadequate information, high costs of moving, or reluctance for non-economic reasons to leave home. And even with the immigration restrictions, laborers do tend to move across international boundary lines, especially between contiguous areas. The case of the Mexican "wetbacks" provides an excellent example. In spite of immigration restrictions, coupled with the efforts of both the Mexican and United States authorities to enforce them, thousands of Mexican workers cross the Rio Grande into this country each year, attracted by the higher wage rates.

In so far as productive factors cannot, or will not, move across national or regional borders in response to economic rewards, the impetus for trade in goods across such borders is increased. For differences in the efficiency and in the proportions of labor and capital make it profitable for nations and regions to specialize in the production of those goods and services for which the resource situation is most advantageous. Interregional and international trade, therefore, resulting from geographical specialization, represents something of a substitute for the movement of productive factors from place to place.

THE GAINS FROM TRADE

David Ricardo, a famous British economist of the classical school, was the first to demonstrate numerically the gain which accrues to both countries which engage in trade. The following model, which has been used by a modern British economist,[1] is constructed in much the manner

	Costs of production	
	In Country I	In Country II
One unit of commodity A............	x	y
One unit of commodity B............	x	$2y$

of Ricardo's original demonstration: A unit of commodity A and a unit of commodity B have been defined in such a way that the cost of each is the same in Country I. In Country II a unit of B, as so defined, costs twice as much to produce as a unit of A. It does not matter whether the method of measuring costs is the same in the two countries; indeed, if the two countries have different currency units, even monetary measures are not directly comparable. The only important point for our purposes is that, whereas the ratio of production costs for the two commodities is

[1] R. F. Harrod, *International Economics* (London: Cambridge University Press, 1933), p. 17.

one to one in Country I, it is one to two in Country II. The two commodities are assumed to be the only ones produced.

Under conditions assumed in the model, it will be desirable for Country I to specialize in the production of commodity B, for Country II to specialize in commodity A, and for the two countries to trade with one another. Country I is said to have a comparative advantage in commodity B and Country II to have a comparative advantage in commodity A. If we assume transportation between the two countries to be costless, trade between them to be free, and pure competition to exist within both countries, it will be not only desirable for the countries to specialize as indicated but *necessary* for them to do so. This is because the prices of input factors in Country II will be based on their marginal revenue productivity in their best use, which is in the production of commodity A. This will mean that any firm attempting to use these inputs to produce commodity B in that country could not do so profitably. Similarly, the prices of inputs in Country I will be such as to make the production of commodity A unprofitable in that country. This is the same reasoning used in Chapter 2 to show why it would be unprofitable to produce sugar beets in Iowa; *i.e.*, the "corn" use of land and labor would make rentals and wages so high as to make sugar-beet production economically infeasible.

If Country I specializes in the production of commodity B and Country II produces nothing but commodity A, it will be necessary for traders to arrive at some exchange ratio between the two goods. This exchange ratio will have to fall somewhere between the limits 1 of B for 1 of A and 1 of B for 2 of A. Since if Country I did not trade with Country II, but produced both commodities for its own consumption, it could get 1 unit of commodity A by giving up 1 unit of B (by shifting resources from B to A), it would be unwilling to trade with Country II if it had to give up more than 1 unit of B in exchange for 1 unit of A. Similarly, if Country II did not engage in international trade, it could get 1 unit of B by giving up 2 units of A. Country II will certainly not pay Country I more than 2 units of A for 1 of B.

The Terms of Trade

Since Country I is specializing in commodity B, the closer the actual exchange ratio approaches the limit 1 of B for 2 of A the more favorable the "terms of trade" are to Country I. Similarly, since Country II is specializing in commodity A, the closer the exchange ratio comes to the other limit, 1 of B for 1 of A, the more favorable the terms of trade are to Country II. The actual exchange ratio which is arrived at by the traders of the two countries will depend on the relative *demands* for the two goods. Any shift in demand would cause the terms of trade to become more favorable to the country which produces the good for which demand increases relative to that of the other. If we assume that Country I is specializing in cloth and Country II in beer, a cold winter might turn the terms of trade in favor of Country I, while a hot summer might make the exchange ratio more favorable to Country II.

Suppose that the actual exchange ratio between commodities A and B in our model turns out to be 1 of B for $1\frac{2}{3}$ of A. Both countries will gain. Country I will produce B at a cost of 1 and receive for it $1\frac{2}{3}$ units of A; she is getting for a cost of 1 what without trade it would have cost her $1\frac{2}{3}$ to produce domestically. And Country II gets 1 unit of B at a cost of $1\frac{2}{3}$, whereas it would have cost her 2 to produce B domestically. Country I, accordingly, saves $\frac{2}{3}$ of a cost unit on each unit of A, and Country II saves $\frac{1}{3}$ of a cost unit on each unit of B.

The highly simplified model which we have examined is designed to emphasize an important point, namely, that by specializing in the commodities for which it has the greatest comparative advantage and trading part of its output with other nations a country can produce a greater volume of goods and services than if it attempted to be self-sufficient. It is more economical to produce many commodities *indirectly* through international trade than to produce them *directly* at home. The specialization on those commodities in which a nation has the greatest comparative advantage, however, does not imply that a country may not produce a part and import a part of its requirements of a given commodity. The United States, for example, imports large quantities of wool, but some sections of this country are well adapted to the production of this commodity, and a significant part of our wool requirements are met from domestic production.

Demand and Specialization

So far we have neglected the effect of demand in the determination of which commodities a country will find it desirable to specialize in producing. In order to see this effect more clearly, let us expand our model by considering a world again consisting of only two countries in either of which any of six commodities can now be produced—in quantities which are limited, of course, by available resources. We may again designate the countries as I and II, and the commodities as a, b, c, d, e, and f. We shall define a unit of each commodity as the amount which can be produced by a given amount of resources in Country I; this cost will be designated x. In Country II, on the other hand, each commodity is produced at a different cost—whether at a greater or smaller cost than in Country I is immaterial. These cost data are summarized in Table 15.1. We may assume that the six commodities are arranged in order of increasing cost in Country II, that is, y_2 is greater than y, y_3 exceeds y_2, etc.

Table 15.1. Two-country Six-commodity Model

Commodity	Cost of production	
	Country I	Country II
a	x	y
b	x	y_2
c	x	y_3
d	x	y_4
e	x	y_5
f	x	y_6

Tariff barriers are assumed not to exist, and transportation between the two countries is assumed to be costless.

Country II clearly has a comparative advantage in the commodity at the top and Country I in the commodity at the bottom of the list. We can be sure that if trade occurs between the countries, Country I will export f while Country II will export a. But without knowing the nature of the demand for the several commodities, it is impossible to determine which country will specialize on the intermediate commodities. Each country will have to pay for its imports with its exports. If Country II's demand for f is sufficiently great, it is possible that Country I could produce only this commodity and pay for its imports of a, b, c, d, and e by exporting f. Or Country I may produce and export d, e, and f and import a, b, and c. A knowledge of the demand side of the international market is necessary for determination of the nature of the commodity specialization as well as the terms of trade. Brazil, for example, exports considerable quantities of cane sugar and citrus fruits in addition to coffee. If, however, the world demand for coffee should increase sufficiently, Brazil might give up the production of sugar and citrus fruits and pay for her imports by exporting only coffee.

It should be kept clearly in mind that the above model is constructed using only assumptions as to the relative cost of the six commodities *within* Country I and their relative cost *within* Country II. No intercountry cost comparisons are involved. Country I may have a poorly educated labor force and a small supply of capital per worker compared with Country II. Yet Country I will be able to trade with Country II because Country II will find that it can enjoy a greater volume of the six commodities by specializing in one or a few for which it has the greatest comparative advantage and securing the others by trade. Country I, even if it is relatively poor in resources, can maximize its own real income by producing the goods for which its resources are best adapted and securing other goods in exchange. Both countries are saved by international trade from the inefficient action of having to produce directly those goods which can be obtained more economically indirectly by trade.

The models used in this chapter to illustrate comparative advantage have been purely hypothetical and highly simplified. They help to answer some important real-world questions, however. Is the American standard of living endangered, for example, by free trade with Japan? The answer is clearly no. Such trade permits us to concentrate to a greater degree on the commodities for which our labor and capital are particularly well adapted and to secure from Japan items for which they have a comparative advantage. Toys which require a great deal of hand labor, for example, have long been a commodity for which Japan is highly suited. While American toy manufacturers and their employees might like to prevent their importation, this action would make it necessary for us to devote some of our resources to tasks for which they are not best suited, and this would do its bit to lower the American standard of living.

As a long-run matter, all countries gain from international trade because of the superior allocation of resources possible with trade compared with that possible without trade. As a short-run matter, changes in the demand and supply conditions under which international trade is carried out can require difficult readjustments. (This is also true of purely internal trade.) If, for example, a commodity which is imported is suddenly reduced sharply in price to American consumers because of a drop in the dollar price of a foreign currency, domestic producers of the same good or close substitutes will find their sales volume reduced. This will have an adverse effect on investors, executives, and labor in the affected domestic industry. They may then press for a tariff or other restrictions on imports. (These matters of political economy will be taken up in Part C.) But it is generally not wise to allow the short-run interests of any producer group to dominate the allocation of resources. To do so reduces the national real income and is likely to be harmful to international political relations.

CHAPTER 16

THE EFFICIENCY OF THE PRICE SYSTEM:
A SUMMARY

With this chapter we conclude Part A, and it is appropriate that we take a brief look to see where our journey through the mysteries of economics has thus far taken us. Probably the most fundamental fact which confronts the student of economics is that human wants are virtually insatiable, whereas the means to satisfy them are limited. We do not drive a ten-year-old jalopy because we prefer it to the latest Cadillac convertible, nor do we eat hamburger because we have no taste for *filet mignon*. The consumer is confronted with a host of desirable goods and services, but each has its price tag. Since the consumer's income is limited, it is necessary for him to decide what he will buy and what he will forgo; in short, he must economize.

The consumer's problem is to allocate his income among the plethora of goods and services which are potentially available to him in such a way that his total satisfaction will be maximized; if it is possible for him to alter his expenditure pattern by spending less on some commodities and more on others and thereby to increase his total satisfaction, he has not allocated his income optimally. The matter of maximizing satisfaction is, of course, a highly subjective operation. One cannot say that the milk shake just drunk provided the consumer with six units of satisfaction, whereas the economics textbook just purchased is likely to provide him only two units—or a negative 632. And it is reasonable to suppose that many consumers, in fact, do a poor job of allocating their incomes. The bride who spends next month's grocery budget on a new dress may very well soon regret yielding to the impulse, and the alcoholic who leaves his pay check with the barkeeper may, after he has sobered up, realize that he has acted unwisely. But we may assume that at the time a consumer makes an expenditure he prefers the commodity he is purchasing to anything else which the same amount of money would buy; any other behavior may quite properly be classified as irrational. At any rate, in a private-enterprise economy the consumer is free to determine how he will spend his money, and the consumer expenditures in the aggregate determine how the economy's resources are allocated. The whole economy faces a problem almost equivalent to that faced by each consumer. The available productive resources are not sufficient to produce all that is desired by consumers (as a matter of fact, this is the reason why consumers are faced with an economic problem in the first place). The job of the price system is to allocate the available resources among alternative uses.

The efficiency of the economic system as a producer of goods may be evaluated by an analysis similar to that applied to the consumer. If resources may be shifted from current employments to other uses and thereby increase what may be called the total social product, the current allocation of resources is not optimum. If all resources are employed and if all similar resource units are yielding the same addition to social product in all uses, the total cannot be improved by shifting. This is one of the prime concepts in economics, and it has been labeled "the economic principle" by Professor Frank H. Knight.[1] It may be stated more generally as follows: When there exists a scarce resource to be allocated among alternative uses, the maximum return from the employment of that resource will be attained when a unit of that resource yields the same return in all uses.

Let us subject the economist's model of a purely competitive private-enterprise economy to this test of efficiency. Pure competition, it will be recalled, implies, first, that there are so many buyers and sellers that all traces of monopoly power have been avoided, and, second, that factors are mobile and may move to the uses and locations dictated by the market.

If resources are free to move, such movements will tend to take place in a purely competitive economy until similar units of resources receive similar rewards in all uses. If, for example, the wage rate for a particular type of labor were higher in one employment than in others, labor would tend to move from the low-wage to the high-wage employment. This sort of movement would tend to raise wages in low-wage employments and lower them in high-wage employments, and the movement would continue until the returns were approximately equal in all employments.[2] Similarly, new investment seeks the highest return, and this tends to equate interest yields in different uses where riskiness is comparable. These adjustments require only that the markets for productive resources be freely competitive on the supply side.

But if, in addition, the market for inputs is free on the buying side, the

---

[1] For an early statement see his *Risk, Uncertainty, and Profit* (Boston: Houghton Mifflin Company, 1921), p. 65.

[2] A slight qualification is necessary here. The rewards which will tend to be equalized are real rewards and not money rewards. If some employments differ in their nonpecuniary attributes, money rewards for like resource units will not be equalized even in the fully competitive equilibrium situation.

price of the input unit will be made equal to the marginal revenue product of that unit to the firm purchasing it since, as we have seen in earlier chapters, firms will find it profitable to continue to hire input units to the point where the addition to total revenue, *i.e.*, marginal revenue product, is equal to the price required to secure the services of that unit. Competition on the supply side of the input markets ensures the equality of returns for all like resource units, and competition on the demand side of the input markets ensures the payment of the full marginal revenue product to each input unit.

Finally, pure competition in the output markets guarantees that equal marginal revenue products of inputs employed by different firms represent equal additions to social product. If a firm buys inputs and sells outputs competitively, it will employ enough inputs to make the value of the marginal product of each type of input equal to the price of that input; that is to say, no alternative use of the input factor would produce an output which consumers would prefer to buy at the prevailing prices, and the total social product, accordingly, could not be increased by a different allocation of productive resources.

In the purely competitive model, accordingly, the optimal allocation of resources is attained.[1] An alternate method for evaluating the efficiency of the purely competitive model is to concentrate on the relationship of output prices and costs rather than on the allocation of resources. If all markets are free, *i.e.*, if all industries are purely competitive, all firms will tend to be of the most efficient size; they will operate plants of the most efficient scale; and plants will be operated in the most efficient way. If this were not true for a given firm, that firm would be selling below average cost and in due course would be forced out of business, since pure competition means that in long-run equilibrium the optimum-sized firm operates the optimum-scale plant at optimum output. Goods are available to consumers at the lowest possible cost as measured in terms of inputs or in terms of sacrificed alternative goods and services.

Prices under conditions of pure competition are equal to marginal costs. This means that as long as the additional cost to the firm of producing additional units of output is less than the price which consumers are willing to pay for the additional output, those goods will be produced. Consumer preferences could not be better served by any possible shifting of resources to other uses.

[1] It is perhaps appropriate to add a further qualification here. This analysis has assumed that the marginal product to the firm is equivalent to the marginal product to society. The possible divergencies between private marginal product and social marginal product may be significant, but they are left out of account in this book. For a discussion see A. C. Pigou, *The Economics of Welfare* (London: Macmillan & Co., Ltd., 1950), 4th ed., Part II. See also K. W. Kapp, *The Social Costs of Private Enterprise* (Cambridge, Mass.: Harvard University Press, 1950).

Prices in pure competition also tend to equal average costs. This means that there are no monopoly profits, and payments to input factors will exhaust the firm's total revenue.

In a perfectly competitive economy it would be impossible for one economic group to exploit another. If one firm refused to pay labor the full value of its marginal product, laborers would refuse to work for that firm and would get jobs somewhere else. If one firm attempted to charge higher than market prices, it would lose all of its customers. If a firm attempted to sell shoddy goods, consumers would take their custom elsewhere. If a laborer insisted on a wage in excess of the value of his product, firms would hire someone else who was available at the going rate.

The purely competitive economy is ruled directly by the desires of consumers. Only those goods and services are produced which consumers desire and for which they are willing and able to pay. Consumers are faced with proper alternatives in the market place. Two goods carrying identical price tags reflect equivalent marginal costs of production. A change in consumers' tastes will be reflected by a change in prices, and this, in turn, will be followed by a shifting of resources from the production of some goods to the production of others. Firms will not need to spend large sums on sales promotion in an attempt to increase demand for their output.

The behavior of a purely competitive economy may be briefly reviewed by consideration of an oversimplified illustration. Suppose that an economy characterized by pure competition in all markets has reached long-run equilibrium and that television is then made available to consumers for the first time. The demand for television sets is great, and in the short run prices exceed average costs of production. Resources are shifted to the television industry, and new firms enter the industry until the short-run profits are eliminated. But if people spend more time at home watching television, they will have less time for reading, movies, and automobile driving, and the demand for the associated commodities will fall. Resources shift away from the industries producing these items, and in the long run some firms will close down. These effects, both positive and negative, generate secondary and tertiary effects throughout the entire economy. The decreased demand for books, for example, decreases the demand for pulpwood. This in turn decreases the demand for woodsmen, and this results in a decreased demand for woodsmen's clothing, axes, and so on. Such derivative effects can conceivably be followed until the initial impact of one change in consumer tastes is traced throughout the entire world economy.

Similar effects may be traced in the actual economic system as well as in hypothetical cases of the sort considered here. A fundamental feature of the modern economic system is the fact that in lesser or greater degree everything depends on everything else. This is reflected for the real world in the national input-output table of Chapter 2. If only one of the many entries in the table is changed, this will generate changes throughout the whole table.

Free markets are responsive to the desires of consumers, but it must be remembered that the effectiveness of these desires is dependent on the relative wealth and income of consumers. The private-enterprise economy is a one-dollar-one-vote system, and wealthy consumers have more control over the scale of values finally established than do poor consumers. Pure competition will maximize the total social product only in terms of the relative value scale established by the actual dollar votes of consumers, and those with the most dollars exercise the greatest influence in determining what relative value scale will be established. That is to say, the free market system guarantees maximum efficiency on the assumption that a particular distribution of income among consumers is taken as given. If the distribution of income is changed, the allocation of resources will be changed. But since a changed distribution of income will itself produce a new allocation of resources if markets are free, the new allocation may then be considered as optimal. The total social product, for example, will include the production of some champagne if there are enough relatively wealthy people who are willing to pay a price which will cover the costs of producing it. If steps were taken to make incomes more nearly equal, less champagne and more beer would probably be produced. The optimum allocation of resources as between champagne and beer would change as the distribution of income changes.

Clear thinking on economic matters requires that the problem of resource allocation be separated from the problem of income distribution. With any given distribution of income, a system of ideally free markets will tend to move resources into the right places. Whether the distribution of income itself is optimal from the point of view of social welfare is another larger and much more difficult question which must be considered independently of the evaluation of the price system as an allocator of resources. Some attention will be turned to this larger problem in Part C.

We have seen that free international trade is necessary if resources are to be allocated in an optimum way even from a national point of view. Since labor and capital are quite immobile between nations, it is necessary to rely on the unhampered international flow of commodities as a partial substitute for resource mobility. Since trade is really a method of indirect production, a country is not fully efficient as a producer if it devotes a portion of its resources to making goods which it could secure with a smaller expenditure of resources by engaging in trade.

Actual conditions in our economy, of course, usually depart in greater or lesser degree from the competitive pattern. Competition, however, is a vitally important force in the real world, and a full understanding of its workings under ideal conditions contributes much to an understanding of actual economic life. The competitive model is also useful in a normative sense. The actual economy can hardly be evaluated except in terms of comparison and contrast with the ideally competitive economy. The task remains to summarize how the appearance of monopoly elements in any area tends to distort the optimal allocation of resources.

Let us assume an economy where in the beginning all markets are purely competitive. Suppose now that one industry comes under the domination of a large firm which represents a merger of all formerly competing firms in the industry, while all other markets remain competitive as before. The whole down-sloping market demand curve for the industry will now be the monopolistic firm's demand curve, and it will find it advantageous to produce less than was produced by the sum of the competitive firms before the industry was monopolized. By restricting output to the point where marginal cost equals marginal revenue the firm will maximize monopoly profits, whereas in the long-run equilibrium position under pure competition goods were sold at average cost. The result is that fewer goods of this type are made available to consumers; prices which consumers must pay are higher; and, since output is reduced, the number of inputs employed is reduced, and the aggregate return to input factors is decreased. Some inputs previously employed in this industry will be forced into other employments. By this movement they will tend to lower marginal revenue products in other industries, and hence the prices of similar resources will be lowered throughout the economy. Resources remaining in the employ of the monopolist will now be producing an output which is valued by consumers at more than the output produced by similar resource units in other employments; i.e., the value of the marginal product will be higher in the monopolistic firm than in the competitive firms. But, since the monopolist is buying inputs competitively, resource units will be paid at the same rate by both monopolistic and competitive firms; consequently, there is no incentive for resources to shift from competitive firms to the monopolistic firm.

The nature of the distortion in the allocation of resources resulting from the monopolization of one industry can also be seen in the relationship between price and marginal cost. In competitive industries, price will always equal marginal cost, whereas in the monopolistic firm, price will always be greater than marginal cost by the amount of a monopoly-imposed differential. The effect of the monopolization of one industry has clearly been to shift resources from the allocation which would produce the maximum social product in terms of the value scale which has been established by consumers. Resource allocation could be improved by the shifting of resources back to the monopolized industry and away from the competitive industries. Effects similar to those just described could be demonstrated to result from monopoly in input markets. The net effect of monopoly (using the term now to include both monopoly and monopsony) is to distort the optimum allocation of resources.

The economy in which we live is permeated with elements of monopoly in many markets. Prices are likely to exceed marginal costs in many instances, which indicates that monopoly power is present. Prices are also likely to be in excess of average costs, which, except during transition periods, indicates the existence of monopoly profits. It would be premature, however, to condemn the modern private-enterprise system as an allocater of resources on the grounds that it is infested with monopoly elements. The purely competitive model is an abstraction, and in it we assumed that static conditions prevailed; the basic wants, resources, and technology were assumed as given in order to keep the analysis as simple as possible. In the real world, on the contrary, conditions do not remain static. Wants, resources, and technology are continually changing. In a dynamic society the monopoly elements are not quite so foreboding as they appear in the static analysis. Significant monopoly profits tend to attract firms to the production of close substitutes and to develop new and better processes of production. There is continuous pressure toward the removal of excessive profits, and, in spite of the departures from the competitive norms which any descriptive analysis of the economy would reveal, the forces of competition still loom large in the underlying structure.

The chief threat to the effective functioning of the private-enterprise system probably lies not in the tendency for business to become monopolistic but in unwise business regulation by government. Government simultaneously enforces "antitrust" legislation to eliminate evils of monopoly and "fair-trade" legislation to encourage the maintenance of monopoly. Government may properly serve to make markets more competitive, but in many instances government intervention is designed instead to foster the monopoly power of pressure groups. In our vastly complex economy there is a vital economic role which governments must play, but whether government participation in economic affairs strengthens or weakens the private economy depends on the kind of decisions which governments make.

It should be recognized that the discussion in Part A has been concerned with the allocation of resources on the assumption that they are fully employed. It has stressed the loss of output which occurs when resources are not used in the right amounts to produce the right commodities. It has not been concerned with the possible unemployment of a portion of available labor and capital. This has often been a serious problem in our economy. Parts B and C will examine this phase of the economic problem, including the part which government should play in securing full employment without disruptive price inflation.

CHAPTER 17

WHAT IS NATIONAL INCOME?

From time to time the American economy seems to be struck with a case of general paralysis. For reasons which are never clear to the man in the street and sometimes appear to mystify the experts, factories close down; prices and wages fall; a large fraction of the working population is un-employed; many who have jobs work only part time; some people, par-ticularly professional workers such as teachers, preachers, and physicians, work full time but may be able to collect only a part of their wages; and morale everywhere is low. The situation would be less deplorable if only the wicked suffered, but, in fact, those who have been thrifty may find their savings wiped out through drastic declines in security and property values, those who have attained skills may discover that there is no de-mand for their special abilities, and the virtuous may have to wait until they get to heaven to reap their rewards. Even a college diploma will not guarantee a person steady employment; during the depression of the 1930's the abbreviation Ph.D. was sometimes held to stand for posthole digger, and some college graduates were unable to find employment even as unskilled manual laborers.

If the economy behaved strictly in accordance with the purely competi-tive model described in Part A, widespread and protracted unemployment of economic resources would be improbable. If prices performed perfectly their proper rationing function, an oversupply of goods or labor would be followed by a decline in prices or wages, markets would be cleared, and unemployment would probably be short-lived. The fact that extensive and prolonged periods of depression have occured in the contemporary economy indicates that there are powerful forces at work which need to be scrutinized with great care.

On the other hand, there are times, such as in the years immediately following World War II, when there seems to be almost too much pros-perity. Everyone is employed and factories are humming, but prices also are moving rapidly upward. Families find that the dollar is continually shrinking in value, and the weekly wage needed to maintain living stand-ards must be constantly increased. Persons living on fixed incomes are extremely hard put to make ends meet and are likely to think that the 1930's were not so bad after all.

The term "business cycle" is frequently used to refer to the fluctuations in the level of business activity, and, although this phrase probably implies a regularity in the recurrence of periods of prosperity and depression which the facts do not bear out, it does quite properly suggest something of the instability of business activity. Some instability may well be necessary in a capitalistic economy (this is a debatable point, but certainly the extreme instability of the past need not and should not be allowed to continue in the future). Widespread and protracted unemployment of the sort experienced during the great depression of the 1930's is tragic in its effects and stands as a tribute to our stupidity. The severe inflation after World War II provides an example of the opposite extreme. If severe depressions and inflations cannot be avoided in a private-enterprise economy, there will be many who want to replace capitalism with some alternative system which promises a greater degree of stability of employment and prices, even if that means a sacrifice of liberties which Americans have traditionally cherished. The United States is even now one of the few major countries in which private enterprise is still the predominant form of economic organization.

Stimulated by the world-wide depression of the 1930's, many economists have in recent years turned their attention to a study of aggregates of economic data in an effort to understand the causes of extensive unemployment and to determine the policies which will minimize the extent of depressions. Rather than concerning themselves with data relative to individual firms or industries, as we did in Part A, these writers have investigated the nature of such aggregates as the national income, total savings, and total investment. This newer branch of economics has been designated "macroeconomics" as contrasted with the "microeconomics" of Part A, *i.e.*, the economics of large rather than of small units. The pioneer work in this field was John Maynard Keynes's book, *The General Theory of Employment, Interest, and Money*, published in 1936. Few books of our time have been more influential than this one, and it is with the concepts and issues developed by Keynes and others that we shall be concerned in Part B.

We begin our study of economic aggregates with an analysis of national income. This analysis will not discuss in detail the factors which determine the upper limit to national real income. That limit is in large part determined by the stock of resources (labor and capital), the state of technology, and the form of the economic and social organization. If the upper limit were always attained, national real income would not change greatly over short-run periods. It would tend to increase gradually as population grew, as capital accumulation took place, and as technical innovations were introduced. The analysis which follows will be more directly concerned with the causes of fluctuations in national income than with factors determining its absolute size.

TWO VIEWS OF NATIONAL INCOME

There are two distinct ways of viewing national income: (1) as the summation of the net value of final goods and services produced during a period; and (2) as the summation of wages, salaries, interest, rent, and business incomes received during a period. The first method amounts to an evaluation of all final outputs of the economy at prevailing prices. The second method must, logically, give the same answer as the first, since the selling value of output must be equal to cost of production plus profits. (This is true for the same reason that the value of total gross output for each industry in the input-output table of Chapter 2 is equal to total gross outlay for the same industry, *i.e.*, profits are included in gross outlays.)

In calculating national income by the first method, it is necessary that only final goods and services (those which are not resold) be counted. A great deal of duplication would be involved, for example, if the value of portland cement were counted when it was sold by the producer, again when sold by a distributor, again when sold by a transit-mix concrete company, and again when sold by a builder to a new home buyer, incorporated in a basement floor. Instead, it is necessary that only the value of the basement floor be counted, since this includes the original value of the cement, the value added in transportation and distribution, the value added by the concrete mixer, and the value added by the builder. Actually, the value of the floor would not be reported separately but would be picked up statistically as part of the value of new residential construction. (Even here the statistician would have to make some "educated guesses," since data in the field of construction are poor.)

In calculating national income, the U.S. Department of Commerce statisticians are guided in part by what is practicable rather than by what should theoretically be included. Conceptually, the national income should include such items as the value of housewives' services; lawn-mowing and maintenance services of all sorts provided by male members of the families; baby-sitting services, whether paid for or furnished gratis by grandparents; and vegetables, fruits, and flowers raised in the home garden and orchard.[1] Since such items cannot readily be estimated in dollars, however, they are omitted, leaving the national income rather substantially understated. This omission probably makes little real dif-

---

[1] The Department of Commerce income estimates include an imputed value for home-produced food for farm families but not for urban families.

ference except when there is an important change in the magnitude of such uncounted income. For example, during World War II millions of women switched from housework, where their services are not counted, to factory work, where their wages and product do count as national income. It has frequently been asserted that civilian consumption was higher throughout World War II than just prior to the war despite the huge volume of munitions output which we attained. This conclusion has been derived directly from the published national-income data but should be viewed skeptically for the reason just given. In a broad sense, leisure is also a type of income as long as it is not available in an excessive amount because of involuntary unemployment. During the war a six-day week was common, leaving many people with less leisure time than they would have chosen had they been able to work only as long as they preferred additional income to additional leisure. This further reduces the wartime significance of the national-income estimates as a measure of national "psychic" income.

Another important respect in which there is a compromise between theory and feasibility is the treatment of durable consumers' goods. If a new automobile will last ten years, for example, only about one-tenth of its original cost (less ultimate scrap value) should be counted as income each year. Actually, the entire value of new cars is counted as national income in the year in which they are produced. In the case of owner-occupied homes, however, the error which would be involved in leaving out the yearly value of housing services consumed would be so great that an estimate of their value is actually made and included in national income.

The above discussion should not cause one to regard the national-income estimates as worthless, but rather it should serve as a warning that due caution must be exercised in their interpretation. Any substantial movement in the national-income figures from year to year undoubtedly reflects important changes. On the other hand, a variation of small magnitude, e.g., a one-billion-dollar decline, should not be taken seriously, since the error probably contained in the estimates plus variations in the unmeasured items is likely to be of greater magnitude.

NATIONAL-INCOME CONCEPTS

The Department of Commerce compiles data corresponding to five different concepts of national income.[1] Like rubbing alcohol, all should be used with caution, for the reasons which have been set forth. While all five are national-income measurements in a broad sense, the term "National

[1] These are designated Gross National Product, Net National Product, National Income, Personal Income, and Disposable Income.

Income" also refers to a particular one of the measurements. National Income in the particular sense and Gross National Product are the most widely publicized measurements. The latter (GNP) is somewhat easier to understand. It is the total output of final goods and services during the year, measured at their market values. The statistical job would be harder, but GNP could also be found by measuring the total outputs of all firms and deducting inputs bought from other firms. This would amount to a summation of the *value added* by each firm to the materials and semiprocessed goods which it processed, the value additions resulting from the application of labor, capital, and managerial skill.

Not all of the goods and services produced in any one year represent "income." Some goods and services must be produced to replace the capital used up during the year if the total stock of capital is not to be reduced. Therefore in order to arrive at a figure for National Income, "capital consumption allowances" must be deducted from Gross National Product. This really amounts to deducting the value of the capital which is "used up" in producing the total income and which, therefore, must be replaced if future income is to continue to be produced.[1]

NATIONAL-INCOME DATA

Department of Commerce estimates of Gross National Product and National Income for selected years are shown in Table 17.1. We have

Table 17.1. Gross National Product and National Income
(In billions of dollars)

	1929	1932	1939	1944	1950	1951	1952	1953*
GNP	$103.8	$58.3	$91.3	$213.7	$286.8	$329.8	$348.0	$367.0
NI	87.4	41.7	72.5	183.8	240.6	278.4	291.6	308.4

* Estimated.
Source: U.S. Department of Commerce.

included 1929 because it was a year of great prosperity, which, however, ended on a sorrowful note after the most violent stock-market crash in our history; 1932 is shown because it was the worst year of the most severe depression which the nation has experienced; 1939 is included because it was the last year prior to World War II, in which United States munitions production was of negligible proportions; 1944 is of interest because it was the year of peak military production; 1950 is shown as

---

[1] United States government statisticians also make other deductions, but these are of little importance to the student's elementary understanding of the national-income concept.

the year in which the Korean War started and rearmament was undertaken in earnest; and 1951, 1952, and 1953 are included in order to show the recent trend.

The severity of the decline of business activity from 1929 to 1932 and the hesitant pace of recovery during the next seven years are shown by both statistical series. The tremendous effect of the war on national product and income are reflected in the comparison of 1944 and 1939 figures, while the high level of rearmament economic activity is seen in the 1950 and later data.

The figures of Table 17.1, however, overstate the fluctuations in real gross product and real income, that is, in the physical volume of goods and services turned out. Prices changed radically over the period covered by Table 17.1, falling sharply from 1929 to 1932 and (except for some rather short-lived setbacks) rising over the next two decades. Because part of the decline in GNP and NI from 1929 to 1932 is accounted for by the drop in prices which occurred, real gross output and real income did not fall so sharply as their dollar measures. Similarly, the real gain after 1932 was less spectacular than it appears, since a sizable part of the recorded rise was due to price inflation.

In order to eliminate the influence of changing prices on such dollar measurements, statisticians "deflate" the data by dividing by appropriate index numbers of prices. As an illustration of the statistical process of deflation (which must not be confused with the other meaning of the term, namely, a general decline in prices), suppose a vendor sells $1,000 worth of $1 neckties in a given year. For the next year he decides to charge $2 a tie instead of $1, and sells $4,000 worth during the year. What has happened to the physical volume of his sales? Obviously, his "real" sales have doubled. Arithmetically, this is determined by dividing $1,000 by $1 and $4,000 by $2 in order to get physical sales of 1,000 and 2,000 ties respectively, in the two years.

When the dollar aggregates pertain to a number of commodities rather than to just one, it is not so simple to find the correct divisors. Conceptually, one should divide by average prices which have been computed by giving to each commodity the same weight (importance) in the average as it has in the dollar aggregate. In practice, such average prices (which are called index numbers when expressed in a percentage relationship to a base period) are only an approximation of the average which is really appropriate. Despite these shortcomings, deflated income aggregates give us a much more correct picture of real economic changes than do the unadjusted dollar data in a period of violent price changes such as have characterized the past quarter century.

Table 17.2 shows Gross National Product adjusted to dollars of 1939 purchasing power—that is, deflated by price indexes which use 1939 as a

Table 17.2. GNP Measured in 1939 Dollars
(In billions of dollars)

1929	1932	1939	1944	1950	1951	1952	1953
$ 85.9	$61.9	$ 91.3	$156.9	$156.2	$167.0	$172.0	$178.3

Implicit price index numbers (1939 = 100)

120.8	94.2	100.0	136.2	183.6	197.5	202.3	205.8

Source: *Economic Report of the President, Jan. 28, 1954.*

base.[1] Even though the purpose of national-income accounting is to measure fluctuations in the real volume of final goods and services produced, it is necessary to use dollars in order to add together the thousands of diverse commodities and services which are measured physically in a very large number of different units (pounds, tons, gallons, quantity per hour, etc.). It is consequently necessary to settle on a dollar of unchanging purchasing power so that the standard of measurement will not change at the same time that the thing being measured is varying. By placing the index numbers used as deflators on a base of 1939 as 100, the statisticians attempt to show what the same volume of goods and services turned out in each of the other years would have sold for had 1939 prices prevailed. Original and deflated GNP for 1939 must be identical, of course. Thus the deflated GNP for 1953, $178.3 billion, can be found by dividing $367.0 billion (from Table 17.1) by the index number 205.8. The latter index number is interesting (and shocking) in itself, since it shows a more than doubling of prices on the average between 1939 and 1953.[2]

Removal of the influence of price changes has a great effect. In actual dollars, the increase in Gross National Product was about 254 per cent from 1939 to 1953. In standard 1939 dollars, the percentage gain was 108 per cent. While the latter is an impressive gain in real gross product,

[1] The "implicit" index numbers shown in Table 17.2 along with deflated GNP are so termed because they have not really been used in this form as deflators. Instead, the actual deflation of components of GNP is carried out in as fine detail as is possible. The separately deflated components are added together to get the results shown in the first row of Table 17.2. Then the statisticians have divided the original GNP figures by the deflated ones to see what price index numbers they would have had to use in order to get the deflated data in a single operation.

[2] The student should distinguish between general inflation and deflation and the rise and fall of particular prices. The latter are a necessary part of the proper operation of the price system; that is, price must change in order to carry out its rationing and production-motivating functions whenever underlying supply-demand conditions change. But general price inflation does more to misallocate than to allocate resources.

it is apparent that rising prices during the period had more influence in raising GNP than did the actual gain in gross output.

GNP Components

Both Gross National Product and National Income can usefully be broken down into major components, and this is a regular part of the Department of Commerce reporting activity. GNP is the summation of market values of final goods and services produced, and it is of interest to see what groups purchase this output and in what amounts. The disposition of the 1953 output is shown in Table 17.3, figures being expressed in 1953 rather than 1939 dollars.

Table 17.3. Major Components of GNP—1953
(In billions of dollars)

Personal Consumption Expenditures	$229.8
Gross Private Domestic Investment	55.7
Net Foreign Investment	−1.9
Government Purchases of Goods and Services	83.4
Total	$367.0

The largest figure, Personal Consumption Expenditures, shows purchases made by individuals and nonprofit institutions for consumption purposes. This includes food, clothing, haircuts, and all sorts of other nondurables plus durable goods such as automobiles and furniture. Residential buildings purchased are, however, excluded and placed instead in the second category—Gross Private Domestic Investment.

Some consumers' goods are secured without the expenditure of money, and national-income statisticians include allowances for such goods in the Personal Consumption Expenditures figures. Food, housing, clothing, and fuel received directly by some workers as part of their pay are included here. Similarly, the value of housing services derived from owner-occupied homes is estimated and included, as is the value of food and fuel which are both produced and consumed on farms. As suggested earlier in this chapter, it would be logical to include the value of household services furnished by members of families and perhaps even the value of leisure time, but Federal officials have not considered it wise to do so.

The second row in Table 17.3, Gross Private Domestic Investment, shows the aggregate purchase of new residential buildings, new machinery, and other durable producers' goods such as power lines and pipelines. Some of these purchases merely serve to replace worn-out buildings and equipment, but it should be remembered from the earlier discussion that no distinction is made between replacement and other items in the computation of GNP. Finally, any net build-up of farm and nonfarm business inventories is counted here. Such build-ups can usefully be thought of as a temporary purchase by farmers and other business-men of their own goods. The temporary inventory accumulations may be either voluntary or involuntary; that is, enterprisers may feel it desirable to carry larger stocks or may end up with larger stocks than they wish because of inability to sell as much as they expected. (This point is of considerable importance in the theory of income determination examined in the next two chapters.)

The third item, Net Foreign Investment, is somewhat more difficult to understand. Roughly, it may be thought of as the excess of our exports over our imports. Actually, the figure is obtained by computing gross dollar receipts by United States residents and subtracting gross dollar payments made to foreigners. Many transactions in addition to merchandise imports and exports give rise to international payments; these were examined in some detail when the international balance of payments was discussed in Chapter 14. For present purposes it is enough to see that our net foreign balance (exports minus imports) is summarized in the term Net Foreign Investment.

It will be noted in Table 17.3 that Net Foreign Investment in 1953 is −$1.9 billion. This seems to indicate that the United States imported more than it exported in 1953. Actually, this was not the case, since Government (Federal, state, and local) Purchases of Goods and Services, $83.4 billion, includes amounts bought by the Federal government and distributed as economic aid and military assistance to foreign nations.

The $83.4 billion of government purchases includes compensation paid to civil and military employees, since presumably their output is commensurate with their pay. It also includes net purchases by the government from domestic businesses and from abroad. Interest on government debt is not included, but this decision is rather an arbitrary one. To the extent that the Federal debt, for example, represents borrowing for purposes of investment in capital goods (factories, power systems, national parks, public housing, etc.), interest on the debt should be counted in GNP and National Income. To the extent, however, that the debt was incurred for such purposes as meeting payrolls during the war and producing munitions which were destroyed by the war, it is perhaps inappropriate to count interest on the public debt as part of the national product and income; it becomes, instead, a "transfer payment," i.e., a transfer of money between persons and institutions which is not associated with current production. All transfer payments (relief to the needy, gifts, inheritances, etc.) are excluded from National Income.

Other difficult problems of classification are connected with government activity. For example, payments to soldiers' dependents are counted in soldiers' compensation, and hence in National Income, but benefits under the GI bills are excluded as being a further reward for past, rather than current, services. Also, work-relief payments, which were large during the depression of the 1930's, should be included or excluded depending on whether the work or the relief was predominant. Here the quality of the planning which goes into work-relief projects is of prime importance.

National Income Components

It is useful also to get an impression of the division of National Income among broadly defined groups of recipients and types of remuneration. Such a breakdown of the 1953 data is given in Table 17.4.

Table 17.4. Distribution of the 1953 National Income
(In billions of dollars)

Wages, salaries, and supplements	$207.6
Corporate earnings	43.2
Earnings of unincorporated business	27.0
Farm income	12.4
Rental income	10.5
Net interest	7.7
Total	$308.4

It will be noted that employees' compensation in the form of wages, salaries, and supplements—the latter term also comprehending such items as employer contributions to social security and private pension plans—amounted to about two-thirds of the total national income. Profits of corporations—a favorite topic of the labor-union leaders in recent years—amounted to a sizable chunk, 14 per cent. It should be recognized, however, that corporations are not ultimate recipients in the same sense as are the receivers of the other listed shares. Part of the profits which remain after taxes are paid out as dividends to stockholders to be spent as they wish (after income taxes), and part of corporation earnings are reinvested by the company officials.

The income shown for noncorporate business includes earnings by professional people such as doctors, lawyers, and public accountants in business for themselves. If they worked for others, their salaries would go instead into the first category. Similarly, a portion of farm income is really compensation for labor services contributed by the farm families which would be added in with wages, salaries, and supplements except for the fact that the farmer is in business for himself.

Rental income includes not only explicit money earnings received by individuals who rent out real property but, it will be remembered, also the estimated rental value of owner-occupied homes, minus depreciation, maintenance, and similar costs. Royalties received on patents and copyrights and from the ownership of such natural resources as oil wells and iron mines are included here.

Interest income, as stated earlier, excludes all interest on government debt. In addition to cash interest received by individuals on nongovernmental bonds and other I O U's, this item includes very substantial earnings received by insurance companies on policyholders' funds but not paid out currently to policyholders.

The size of the national income is of vital importance to the nation, and national-income theory, to be developed in the next three chapters, consequently constitutes an important part of modern economics. It should always be kept in mind, however, that aggregative data inevitably conceal important information regarding the constituent elements. This is true even when a broad breakdown is attempted, as in Table 17.4. Many Americans live in poverty even when national income is high, and many groups, such as retired persons and white-collar workers, may face declining standards of living even when national real income is rising. Much of what is termed "political economy" in Part C of this book is an outgrowth of a great tug of war between different organized groups in the nation, each trying to get a larger share of the national income.

CHAPTER 18

HOW IS NATIONAL INCOME DETERMINED?

The national-income data compiled by the Department of Commerce provide us with a reasonably accurate measure of the level of economic activity, and fluctuations in national income reflect movements in employment, production, and prices. This chapter will discuss the forces which determine fluctuations in national income. We know that serious fluctuations have occurred in the past and may recur in the future. What forces generated the tragic depression of the 1930's? How could the same economy undergo deflation and depression in the 1930's and inflation in the late 1940's and early 1950's?

First of all, a distinction must be made between national real income and national money income. As the last chapter indicated, goods and services produced in the economy can be "added up" only in value or money terms. But an increase in money income may not represent an increase in the amount of real goods and services produced; it may result from an increase in the level of prices. We are, of course, interested in both money income and real income. When real income is considerably below that which our available resources might produce, the economy is plagued with depression. When money income is too high relative to the real goods and services produced, inflation is present.

In order to discover the causes of fluctuations in real income, we shall first discuss the causes of fluctuations in national money income. Then the conditions under which fluctuations in national money income are likely to be accompanied by shifts in real income will be outlined.

THE MONEY-INCOME WHEEL

The wheel of income was introduced in Chapter 2 and was discussed again in Chapter 10. The money-flow portions of this wheel are reproduced in Figure 18.1 with some differences to be explained. We are assuming for the time being that individuals (families) and business units are the only important economic entities. We are leaving aside the effects of government. As before, the money flow in the lower half of the wheel represents payments made by business units to private families in the form of wages, salaries, rents, royalties, dividends, etc. This flow represents one view of national money income, as was mentioned in the last chapter, and the summation of these various shares is one means of estimating it (see Table 17.4). In Figure 18.1, the magnitude of this flow is indicated by the width of the "pipe." As this income is received by individuals (families), all of it ultimately must be disposed of in one of two ways. It will be spent for goods and services, or it will be saved. The income spent by private families is for consumption goods and may be called "consumption."[1] If we let the national money income be represented by Y, consumption expenditure by C, and savings by S, we can set up the equation $Y = C + S$.

That part of income which is spent on consumer goods and services (C) reenters the money flow shown in the upper half of the diagram and returns to business units as payment for goods and services. Goods and services purchased by private families (consumers) are not, however, the only kind produced by business units. A significant share of total national production takes the form of goods which are designed to be utilized in the further production of other goods. These are normally characterized as capital goods—buildings, machinery, equipment, inventories. Goods of this sort are not purchased by private families, but instead they are purchased from business units by other business units. The expenditure on goods of this type is called "investment expenditure," and the act of "investment" comprises the purchase of capital goods.[2] Business firms undertake investment to replace worn-out plant and equipment, to expand existing facilities for production, to construct completely new plants, and to launch new projects. The total investment expenditure added to the total consumption expenditure must be equal to the total value of all goods and services produced, provided that the accumulation of business inventories, including finished-goods inventories retained by producing firms, is counted in "investment expenditure." This total value of all goods and services produced in the national economy is called Gross National Product. (Remember that we are neglecting government and foreign investment at this point.)

[1] This does not precisely agree with the definition of consumption expenditure employed by the Department of Commerce. Expenditure by private families on residences is called "investment." However, for purposes of making the theory of income determination as clear as possible, we shall find it convenient to think of all expenditure by private families as "consumption" and all expenditure on capital goods (including inventories) by business firms as "investment."

[2] "Investment" as thus used in national-income theory should be distinguished from the common usage of the term. In common parlance, the act of investment means the purchase of any earning asset—stock, bond, or physical unit of capital goods.

The Two Income Equations

All that is necessary in this simplified model to arrive at national income from Gross National Product is to deduct the expenditure for capital goods which was required to replace "used-up" capital. In estimating national income, therefore, there needs to be added to consumption expenditure only "net" investment expenditure, *i.e.*, total investment expenditure minus full depreciation charges. If we use the same symbols as before for income and consumption, and if we let I represent net investment expenditure, the equation $Y = C + I$ may be derived.

Now we have two equations for national income. The first ($Y = C + S$) concentrates on the disposition of income as it is received by individuals. It is either spent or saved. The second ($Y = C + I$) concentrates on the expenditure for goods and services produced. If we think of business units as receiving revenue from sales and then paying out all these receipts in the form of income shares (wages, salaries, rent, interest, dividends, and profits), then it is clear that we are representing the same money flow in both simple equations. By deducting from the revenue side the expenditure made to replace "used-up" capital and from the payments side the reserve for depreciation of capital, and assuming these two items to be both correct and equivalent, then the same national money income may be represented in both equations. The Y in the two equations is the same. We can also see that the C item in each equation must be the same. This is true because what private families spend for consumption goods and services (the C in the first equation) must be equal to what business firms receive as total expenditure on consumption goods and services (the C in the second equation). If the Y and the C are the same in the two equations, it follows that the third terms must be equal. Savings must be exactly equal to net investment expenditure ($S = I$). Returning to the money-income wheel of Figure 18.1, this means that the drainage from the money flow on the left through savings must be exactly offset by the addition to the money flow through investment on the right.

THE EQUALITY OF SAVINGS AND INVESTMENT

Why must the amount of income saved be identical with the amount of net investment expenditure? This is one of the central points in the modern theory of income determination, and it is therefore essential that the answer be made quite clear. The act of saving is undertaken by both individuals and business units. Saving by families is represented by putting a portion of income aside for a rainy day, for old age, to meet certain unexpected contingencies, etc. Saving by business firms represents the retaining of some profits rather than paying them all out to owners. Saving may take several forms: Irrationally cautious people may bury a few dollars of each monthly income in a fruit jar in the back yard or sew it up in a mattress; others may rent strongboxes. But more frequently, saving by both individual families and business firms takes the form of increased bank deposits, increased share purchases in building and loan associations, increased purchases of government securities, etc.

The act of investment in the sense defined here is of a different nature from that of saving. Investment and saving, in large part, are carried out by different sets of people for different reasons. Investment is the purchase of capital goods and as such is largely undertaken by business firms. Only for that portion of total saving which is carried out by certain types of business firms are the decision to save and the decision to invest made by the same people. There would seem to be, therefore, no reason why the amount of net investment expenditure must always be equal to the amount of saving in any given time period, even in the very simplified analysis we are discussing here.

The banking system, which will be examined in subsequent chapters, does provide a mechanism through which savings may be channeled into actual investment. If individuals save and increase their bank deposits, a greater amount of loanable funds becomes available to banks—funds which may be loaned to business firms seeking to purchase capital goods, i.e., to invest. But the banking system does not operate to keep the two magnitudes, savings and investment, in exact equality or even moving toward equality. Economists of a few decades ago did think that the banking system tended to keep the two equal. Their reasoning was as follows: If savings became greater than the amount of investment expenditure undertaken by businessmen, banks would find themselves unable to lend all that they desired. The supply of loanable funds would then exceed the demand for them at the going rate of interest. The divergence between demand and supply would force the rate of interest down. With the lower rate of interest, more investment would be undertaken and less saving would be forthcoming. The interest rate would fluctuate in this way until the supply of savings and the demand for them, i.e., investment, were brought into equality. This chain of reasoning is not entirely wrong, but the forces of adjustment included are not strong. Investment expenditures are to some extent financed out of bank credit, but the amount of bank credit at any time depends only remotely on the amount of savings. In addition, the response of investment expenditure and savings to changes in the interest rate (as was mentioned in Part A) may not be strong and, in some cases, may not even be in the direction indicated by the above line of reasoning.

Income Fluctuations Equate Savings and Investment

There is a much more important variable connecting the amount of saving and the amount of investment and operating so as to make the two necessarily equal. This variable is the national money income itself. Fluctuations up and down in national money income serve to keep savings and investment equal. For this reason the savings-investment relationship looms as extremely important. In order to be able to discuss more clearly the nature of this relationship and its effect on the determination of national income, a time-period method of analysis will be introduced. Thus far we have referred to the equality of savings and investment during any given period without specifying the dimensions of the time period. In reference to the money-income wheel of Figure 18.1, we have assumed implicitly that the money flows in both the upper and lower parts of the wheel take place in the same time period. Actually, this is not the case; individuals must receive income before they can spend it. People receive income in one period but do not spend it until the next one. In addition, businessmen make investment plans partly on the basis of consumption expenditures in the past period.

Without at the moment asking why, assume that the amount of saving is just equal to the amount of net investment expenditure. This is the case represented by Figure 18.1. National money income is in a position of full equilibrium. Equilibrium carries with it the same idea here as in Part A; it indicates a position which, once reached, will be maintained unless underlying forces shift. In this case, there will be no tendency for national money income to shift up or down. Businessmen will be fully satisfied, since they find that they are able to sell all the goods and services produced for sale at the prices which were expected. Consumers will be satisfied, since they will find themselves able to purchase all the goods and services which they intended to purchase at the prices which they expected would prevail. As long as the savings flow and the investment expenditure remain equal in the volumes indicated, national money income will remain at the level shown by the width of the flow-of-payments "pipe" in the lower half of the money-income wheel. The total money expenditure for goods and services produced over and above replacement of used-up capital $(C + I)$ is just equal to the total of the payments made to individuals by business firms $(C + S)$.

In order to see how this equilibrium position might be disturbed, let us assume that individuals, for some reason, decide to save a greater share and spend a smaller part of their incomes than previously. It should be clear, of course, that particular individuals may save more without this action resulting in more total saving, since, if some other individuals save less, the total may remain unchanged. We are dealing here with aggregates, however, and are therefore concerned only with changes in total saving. Our assumption is simply that people decide to increase their aggregate net saving. Let us employ our customary helpmate, *ceteris paribus.* In this case, the principal other thing that must remain unchanged is the amount of investment expenditure that business firms plan to undertake in the succeeding time period. Businessmen, we shall assume, do not anticipate the change in saving (and thus in consumption expenditure) and therefore plan to produce capital goods and consumption goods at the same rate as during the preceding period when national money income was in equilibrium. Thus, investment plans and national income remain unchanged, but a greater amount of saving is attempted.

Planned Savings and Planned Investment

This divergence between the savings plans of individuals and the investment plans of firms means that someone is going to be disappointed. For as people begin saving more, *i.e.*, putting a greater portion of their income in bank deposits, government bonds, etc., their expenditure on consumption goods and services must be correspondingly reduced. Therefore, a smaller money flow will begin to enter the upper half of the money-income wheel as expenditure on consumption goods and services. Business firms will begin to experience difficulty in selling goods; they will find their shelves and warehouses filling up. It will not be possible for them to sell at going prices all the goods and services that have been produced and prepared for sale. For it must be remembered that the goods and services were produced with the expectation that consumer expenditure would remain at its earlier and higher level. So inventories will accumulate as a result of the decline in consumer buying. This net addition to inventories is also "investment" under the meaning employed here. But this type of investment is of a different sort from the more normal expenditure for capital goods. This net increase in inventories above their normal level was not anticipated or planned. Business firms had expected to sell more goods and services than they now find themselves able to sell. They are left holding the bag, so to speak, full of extra and unsold goods. They are therefore disappointed because their plans have not been carried out. They have really "invested" more than they had intended.

The situation prevailing at this stage is shown in Figure 18.2. The consumption expenditure entering the income stream is lower than that in Figure 18.1, which depicts the earlier equilibrium level of national money income. Planned investment expenditures are unchanged. But the shaded area represents investment in unsold goods, or inventories, an investment which was not anticipated. This amount of unintended investment is precisely equivalent to the difference between the planned savings (which is actual saving in this case) and planned investment. The unintended in-

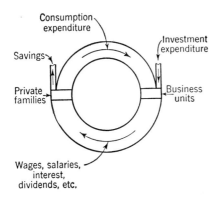

Figure 18.1. INITIAL EQUILIBRIUM—
Planned Saving =
Planned Investment
Actual Saving = **Actual**
Investment

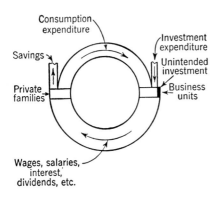

Figure 18.2. BUSINESSMEN DISAPPOINTED—
Planned Saving Exceeds Planned
Investment
Actual Saving = Actual Investment

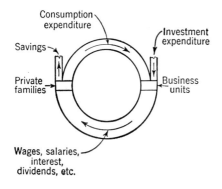

Figure 18.3. NEW EQUILIBRIUM WITH LOWER
NATIONAL INCOME—
Planned Saving = Planned Investment
Actual Saving = Actual Investment

vestment is the item which equates the realized or actual savings with the actual investment. We may now state an important result of our analysis so far. Planned savings can be greater or less than planned investment, but realized savings must be equal to realized investment at the end of any time period. Not all of the savings and investment actually carried out need have been planned, and that which was planned does not need to have been actually carried out.

Consumption, savings, and investment plans for subsequent time periods will be made on the basis of the situation prevailing at the stage shown in Figure 18.2. If the initial change in saving is permanent, consumers will again plan to save the larger amount, since national income has not yet changed. But businessmen will note the reduced rate of consumer spending and the accumulating inventories. If they expect this change in consumer buying habits to be relatively permanent, it is clear that they are not going to allow inventories to be continually built up. They are extremely likely to make some changes in plans. There will be a tendency for them to reduce prices in order to sell more goods. Prices will fall somewhat, but, at the same time, a more significant adjustment will take place in the rate of production. Rates of output will be reduced for many commodities, since many firms will prefer a reduction in the rate of production to drastic price cuts. This stems from two causes. First, many producers have at least some degree of monopoly power, *i.e.*, some control over the prices which they charge. They realize that the reduction in production will allow them to maintain prices at higher levels. Other firms are members of oligopolistic industries in which price cutting might lead to price wars (see Chapter 8). Second, even if firms were willing to cut prices drastically to move unsold goods, they would be able to do so readily only in those instances where prices are high in relation to average variable cost. If variable costs are to be lowered, prices paid for the productive services employed must be lowered. The most important of these inputs is labor; therefore, a general reduction in variable costs would be possible only if labor were willing to accept wage reductions. But money-wage-rate reductions are likely to be almost impossible in the short run, especially in industries in which labor is highly organized. For these two main reasons, prices and costs are often extremely slow in adjusting to downward movements in demand. The primary adjustments will accordingly be in terms of output. The reduction in the rate of output is accompanied by a reduction in the rate of input of productive services. This involves layoffs and unemployment. The initial reduction in consumption expenditure will, therefore, create unemployment through its effects on the plans of business firms. Money incomes and real incomes are both reduced as a result of the attempts of business firms to adjust to the new situation facing them.

This adjustment process will continue until excess inventories are no longer present, *i.e.*, until planned investment is equal to planned saving. The new equilibrium level of income is approached in the following way. As employment and/or rates of pay are reduced, total money payments to owners of productive services are reduced, *i.e.*, personal incomes are lowered. Out of the lower incomes, individuals will be able to save less than before. This reduction in the money-income flow is the primary mechanism which serves to bring planned savings into equality with planned investment. National income will fall, in our example, until people's ability to save is reduced enough to conform with the new investment plans of firms. The initial attempt made by individuals to increase total savings may actually result in their saving less, because the changed pattern of spending generates a reduction in income.

The situation prevailing after the adjustment process is completed and the new lower equilibrium level of income is reached is represented in Figure 18.3. Once again the drainage from the income stream into savings is just equal to the addition to the income stream through investment; there is no unintended saving and no unintended investment. Thus, the situation is identical with that shown in Figure 18.1 except that the size of the income flow is different. National money income is lower than it was before the change in saving was attempted.

Other Types of Adjustment

The example employed above traced the effects of a change in the savings plans of consumers on the level of national money income. This is only one of several changes which might affect the level of income. The model used here could be employed to trace through the effects of other types of changes. It should not be difficult to see that a reduction in planned investment expenditure with no change in savings plans would have had almost identical effects as those in the example above. The major difference would have been in the industries primarily affected. With the reduction in consumption spending traced above, consumer-goods industries were the first to feel the impact; with the reduction in investment spending, capital-goods industries would be the first affected.

The analysis may be reversed to show the causes of an increase in national money income. An increase in planned consumer spending, which is the same as a reduction in planned saving, would tend to deplete business inventories, making investment less than had been intended. Or, if inventories are not sufficiently large, not all of the planned purchases may be carried out, and this will necessitate some unplanned saving. The newly increased demand would cause firms to place additional orders, adding to investment expenditure. Income payments would go up. At a higher money income, savings would be greater. The upward movement in national money income would continue until planned saving and planned investment were once again in equality.

Similar effects would be forthcoming following an increase in investment expenditure with no change in savings plans. Changes up or down in the level of investment expenditure are considered by economists to be a major determinant of the level of national money income. This is true because consumers' spending and saving habits have been generally assumed to be more stable over time than the investment plans of business firms. Investment plans, depending as they do in large part on the state of business expectations, may be subject to considerable variation in relatively short periods of time. The presumed stability of consumption spending over time will be considered in some detail in the following chapter.

An upward movement in money income, generated by either an increase in investment or a decrease in savings, may or may not cause similar movements in real income, and thus employment. The upward and downward movements in money income are not precisely symmetrical in their effects on real income. In the case of an upward shift, the effects on real income and employment depend on the level of real income upon which the change is imposed. If unemployment is present, increased spending by either consumers or firms will tend to call forth additional production and employment. But if the economy is running along fairly prosperously, with most of its productive resources employed, the primary effect of the increased rate of spending will then be an increase in the level of prices, both of final products and of productive services. Consequently, an increase in national money income is desirable only when accompanied by an increase in real income; it is undesirable if accompanied merely by inflation.

This chapter has summarized the forces determining fluctuations in national income in a simple model which has omitted the effects of government. This major income-determining force must be brought into full account later. Before this is done, however, a further investigation of the income-determining forces is necessary.

CHAPTER 19

THE INCOME-DETERMINING FORCES
ARE ANALYZED

The preceding chapter showed that fluctuations in national money income (and also real income) may be caused by changes in the spending plans of individual families or business firms. The analysis is useful as a general explanation of why fluctuations occur. A somewhat more detailed formulation of the theory is useful, however, in spelling out more fully the nature of the variables upon which the government must work in order to attempt to offset unfavorable movements in national income. In order to do this, the theory of income determination must include an examination of the underlying forces affecting the saving-spending plans of individual families and the investment plans of business firms.

THE CONSUMPTION FUNCTION

One of the major innovations made by Lord Keynes when he developed the structure of the modern theory of income determination was the introduction of the "consumption function." This was simply the recognition that the amount of consumption spending (and thus saving) depends primarily upon the level of income.[1] The functional relationship between the amount of consumption spending and income (in either money or real terms) is called the consumption function.

The next step, accordingly, involves an examination of the nature of the relationship between consumption expenditure and income. It is evident that, for most families and therefore for the whole economy, the higher the income the greater the amount of consumption spending. An increase in money income makes possible a greater amount of consumption spending. But although consumption spending increases as money income increases, it does not increase so rapidly. This means simply that, as a family's income rises, not all of the increase will be spent. The higher the income the

[1] Earlier economists believed that the amount of saving (for any one family or for the whole economy) was largely determined by the rate of interest.

greater the proportion of income which will be saved. This proposition may also be stated for the whole economy: A greater proportion will be saved out of a high national money income than out of a low national money income.

The relationship between scheduled consumption spending and money income is illustrated geometrically in Figure 19.1. The money income received by an individual family is represented on the x axis, consumption expenditure on the y axis. The line cc represents the consumption function. If money income is OM, MB is the amount of consumption expenditure which will be undertaken. The fact that consumption spending increases as income increases requires that the line cc slope upward to the right.

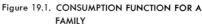

Figure 19.1. CONSUMPTION FUNCTION FOR A FAMILY

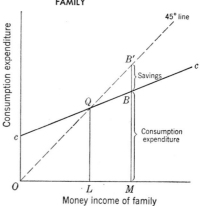

The *ratio* of consumption expenditure to income may also be shown in Figure 19.1. If consumption expenditure were the only means of using money income so that all of one's income were always spent for consumption goods, then the line cc would lie along a line drawn at a 45-degree angle from the origin. At any point on this 45-degree line the ordinate is equal to the abscissa, that is, the distance above the x axis is always just equal to the distance to the right from the y axis. If the entire income OM were spent, consumption expenditure would be MB' instead of MB; OM is exactly equal to MB'. By comparing the actual amount of income expended for consumption goods and services with the maximum amount which could have been spent if all the income received were used in this way, that is, by comparing MB with MB', the ratio of consumption spending to income may be derived.

The difference between the amount of consumption expenditure and the total money income received represents savings. Therefore, savings can also be seen in relation to money income in Figure 19.1. At income OM, savings are represented by BB'. At any income, savings are represented graphically by the distance between the line cc (the consumption function) and the 45-degree line.

It may be noted that Figure 19.1 is so drawn that at an income level shown by OL all the income received is spent for consumption goods and services ($OL = LQ$). OL represents, of course, a very low income level, and it is realistic to assume that at very low incomes families must spend all they can get and are unable to save anything. At incomes lower than

OL, the figure is drawn so as to show that the expenditure on consumption goods and services is actually more than money income received; the line *cc* lies above the 45-degree line. This implies that, at extremely low incomes, families must beg, borrow, or steal in order to survive. If incomes are extremely low for only a short period, a family can live on previous savings, or borrow, until a higher level of income is again attained. Over a longer period of time, previous savings would be wiped out, and the family would no longer be able to borrow. But with modern welfare institutions operating, these families would qualify for relief, community-chest assistance, etc. At incomes lower than *OL*, negative savings may be said to be present. Not only is all the money income which is received in exchange for productive work spent, but more is spent.

The fact that consumption spending does not increase as rapidly as income increases is indicated in Figure 19.1 by the relative slopes of the *cc* line and the 45-degree line. The line *cc* has a smaller positive slope than does the 45-degree line. This means that the proportion of income spent for consumption is lower at a higher income than at a lower income. Turning this around, the ratio of savings to income increases as income increases. This proportionate increase must be distinguished from an absolute increase in savings as income increases. Even if the proportion of income saved did not change as income increased, there would still be a greater absolute amount of savings at higher incomes.

Figure 19.1 represents the consumption-income relationship for an individual family. The aggregate consumption-income relationship for the whole economy is required for extending the analysis. This aggregate consumption function may be derived conceptually by adding the schedules for all individuals. For use in actual prediction, it is derived by relating the estimated consumption expenditure to national money income over as long a time span as available data will permit.

INVESTMENT EXPENDITURE AND INCOME

Investment spending must also be examined in more detail than it was in the last chapter. It seems probable that the decisions of business executives to purchase additional inventories or new equipment, to construct new buildings or repair old ones, etc., are not so closely tied to current or recent income levels as are the decisions of consumers. Instead, investment decisions are primarily dependent on the state of business expectations. If the business community expects consumer spending to be high and the economy generally to be prosperous, firms will normally decide to invest substantial sums in replacing and modernizing plant facilities and in expansion. If, on the other hand, there is a general expectation that a recession is on its way, little investment will be undertaken. Investment spending probably depends more on the way in which income is expected to change than on the level of income at any time.

Nevertheless, there is probably a direct relationship between the level of income and the amount of investment spending which will be scheduled, since the expectations concerning future incomes depend in part on the size of current income. Investment plans of businessmen are closely related to business profits. If substantial profits have been received during a period, it seems probable that businessmen will expect such profits to continue to be received in the future. And it is during periods of high incomes that aggregate profits are highest. In this somewhat indirect way, periods of high income are associated with high investment expenditure. High profits not only provide the incentive for new investment but also provide the funds for such expenditures to the extent that earnings are "plowed back." On the other hand, if profits are not being made, as is the case for most firms during depressed periods of low income, firms' managers tend to be pessimistic. Few of them will foresee prosperity, and firms generally are likely to contract investment expenditure.

In addition to the relationship between the level of national income and the volume of investment expenditures due to businessmen's expectations, a second factor may operate to tie investment spending directly to income changes. As income increases, consumption spending also increases. This increase in the demand for consumption goods will tend to cause firms to demand more capital equipment which goes into the manufacture of such goods unless excess capacity is initially present. This derived demand for capital goods may affect the capital-goods industries more significantly than the consumption-goods industries are affected.

This may be shown by a simple example. Suppose that the daily rate of sales of Coca-Cola in a small Southern town is 2,500 cases. Suppose further that it takes 10 bottling machines to produce 2,500 cases, or 1 for each 250 cases. Suppose further that the average length of life of a bottling machine is ten years, and, on the average, 1 unit is replaced each year. Then the normal annual production of these units of equipment for sale in this town is 1 per year.

Now suppose that consumers increase the quantity purchased by 20 per cent because of an over-all increase in income. This means that 3,000 cases instead of 2,500 will be demanded. To produce this amount, 12 instead of 10 units of capital equipment will be required. So 2 additional bottling machines must be produced to supplement the initial 10, plus the 1 which is produced to meet the normal replacement requirement. If this situation is representative of the economy as a whole, the capital-equipment industry must expand by 200 per cent as a result of an increase in final product demand of 20 per cent.

This is, of course, an extremely abstract and oversimplified example. If consumer-goods industries possess excess capacity, there may be no increase in the demand for capital equipment. Furthermore, capital equipment need not remain in a fixed ratio to final output. In spite of these necessary weaknesses, the acceleration principle is useful in indicating the manner in which a change in consumer spending may generate subsequent demand for investment and in showing why fluctuations in capital-goods industries may be more violent than in consumer-goods industries.

The Investment Function

The investment function may be shown geometrically in Figure 19.2. In this case, this relationship can better be considered initially to be in aggregate terms, that is, we are relating total net investment expenditure by all firms to total income of the economy. National money income is measured along the x axis and total net investment expenditure along the y axis. The line II represents the investment function. Any point on II shows the amount of investment spending which business firms will be planning to undertake at that level of income. Thus, if national money income were OM, investment spending undertaken would be MD. By drawing in the 45-degree line as before, the ratio of investment expenditure to income may be seen. Since MD' is equal to OM, this ratio at income OM is MD to MD'.

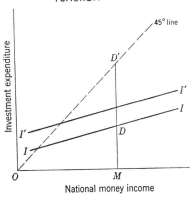

Figure 19.2. AGGREGATE INVESTMENT FUNCTION

THE DETERMINATION OF NATIONAL MONEY INCOME

The way in which national money income is determined in this simplified model may now be indicated. By adding the aggregate consumption function and the investment function, an aggregate expenditure-income relationship may be derived. This is illustrated geometrically in Figure 19.3. The aggregate consumption function is drawn as C. To the amount of consumption expenditure indicated by this function is added the amount of investment expenditure at each income level. In this manner, the aggregate expenditure-income function is derived; this function is labeled as $C + I$ in Figure 19.3.

If the usual 45-degree line is drawn in, it may be shown that the level of national money income will tend to be that represented by OX. The point

X is determined by the intersection of $C + I$ and the 45-degree line. This level of income will tend to be established, since it is the only level at which planned savings and planned investment are equal. Since the vertical distance between the consumption function and the 45-degree line represents aggregate planned savings, any other income level would not be an equilibrium one. At income OX (which is equal to XK), planned consumption spending is XJ, planned saving is JK, and planned investment is also JK.

In order to explain fully this process of income determination, let us again start with an initial position of income equilibrium as we did in the

Figure 19.3. NATIONAL INCOME IS DETERMINED—
Where Total Spending and 45-degree
Lines Meet

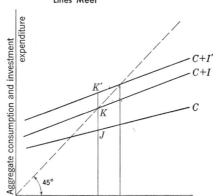

preceding chapter, assume a change in spending, and examine the process by which income shifts to a new equilibrium level. Let us assume that national money income initially is in equilibrium at OX. Consumers are successful in spending and saving in accordance with plans, and business firms are able to carry out all the investment expenditure that is attempted. For some reason, which need not concern us here, the business community becomes more optimistic about future events (perhaps as a result of the favorable outcome of an election). They make plans to step up the rate of investment expenditure. The investment function shifts to the position shown by $I'I'$ in Figure 19.2. This shift in the investment function shifts the aggregate expenditure function upward from $C + I$ to $C + I'$ in Figure 19.3.

People continue to try to spend an amount XJ on consumption goods and services. But business firms are now attempting to spend JK' on investment. If income were to remain at OX, aggregate spending plans would have to be curtailed by the amount KK'. If inventories in the capital-goods industries were large when the initial shift in investment plans occurred, the adjustment might be primarily in such inventories. The increase in planned investment would deplete inventories of the capital-goods industries below normal (*i.e.*, would involve disinvestment) by an amount KK', making actual net investment only JK instead of JK'. Or if these inventories were not sufficient for this result to be forthcoming, some of the plans for purchasing capital goods might not be carried out. A third alternative might be that consumers would be unable to spend all they desired. They might be forced into unintended savings. In any event, income could not long remain at OX, for some or all groups would be unsatisfied. Some group would be spending less than it wanted to spend.

In subsequent periods, income will tend to rise in a manner similar to that discussed in the last chapter. Faced with depleted inventories or with unsatisfied orders from consumers, business firms will try to expand production. If unemployment is present, production and employment will go up, increasing real as well as money incomes. If no unemployment is present, the attempt to expand production will bid up the prices for productive services. Wages will go up, and money income will rise. In this case, real income will not increase significantly since the economy was already operating at a capacity level.

The upward movement in money income will continue until the spending plans of all groups are satisfied. As income increases, a greater amount of savings is made possible, so that a new equilibrium level may be approached. In Figure 19.3, the final equilibrium level of income is shown as OX'. At this income, all plans are fulfilled; intended savings equal intended investment.

The type of analysis used here can be applied to any of the three other possible causes for a change in the level of income. If planned investment should be reduced, a fall in income would result. This might best be analyzed by assuming the initial equilibrium income to be OX', and for the investment function to shift downward from $I'I'$ to II in Figure 19.2. Income would, of course, tend to fall to the new equilibrium level OX. Or a shift in the consumption function (*i.e.*, in the spending-saving plans of consumers) upward or downward with investment unchanged would generate changes in income. The example used in the last chapter to illustrate the process of income change could equally well have been discussed with the help of Figures 19.2 and 19.3.

The analysis of this and the preceding chapter should indicate that there appears to be nothing which tends to cause the equilibrium level of national money income to approximate that which is most desirable. The equilibrium level might well be one of inflationary magnitude, or it might be one low enough to generate a significant degree of deflation and unemployment. All the theory does is to define that level of national money income which will tend to be established in an economy in which the government is truly neutral, or conceptually nonexistent. The only factors determining this equilibrium-level income in such a model economy are the plans of consumers concerning spending and saving of the income received and the plans of business firms concerning investment.

If the relationship between consumption spending and income (the consumption function, represented by the line C in Figure 19.3) remains relatively stable, the equilibrium level depends largely on the level of investment. The investment variable is likely to prove more unpredictable and subject to more erratic shifts than the consumption variable. But the equilibrium level of national money income in an economy is determined by more variables than those included in the simple model of these two chapters; major influences have been left out of account. These will be considered in the following chapter.

CHAPTER 20

SOME COMPLICATIONS ARE INTRODUCED
INTO INCOME THEORY

The forces operating to fix the equilibrium level of money income in a simplified model were discussed in the last two chapters. The purpose of assuming such unrealistic models is to enable the student to understand the interaction of the various forces in the simplest possible cases. Once this is accomplished, additional influences determining the level of income may be introduced and the model thereby made more realistic.

THE GOVERNMENT IN THE ECONOMY

The major factor now to be introduced is the activity of the government, which exerts a major influence on the flow of income in the modern economy. The total spendings stream is not composed of private consumption expenditure and investment expenditure alone; to these we must add government expenditure on goods and services. This third expenditure item has become an extremely important one in these days. So, in terms of total expenditure for goods and services, we now have three items to add: consumption spending, investment spending, and government spending. The equation $Y = C + I$ in our earlier discussion now becomes $Y = C + I + G$, where G represents government expenditure on goods and services. The G does not include all the government actually spends, since a large part of government spending goes for transfer payments such as social-security benefits, interest on the public debt, and veterans' benefits, i.e., payments to people which are not made in exchange for real goods or services currently produced. The G as used in income theory includes only government expenditure on real goods and services such as the construction of post-office buildings, the maintenance of highways, the collection of statistical data, etc.

The government also reduces potential consumer spending by the imposition of taxes, which decreases the disposable income of individuals. Once government is brought into the picture, there are three rather than two potential uses of income. Income may be either spent, saved, or paid in taxes to the government. In terms of the disposition of income, the equation $Y = C + S$ becomes $Y = C + S + T$, where T represents personal taxes. The transfer payments of government which were left out of G are included in T as negative taxes. A man paying an annual personal tax of $1,000 and receiving interest on government bonds of $1,000 would not affect the aggregate T at all, since the positive and negative items would, in his case, cancel out. Some difficulty arises when business taxes are to be taken into account. These taxes are collected from business firms and thus do not directly reduce the stream of money-income payments made to individuals. For our purposes, however, we may make the simplifying assumption that the amount collected in business taxes would have been paid out to individuals as dividends if the taxes had not been levied. This allows all taxes to be included in the T above, and our analysis is not disturbed.

The total amount of taxes collected by government need not match precisely the expenditures made by government on goods and services. If the government adds more in expenditure than it collects in taxes, there is a net government addition to the spendings stream. Contrariwise, if taxes collected exceed government expenditure, a depressing influence on money income is exerted. The government budget thus becomes a powerful instrument in influencing both the level of and changes in national money income. This whole problem of purposefully manipulating the budget to influence income will be discussed more fully in Part C.

Once it is recognized that government expenditure on goods and services need not equal taxes collected, it can no longer be said that the equality between planned savings and planned investment is the required condition for maintaining stability in the level of national income. With the government taken into account, we may say that planned saving plus planned tax collections must equal planned investment expenditure plus planned government expenditure. If the government intends to spend considerably more than it intends to collect in tax revenues, planned private savings must exceed planned private investment expenditure if national money income is to be prevented from rising. For example, if the government budget calls for a deficit of $9 billion, planned private saving must exceed planned investment by this amount if national money income is to be kept on an even keel. On the other hand, if the government intends to collect more in taxes (a purely hypothetical supposition?) than it intends to spend, planned private investment expenditure must exceed planned savings if national money income is not to fall. Only if the government budget is to be kept balanced, and at a stable level, will the equality of planned savings and planned private investment ensure income stability.

Taxation will reduce the disposable income of individuals and, consequently, the amount of consumption spending out of each possible level of income. But it will reduce consumption spending by less than the amount of the taxes collected. This is because a portion of the taxes collected would have been saved if left in private hands. Therefore, even if the government spends only the total tax revenues, total spending, private and public, will be greater than before the imposition of the tax. For this reason, an increase in government spending, even if fully financed by taxation, will tend to increase total aggregate spending and thus push national money income upward. Conversely, a reduction in government spending,

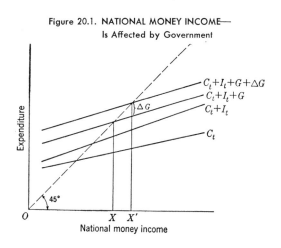

Figure 20.1. NATIONAL MONEY INCOME—
Is Affected by Government

even if accompanied by a dollar-for-dollar tax reduction, may tend to reduce total spending and cause an income shift downward. Some of the dollars received as tax reduction by individuals will be saved, whereas had the government collected them in taxes they would surely have been spent. For these effects to be present, it must be assumed that investment expenditure is not indirectly affected by the size of the government budget. This may or may not be an acceptable assumption. The main point to be remembered is this: Not only is the balance or unbalance of the government budget important in influencing the level of national money income, but in addition the absolute size of the budget is significant.

The geometrical analysis employed in the last chapter may readily be expanded to include the effects of government budgetary policy. This is shown in Figure 20.1, which is similar to Figure 19.3. National money income is represented on the x axis and the various spending components on the y axis. Aggregate consumption spending out of each income level is shown by C_t. The subscript t denotes that taxation has been taken into account. Consumption spending plus investment is shown as $C_t + I_t$. To these is added government expenditure on goods and services G. The aggregate spendings function is thus shown as the line $C_t + I_t + G$. The equilibrium level of national money income is again shown as OX, which is determined graphically by the intersection of the total spendings function and the 45-degree line.

THE FOREIGN-TRADE BALANCE

Another important influence on the level of national money income has so far been neglected. The analysis of this and the two preceding chapters has assumed that the economy was a closed one and that no foreign trade was carried on. In the real world, foreign trade does take place, and the effects of the existence of trade among nations on the level of income within any one nation must be taken into account. Foreign purchases made in this country constitute expenditure on home-produced goods and services. On the reverse side, income earned in this country but expended for foreign-produced goods and services constitutes a net drainage or leakage from the domestic-payments stream. There are now four means of disposing of income: consumption spending, saving, paying taxes, and purchasing foreign goods and services (importing). There are now also four components of total spending: consumption, investment, government, and foreign expenditure on domestically produced goods and services. If the terms are carefully defined so as to include all relevant items, foreign purchases may be called "exports" and purchases made in foreign countries "imports." The impact of foreign trade upon national income may be combined in a single item called "net foreign balance," which is defined as "exports minus imports." If exports exceed imports in value, the net foreign balance is positive. This means that international transactions exert an upward influence on national income, adding to the stream of total spending. If imports exceed exports, foreign trade exerts a depressing influence on the level of national income. Any complete analysis of the determination of national money income must therefore include the possible difference between exports and imports. These two items may be expected to remain roughly in balance unless one country is investing in other countries. Foreign countries can buy in the United States only if they are selling something to us or borrowing from us; otherwise, they do not have available the dollar exchange with which to purchase American goods and services. A long-term difference between the export and import items must involve some creation of the wherewithal with which the deficit country may purchase. A leading reason why the United States was able to import more in dollar value than she exported in the nineteenth century was that British businessmen were investing capital in the construction of American railroads. Since World War I, our exports have been greater than our imports because we have been lending or giving large sums to foreign governments. In this case, we are "investing" abroad.

The foreign-trade influence could easily be incorporated into the geometrical illustration of Figure 20.1. If the balance were positive, the total spendings function would be shifted upward; if negative, it would be shifted downward; if zero, there would be no shift.

AN EVALUATION OF THE THEORY

National money income at any one time has been shown to be determined by the decisions of consumers to spend and save; the decisions of businessmen to purchase investment goods; the decisions of legislative bodies and government officials concerning the size and balance of the government budget; and the decisions of both natives and foreigners relating to purchases of home-produced and foreign-produced goods and services. The first question to be asked in any evaluation of this theory is: Is it useful in helping to understand the causes of and to predict changes in income? The ability to predict is the basic test of any theory, and it is especially important here. If undesirable fluctuations are to be prevented, it is essential that movements of the important determining variables be predicted in advance with reasonable accuracy. For this requirement to be fulfilled, the economic variables must not be subject to unexpected and random changes. The most important of these variables in magnitude is consumer spending. *If* the relationship of consumer spending to income remained relatively stable over time, an estimation of income payments would make possible a rough prediction of consumer expenditure. The government item is relatively predictable and controllable. And, for this country, year-to-year changes in the foreign-trade item are not appreciably large. This leaves investment expenditure as the variable most subject to erratic fluctuations, and therefore this variable is held by some to be the major determinant of changes in the level of income. Fluctuations up and down in money income are held to be largely the result of waves of optimism and pessimism pervading the business atmosphere. National money income is considered to be a direct function of investment expenditure.

The "if" mentioned in the preceding paragraph proves, however, to be a big one. Between the years 1929 and 1940 there was a steady correlation between consumption spending and income. But this relationship was greatly disturbed during and after World War II. As a matter of fact, a group of Washington economists made a serious error in predicting a significant depression in late 1945 and early 1946 largely because they were using the consumption-income function of the 1929-to-1940 period as the basis of their predictions. But consumption spending proved to be greater in 1946 than this earlier relationship would have indicated. As a result, inflation rather than depression became the actual postwar problem. Since this time, economists have become much more cautious concerning their ability to predict with any degree of accuracy the swings in income by the use of statistics based on the theoretical analysis presented above. Although it is admitted that income is a major factor determining the amount of consumption spending, it is now recognized that other important variables affecting such spending are also present which are not explicitly accounted for in the analysis. These may include past income, expected income, the price level, and the real value and liquidity of assets owned. The consumption function shifted upward in 1946 from its 1940 position largely because people had accumulated large cash and government-bond holdings during the war period and had also built up unsatisfied desires for goods which had been unavailable for several years.

THE INCOME MULTIPLIER

Concentration upon the flow of income around the money-income wheel has provided the basis for the development of the "multiplier" concept. The wheel shows that a large portion of income received by individuals returns directly to the income stream as expenditure on consumer goods and services. This suggests that the addition of a new dollar of spending anywhere in the income flow will generate "multiplying" effects on income as it moves around the money-income wheel during succeeding spendings periods.

If individuals may be presumed to spend a rather fixed proportion of additional income received, a degree of arithmetical precision is given to the multiplier. Suppose, for example, that people spend, on the average, $9 and save $1 out of each additional $10 of income they receive.[1] Now suppose that, without anything else changing, some business firm expands its investment by $1. If new savings in the amount of $1 are to arise to match the additional investment, income will have to expand by $10. The new investment dollar will have to generate a tenfold increase in income; the value of the multiplier must be 10. This value depends only on the ratio of additional consumption to additional income.

The concept may be clarified by a more detailed look at the multiplying process in our example. The firm purchases an additional dollar's worth of machinery. The sellers of the machinery receive an additional dollar in

[1] This ratio between the additional amount of consumption expenditure and the additional income is technically defined as the "marginal propensity to consume." Mathematically, it is represented as $\Delta C/\Delta Y$. Geometrically, it is the slope of the consumption function. It is distinguished from the "average propensity to consume," which is simply the ratio of total consumption expenditure to total income, or C/Y.

revenue. They pay out this dollar in wages, dividends, or other forms of payment. Since we have assumed that people spend $\frac{9}{10}$ of any additonal income, those who receive the dollar will spend 90 cents and save 10 cents. The 90 cents is spent for consumer goods and again becomes income (in the form of wages, dividends, etc.) to private families. Out of the 90 cents received as income, 81 cents is spent, and 9 cents is saved. This will continue until income measured over the whole period of the multiplying process has expanded by the full $10. The multiplying effects in any one spendings period become smaller as more periods are passed. The multiplying effect will finally vanish when the full amount of the $1 has "leaked" out of the spendings stream into savings, either personal or business. At this point, the effects of the initial increment in investment will have spent themselves, and national income will again be generated at a rate equal to that prevailing prior to the injection of the additional investment dollar. Table 20.1 illustrates the multiplier process resulting from a $1 increment in investment.

Table 20.1. Multiplier Effects of $1 Increment in Investment
(Marginal propensity to consume equals $\frac{9}{10}$)

Spending period	(ΔY) Income	(ΔC) Consumer expenditure	(ΔS) Savings
1	$ 1.00	$0.90	$0.10
2	0.90	0.81	0.09
3	0.81	0.729	0.081
4	0.729	0.6561	0.0729
5	0.6561	0.59049	0.06561
6	0.59049	0.531441	0.059049
7	0.531441	0.4782969	0.0531441
8	0.4782969	0.43046721	0.04782969
9	0.43046721	0.378420489	0.043046721
..	. . . .	. . . .	. . . .
n			
Total....	$10.00	$9.00	$1.00

Only if the $1 increment in investment continues in successive spending periods will income in any one period tend to rise by the full amount indicated by the multiplier. This will be accomplished when the additional spending is made up of the $1 increment to investment, plus the 90 cents second-round effects of the $1 increment in the preceding spending period, plus the 81 cents third-round effects of the $1 increment made to investment two periods back, etc. In this way the secondary effects of the increment to investment in each of the preceding periods will be concentrated in one period, and the income of the period will be greater by the full $10 in our example.

It should be emphasized that the multiplier effect may work negatively as well as positively. A reduction in investment with other things unchanged will generate a multiple contraction in income.

The multiplier concept should not be taken to represent too much. It really says little more than was said in earlier chapters, that is, a change in investment expenditure will tend to generate an increase or decrease in income. The arithmetical exactitude of the value of the multiplier depends solely on the presumed stability of the marginal propensity to consume. The concept is extremely useful, however, if not taken too strictly, for it does tend to focus attention on the cumulative effects of initial changes in spending.

The concept should not be limited to investment alone, since it applies equally well to any change in spending. The additional spending of a dollar on consumption goods would likewise have generated a tenfold increase in income in the example above. The concept is especially useful in indicating the cumulative effects of changes in the economic variables which are subject to control by government. A change in the government's expenditure without any increase in taxes will serve to increase income by some multiple of the change in the government deficit, provided that private investment plans are not directly affected by the deficit financing.

The effects of a change in the size of the government deficit may be shown in Figure 20.1. An expansion in the rate of government spending which is maintained without an increase in taxes, and with no other offsetting effects, would shift the aggregate spending function upward. The line $C_t + I_t + G$ would shift upward by the amount ΔG, where ΔG represents the increment in government spending. National money income would tend to increase to OX'. The increase in national money income XX' may be seen to be greater than the increase in government spending. The ratio between the increase in income (XX') and the initial increase in government spending (ΔG) is the multiplier. It may be seen that the value of this ratio depends on the slope of the aggregate spending function.[1] The greater the slope, that is, the greater the proportion of an increment in

---

[1] If investment were independent of income, and constant at all levels of income, the slope of the total spending function would be equal to that of the consumption function (assuming also that government spending does not depend on income). This is normally assumed in dealing with the multiplier concept and was employed in the arithmetical example above. However, since we have said that investment expenditure probably increases as income increases (Figure 19.2), the slope of the aggregate spendings function is dependent on the slope of the I function as well as the C function. The multiplier is determined, therefore, by the marginal propensity to spend, not the marginal propensity to consume.

income that will be spent, the greater will be the multiplier effects of a government deficit. If the government decides to cut down its spending without changing the tax rate, a negative multiplier effect will be introduced, and a cumulative reduction in income will set in.

SUMMARY

We may summarize our discussion of national-income theory up to this point by saying that the aggregate expenditure of individuals, firms, government, and foreigners is the primary determinant of national money income. If this total expenditure remains roughly constant over time, national money income will tend to remain stable. If total expenditure on goods and services increases, national money income will tend to increase, and, if total expenditure falls, national money income will fall. Since the expenditure magnitude depends upon the independent decisions of many spending units, there is nothing to ensure stability in the aggregative sense. For this reason, national money income is liable to fluctuate if no positive stabilizing influence is exerted, and such fluctuations in turn generate depression on the one hand and inflation on the other. It is essential that the government exert a positive, instead of merely a passive, role in keeping the national money income at a desirable level. Before we examine this role in more detail, however, we must examine still another important income-determining factor as yet left out of account.

CHAPTER 21

MONEY AND PRICES ENTER THE PICTURE:
THE EQUATION OF EXCHANGE

A major weakness in the theory of income as it was discussed in the preceding chapters is its failure to include monetary factors as important
determinants of the fluctuations in national money income. While concentrating on spending decisions of firms, individuals, and government,
it largely neglects the monetary system and the monetary policy of the
government. This neglect must now be remedied, for the theory is incomplete as it now stands. Monetary factors may act to influence the level of
money income in several ways, and since movements in real income are
likely to accompany shifts in money income, it follows that monetary
factors can also influence real income.

MONETARY POLICY AND DECISIONS TO SPEND

The theory of income determination does not completely leave out of
account monetary influences. A more appropriate statement would be to
the effect that the theory assumes (without making the assumption explicit) that a particular type of monetary system is in existence and that
a certain kind of monetary policy is being followed. It assumes a monetary
system and a monetary policy which will allow decisions to spend to be
carried out without difficulty. For example, when we traced through the
effects of a change in investment expenditures on income, it was assumed
that business firms would have no difficulty in securing the additional
funds required. This is a reasonably realistic assumption in the modern
economy: an expansion in investment expenditure may be carried out by
increased borrowing from the banking system. But the monetary and
banking system in its present form is only one of many conceivable systems which could be utilized. The particular monetary system which does
exist in our economy and some of the alternative monetary policies will
be discussed more fully in later chapters. It will be sufficient here to show
briefly how a change in monetary policy might influence income.

Suppose that national real income is at such a high level that further increases in national money income would lead only to inflation and hence would be undesirable. The analysis of the preceding chapters has shown how a further increase in money income might be prevented by a reduction in government spending or an increase in taxation. But monetary policy can also be effective in accomplishing this objective. Suppose that businessmen (perhaps expecting even more inflation in the future) plan to invest considerably more in subsequent time periods than they are now investing. Anticipating the expanded investment, the government might inaugurate a restrictive monetary policy through its control of the banking system. This would probably take the form of making the borrowing of funds more difficult, for example, by increasing the rate of interest to be charged on bank loans. The way in which the government could curtail borrowing will be explained in some detail in later chapters.

Investment decisions depend to some degree upon the rate of interest. If a project under consideration is expected to yield a return substantially above the rate at which money can be borrowed, sound business practice would indicate that the money should be borrowed and the project undertaken. Consequently, while many potential projects might prove profitable at interest rates of 2 or 3 per cent, these same projects might well prove unprofitable at 5 or 6 per cent rates. Investment expenditure is related to the level of interest rates in an inverse fashion. It was shown in Chapter 12 that the anticipated marginal revenue product of capital goods, along with the interest rate on money capital, affects a firm's investment decisions. If other things are the same, a higher rate of interest will reduce the amount of investment expenditure and thus lower national income.

Not only does the level of interest rates affect spendings decisions of firms; individual families are also affected. Especially important is the influence of the rate of interest on expenditure for residential construction. If money can be borrowed on long-term mortgages for 4 per cent (as was possible for a few years after World War II under the GI home-loan guarantee), the monthly costs of owning a home will be significantly lower than if the money could be borrowed for no less than 6 per cent.

The influence of monetary policy on spendings decisions of firms and individuals is not limited to the effects generated by direct operations on the interest rate. The supply of money can be varied, and this may affect the rate of interest, a large supply tending to make people more willing to give up money, thus lowering the interest rate. The money supply may also have a direct influence on spendings decisions. In addition, as was mentioned earlier, the amount of consumption expenditure depends partly on the real value of assets held by consumers, especially the total purchasing power of their money and government bonds. Monetary policy designed to increase the cash holdings of individuals may, therefore, have a tendency to increase consumption spending and thus to raise income.

THE PRICE LEVEL AND DECISIONS TO SPEND

The theory of income determination sketched in the three preceding chapters utilizes the consumption function, that is, the relation between consumption spending and national money income. Changes in national money income may reflect changes in real income, changes in prices, or some combination of the two. It should now be noted that the consumption function is somewhat affected by the price level; that is, when national income changes it makes some difference whether the change is due just to an altered volume of goods and services or partly to changes in their prices.

The effect of price-level changes on consumption spending was neglected in the discussion of income determination. However, it appears that the whole relationship between consumption spending and money income is influenced significantly by changes in the level of prices. A general reduction of prices will cause an increase in the purchasing power of the relatively liquid assets held by individuals. On the other hand, a general increase in prices reduces the real value of such assets as cash balances and government bonds, and this may cause a shift in the consumption function. It should be recognized, however, that these effects of price-level changes also depend to a great degree on expectations concerning the future movement of prices. That is, if prices fall and consequently increase the real value of cash balances, people may on this account have no greater disposition to consume than before if they expect prices to fall still more.

THE THEORY OF THE PRICE LEVEL

Since monetary and price-level factors, both of which are important in influencing economic fluctuations, are partially left out of account in the theory of income, for many purposes an alternative theory may yield more productive results. The alternative theory concentrates directly on the money supply and people's desires to hold money and tries to explain economic fluctuations in terms of the general level of prices rather than in terms of income.

The monetary approach begins with a fundamental equation which ties together the important variables affecting the general level of prices. If P represents the general level of prices, T the total volume of transactions carried out during the period under study, M the quantity of money, and

V the velocity of circulation of money, *i.e.*, the rate at which money turns over, the equation takes the form $MV = PT$.[1] This is sometimes called the "equation of exchange." From one point of view, the equation states the obvious fact that the amount expended during any period MV equals the value of the goods and services sold PT. The fact that the equation may be a truism does not prevent its being extremely useful.

The equation serves to place the important monetary variables in a precise relationship to each other. In so doing, it allows a logical chain of reasoning on monetary matters to be followed. A glance at the equation shows that an increase in the quantity of money M must be accompanied by either a decrease in velocity V, an increase in the general level of prices P, or an increase in the volume of transactions T. That is, if the supply of money increases, people may either hold it for longer periods on the average, thus decreasing velocity, or they may spend more. If they spend more, the money demand for goods and services is increased. If the supply of goods and services remains unchanged, the increase in money demand will cause prices to be bid up, increasing the price level P. If the increased spending is accompanied by an increase in the volume of goods and services T, as would perhaps be the case in times when resources were unemployed, the price level need not be increased. The equation thus shows that an increase or a decrease in the quantity of money may be counterbalanced by changes in either one or all of the other variables.

If national output is high and resources are fully employed, it is not likely that the physical volume of transactions can be increased a great deal.[2] In addition, it is probable that people will not, in such situations, substantially change their habits concerning the average length of the period for which a unit of money is held; *i.e.*, velocity will not change substantially. In these circumstances, an increase in the quantity of money (and/or money substitutes such as government bonds) will probably exert a primary effect on the level of prices, serving to generate inflation.

On the other hand, if there is significant unemployment and business generally is in a depressed state, an increase in the quantity of money

---

[1] Serious problems are involved in the precise definition of the form of the variables in the equation. Properly, each variable must be in terms of an index number of the composite magnitude represented, and each index number must be related to the same base. See Clark Warburton, "Elementary Algebra and the Equation of Exchange," *American Economic Review*, Vol. 43, pp. 358–361 (June, 1953).

[2] A qualification must be introduced here. Since T represents an index of the total volume of transactions, it includes financial as well as real output transactions. The inclusion of financial transactions creates difficulties in the use of the equation, since an increase in T could come about without an increase in real output, for example, in a stock-market boom. These difficulties may be substantially eliminated in a more rigorous version of the equation, but this cannot be elaborated here.

may exert its primary effect on increasing the volume of transactions with little or no effect on prices. If the increased quantity of money induces more spending, the demand for goods and services will increase. This increased demand need not cause prices to rise, however, if it generates an increase in supply to match the increase in demand. The increased spending will thus serve largely to increase production and employment. However, if expectations are extremely pessimistic, there is the possibility that an increase in the quantity of money may not generate an increase in total spending; the right-hand side of the equation will not be affected at all if velocity declines sufficiently to offset the increase in M. In this case, an increase in the quantity of money would serve merely to increase the cash balances of those groups holding money for longer periods. People, on the average, would simply turn over their money more slowly. Although a decline in velocity might offset an increase in the money supply to some degree, it seems highly unrealistic to assume that it will ever fully do so. An increase in the quantity of money will, therefore, normally generate some increase in spending, thus increasing either the general level of prices or the volume of goods and services produced, or both. A decrease in the quantity of money (or money substitutes) would have effects in the opposite direction from those traced above, serving to decrease the level of prices or the volume of real output unless offset by an increase in the velocity of circulation of the reduced money stock.

The emphasis on the quantity of money as the causal variable in the equation of exchange stems from the fact that it is the one most susceptible to control by the government. Independent shifts in any of the variables may also cause changes in any or all of the others, including the quantity of money. If the average wage earner suddenly decides to hold a larger cash sum in his pocket than he did before, for example, the velocity of the existing money supply will be reduced. This change might cause the banking system to expand the money supply in an offsetting fashion, but if not, a reduction in spending would ensue. Or, in the converse case, if a law were passed requiring that all wage earners be paid daily instead of weekly, the velocity of circulation would be increased. With more frequent pay periods, the typical family would keep the average income dollar on hand for a shorter period of time. Fewer dollars would do the same amount of work in exchanging goods and services. Unless a reduction in the quantity of money accompanied the changed length of pay period, an increase in spending, and consequently an increase in the price level or in the volume of transactions, would result.

Just as with the model used in the theory of income discussed in the preceding chapters, the real usefulness of the equation of exchange depends on its ability to facilitate prediction. This ability depends on whether or not the proper variables have been included and whether or not these variables can be measured and their changes predicted. The equation does bring together important variables. Some of these are, however, extremely difficult to compute statistically, and such a computation would be required for prediction. The equation of exchange has been employed for prediction purposes in the so-called "quantity theory of money." The proponents of this theory generally assume that the velocity of circulation is approximately constant over short time periods. They further assume that the volume of transactions remains unchanged (an assumption which is approximately valid only when the economy is operating at full capacity). With these restrictions placed upon it, the equation of exchange then indicates that an increase or decrease in the quantity of money will exert a direct influence on the level of prices. This version of the "quantity theory" has been properly criticized for neglecting possible shifts in velocity and changes in the volume of transactions.

COMPARISON OF THE INCOME THEORY AND THE EQUATION OF EXCHANGE

The velocity of circulation occupies a position in the monetary theory of economic fluctuations which is similar to that occupied by the consumption-income relationship in the income theory. If velocity does not remain relatively stable over short-run periods, i.e., if people's habits concerning cash holdings do not remain approximately stable over time, changes in total spending cannot be predicted from changes in the quantity of money. Similarly, if the consumption-income relationship is not stable but is subject to erratic fluctuations, changes in money income cannot be predicted directly from changes in the volume of investment expenditure. The appropriateness of these two different theoretical approaches to economic fluctuations depends in part on the relative degree of stability in these two variables, i.e., velocity of circulation and the propensity to consume.

The choice between using the income theory and the monetary theory of economic fluctuations also depends on the purposes which are to be accomplished. The income theory concludes that the decisions of people to spend or save, the decisions of businessmen to invest or not to invest, and the decisions of government budget makers are the active determinants of national money income and thus of the level of real income and prices. This conclusion implies the corollary assumption that the monetary variables (the quantity and velocity of money) are passive, that is, that the monetary system is of such a nature that it adjusts automatically to changes in the spendings decisions. As the following chapters discussing the monetary system will make clear, this assumption is a relatively realistic one in the economy today. This may be shown by a single example.

Suppose that a wave of confidence causes businessmen to expand their investment plans. To finance the added investment, additional funds will be required. These funds may come from expanded bank loans, security sales, or reductions in the cash reserves of firms. In the first case, the money supply (which includes currency and bank deposits) is increased. The increase in M would indicate by way of the equation of exchange that either the price level or the volume of transactions or both would increase. The monetary approach therefore arrives at precisely the same conclusion as the income approach, *i.e.*, that national money income would increase if investment increased. In this example, however, the income approach is the more descriptive, because the initiating force is the decision made by businessmen to increase investment. The increase in the money supply was secondary to this decision and was effected by the additional demand for bank loans.

For other than purely explanatory purposes, however, the monetary approach frequently proves to be more useful. In the example just considered, the added investment expenditure is able to exert an effect on money income only because the supply of money is adjustable. And while the investment decisions are made by private individuals and, therefore, are not directly controllable by government in a free economy, the regulation of the quantity of money has traditionally been accepted as an appropriate governmental function. The monetary approach becomes superior in that it concentrates on the one variable which may be directly controlled, the money supply. The velocity of circulation cannot, of course, be so readily controlled. Decisions to transfer funds from active to inactive accounts, and vice versa, are decisions made by private individuals. But such shifts may be offset by opposite shifts in the quantity of money.

From the comparison of the two approaches, it should be evident that they are alternative and complementary to each other. The theory of income is incomplete unless the influence on total spending exerted by the supply of money and the price level is taken into account. The theory of the price level is incomplete unless shifts in velocity brought about by changes in saving-spending decisions are included.

THE INFLATIONARY PROCESS

It is necessary to discuss more carefully than we have done heretofore the meanings of the terms "inflation" and "deflation." In the first chapter of Part B, the idea of the general price level was introduced. When the general price level is increasing, inflation is said to be occurring. It should be emphasized that the movements in the general or "average" level of prices should be distinguished from movements in individual prices. During inflation, not all individual prices need be increasing, and among those which are increasing the rate of increase need not be uniform. As was shown in Part A, any individual price is set by the particular supply and demand forces affecting that product or service. Some prices may be remaining stable or even declining, while the total economy is experiencing inflation. For example, the prices of automobile tires remained roughly stable during the inflation accompanying and following World War II. This came about because supply increased as rapidly as demand in this particular industry. Inflation is taking place whenever enough prices of important commodities and services are increasing to cause a general index of prices to rise.

Another way of stating the same thing is in terms of the value or purchasing power of money. Inflation is occurring when the purchasing power of the monetary unit is falling. The general price level and the value of money are really two sides of the same coin.

Inflation occurs when an increase in the total money demand for goods and services, total spending, is not offset by an increase in the total supply of goods and services. The increase in total spending may come from any of several sources—investment spending, consumption spending, or government spending. It may be accompanied by an increase in the quantity of money or by an increase in the velocity of circulation or both. The increase in money demand will not affect all goods and services alike, and this fact points up one of the major evils of inflation. Some prices tend to rise faster than others. It is likely that final product prices will be the first general category affected. There may be considerable time lags between the increases in final product prices and increases in the prices of productive services. This time lag may be shortened, however, if sellers of productive services anticipate the increases in product prices, as some labor unions have done, and exert pressure for wage increases in advance.

Let us trace through in very simple terms the effects of an increase in money demand for consumers' goods. Firms will find inventories dwindling and will be quick to realize that they can increase selling prices. The increase in prices will serve to increase business profits in several ways. First of all, inventories may have been purchased at preinflation prices. A profit is secured by merely holding inventory. But this type of profit has sometimes been called "paper profit," because when firms find it necessary to replace inventory they will increase the demand for goods at the wholesale level. Wholesale prices will go up, and the pure inventory profits will vanish. A second source of profits is found in the type of contracts used in purchasing inputs of productive services. Many inputs are purchased on the basis of long-term contractual arrangements. For example, having agreed to pay for labor services at a certain wage rate for a year, the firm is assured of constancy of labor input prices during the contract period even though output prices may increase. Prices of such inputs as utility services are likely to move upward slowly because of regulation by government agencies. A third source of inflationary profit is associated with the capital investment which has been made in fixed plant and equipment. If the capital goods were purchased during a pre-inflation period, depreciation charges are fixed over the length of the life of these assets and do not go up as output prices rise. When replacement becomes necessary, however, the depreciation reserve may not be sufficient to replace fully the fixed capital used up. In this sense, the high profits reported by business firms during periods of inflation reflect in part the failure of the accountants to deduct "true" depreciation charges from gross profits.

While final product prices and profits tend to increase before the prices of productive services or inputs increase, among the various inputs there is a great difference in the rates at which prices rise. In recent years, escalator clauses have been included in some wage contracts. These clauses are designed to tie the rate of wages directly to the cost-of-living price index. But whether or not escalator clauses are used, most strongly organized labor groups are able to keep wage rates roughly in line with upward movements in product prices. Many farmers have been able to secure government guarantees against both inflation and deflation through the device of "parity prices."

Other groups are not so fortunate, and upon them really rests the incidence of the inflationary process. Inflation is extremely harmful to the class of so-called white-collar workers. This group is largely unorganized and is unable to exert political and economic pressure in its own behalf. Wages and salaries paid to this group tend to move slowly during inflation, lagging far behind the upward movement in product prices (the cost of living) and in wage rates for strongly organized groups. But the most severely hit of all groups during inflation is that composed of individuals and families living on relatively fixed incomes. This group includes those living on pensions, beneficiaries of annuity contracts, recipients of bond interest, social-security beneficiaries, etc. For this group, an increase in the general level of prices is equivalent in result to the imposition of a tax which cannot be shifted to anyone else. In one sense, the best way of looking at the redistributive effects of inflation is through a comparison of its results with a tax and expenditure scheme which would have the same effects. A tax levied on all people with relatively fixed incomes, with the proceeds of the tax to be paid out to all people with more flexible incomes (stockholders, organized wage earners), would produce redistributive effects precisely equivalent to inflation.

In addition to these harmful redistributive effects, general inflation contains other evils. One of the greatest of these is the ever-present potential danger that a runaway or explosive inflationary process will be developed. If inflation continues long enough or rapidly enough to convince the general public that the upward movement in prices is permanent and will continue without reversal, explosive inflation is apt to ensue. If an individual expects prices to keep on rising, he will change his spending pattern and make every effort to transform his assets so as to take advantage of the expected price increases. Cash will be a highly undesirable form of asset in such cases; individuals will try to convert cash assets into real property, such as land, buildings, automobiles, or equity shares such as common stock. This very attempt to convert cash into other assets (increasing velocity of circulation) will drive up the price level, and the expectation of rising prices will be fulfilled. This is an example of a situation in which people's thinking that something will happen and acting accordingly will itself ensure that the expected will happen.

It should be recognized that the stability that is present in the general level of prices stems always in part from the continued faith of the people in stability. There always exists in the public mind some vague sort of idea concerning "the value of the dollar," usually based on the average purchasing power of money over several years. The mere existence of this idea serves to keep people from losing faith in the monetary system and letting inflation become explosive. If this faith is lost, however, prices skyrocket and economic chaos is the almost inevitable result.

A type of inflation slightly different from that just discussed has come to be recognized in recent years; this is "repressed" inflation. It usually comes about when the money supply expands but this expansion is not allowed to exert the usual effect on prices because of direct controls imposed on prices by the government. In this case, the excess purchasing power will result in added expenditure on goods and services not subject to control, in the appearance of black markets, in expanded security purchases, and in the accumulation of cash balances creating a source of inflationary spending once the controls are removed. The whole problem of direct controls over prices will be discussed more fully in Part C.

THE DEFLATIONARY PROCESS

"Deflation" is said to be occurring when the general price level is falling. The deflationary process, however, is not symmetrical to the inflationary process, as we have indicated. With a net reduction in total spending, downward pressure is exerted on prices, but many prices do not move downward as readily as they move upward. This difference may be attributed to several causes.

First of all, the character of markets is important here. In the case of upward shifts in money demand, prices will tend to be increased regardless of the type of market. In the case of downward shifts in demand, however, the markets which are monopolistic must be distinguished from those which are competitive. If all markets were fully competitive, prices would be set by the impersonal forces of demand and supply, and they would move downward as easily as upward in response to demand shifts. In the real world, however, few markets are fully competitive. Sellers generally do possess some control over price and, therefore, may not immediately respond to a reduction in demand with price reductions. Many will prefer to adjust output rather than price. There will be some price reductions, but, in general, prices are likely to be slow in moving downward. Firms in industries which are oligopolistic will be fearful of setting off price-cutting wars by initiating price reductions.

Another reason for the failure of output prices to move downward readily is the stickiness of input prices to firms. If a firm is to reduce output prices substantially, it must be able to reduce variable costs. This requires a reduction in input prices. But sellers of inputs, notably labor, may choose to accept unemployment and layoffs rather than take wage cuts.

The longer the deflationary process continues the more probable it is that significant price reductions will extend to all markets. And there are other steps which amount to almost the same thing as price reductions. Services are expanded and merchandise is frequently improved in quality.

The redistributive effects of deflation are similar to those of inflation, except, of course, in the opposite direction, but they are not likely to be so significant because of the stickiness in prices. Those in the fixed-income group stand to gain at the expense of other groups in society. This remains true, however, only so long as they can retain their source of income. The white-collar workers may gain in relative income position. But the threat of unemployment is constantly present during such periods, so any gains made are precarious ones. As a matter of fact, there are few groups who actually gain during a period of deflation and depression. It is also important to note that those who might gain are not powerful politically. This is another way in which deflation is not symmetrical with inflation. Many groups which are politically powerful feel that they have a vested interest in inflation and, therefore, seem likely to support governmental policies which are designed to encourage it. But after the great deflation-depression of the 1930's, there will be little support in the foreseeable future for policies aimed actively at promoting deflation or allowing deflation to continue once it has started.

The deflationary process affects expectations as does the inflationary process, but, again, in the reverse direction. If people once get the idea that prices are going to continue to fall, their own actions will ensure that prices will fall. With the expectation of falling prices, cash will become desirable as an asset form. Real property and equity shares will become undesirable and will fall in price. Under such circumstances, little may be gained from a policy aimed merely at increasing the money supply. The increase may be absorbed by additions to inactive cash balances and may affect total spending and, therefore, prices and incomes, little if at all. This point will be seen to be of considerable importance in Part C, where the relative effectiveness of monetary policy and of fiscal policy are compared.

CHAPTER 22

BANKS CREATE MOST OF OUR MONEY

An economist has been described as a man who knows all about money and does not have any of it. Like most epigrams, this one states only a partial truth. The fact is, of course, that the economist does not know all about money. It might be more accurate to say that an economist is a man who knows that what most people believe about money is not true.

One of the popular misconceptions is the belief that money is valuable because it is "backed up" by something of value. It is pointed out, for example, that one can take a dollar bill to the bank and get in exchange a silver dollar, and the silver, it is supposed, has some kind of intrinsic value. While it is true that the silver in a silver dollar is worth more than the paper in a paper dollar, it would be a mistake to assume that the value of the paper dollar results from the value of the silver with which it is backed up, and this for two reasons.

In the first place, much of the value which the silver dollar possesses derives from the fact that silver is used as money; if silver were to be demonetized, much of the demand for silver would disappear, and silver would lose a considerable fraction of its worth. It can scarcely be argued that paper money is valuable because it is redeemable in silver, and silver, in turn, is valuable because it is used as money.

A second point to be made in this connection is that a silver dollar contains considerably less than a dollar's worth of silver, the exact value of the silver in a dollar fluctuating with each change in the market price of silver. If one wished to buy silver, he would do better to buy it on the silver market than to get it at the bank. And what may be even more disturbing is that there is less silver in ten dimes, four quarters, or two half dollars than there is in a silver dollar. Since ten dimes do, in fact, exchange for a silver dollar, it seems reasonable to suppose that the value of neither the dimes nor the dollars is determined by the value of the silver which they contain. A paper dollar and a silver dollar are not fundamentally different; the only significant difference is that the silver dollar uses a somewhat more expensive raw material than the paper dollar uses.

But both are "token" money; both are valued far beyond the worth of the materials used in their manufacture.

Since January 31, 1934, the U.S. dollar has been defined as $15\frac{5}{21}$ grains of gold $\frac{9}{10}$ fine, which is equivalent to $35 per fine ounce. If the dollar is by definition $\frac{1}{35}$ of an ounce of gold, then $\frac{1}{35}$ of an ounce of gold must be worth $1, and the price of gold will not fluctuate below that price as long as the legal definition of a dollar remains unchanged. If one could take a $5 bill to the bank and get in exchange for it a $5 gold piece containing $\frac{5}{35}$ of an ounce of gold, he could get $5 worth of gold for his paper money. Prior to 1934, one could redeem his paper money in this way and receive in exchange for paper its face value in terms of gold. But since that time gold coins have not been permitted to circulate. If one cannot get gold in exchange for paper money, it is clear that paper money is not valuable because it is secured by gold.

As a final confusing element it may be observed that the Federal Reserve Banks are required to hold reserves against Federal Reserve notes consisting of 25 per cent in gold certificates and the remainder in acceptable securities of the United States government and business firms. That is to say, our most important type of currency is backed up mainly by I O U's of businessmen and government—promissory notes and government bonds; our money is backed up by debt! The relative importance of the several kinds of money in circulation in the United States is indicated in Table 22.1.

Table 22.1. Kinds of Money in Circulation in the United States, November, 1953
(In millions of dollars)

	Amount	Per cent of total
Gold certificates...................................	$ 36	0.03
Credit money issued by the government:		
Token coins......................................	1,816	1.26
Silver certificates................................	2,121	1.47
U.S. notes.......................................	321	0.22
Credit money issued by the Federal Reserve Banks:		
Federal Reserve notes............................	26,249	18.19
Federal Reserve bank notes.......................	192	0.13
Credit money issued by other banks:		
National bank notes..............................	72	0.05
Demand deposits.................................	113,480	78.65
Total...	$144,287	100.00

Source: *Federal Reserve Bulletin.* The figures show amounts outside the Treasury and the Federal Reserve Banks. Federal Reserve bank notes and national bank notes are being retired from circulation. The $36 million worth of gold certificates represents the amount which has been lost, destroyed, or sent abroad; gold certificates do not actually circulate.

Since silver certificates are backed up by silver dollars which do not contain a dollar's worth of silver, and since gold certificates do not circulate anyway and are backed up by gold which is not permitted to circulate, and since Federal Reserve notes are backed up by gold certificates and instruments of debt, what does determine the value of money?

By the value of money is meant essentially the same thing as is meant by the value of anything else; *i.e.*, the quantity of other things which it will command in exchange. If a given amount of money will exchange for a considerable quantity of other goods, money may be said to have a relatively high value; if the quantity of other goods which can be obtained with the given amount of money decreases, the value of money may be said to be decreasing. That is to say, if the price level is high, the value of money is low; if prices are low, the value of money is great. What the value of money is at any particular time is the resultant of the several complex forces which were described in the preceding chapter. Among these factors is the quantity of money. If there is an oversupply of money relative to the work it has to do, whether the currency is backed up dollar for dollar with gold coins which are allowed to circulate freely or whether the money supply consists of unredeemable paper, prices will be high; *i.e.*, the value of money will be low.

SOURCES OF THE MONEY SUPPLY

In the United States at the present time, only about 3 per cent of the money supply is issued by the United States Treasury; about 18 per cent is issued by the Federal Reserve Banks, and the remainder—almost 80 per cent—is issued by private banks. *Demand deposits held in local banks represent the bulk of our money supply.* If the total quantity of money becomes too great or too small, the perils of inflation or deflation become real. As we observed earlier, the quantity of money is important because it is the one variable affecting the level of prices and incomes which is most easily controllable by government. It is, indeed, a major function of the Federal Reserve System to control the supply of money in such a way that neither too much nor too little is in circulation.[1] This suggests several questions which need to be answered. What actually determines the amount of money in existence? What is meant by demand deposits, and why are they included as a part of the money supply? How does the

---

[1] *Cf.* "Statement before the Subcommittee on General Control and Debt Management of the Joint Committee on the Economic Report, 82nd Congress," by Malcolm Bryan, President, Federal Reserve Bank of Atlanta, Mar. 19, 1952, p. 6: "The Federal Reserve System, as a central banking organization, has only one fundamental power, the power to create and to extinguish bank reserves, either through its own investment account or by lending to commercial banks, and thus to influence the supply of money. All other powers are merely incidental or facilitating."

central bank influence the amount of demand deposits held by local banks? These questions will be considered in this and following chapters.

The American commercial-banking system consists of two sets of banks: the local banks ("state" or "national" banks) and the Federal Reserve Banks. All national banks are "members" of the Federal Reserve System, and state banks which qualify may join the System. The local banks are commercial banks; *i.e.*, their primary function is to accept deposits of individuals and firms and to make loans for relatively short periods, usually thirty to ninety days. There are twelve Federal Reserve Banks located throughout the country. These are "bankers' banks," which deal primarily with the member banks, the United States Treasury, and foreign governments. All member banks are required to buy stock in the Federal Reserve Bank of their district and to maintain a deposit there. The member bank's deposit in the Federal Reserve Bank serves two important functions: (1) it assists in the "clearing" of checks drawn on one bank and deposited in another, and (2) it serves as the "reserve" which the member bank must maintain against its own demand deposits. Both of these functions will be explained in the discussion which follows.

THE FORMATION OF A COMMERCIAL BANK

We shall illustrate the operation of the commercial-banking system by supposing that we organize a local bank and by observing the changes that take place in its balance sheet as it engages in various transactions. The balance sheet is the statement of assets, liabilities, and net worth of the bank listed by major categories.[1] The principal liability consists of deposits, since a bank can be considered to owe that amount to its depositors.

Suppose that we are able to interest local investors in organizing a new bank in our town. We form a corporation and issue 4,000 shares of capital stock with a par value of $100, thus acquiring $400,000 in cash.[2] At this early point in the bank's history, the balance sheet will look like this:

ABC National Bank
Balance Sheet No. 1

Assets		*Capital and liabilities*	
Cash	$400,000	Capital Stock	$400,000
Total	$400,000	Total	$400,000

[1] See Appendix A.

[2] National banks actually sell their stock above par, which gives rise to "paid in surplus." To simplify the balance sheets, this has been neglected here.

The next step is to find a place to do business. Since we want people to have faith in the security of their deposits, we want to buy an impressive building, perhaps one with a marble front. Suppose that we purchase such a building which costs us a total of $382,000; in addition, we purchase $12,000 in stock in the Federal Reserve Bank, since all member banks are required to do so in the amount of 3 per cent of their own capitalization. The balance sheet now takes on the following form:

ABC National Bank
Balance Sheet No. 2

Assets		Capital and liabilities	
Cash......................	$ 6,000	Capital stock...............	$400,000
Land and building...........	382,000		
Federal Reserve stock........	12,000		
Total...................	$400,000	Total....................	$400,000

Our bank is now ready to begin business. We announce a grand opening day and invite everyone in to see our fine new facilities. We decorate the bank with flowers sent to us by well-wishers; we put on our company manners and behave like fraternity men during rush week. We proudly show off our new vaults, pointing out the thickness of the walls and the extreme care we have taken to make the building burglar-proof. We take special pride in our drive-in window where customers may make deposits and cash checks without leaving their cars, and during the course of the day we persuade a number of people that this is the bank with which they should do business. By the end of the day we find that a total of $100,000 in cash has been deposited with us. For simplicity, let us assume that these are all "demand deposits" subject to check; our savings department is not yet ready to do business. The $6,000 cash which we had before the opening will probably suffice as "till money." Consequently, we shall deposit the entire $100,000 in new cash in the Federal Reserve Bank. These actions are reflected in the third balance sheet.

ABC National Bank
Balance Sheet No. 3

Assets		Capital and liabilities	
Cash......................	$ 6,000	Capital stock...............	$400,000
Deposits in Federal Reserve..	100,000	Demand deposits............	100,000
Land and building...........	382,000		
Federal Reserve stock........	12,000		
Total...................	$500,000	Total....................	$500,000

If the legal reserve requirement is 20 per cent, our bank must maintain a deposit in the Federal Reserve Bank equal to at least 20 per cent of our demand deposits.[1] The legal reserve against our present deposits of $100,000 would be $20,000. Since at the moment we actually have a deposit in the Federal Reserve Bank of $100,000, we have excess reserves of $80,000. This is shown in step 1 of Exhibit 1. For convenience, only that part of the balance sheet necessary to an understanding of the process of deposit creation is shown in Exhibit 1.

THE DEPOSIT MULTIPLIER

As shown in step 2, our bank can safely lend $80,000—the amount of its excess reserves. The borrowers will probably take the proceeds in the form of checking accounts at the ABC Bank.[2] But they are unlikely to leave these sums in the bank long, since they have borrowed and are paying interest in order to be able to make purchases, for example, of merchandise with which to replenish stocks. (We are assuming that the original $100,000 in deposits will remain in the bank somewhat longer, since it is made up in part of funds placed in the bank for safekeeping or to be held as a reserve for contingencies.)

Step 3 assumes that all of the checks drawn against the loan-created demand deposits in the ABC Bank are deposited in other commercial banks. This would cause our bank to lose $80,000 in reserves at the Federal Reserve Bank, since checks in that amount would be charged to

---

[1] The pattern of legal reserve percentages in effect in February, 1954, is given in the table below:

Bank	Net demand deposits			Time deposits		
	Legal mini- mum	Legal maxi- mum	Actual	Legal mini- mum	Legal maxi- mum	Actual
Central Reserve City.....	13	26	22	3	6	6
Reserve City.............	10	20	19	3	6	6
Country.................	7	14	13	3	6	6

Source: *Federal Reserve Bulletin.*

[2] For the sake of simplicity, we shall ignore the amount of interest collected by the bank. If interest is charged at the annual rate of 4 per cent and the loans are made for 90 days, the interest or "discount" on loans of $80,000 would be $800. Normally the discount is applied at the time the loan is made, and the Loans and Discount account would be $80,000, demand deposits would be increased by $79,200, and the $800 would be placed in Interest Collected but Not Earned, a liability account. At the end of the 90 days, the interest collected would go into the Undivided Profits account. It should be noted that this system makes it possible for the bank to advertise a 4 per cent interest rate while actually charging more, since borrowers do not actually secure use of the full $80,000.

Exhibit 1
Expansion of Money Supply by Banking System
(Assuming uniform 20 per cent reserve requirement)

Step 1. ABC National Bank has $80,000 in excess reserves

ABC NATIONAL BANK

Federal Reserve account.. $100,000	Deposits....... $100,000

Step 2. And can safely lend this amount, building up borrowers' deposit accounts

ABC NATIONAL BANK

Federal Reserve account.. $100,000	Deposits....... $180,000
Loans................. 80,000	

Step 3. The newly created deposits are likely to be quickly checked out. In clearing process ABC's reserves may be reduced to minimum

ABC NATIONAL BANK

Federal Reserve account... $20,000	Deposits....... $100,000
Loans................. 80,000	

Step 4. But checks on ABC Bank are deposited in various banks which, in the clearing process, secure larger Federal Reserve accounts

STAGE II BANKS

Federal Reserve accounts.. $80,000	Deposits........ $80,000

Step 5. Having excess reserves of $64,000, these banks can safely lend that amount

STAGE II BANKS

Federal Reserve accounts.. $80,000	Deposits....... $144,000
Loans................. 64,000	

Step 6. As newly created deposits are checked out, reserves are reduced to legal minimum

STAGE II BANKS

Federal Reserve accounts.. $16,000	Deposits........ $80,000
Loans................. 64,000	

Step 7. But banks in which checks are deposited can, in turn, extend credit and create deposits

STAGE III BANKS

Federal Reserve accounts.. $64,000	Deposits....... $115,200
Loans................. 51,200	($64,000 + $51,200)

And so on, until a theoretical maximum of $500,000 in deposits can exist in the system because of the $100,000 in cash originally deposited in the ABC National Bank. (The $500,000 in deposits includes this original deposit.) Loans will total $400,000, since all but the first deposit have been created through bank loans.

the ABC Federal Reserve account in the clearing process. The amount would be credited to reserve accounts of banks in which the checks were deposited. As shown in step 4, these "Stage II" banks now have new deposits and new reserves of $80,000, of which $64,000 are excess reserves by virtue of our assumed 20 per cent legal reserve requirement.

New loans can safely be made in the amount of these excess reserves. Thus deposits in Stage II banks can be increased by $64,000 to $144,000. As the newly created deposits are checked out, reserve accounts are lowered to the legal minimum of $16,000, but Stage III banks now have excess reserves, permitting them to lend $51,200, as shown in the last partial balance sheet of Exhibit 1.

Eventually a theoretical maximum of $400,000 in new loans and new deposits can be created by the system. Counting the $100,000 originally deposited in the ABC National Bank, there would exist $500,000 in deposits, which would be based on the original $100,000 cash deposit. The $100,000 will all have become required reserves, the ownership of which will have been spread among a large number of banks as shown in the third column of Table 22.2. The table also summarizes the new deposits

Table 22.2. Deposit Expansion by Commercial Banks

	New deposits	New loans (80%)	Reserves kept (20%)
ABC Bank....................	$100,000	$ 80,000	$ 20,000
Stage II banks.................	80,000	64,000	16,000
Stage III banks................	64,000	51,200	12,800
Stage IV banks................	51,200	40,960	10,240
Stage V banks.................	40,960	32,768	8,192
Stage VI banks................	32,768	26,214	6,554
Stage VII banks...............	26,214	20,971	5,243
....	....	....	....
Other banks...................	104,858	83,887	20,971
All banks.....................	$500,000	$400,000	$100,000

and loans which would appear at each of the stages in the expansion. It should be noted that the deposits which remain after newly created deposits are checked away are the ones which are counted at each stage in this table. (Those which are checked away come to make up the more stable deposits which are counted at the next stage.)[1]

The assumptions upon which the foregoing bank-credit expansion process was based were kept somewhat unrealistic in order to simplify the illustration. No additional cash was assumed to be required for till money

[1] It may be noted that the deposit multiplier discussed here is analytically similar to the income multiplier discussed in Chapter 20. The ratio of additional saving to additional income occupies the same place in the income multiplier that the required-reserve ratio does in the deposit multiplier.

by the bank despite the build-up of deposits. Actually there would probably be some increase in this use of cash, so that less than $100,000 of the new cash would find its way into the Federal Reserve Banks to serve as new reserves. It was also assumed that all checks drawn were deposited in banks *other* than those against which they were drawn. Actually, some checks are redeposited in the same bank. If officials of the ABC Bank, for example, had been willing to take a chance that this would happen, they could have expanded loans by somewhat more than $80,000. Had they done so, however, the expansion possible in Stage II would have been less than that shown. The ultimate result would have been the same—a theoretical maximum of $500,000 in deposits throughout the system because of the $100,000 in new cash made available by depositors to any one bank or any combination of banks.

Contractions of the Money Supply

The multiple expansion of deposits by the banking system based on the acquisition of new reserves can (and frequently does) work also in reverse. A *loss* of reserves can force a multiple *contraction* in loans and demand deposits and hence in the nation's money supply.

Using the same simplifying assumptions as before, suppose that $10,000 in cash is withdrawn from the ABC National Bank and remains outside the banking system. Assume that the position of the bank prior to this withdrawal was as follows (with respect to the key accounts):

ABC National Bank

Federal Reserve account	$20,000	Deposits	$100,000
Loans	80,000		

In order to secure the $10,000 cash which depositors demand, the ABC Bank will withdraw that amount from its Federal Reserve account. Its position will then be as follows:

ABC National Bank

Federal Reserve account	$10,000	Deposits	$90,000
Loans	80,000		

The ratio of reserves to deposits is now below the required 20 per cent—a condition which must quickly be rectified. Our bank will be obliged to tighten up on credit in order to secure a net repayment of loans so as to obtain the funds needed to build up the reserve account. Since deposits are now $90,000, the reserve account must be brought up to $18,000 (20 per cent of $90,000). Loans outstanding must be reduced by $8,000 to raise the bank's Federal Reserve account by this amount. For simplicity, we are assuming that all checks paid to the ABC Bank in retirement of loans are drawn against other banks. Our bank would then have a favorable clearing balance of $8,000 at the Federal Reserve Bank; this would build its reserve account up to the required $18,000, the key accounts appearing as follows:

ABC National Bank

Federal Reserve account	$18,000	Deposits	$90,000
Loans	72,000		

Since other banks would lose $8,000 in reserves due to unfavorable clearing balances, they, in turn, would be forced to reduce loans under the assumption that they had loaned as much as possible. They would be forced to reduce loans outstanding by $6,400; their deposits would be down by $8,000. The induced contraction of loans in the next stage would be $5,120, and deposits in this stage would fall by $6,400. The end result of the process would be a maximum theoretical contraction of $50,000 in demand deposits and $40,000 in bank loans as a result of the $10,000 loss of cash to the banking system. In this way a fractional-reserve banking system tends to be subject to sharp contractions as well as expansions of deposits and loans. The nation's money supply may be subjected to large fluctuations resulting from attempts made by the public to change the form of their asset holdings from demand deposits to cash or from cash to deposits.

SUMMARY

The models of deposit expansion and contraction which have been used in this chapter have been artificially simplified in order to bring some essential elements into bold relief. The fundamental fact is that most of our money supply is not issued directly by the United States Treasury but is created (and destroyed) by the commercial banks. Actually, the Federal government, through operations of the Treasury and Federal Reserve System, has a good deal of control over the money supply (as will be explained in the next chapter). The fact remains, however, that under our banking system the money supply is governed to a substantial extent by the actions of bankers and private borrowers. When waves of optimism or pessimism affect their actions, the fractional-reserve system permits sharp increases or decreases in the money supply to occur.

As was pointed out in Chapter 20, an increase in the supply of money, under conditions of full employment, will probably not be offset by a reduction in velocity or an increase in transactions and will consequently exert an inflationary effect. A sharp contraction in the money supply, on the other hand, is likely to cause a general fall in prices. Thus the commercial-banking system, operating on a particularly vulnerable fractional-reserve basis, exerts a powerful influence on our economic well-being. This has led to a measure of central regulation of the banking business which will be described in the next chapter.

CHAPTER 23

THE FEDERAL RESERVE SYSTEM CONTROLS
THE MONEY SUPPLY

Some notice was taken of the Federal Reserve System in the last chapter, but its role there may have appeared to be only a passive one of holding legal reserves for member commercial banks and acting as a clearinghouse for checks. Actually, the System has the important positive power of influencing the lending operations and consequently the money-creating capacity of commercial banks throughout the nation. In large measure this control power is exercised by means of actions which increase or decrease the reserve accounts of member banks in the Federal Reserve Banks.

The principal controls utilized by the Federal Reserve System are summarized in the following listing. Each will be discussed in some detail:

1. Adjustments in rediscount rates
2. Changes in legal reserve requirements of member banks
3. Open-market operations
4. Moral suasion
5. Selective credit controls

ADJUSTMENTS IN REDISCOUNT RATES

When an individual borrows from a commercial bank, the latter frequently "discounts" the loan by the amount of interest charged, turning over to the borrower only the remainder of the capital sum. The bank may, in turn, "rediscount" the businessman's note at the Federal Reserve Bank in its district, that is, borrow and leave the note as collateral. This action adds to the reserve account of the borrowing bank, thus increasing its ability to make further loans. Since the commercial bank's discount rate generally exceeds the Federal Reserve's rediscount rate, the operation is profitable to the former as long as the demand for loans by businessmen is sufficiently brisk.

Instead of rediscounting commercial paper (businessmen's notes), a commercial bank may borrow from the Federal Reserve Bank on its own note. In either case, the Federal Reserve credit extension builds up the commercial bank's reserve, permitting the bank to make additional loans of approximately the amount of its borrowing and making possible a much greater expansion of deposits by the banking system as a whole (in the manner described in the last chapter).

Although the Federal Reserve Banks are not required to lend to member banks upon application, they have almost invariably been willing to do so provided that satisfactory collateral is offered. Consequently, an important method by which the System is able to encourage or discourage borrowing by the banks is through adjustment of the rediscount rate. Lowering this interest rate tends to make borrowing by the banks more profitable, while raising the rate discourages bank borrowing.

When the Federal Reserve System was established in 1913, it was thought that the rediscount rate would be a powerful device in the hands of the central-banking (Federal Reserve) authorities, permitting them to check the expansion of bank credit, and consequently the money supply, in periods of inflation and to encourage the expansion of commercial loans when deflation threatened. In part, this expectation has been fulfilled, but it has been found to be more difficult to encourage expansion of credit by this device than to inhibit credit extension. When excess reserves of the banking system are large, as they were during the 1930's, the rediscount rate is of little significance, since banks do not need to borrow. In addition, the large volume of "near reserves" acquired by the banks during and after World War II in the form of government securities diminished their need to borrow and hence reduced the importance of the interest rate charged by the Federal Reserve Banks, as will subsequently be explained. During the early 1950's when reserves were smaller, there was some revival of the efficacy of the rediscount, or borrowing, rate as a control device.

CHANGES IN LEGAL RESERVE REQUIREMENTS

It should be easy to see that a very direct and powerful method of government control of the supply of bank money is the changing of the percentage reserves required to be held against deposits. If the commercial banks have large excess reserves on deposit with the Federal Reserve Banks, and hence are in a position to make loans and investments in large volume, the authoritative raising of reserve requirements can wipe out millions of dollars in excess reserves at the stroke of a pen.

The power of the Board of Governors to change legal-reserve ratios is limited by Congressional authorization. As indicated in the previous chapter, reserve requirements in relation to demand deposits as of February, 1954, were 22, 19, and 13 per cent, respectively, for Central Reserve

City (New York and Chicago), Reserve City, and Country banks. Historically, required ratios have almost doubled; they were 13, 10, and 7 per cent, respectively, in 1917; these percentages correspond with the minimum ratios which the Federal Reserve Board could now legally impose.

The changing of required reserves is a device which is used infrequently. Congress is not always willing to authorize the changes in maximum reserve ratios which Federal Reserve authorities deem desirable. Even apart from the matter of Congressional authorization, there remains the problem of the uneven status of the various commercial banks within each of the three categories. At the same time that some banks have large excess reserves, others may have little more than the minimum needed against their deposits. A raising of legal ratios then places the latter banks in a difficult position, necessitating such measures on their part as the liquidation of securities or borrowing from the Federal Reserve Banks. The Federal Reserve authorities are generally reluctant to impose controls which have a very uneven impact on the operation of different banks. The raising of legal-reserve ratios is consequently not so practicable a measure as it at first appears to be. At times, however, it has been employed effectively. There are no comparable problems in lowering reserve requirements, but, if banks generally already have excess reserves, this action may have little influence upon the expansion of loans.

OPEN-MARKET OPERATIONS

The most interesting, and in recent years most important, method by which the Federal Reserve System through its Open Market Committee exercises control over bank credit is the purchase and sale of government securities in the "open market" (*i.e.*, in the ordinary markets in which existing securities change hands). The Federal Reserve Banks generally do not buy new government issues directly from the United States Treasury.[1] However, their investment portfolio included about $26 billion of United States securities in early 1954, the bulk of which were purchased in the open market for securities.

When the Federal Reserve authorities wish to encourage the further expansion of bank loans and consequently of the money supply, they can do so by *buying* bonds on the open market. Suppose they buy bonds directly from a member bank: the Federal Reserve Bank simply credits the selling bank's reserve account with the proceeds, placing that bank in an improved position to create new deposits by means of loans or

[1] During World War II, however, the Federal Reserve authorities bought a large volume of bonds directly from the Treasury. The inflationary effect is about the same whether the Federal Reserve System buys new or "secondhand" bonds.

investments. (The banking system is then able to engage in total-deposit expansion to a multiple of the newly created reserve if a sufficient demand exists for bank credit.) If a Federal Reserve Bank buys government bonds from private owners, the result is the same. Normally the seller will deposit the Federal Reserve check or Federal Reserve notes (paper money) which he receives for his bonds in his account at a commercial bank. When his bank, in turn, deposits the Federal Reserve check or notes in its own account at the Federal Reserve Bank, it will build up its excess reserves and be in a position to make further loans. Open-market purchases by the Federal Reserve System thus encourage bank-credit expansion, since their result is to convert United States government bonds held by commercial banks, business enterprises, and individuals into reserves of the banking system.

If the Federal Reserve authorities wish to tighten up on bank credit (curb the creation of money by the commercial banks), they can do so by *selling* United States government bonds or other assets. If commercial banks buy these securities, their reserve accounts are directly reduced by their market value. If individuals and firms buy them, they normally pay by means of checks drawn against their deposits in commercial banks. When such a check clears through the Federal Reserve Bank, it becomes a charge against the reserve account of the bank upon which it was drawn. This reduces the bank's reserve and places the commercial bank in a poorer position to make loans. New applicants for bank loans are more likely to be turned down, some old borrowers may be unable to renew their loans as they come due, and those who are able to secure loans may have to pay a higher rate of interest. As was seen in the previous chapter, a one-billion-dollar reduction in bank reserves, for example, can necessitate something like a five-billion-dollar decrease in demand deposits and hence in the supply of money. This occurs, however, only if banks have loaned to the limit prior to the open-market sales, *i.e.*, if excess reserves were negligible.

Federal Reserve Support of the United States Treasury

The general mechanics of open-market operations have been discussed, but the student cannot understand recent Federal Reserve policy without studying the place of the United States Treasury in the banking picture. A very important job of the Treasury consists in administering the huge national debt ($275 billion early in 1954), that is, selling new United States securities, paying off those which mature (or are redeemed before maturity, in the case of Series E savings bonds), and making interest payments on the public debt (about $6 billion per year). While the Treasury made a strong effort during and after World War II to place United States securities in the hands of individuals, firms, and nonbanking institutions, it was found necessary to sell a very large volume to the commercial banks and to a much lesser extent directly to the Federal Reserve Banks.

When commercial banks buy newly issued government bonds, they are extending credit to the United States Treasury in the same way that they regularly extend credit to businessmen. In exchange for the United States bonds, the Treasury secures demand deposits against which it can draw checks to pay its bills. These Treasury deposits may be in either the Federal Reserve Banks or the commercial banks.

To illustrate the process by which the commercial banks acquire government bonds, suppose the ABC National Bank, which we assume is subject to a 20 per cent legal reserve requirement, has excess reserves of $0.2 million and is consequently in a position to make further loans to business or government. The important accounts might look like this:

ABC National Bank
(In millions of dollars)

Federal Reserve account......... $1.2	Demand deposits............... $5.0
Loans and securities............. 4.0	

Suppose now that our bank wishes to buy additional newly issued United States securities in the amount of its excess reserves. It may do so through the Federal Reserve Bank in its district. The Federal Reserve Bank simply shifts $0.2 million from the ABC Bank's account to the Treasury's account and turns over the new United States securities to the ABC Bank. The key accounts in our bank's balance sheet will then look as follows:

ABC National Bank
(In millions of dollars)

Federal Reserve account.......... $1.0	Deposits....................... $5.0
Loans and securities............. 4.2	

As the United States Treasury pays its bills by drawing down its new $0.2 million in deposits at the Federal Reserve Bank, its checks will be deposited in various banks which will then find themselves with excess reserves in the manner described in the previous chapter. They can then make additional loans to businessmen or to the United States government: to the extent that they lend to the government they will acquire additional United States securities. Thus a maximum of about $1 million in government securities might be acquired by the commercial banks as a whole based on the original credit extension to the government by the ABC National Bank. This illustration indicates the process by which the banks have simply created much of the money with which they have acquired over $60 billion in government securities.[1] This has been made possible by the fractional-reserve banking system and, of course, by the deficit financing on the part of the United States government during the decades of the forties and fifties.

The Federal Reserve Banks during the war and for some years after stood ready to buy all United States securities offered for sale on the open market by banks and others at definite prices which were seldom allowed to change. Why did the Federal Reserve authorities support the United States bond market in this way? They did so in order to aid the Treasury in its tremendous job of debt management. By supporting government-bond prices, the Federal Reserve Banks held down interest rates both on existing bonds and on new bond issues. If U.S. bonds had been permitted to fall in a free market they would have yielded higher rates of return to buyers, and these higher interest rates would have had to be matched by the United States Treasury in selling new bonds.

In addition to the Treasury's desire to keep down interest rates, there is pressure from owners of government bonds to keep their prices from dropping. Bond owners do not wish, of course, to suffer capital losses on securities which they hold, and if such losses are threatened they may be reluctant to subscribe to new government-security issues.[2] During and after World War II, the Federal Reserve System found itself operating a price-support program somewhat akin to the farm-price-support program —it was forced to acquire a large inventory of government securities in much the way that the Commodity Credit Corporation acquires stocks of farm products which no one else wishes to own.

United States Treasury and Federal Reserve officials reached a highly publicized "accord" in March, 1951, which temporarily, at least, permitted the Federal Reserve System to operate with a greater degree of independence. The result was a general (though modest) rise in interest rates on Federal securities and private loans as the Federal Reserve more nearly allowed United States securities to seek their own (lower) price levels. The recent history of the Treasury–Federal Reserve relations will be examined in Part C.

[1] In our example we have assumed that the commercial banks initially had excess reserves. It should be pointed out, however, that even if this were not the case, excess reserves could have been easily created by the sale of securities to the Federal Reserve Banks. This was, in fact, one of the reasons for the sale of new securities to the Federal Reserve System during World War II.

[2] When interest rates rise and bond prices fall, bondholders suffer actual capital losses only if they choose to liquidate their holdings prior to maturity. Regardless of the fluctuations in bond prices, no owner suffers a capital loss if he holds his bonds until the stipulated maturity date, when the Treasury will pay off at full face value. Thus actual capital losses are suffered more often on long-term bonds than on short-term securities. Some analysis of the importance of this point will be made in the next chapter.

MORAL SUASION

The fourth type of Federal Reserve control, frequently designated "moral suasion," consists in the occasional Federal Reserve practice of requesting that member banks exercise more or less restraint in the granting of business loans. The American Bankers Association cooperates in requesting banks' compliance with such requests.

Like other voluntary controls sometimes attempted by government, moral suasion is often relatively ineffective, since the desired action may be contrary to the profit-seeking ends of the member banks. The exercise of certain types of government economic control over individuals and firms is frequently questionable as a matter of policy. If controls are imposed, however, they should be mandatory, uniform in their operation with respect to similarly situated firms, and adequately enforced. Moral suasion on the part of the Federal Reserve authorities fails to meet these tests, especially because some bankers may try to comply with the request while others disregard it. Nevertheless, moral suasion cannot be written off as being entirely impotent, particularly when it is backed by a threat of more direct action such as the denial of loans to noncooperating banks.

SELECTIVE CONTROLS

The controls discussed so far are all *general* credit controls, in that their basic purpose is to affect the commercial banks' capacity to make loans for all sorts of purposes and hence their capacity to create or destroy money. During and after World War II, *selective* credit controls were frequently used by the Federal Reserve System. These selective controls specify credit terms upon which banks may make loans for particular purposes, especially for financing installment purchases by consumers.

Wartime regulation W of the Federal Reserve System imposed a twofold restraint: It specified minimum percentage down payments on listed articles and maximum periods within which loans had to be repaid. The purchaser of an automobile, for example, had to make a one-third down payment and pay the balance within eighteen months. Consumer-credit restrictions applied also to lenders outside the banking system. Personal-loan companies, department stores, appliance dealers, and others who might grant consumer credit were subjected to Federal Reserve regulations. Selective credit controls were terminated November 1, 1947, reimposed in 1948, and removed again in 1949. They were reimposed in 1950 after the outbreak of warfare in Korea, and again were terminated in 1952.

To the extent that selective credit controls curtail bank loans, they tend to hold down the total supply of money. This is not their primary purpose, however. They are designed to restrict consumer demand for the particular articles to which they apply. This has a twofold result: (1) it reduces the upward pressure on the prices of houses, automobiles, household appliances, and similar "hard" goods which is likely to exist during a period of national emergency; and (2) it tends to shift resources out of these consumer-goods fields into munitions production by reducing the profitability of the civilian items to producers. The saving in civilian consumption of such metals as steel, copper, and aluminum is especially important because of their heavy use in war production. It should be noted, however, that selective credit controls are a less certain device for limiting civilian output and forcing a redirection of resources toward the munitions fields than are such non-Federal Reserve controls as limitation orders, priorities, and material allocations (which will be discussed in Part C).

Another type of selective control administered by the System is that over margin requirements for stock purchases. The basic purpose is to limit the use of bank credit for security speculation. During the 1920's, speculators could purchase stocks on as little as 10 per cent margin, borrowing the remaining sums from brokers (who, in turn, borrowed from the banks). This practice has been held partly responsible for the great price boom in securities and the devastating 1929 crash. Stock prices also rose during World War II, causing the Federal Reserve authorities to impose 50 per cent, then 75 per cent, and finally 100 per cent margin requirements. The margin requirement was dropped to 75 per cent in February, 1947, and to 50 per cent in February, 1953.

FEDERAL RESERVE NOTES

So far the discussion has been concerned chiefly with Federal Reserve control over the volume of demand deposits; little notice has been taken of Federal Reserve notes, which constitute most of our supply of currency. Demand deposits and their fluctuations are of much greater importance in the total money supply, but changes in the volume of currency are not without significance.

Federal Reserve notes are paid out by the twelve Federal Reserve Banks to member banks whenever the latter require more cash. Reserve accounts of the member banks are charged for the amount of notes paid out; one sort of Federal Reserve liability is substituted for another type of liability. The only limitation on the issue of Federal Reserve notes is that the Federal Reserve Banks must have on hand gold certificates amounting to at least 25 per cent of the combined total of notes and deposits. Government bonds and other assets owned by the Federal Reserve Banks serve as the additional collateral behind Federal Reserve notes. The 25 per cent reserve requirement does not actually constitute an important check on either the issue of Federal Reserve notes or aggregate deposits (and hence member-bank reserves), since the Federal Reserve Banks have a large excess of gold certificates and since in any event Congress can readily lower the required reserve ratio—and has done so in the past.

In summary, Federal Reserve notes—which constitute our principal hand-to-hand currency—are "backed" principally by government securities, *i.e.*, by national debt, although gold certificates play a secondary and changeable role. The quantity of notes which circulate depends mainly on the need of the country for currency as gauged by the commercial banks. Since the commercial banks secure additional Federal Reserve notes at the cost of reducing their reserves, they have an incentive not to demand unnecessarily large amounts of currency from the Federal Reserve Banks. Also, they have the necessary incentive to turn in Federal Reserve notes which they acquire in excessive volume, since this action will build up their reserve accounts, or, alternatively, pay off debts which they have contracted by borrowing from the Federal Reserve Banks.

GOLD AND THE FEDERAL RESERVE SYSTEM

Since 1934 the United States government has followed the policy of paying $35 per ounce for all gold bullion offered to it for sale. This represents a sharp increase above the value of approximately $21 per ounce which prevailed while the country was on a full gold standard prior to that year.[1] Much of the gold newly mined in this country is sold to the United States Treasury to be buried (again) at Fort Knox, Kentucky. Much new gold from South African, Canadian, and other foreign mines is also sold to the Treasury. Gold movements between countries are one means of settling international balances. When private firms in this country receive gold from abroad, they are also obliged to sell it to the United States Treasury at $35 per ounce.

It is important to see how the Treasury's purchase of gold affects the banking system. When the Treasury buys gold, it pays with a check drawn against its account at a Federal Reserve Bank. It then issues gold certificates against the gold and deposits them in the Federal Reserve Bank in order to replenish the Treasury account there.[2] The United States govern-

---

[1] The price of gold was raised in part because of the peculiar belief of those in authority that raising the dollar price of gold would raise the price of all commodities above their depressed levels. It was also designed (more rationally) to stimulate United States exports by cheapening our dollar relative to foreign monies and to "export unemployment" to foreign countries.

[2] To save the cost of printing actual gold certificates, the more common practice is actually merely to give the Federal Reserve Banks credit on the Treasury Gold Certificate Book.

ment thus virtually acquires the gold "for nothing," but this should not be surprising, since a central government can always issue money in order to buy what it wishes. From a broader point of view, however, the gold is not free, since its sale gives gold sellers command over real goods and services produced in the United States. Its artificially maintained price gives producers a continuing subsidy to the extent that gold sells at a price above what it would sell for if it were not government supported.

Ordinarily, the gold seller deposits the Treasury's check in a commercial bank, which in turn sends it to the Federal Reserve Bank and secures a corresponding addition to its reserve account. Thus the gold purchase increases both deposits in commercial banks and their deposits in the Federal Reserve Banks. Under the system of fractional-reserve requirements, this builds up excess reserves upon which the banking system can base an expansion of deposits to a multiple of the value of the gold purchase.

The effect of gold purchases by the United States Treasury is thus similar to that of open-market purchases, loans by the Federal Reserve Banks to member banks, or the deposit in banks of cash previously hoarded by individuals. In years when a large inflow of gold from abroad occurs, the control job of the Federal Reserve authorities is made more difficult, since this is a money-creating force outside of its jurisdiction. At times the Federal Reserve Banks have been able to offset the gold inflow by means of open-market sales, but the chronic opposition of the Treasury to this activity generally makes it infeasible. The raising of reserve requirements to offset the effect of a gold inflow can only occasionally be resorted to, as pointed out earlier, and the raising of interest rates charged member banks is not very effective, since banks rely less on such borrowing than they did during the first decades of the Federal Reserve System.

FEDERAL RESERVE ACCOUNTS

It may be useful by way of summary to examine a highly consolidated balance sheet for the twelve Federal Reserve Banks (Table 23.1). Inspection of the asset side shows gold certificates held by the Federal Reserve Banks amounting to $20.5 billion. It should be remembered that they must hold gold certificates equal to at least 25 per cent of notes and deposits. The latter accounts, as can be seen on the right-hand side, totaled $48.6 billion. Hence the value of the gold certificates was actually more than 42 per cent of notes and deposits. This illustrates the difference between Federal Reserve and commercial banks' operations. The Federal Reserve System, which makes no attempt to maximize profits, generally has large excess reserves. Member banks, on the other hand, frequently carry small excess reserves. Member-bank reserves of $20.1 billion, as shown among the liabilities of the Federal Reserve Banks, were only about

$0.8 billion in excess of the amount actually needed to be held against demand and time deposits. It is not profitable for the commercial banks to carry substantial excess reserves, since they receive no interest on their deposits in the Federal Reserve Banks. Federal Reserve assets included $25.9 billion in United States government securities—almost $\frac{1}{10}$ of the Federal debt. Discounts and advances were much smaller in magnitude ($0.4 billion), but loans to banks are of greater importance than they were a few years ago.

Federal Reserve notes outstanding of $26.8 billion represent the largest single liability of the System. The volume of such notes increased sharply during the war years and was maintained in the postwar period. The increase in notes compared with prewar years reflects in large part the need

Table 23.1. Combined Federal Reserve Banks Consolidated Balance Sheet as of December 23, 1953
(In billions of dollars)

Assets		Liabilities and capital	
Gold certificates.	$20.5	Federal Reserve notes.	$26.8
U.S. government securities.	25.9	Deposits:	
Discounts and advances.	0.4	Member bank reserves.	20.1
Other assets.	6.0	U.S. Treasury.	0.8
		Foreign and other.	0.9
		Other liabilities.	3.1
		Capital paid in.	0.3
		Surplus	0.8
Total assets.	$52.8	Total liabilities and capital.	$52.8

Source: *Federal Reserve Bulletin.*

for more hand-to-hand currency because of price inflation. To a lesser degree, the increase in such currency has itself been a cause of the inflation.

The final item of particular interest is the United States Treasury deposit ($0.8 billion). The modest amount of this item may be misleading, since it does not reflect turnover (velocity). As was pointed out earlier, the Treasury generally pays for gold by drawing checks against its Federal Reserve accounts, and replenishes these accounts with gold certificates. The Treasury maintains the bulk of its demand deposits in designated commercial banks and as a rule maintains only a minimum operating balance at the Federal Reserve Banks. Usually its deposits in commercial banks are transferred to the Reserve Banks as they are needed, and checks are drawn against them there.

SUMMARY

In this chapter we have noted that substantial changes have taken place in the types of control operations emphasized by the Federal Reserve System. After four decades the System remains an important institutional device through which a measure of central control can be exercised over the nation's money supply. The Federal Reserve Board's performance of this function has been greatly complicated, however, by the great growth in the national debt, by the vast security holdings of the commercial banks, and by the United States government's policy of buying gold at a fixed price. Perhaps the most important danger which is involved in the huge national debt is to be found in the restrictions which it tends to place on the power of Federal Reserve authorities to control inflation.

CHAPTER 24

UNCERTAINTY AFFECTS ASSET HOLDINGS

The national-income and monetary analysis with which Part B has been primarily concerned deals basically with flows of money or of goods and services over time. Some interesting and important economic analysis deals instead with the ownership of capital goods and other assets at a point of time. An understanding of the factors which affect the pattern of asset holdings by individuals and firms is useful to a fuller understanding of national-income determination and possibilities of public control of the over-all level of economic activity.

The first idea which is fundamental to this chapter is the simple one that all assets which exist in the economic system at any time must be owned by someone. These assets consist of all the money (currency and bank deposits), all the securities and other certificates of ownership and debt (*e.g.*, common stocks, bonds, bankbooks, and accounts receivable), and all material wealth (ranging from bread to battleships). Total assets are thus much larger than total capital, or wealth, since the latter consists only in the aggregate of valuable material objects.

SPECULATION

All holders of assets are necessarily speculators. The money value of any asset except that of cash itself may vary through time. And the value of cash in terms of goods for which it will exchange also varies. It was noted especially in Chapter 21 that the value of money rises and falls with decreases and increases in the general level of prices. Fluctuations in security prices are known to be common and sometimes are of dramatic magnitude, as during the 1929 stock-market crash. Inventories, buildings, land, and other items of material wealth frequently change markedly in value.

Even the conservative individual who holds most of his wealth in the form of a deposit in a savings bank, in Series E government bonds, or in life-insurance policies with cash surrender value is speculating (probably without realizing it), since the real value of his savings may be impaired by an inflation, or increased by a deflation, of prices in general. Similarly, the profit position of a manufacturer may be affected more during a given year by changes in the value of his raw-material inventory than by his manufacturing and selling operations. Banks, insurance companies, and other institutions which hold large volumes of securities for purposes of earning interest are highly aware of changes in their market prices.

Professional Speculation

On the other hand, persons known as professional speculators buy and sell securities and commodities solely in the hope of selling at prices higher than those at which they buy. Their purposive speculative activity relates to *particular* price changes rather than to changes in the *general* price level, as is the case with the holder of cash or Series E government bonds. Professional speculation is greatly facilitated by the existence of well-organized security and commodity markets such as the New York Stock Exchange, American Stock Exchange, New York Cotton Exchange, and Chicago Board of Trade.

The professional speculator who feels "bullish" about a particular asset (*i.e.*, expects its price to go up) will purchase the asset and hold it until he feels that the time to sell has arrived. His position during the interval between purchase and sale is known as a "long" one. His profit, if any, is the excess of the selling over the buying price, minus commissions and taxes.

In terms of asset preference, the speculator can be said to show preference for a security or commodity compared with money when he makes his purchases. When his desire for more liquid assets, his "liquidity preference," becomes sufficiently great, he converts the security or commodity into cash by selling it. The buyer, on the other hand, must prefer the security or commodity to cash at the price paid. A general increase in liquidity preference would clearly bring a wave of selling orders, which would lower security prices. This, of course, was the situation during the 1929 crash and in the early years of the great depression of the 1930's.

If a speculator feels "bearish" (*i.e.*, expects a fall in prices), he can, if correct, translate his expectation into a capital gain by taking a "short" position in a security or commodity. This means that he sells first at a specific price and commits himself to make delivery at a later date. He will profit if the asset falls in price so that he can subsequently buy it for less than the price at which he has already sold it.

In the security markets, the short seller first borrows the desired number of shares of the particular security from his broker. (Brokers regularly have possession of a considerable volume of securities which they are holding for the owners, and they cooperate with one another in making such shares available to short sellers.) Next he sells the security at the market price and receives a credit for the amount of the sale to his account with the broker. At a later date he must "cover" his sale by buying the same number of shares of the same security in the market, thus being able to return them to the broker. If his expectation of a price decline was correct, he profits by the transaction.

Dealings in commodities such as wheat, corn, cotton, and eggs are somewhat different, because of the quoting of "futures" prices as well as "spot" prices. Spot prices are simply prices quoted for immediate delivery of the commodity. (These are the only prices quoted for securities.) Futures prices are presently quoted prices applicable to delivery at a future date. For example, the spot price of a particular grade of wheat might be $2.35 per bushel on November 1. On the same day the price of wheat to be delivered in December may be $2.38, March wheat may sell at $2.45, May wheat at $2.48, and July wheat at $2.47. These futures prices quoted on November 1 may be thought of as the spot prices then expected to prevail when those future dates arrive. Different persons, of course, have unlike expectations as to what spot prices will be, but the futures prices reflect a sort of net opinion determined by traders' buying and selling actions.

A grain speculator who possesses storage capacity and who entertains bullish expectations regarding prices can, if he wishes, buy spot grain and store it until a future date in the hope of selling it at a capital gain (even after paying for the storage services). If he does not possess the storage space, he may rent it. A simpler practice, however, is to make use of the futures market. If the speculator were confronted on November 1 with the price quotations indicated above, but believed that next July spot wheat would sell for more than $2.47 per bushel, he could buy July wheat, thereby contracting to accept delivery of a designated quantity next July and to pay $2.47 per bushel upon delivery. If he acts on this opinion and it turns out to be right, he can profit by the difference between the $2.47 which he will pay and the higher spot price at which he can sell the wheat in July.[1] Conversely, if he believes on November 1 that the price in July will be below $2.47, he can sell July wheat. If this bearish position (similar to a short position in the stock market) is correct, he will profit by delivering wheat for $2.47 a bushel which he can actually buy in July for a lower figure.

Speculation has often been criticized, and it has been made the scapegoat by some politicians for depression, unemployment, inflation, and almost every other economic evil. Prices in the speculative markets (security and commodity) do depend to a greater degree on expectations than prices in other markets. For this reason, if a threat of deflation causes traders to become pessimistic (bearish), the speculative markets may

[1] Actually, the contract may change hands many times between November and July, finally coming into the possession of someone who actually wants to accept delivery of the wheat.

aggravate the downswing, and security prices may fall faster than other prices. On the other hand, if inflation is in the offing, and this is anticipated by professional speculators, security prices tend to lead the general price increase and in this way make the inflation worse by creating unduly optimistic expectations.[1]

It is clear, however, that the existence of organized security and commodity markets along with the activity of professional speculators serves a positive social function. Speculators in securities create a more active market which facilitates purchases and sales by individual investors. The availability of such a market tends to encourage the flow of personal savings into equity shares (common stocks). The social usefulness of commodity speculation is even more evident. First of all, it allows the rate of consumption of periodically harvested commodities to be regulated without governmental interference. Second, commodity speculation permits some types of business firms to remove some uncertainty by "hedging," which will be discussed later.

Regarding the first point, it is clear that, if price is to carry out its rationing function properly with respect to agricultural crops which appear at particular seasons, the price must move in such a way as to retard consumption which is proceeding at too fast a rate and to encourage consumption if stocks are being used too slowly. Suppose the rye crop is being consumed too rapidly. Speculators, anticipating a price rise prior to appearance of the next harvest, can (1) buy spot rye and store it and (2) buy rye futures. Both actions tend to raise spot prices for rye. In the first case the increased demand directly raises spot prices. In the second case the increased demand raises futures prices, and this, in turn, makes it more profitable for speculators to buy spot rye and store it, thus indirectly raising spot prices. Higher spot prices retard the rate of use of the existing stock. Thus speculators' vigilance, based on self-interest, promotes a more even utilization of supplies. A similar force operates to increase the rate of use of agricultural stocks when they are being consumed too slowly, spot prices being depressed by speculators' selling orders in the spot and futures markets.

HEDGING

As has been indicated, professional speculators are useful in making possible, in some lines of business activity, a pattern of asset holding known as hedging. Hedging can be defined roughly as betting in two opposite ways on the same thing. Normally, however, this does not make sense, especially if the odds are the same on each bet. If, for example, the

---

[1] The inflation following World War II was not characterized in this way. This inflation was prevented from becoming worse than it actually was by a sort of "depression psychosis" born out of the long depression of the 1930's.

betting odds on an election were even, it would not make sense to bet $50 on the Republican candidate and $50 on the Democrat. However, if you were under some sort of outside compulsion to bet on one candidate—for example, if the Democrat were your father-in-law—it might be desirable to hedge by surreptitiously betting an equal amount on the Republican. Whoever won, you would break even, but at the same time you would be taking no risk of upsetting the harmony of your household by revealing a lack of confidence in your wife's father.

The above example illustrates a fundamental reason for hedging by businessmen; namely, to offset speculative positions which they are forced to assume as incident to carrying on their regular business. The purchase of insurance is a type of hedging. If a businessman owns a building and takes out fire insurance, he is, in effect, placing a bet that his building will burn down. Since the premium is relatively low, because of the small proportion of buildings which actually burn down during any given year, his asset position will not be drastically impaired whether or not the event insured against occurs. Similarly, the purchase of life insurance (which should really be called by the more sinister name "death insurance") is a hedge against complete loss of income to the family in the event of the insured's demise.[1] It is essentially a bet with the company that one will die during a certain period—a sort of heavenly hedge.

The varieties of hedging which are of greatest economic interest consist of actions taken as protection against *unfavorable price changes*. A person of considerable wealth, for example, can hedge against unfavorable changes either in individual prices or in the general price level by keeping part of his wealth in a highly liquid form such as bank deposits and the rest in such assets as real estate and common stocks. In a period of inflation, his cash will decline in real value, but his real estate and stocks will probably maintain their real value. In a period of deflation, the gain in real value of his cash will tend to offset the reduction in dollar value of his other holdings.

Hedging is frequently practiced in businesses in which storage of a commodity is a regular part of their operations. For example, eggs are regularly placed in cold storage during the spring and early summer months when production exceeds consumption. If a firm is to be in the cold-storage business, it must take a "long" position in eggs, that is, hold inventories which may either increase or decrease in value with changes in the market price of fresh eggs. In order to minimize the risk of a price decline, the firm can take an offsetting short position. It can sell egg futures in approximately the amount of its egg inventories. If egg prices fall,

---

[1] Insurance should not be bought against the life of (ordinary) children, since, from an economic point of view, they are liabilities rather than assets. (Farm children are sometimes an exception.)

the loss in inventory value will be approximately offset by the gain on the futures sale, since when the delivery date arrives the storage firm's obligation can be met by the delivery of eggs which are worth less than the buyer of eggs has agreed to pay. The speculative risk is largely shifted from the cold-storage firm to a professional speculator. Normally the egg company will secure the going rate of return on the capital it has invested in storage capacity, since the "spread" between futures and spot prices is usually about equal to the cost of storage from that date to the future date.

HEDGING BY FINANCIAL INSTITUTIONS

The asset holdings of financial institutions such as insurance companies, building and loan associations, investment trusts, and commercial credit corporations, like the egg dealer's inventory, are subject to value fluctuations; consequently, hedging is often vitally important to conservative management. The hedging process in this case does not involve the use of futures markets but consists rather in arriving at a pattern of asset holding which offers some protection against a decline in security prices.

Managers of financial institutions are constantly torn between two conflicting desires. On the one hand, they like to see interest rates rise so that they can secure a greater return on *new* funds placed in their care or on cash which becomes available when maturity dates are reached for bonds which they own. On the other hand, higher market interest rates mean lower market prices for bonds already in their portfolios. These paper capital losses would be transferred into actual capital losses if the bonds were sold.

In order to make this important point clear, let us consider a corporate bond with a $100 face value which pays $4 per year in interest. This indicates that if the bond were originally sold at par, the market rate of interest at the time of issue was 4 per cent for bonds with similar risk characteristics and maturity dates. Suppose the market rate of interest rises to 5 per cent. The bond which we are considering must fall in market price; no sensible buyer will now pay $100 for it, since it pays $4 per year in interest whereas $100 used to purchase a newly issued bond will yield $5 per year. If the older bond had no maturity date (as was true of British "consuls"), it would fall to $80 in market price ($C = \$4/.05$). If it had a very distant maturity date (say 1999), it would fall nearly that much in price. If, however, it was due to mature (*i.e.*, return the $100 face value) in the near future, it would fall only slightly in price. Financial institutions and other holders of marketable bonds are fearful of increases in interest rates to the extent that they hold bonds which bear distant maturity dates. At the same time, as we have just said, they favor higher interest rates in so far as they have new funds with which to purchase securities because of the favorable income effects.

Hedging on the part of financial institutions is inherently more difficult in nature than the variety previously discussed where futures markets were involved. The manager of the financial institution has available no clean-cut transaction which will neatly counterbalance an unfavorable price movement. He is forced by the nature of the business to take a substantial long position in bonds in order to secure interest income. But if he wishes to be conservative, he must keep a part of the company assets in the form of cash or short-term securities. The cash will not be affected in value by a change in interest rates, and short-term bonds will fall only slightly in market price if interest rates rise. (Also, if the latter are held for a short period until maturity, no capital loss at all need be taken if they were bought at par.)

Suppose the cash and bond holdings of a financial institution (other than a bank) are as follows:

Cash....................	$10,000
Short-term bonds..........	20,000
Long-term bonds..........	50,000

No interest will be earned on the cash, a low rate of return will probably be earned on the short-term bonds, and a higher rate of interest will be earned on the long-term bonds. Some of the cash may be needed as a working balance to carry on current transactions, but the remainder and the short-term bonds should be considered a hedge against the possibility of a rise in interest rates (fall in bond prices). The cost of the hedge is the additional interest which could be earned if only long-term bonds were held.

Bullish or bearish sentiment, that is, expectations of increases or decreases in security prices, will also affect the pattern of asset preference. If bond prices are expected to rise, the desire to hold cash is diminished. If bond prices are expected to fall, the desire to hold cash will be greater.

LIQUIDITY PREFERENCE AND INTEREST RATES

Because of uncertainties regarding the future, the desire to hold cash is affected by the present level of interest rates. The income sacrificed by holding cash is less, the lower the interest rate. Hence the aggregate demand for cash balances can be related to the rate of interest.[1] This concept

---

[1] Actually, there is no such thing as *the* rate of interest, since interest rates differ according to length of loan, risk of default, and other factors. When for convenience we speak of the interest rate, it must be taken to refer to that yielded by a representative variety of security. Further, in relating the demand for cash balances to the interest rate, we must assume a given state of expectations and uncertainty, since these also affect the demand for cash.

is represented in the demand curve of Figure 24.1. At any moment a certain amount of money is in existence due to the activities of the United States Treasury and the banking system; this quantity is assumed to be OA. The supply curve for money is labeled S. The interest rate OR can be considered to be determined by the supply of and demand for money. At the interest rate OR, the aggregate amount of money which individuals, firms, and government agencies are willing to hold is equal to the amount of money which is in existence.

Suppose the supply of money is increased, say to OB, while the demand for money remains unchanged. All of it must be held in cash balances within the economy, but some who find themselves in possession of additional cash will then feel a desire to increase their purchases of consumers'

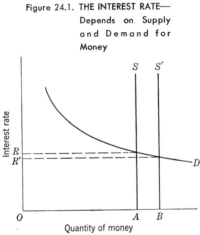

Figure 24.1. THE INTEREST RATE—
Depends on Supply
and Demand for
Money

goods and services, capital goods, and securities. To the extent that the larger money supply causes the demand for securities to increase, however, it will lower interest rates by raising security prices. The addition to the money supply will also make available more funds for lending which will tend to lower interest rates. The decline in interest rates will continue until a new equilibrium rate OR' is reached. At this lower interest rate, persons and firms will be willing to hold all the money which is now in existence.

The demand curve for money D can be considered to reflect the general state of liquidity preference, $i.e.$, the strength of the desire to hold cash rather than other assets. From the discussion of hedging by financial institutions (which is also applicable to any other conservative owner of such assets), it should be seen that an increased fear of lower bond prices in the future would increase liquidity preference.[1] Such an increase in liquidity preference is shown as an upward shift in the demand for money in Figure 24.2. The upward shift means that people will hold a given amount of cash at a higher interest rate than before—that is, will be willing to sacrifice more interest income than before in order to be liquid. The interest rate will then rise because some bondholders will wish to convert

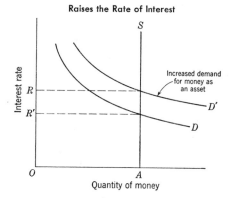

Figure 24.2. AN INCREASE IN LIQUIDITY PREFER-
ENCE—
Raises the Rate of Interest

their securities into cash. The sale of bonds will lower their prices and thus raise interest rates.[2] Present interest rates are, therefore, affected by altered expectations with regard to security prices even though there is no change in the supply of money.

[1] This can perhaps be more easily understood from consideration of the more common idea of an expected rise in a commodity price. When people expect the price of a commodity to rise, their demand for the commodity is increased as they hurry to buy before the price increase. In the case being examined here, people expect interest rates to rise, so they hurry to sell bonds before they fall in price—that is, their liquidity preference goes up.

[2] In Chap. 12, interest was looked upon as the net return from investment in capital goods, such as apartment buildings; in the present chapter, it is being considered the yield of securities. Both are useful points of view, but the former is more fundamental, since new securities are sold in order to secure funds to buy capital goods. Also, interest would exist in a simple barter economy without either money or securities. If we disregard the factor of uncertainty, there is a tendency for the interest rate obtainable by investment in capital goods to equal that which can be secured by buying securities. Thus a reduction in the interest yield on bonds makes it cheaper for firms to secure funds for investment in capital goods. Net interest yields on capital goods are then lowered because of additions to the stock of such assets and tend to be equated to those on securities.

ASSET PREFERENCE AND FEDERAL RESERVE OPERATIONS

In the previous chapter, primary emphasis was placed on the effect of Federal Reserve actions upon the amount of commercial-bank reserves and hence upon the ability of the banking system to create money. A more complete picture of the influence of the central bank can be obtained by considering also its effect on the pattern of asset holding which will be preferred by banking and nonbanking financial institutions.

Suppose that the Federal Reserve Banks, wishing to tighten up on credit, sell government securities in the open market. (They may simultaneously raise the rediscount rate in order to reinforce the effect of this action.) It was pointed out in the preceding chapter that bank reserves will be decreased by the open-market sales; this is likely to reduce the availability of bank credit and may cause interest rates on bank loans to be raised. In addition, the open-market sales will tend to raise interest rates on government securities by depressing their prices. The direct effect will be on interest yields of existing securities, but the United States Treasury will also be forced to pay higher interest rates on new issues, since persons and institutions will not otherwise subscribe to them. Similarly, corporations, states, municipalities, and other issuers of bonds will have to raise interest rates on new issues in order to compete with yields on United States securities (which have assumed great importance because of the magnitude of the national debt).

Federal Reserve open-market sales will probably cause some officials of financial institutions to anticipate further sales and a further fall in security prices. These bearish expectations will cause officials to wish to make their institutions more liquid, i.e., to substitute cash and short-term securities to some extent for long-term bonds, both government and private. The result will be a decrease in the amount of long-term credit made available by life-insurance companies, building and loan associations, and other lenders. In this way the Federal Reserve open-market sales will tend to reduce the availability not only of bank credit but also of nonbank credit. This is an important matter, especially because of the tremendous volume of personal savings which are regularly placed in the keeping of life-insurance companies.[1]

Federal Reserve open-market sales are especially likely to reduce the amount of mortgage money made available by building and loan associations, insurance companies, and others when the interest rates on such loans are established governmentally. For example, GI home loans and

---

[1] Life-insurance companies are seldom anxious to sell pure insurance (term insurance). Rather their salesmen generally try to sell the more profitable "straight-life," "twenty-pay life," "thirty-pay life," and endowment policies. These all combine saving and insurance.

loans insured by the Federal Housing Administration have interest-rate ceilings established by law. When government bonds yield higher interest rates, such home loans become relatively less attractive to lenders than before. The credit-tightening objective is thus achieved.

Suppose the Federal Reserve Banks buy rather than sell on the open market. Government-security prices will tend to go up and interest rates down. Bank credit will probably become easier to obtain because bank reserves will increase. Further, the rise in security prices may create definite expectations of a further rise in security prices in some minds and will at least allay fears of an increase in interest rates on the part of other financial officials. The holding of assets in the form of cash will become less desirable. Securities will be bid up in price, and interest rates will consequently fall. Credit will more readily be made available by nonbank lenders as well as by banks.

It should be apparent, in summary, that a variety of rather different types of actions on the part of individuals and firms in a private-enterprise economy are essentially speculative in nature or else are designedly nonspeculative, that is, designed as a hedge against unfavorable contingencies. In large measure these actions are directed toward taking advantage of, or guarding against, changes in the general level of prices or in particular prices, although hedging is a type of action applicable to many nonprice phenomena as well. Federal Reserve actions derive part of their effectiveness from the speculative and hedging actions which banks and other financial institutions can be induced to take.

CHAPTER 25

THE ECONOMY AS A WHOLE: A SUMMARY

This chapter completes Part B, and it may be useful at this point to step back a bit in order to view the section as a whole. We have taken what is often called a "macroscopic" view, as opposed to the "microscopic" view of Part A. That is to say, we have in Part B focused our attention on the operation of the economy as a whole rather than on particular markets for inputs and outputs. Both views are important to the attainment of an understanding of the workings of a private-enterprise economy and are prerequisite to a study of some major problems of political economy which will be undertaken in Part C.

Part A was concerned with the allocation of resources. It was shown that, in the absence of monopoly elements in the sale of outputs and inputs, there is both an incentive and a compulsion for individuals and firms to act in such a way as to bring about an extremely efficient use of resources. In the entire analysis the question of the aggregate employment of resources was not raised; this is a simplifying omission which was necessary in order to make the analysis manageable. The question is explicitly considered in Part B, and a broader, somewhat less precise type of analysis is utilized in order to study important over-all problems, including the levels of income, employment, and prices. This approach is in some respects supplementary to that of Part A, since an efficient use of resources requires not only that those productive services which are employed be utilized effectively but also that substantially all resources be employed.

In studying the theory of national-income determination, we saw that national money income can be considered to depend on the aggregate spending of individuals, firms, and governmental bodies. Individual purchasing power derives largely from payments for productive services, and the propensity of income recipients to consume or save raises or lowers spending. Such factors as changes in the level of consumer demand, innovations, and interest rates affect profit expectations and consequently influence investment spending. The government budget exerts a powerful influence on national money income, and the analysis of this influence paves the way for an examination of the use of fiscal policy as a device for controlling the over-all level of economic activity.

If all input and output prices in the economy were highly responsive to altered supply-demand conditions, a decline in national money income would not necessarily be accompanied by a serious decline in real income and employment. Wage rates, for example, would tend to fall, thereby reducing the amount of unemployment generated by the decline in money income. And output prices would decline in such a way as to work off excessive inventories quickly. But in the real world, most prices are more or less "sticky." Price inflexibility is promoted by monopoly at many points. Thus, monopoly, which was the villain in Part A, again rears its unlovely head as a factor which promotes unemployment and a lowered standard of living whenever total spending falls.

The national-income approach also throws a good deal of light on the problem of inflation which was a matter of more concern during the 1940's and the early 1950's than was the opposite problem of deflation and economic slack. When the nation's productive resources are fully utilized, further increases in national money income, occasioned by greater total spending, can only cause an inflation of prices. That is, real income can no longer be increased, since there are no unused factors of production to put to work. National money income, which can be thought of as aggregate real income multiplied by the average price level, can only be increased by a rise in prices. Measures designed to reduce total spending are useful in combating inflation; these include reduction in the money supply, higher interest rates, restriction of the availability of credit to businessmen and consumers, and increases in taxation relative to government expenditure.

The equation of exchange $MV = PT$, which is an older device than the national-income analysis, was included in Part B because it is a supplementary and in some ways an alternative view of the economy as a whole. It is useful especially because it gives a prominent place to the total money stock which is a strategic economic variable quite susceptible to control by the Federal authorities. (Money is not a prime active variable in the income analysis; it comes in through the back door, in that money affects interest rates which influence investment which, in turn, affects national income.) The equation of exchange shows clearly that an increase in the money supply will raise the price level unless it is offset by a decline in velocity of money or by a sufficient increase in the number of transactions. Since transactions T are defined to include purchases and sales of securities as well as goods, an increase in the supply of money will probably also increase the demand for securities, thus causing their prices to rise and interest rates to fall. Since the aggregate volume of production is a prime determinant of T, it is quite clear that an increase in the money supply is more likely to cause inflation when employment is full, and the aggregate volume of output can no longer be increased, than when considerable unemployment exists.

It is especially easy to see from the equation of exchange that the fractional-reserve banking system is well designed to aggravate upward and downward movements of prices through the power which it gives the banking system to expand and contract the total volume of demand deposits. The Federal government has rendered its constitutional obligation to regulate the value of money extremely difficult to fulfill by allowing the banking system the power to create and destroy the circulating medium. A degree of regulation is made possible by the central control over the banking system exercised through the Federal Reserve. The type of banking system which we have makes it easy for Treasury officials to inflate the money supply indirectly by selling securities to the commercial and Federal Reserve Banks. Public opposition to this indirect creation of money tends to be much weaker than to the more easily understandable direct printing of currency by the Treasury.

We have seen that the huge national debt tends to make the exercise of anti-inflation powers by the Federal Reserve System much more difficult. Large-scale selling of government securities on the open market would tend to depress their prices and raise interest rates sharply. This would make the Treasury's job of debt management more costly by increasing the aggregate amount of interest which must be paid annually on the national debt.

The deflation-control powers of the Federal Reserve authorities are probably strengthened by the large national debt and the widespread ownership of government securities. If open-market purchases cause managers of financial institutions to anticipate further increases in security prices, such purchases will serve, at least temporarily, to cause insurance companies and other financial institutions to expand their lending. Open-market purchases not only increase bank reserves but may also stimulate loans by reducing the liquidity preference of individuals and financial institutions of various types.

An analysis of the economy as a whole has necessarily involved some consideration of the powers of government. This leads directly to Part C, which examines the role of government in the economy in a more complete and more critical sense. The analysis of both Parts A and B will be applied to several major problems of political economy. The final section will begin with a consideration of the fiscal and monetary policies of the Federal government.

PART C

POLITICAL ECONOMY

CHAPTER 26

FISCAL POLICY AND ECONOMIC STABILIZATION

In Part B we discussed the forces which determine the levels of national income and prices, and we examined the ways through which government may act to influence either the level of income or the level of prices. In this and the following chapter we shall approach the problem of income and price-level stabilization primarily from the point of view of governmental policy. The analysis developed in Part B, along with the policy tools mentioned briefly there, will be applied to the actual problems facing government. This requires, first of all, an outlining of the goals which government should attempt to achieve in influencing income, employment, and prices. After these goals are discussed, the application of available fiscal and monetary tools in attaining these goals will be examined. Finally, the possibilities of long-run structural reforms, which include a modification of the policy-making institutional structure itself, will be briefly considered.

THE GOALS FOR POLICY

An outstanding fact that should have been made clear by a study of the analysis of Part B is that there is no automatic mechanism in the real-world economy which guarantees stability in the aggregative, or over-all, sense. The level of income is determined by the spending and saving decisions of individual families, business firms, and government. These decisions may or may not interact to produce an income that is high enough to provide reasonably full employment without at the same time producing pressures toward inflation. The same conclusion appears if the aggregate economy is discussed in terms of the price level or the value of the monetary unit. The price level is determined by the stock of money, the rate at which this stock is turned over (velocity), and the amount of work this money is required to do (volume of transactions). There is no assurance that these factors will generate a stable price level, even if the stock of money remains constant. And we have seen that the stock of money itself is subject to rather severe fluctuations due to the importance of bank-deposit money in the total supply.

If the premise is accepted that the private-enterprise economy provides no automatic stability in either income or the price level, the next question becomes one of deciding whether or not stability in these two magnitudes is desirable. There would seem to be little doubt concerning the answer to this question. Because of the inherent rigidities in the price and wage structure, a reduction in money income is accompanied by a reduction in real income. A reduction in real income (production) means a reduction in employment. And, after the severe unemployment of the 1930's, the maintenance of reasonably full employment has become one of the most sought-for social goals. If, on the other hand, money income is pushed too high, the price level will tend to rise sharply; inflation will result. The inflation of the years following World War II should have impressed clearly on everyone's mind the desirability of price-level stability. Stability in both employment and prices may be taken as desirable social goals, and governmental policy then should be aimed at the accomplishment of these objectives.

There may be difficulties, however, in attaining both these goals at once. Governmental policy aimed at maintaining full employment may at the same time promote inflation. On the other hand, governmental policy aimed solely at keeping the value of the dollar stable may not guarantee reasonably full employment. For society, and thus for the government, a choice may have to be made between these two goals.

Full-employment Goal

Let us see how these two objectives, each desirable in itself, may come into conflict when both are set up as direct goals for policy. Let us suppose that the government adopts the policy of guaranteeing full employment of the labor force at all times. It plans to accomplish this objective by keeping aggregate total expenditures at whatever level is required to do the job. (Later in this chapter we shall discuss fully the ways in which government may influence aggregate total expenditures.) Assume that the government accomplishes its declared task in any given year so that total expenditures on goods and services—i.e., consumption, investment, and government—are sufficient to employ approximately all the available labor[1] at the prevailing level of wages. Now suppose that the strongly organized labor groups exert pressure for wage increases in excess of the increases which have occurred in labor productivity and that these groups are successful. This will raise labor costs for business firms, which will be forced to lay off workers unless the demand for their products also increases commensurately. Workers will tend to be forced into unemploy-

[1] Excluding those who are in the process of shifting jobs at any given time. This type of unemployment is called "frictional," and could never be eliminated in a free society, even should its elimination be deemed desirable.

ment as a result of the wage increase. But here the government will again enter the picture, for it has adopted the policy objective of maintaining full employment. It will cause expenditures to expand (via either fiscal or monetary policy or both). This increase in total expenditures will increase demand for goods and services sufficiently to allow firms to reemploy all the labor previously laid off. But the expansion in demand will also have increased the level of product prices. Full employment will have been secured only at the expense of a rising price level, *i.e.*, inflation.

Price-level Stability as a Goal

On the other hand, let us assume that the government adopts a policy of keeping the price level, or the value of the dollar, roughly stable. Now suppose, as before, that strong labor groups are successful in securing wage increases in excess of the increase in labor productivity. This would increase costs to business firms, and, again, they would be forced to lay off workers unless the demand for their products were correspondingly raised to offset the increase in costs. But under the policy of keeping the price level stable, the government would not increase expenditures in this situation. Hence, the demand for products would not increase, and the layoffs would be turned into permanent unemployment as long as the wage rate remained at the high level. A policy of price-level stability, accordingly, may be consistent with less than full employment, and a policy of full employment may be consistent with a constantly rising price level. This conflict will be present as long as the economy is characterized by strong monopoly pressures among labor groups which are able to force wages above competitive levels. The inherent policy conflict may be summed up in the statement that society can have any two of the following: (1) full employment, (2) a stable level of prices, and (3) strong monopoly labor groups.[1] It cannot have all three. It must decide which of the three it will abandon and which it will retain. If wages are allowed to move up only in accordance with productivity as would tend to be the case in free input markets, full employment and a stable price level do not conflict as policy alternatives. If union pressures are not checked and wages are allowed to move upward at a faster rate than this, a governmental policy of full employment will be attained at the expense of a rising price level, that is, a continually falling value of the dollar. This appears to be the probable alternative which our society will adopt, although clearly the more desirable policy would be one aimed at limiting

---

[1] Monopoly in the labor market is significant here because "full employment" primarily implies full employment of the labor force. Of course, monopoly in other segments of the economy will alter both the allocation of resources and the distribution of income and, in so doing, may make "full employment" more difficult to achieve.

the monopoly power of unions[1] along with, of course, a more general attack on monopoly in all forms. Here we find yet another reason for seeking to maintain competition in all markets. Monopoly not only is harmful in distorting the allocation of economic resources among various uses but also serves to interfere with the accomplishment of other desirable social goals for the whole economy.

THE LIMITATIONS OF FISCAL POLICY

Now that we have discussed the goals for policy, namely, employment stabilization and price-level stabilization, the next step must be an examination of the policy tools available to government. These may be subdivided into two broad categories, fiscal policy and monetary policy, although, as we shall see later, the distinction between the two is not always sharp. These categories are distinguished not by the goals which they are designed to accomplish, for these are, or may be, the same for both. Rather they are distinguished by the devices employed in accomplishing these goals.

Operations on the budget of government are defined as fiscal policy. Operations on the stock of money, on its rate of turnover, and on its close substitutes are defined as monetary policy. The government debt exists as a bridge between these two policy areas. This follows from the fact that debt is originally brought into existence by differences in the two sides of the budget, that is, by fiscal policy, but once government debt is created it becomes a money substitute, or near money, and operations on debt instruments are similar in effect to those on the money stock. Consequently, a considerable portion of what follows in this and the next chapter is concerned with the creation, retirement, and manipulation of the government debt.

The first major category to be discussed is fiscal policy. This type of policy is of more modern vintage than its brother, monetary policy, and it has been popular only since the great depression of the 1930's and since the introduction of the theory of income determination outlined in Part B. It is not difficult to see why the development of the theory of income led directly into the advocacy of fiscal policy as the most important single

---

[1] Some students of this problem believe that, upon adoption of a genuine employment-stabilization policy by government, union officials will see that it is to their own interest to keep wage increases approximately in line with productivity increases. Should this happen, we might have all three of the things listed, but the monopoly power of labor would be left unused. Other students of this problem (notably Professor A. P. Lerner) have recognized the inherent policy conflict and have proposed schemes for government regulation of wages to keep them in line with productivity. See A. P. Lerner, *Economics of Employment* (New York: McGraw-Hill Book Company, Inc., 1951), Chap. 14.

stabilizer in the economy. For this theory concludes that income is determined by the interactions among the spendings and savings decisions of individuals, business firms, and government. The theory also concludes that the level of income so determined need not be the most desirable one. It follows that since the spending and taxing policies of government are subject to control by government, these should be employed where possible to attain the desired stabilization goals.

The Balanced-budget Rule

The use of the government budget to achieve economic stabilization, however, means that the time-honored rule of budget balance is discarded. This rule holds that government expenditures should be covered by tax revenues. Since Congress normally approves budgets each year, the rule generally has been interpreted as requiring a balance between expenditures and revenues each fiscal year. This traditional fiscal rule did serve as an important check on irresponsible policy. It is always easy to secure political support for expanded government expenditures and for reduced taxation. The typical congressman desires two things: first, to increase the number of Federal projects (veterans' hospitals, drainage canals, Air Force installations, etc.) in his district, and second, to reduce the Federal taxes paid by his voting constituents. The advocates of fiscal policy as a stabilization instrument have perhaps underestimated the importance of the checks on government spending imposed by the old balanced-budget rule. But for fiscal policy to be effective in attaining economic stabilization, no predetermined relationship between total expenditure and total taxes must be rigidly maintained. Instead, the budget itself must be flexible, and it must be changed in accordance with the criteria of income and price-level stability.

Some Problems in Fiscal Policy

Even if the stabilization use of the government budget is accepted, it should be recognized that this provides a powerful but rather unwieldy weapon. Fiscal policy in attacking depression or inflation may be considered similar to a shotgun broadside rather than a rifle bullet. This is true because of the difficulties involved in predicting changes in the income-determining variables, which were discussed in Part B. Fiscal policy cannot be turned on and off or shifted in direction, except after considerable time has elapsed. The legislative branch of the national government holds the authority to initiate changes in either the expenditure or the taxation side of the budget. And the mills of the legislative process grind exceeding slow. For fiscal policy to be an exact and precise weapon in combating economic fluctuations, predictions as to consumption spending, saving, and investment would have to be reasonably accurate for at least eighteen months to two years in advance. Another factor making for inexactness and lack of precision in this sort of policy is the instability of the income multiplier. Even if conditions did indicate, for example, that national money income was to be generated at an annual rate of fifty billion dollars in excess of that desired, it would be difficult to determine by just how much fiscal policy, through government-expenditure reduction or tax increases or both, should reduce total expenditure. This would depend on the value of the multiplier, working negatively in this case. If this value were stable at five, for example, then fiscal policy should aim at reducing total spending by ten billion dollars in each of the several succeeding spending periods. But if the very initiation of this contractionary policy should, for any reason, cause a shift in other important income-determining magnitudes, the expected result might never be realized. For example, if decreased government expenditures cause business expectations to become unfavorable, investment spending may fall off in an unpredicted way, and the ten-billion-dollar reduction in spending accomplished by fiscal policy might serve to plunge the economy into depression rather than merely preventing inflation.

Another difficulty, which will be more completely discussed later, is the proper meshing or coordinating of fiscal and monetary policy. Proper fiscal policy can be based only upon precise knowledge of the kind of monetary policy that is being, and will be, followed. The favorable effects of fiscal actions may be more than offset by monetary policy working in the opposite direction. This was substantially the case in the 1947–1948 inflation. Fiscal policy, albeit largely accidentally, did exert pressure toward contraction through creation of budget surpluses. But these effects were more than offset by an inflationary monetary policy.

In outlining the difficulties of securing proper action via fiscal policy, we do not mean to imply that the budget should not be adjusted with a view to economic stabilization. But we should, first of all, recognize the problems in carrying out appropriate policy once political difficulties are surmounted, and second, we should never disregard completely the political processes through which such policy must be framed. The analysis of income determination provides us with nothing more than an extremely crude basis upon which actual policy proposals may be constructed. But the analysis does point up directions in which action must be taken, and a thorough understanding of such analysis is essential to sound thinking in this area. Therefore, it will be useful to develop the policy implications of the rather simple models of income determination constructed in Part B. We shall first discuss the fiscal policy indicated as appropriate during periods of depression and unemployment. This will be followed by a discussion of fiscal policy during inflation.

FISCAL POLICY IN DEPRESSION

If income is lower than that required to maintain either high-level employment or price-level stability, as was the case in the early 1930's to a tragic degree, the government budget provides a powerful means by which a higher national income may be realized. (1) Expenditures may be raised relative to taxes. This can be accomplished in a number of ways, *e.g.*, by raising expenditures while holding taxes constant or by reducing both taxes and expenditures but reducing taxes by the greater amount. (2) Both expenditures and taxes may be increased but kept equal in their totals. In the first way, a budget deficit is created; in the second, the budget remains balanced at a higher level.

Expenditure Increase

Let us suppose that the government decides to create a deficit by expanding expenditures without raising taxes. (The precise manner in which the extra expenditure is made, whether for bridges or school lunches, for flood control or unemployment relief, is an important factor in determining the aggregate effect, but these differences may be neglected in this initial discussion.) This will increase total spending by the amount of the deficit. The increase in total spending will increase national income. But the increase in national income will be larger than the amount of the deficit, especially if the deficit is maintained during several spending periods. This was illustrated in Figure 20.1. The ratio of the increase in income to the initial increase in spending is, of course, the income multiplier, and it depends for its value on the marginal propensity to spend, *i.e.*, the ratio of additional spending to an additional increment of income.

Tax Reduction

As one alternative to the expenditure-expansion policy, the government may leave its spending unchanged and lower taxes. This will also create a deficit. The disposable income of private individuals and firms will be increased by the tax reduction, and with a higher income, spending by these units will be increased. But it is probable that the deficit required to generate a given increase in national income will be greater in this case than in the case of public expenditure expansion. This is true, since some of the addition to disposable income resulting from the tax reduction will be saved, *i.e.*, not spent. So total spending in the economy will not increase by the full amount of the deficit. The exact amount of the increase depends again on the marginal propensity to spend. If, for example, national money income is twenty billion dollars less than the desirable "full-employment" level, and if the marginal propensity to spend is $\frac{4}{5}$, a tax reduction of five billion will cause a four-billion-dollar increase in spending by individuals. This four-billion increase in spending would ultimately generate the required increase of twenty billion through the multiplier effect (if the marginal propensity to spend is $\frac{4}{5}$, the multiplier will, of course, be five). Thus, a five-billion-dollar deficit would be required to generate a twenty-billion-dollar increase in national income in the tax-reduction case, while only a four-billion deficit would be required in the expenditure-expansion case. This conclusion assumes, however, that investment plans are the same in the two cases. There seems to be some reason for believing that business firms will react more favorably to tax reductions by government than to an expansion of public expenditures. If this is true, the marginal propensity to spend will be higher in the tax-reduction case, and the necessary deficit may be no larger, and perhaps even smaller, than in the expenditure-expansion case.

The reduction of taxes is, in some respects, a more desirable weapon of antidepression fiscal policy than increased government spending. First of all, taxes can be adjusted more quickly than can public expenditures. Second, the area of government activity is kept within sharper limits, always a desirable feature in a freedom-loving society. It is true, however, that the real costs of government services are much lower during depression periods when unemployment is present, and this is a point in favor of expenditure expansion instead. (This will be discussed more fully in Chapter 28.) The appropriate antidepression fiscal policy, therefore, would seem to be one of using both expenditure expansion and tax reduction as weapons in increasing total spending in the economy.

Budget Balanced at Higher Level

Still another possible way of increasing total expenditures is keeping the government's budget balanced but increasing both public expenditures and taxes. Suppose that as an antidepression measure government expenditures are increased by ten billion dollars and taxes are also increased sufficiently to bring in an additional ten billion dollars of revenue. This action will increase total spending, because the ten-billion-dollar increase in taxes will reduce private spending not by ten billion but by somewhat less than that amount. Some of the money collected in taxes would have been saved rather than spent if it had been allowed to remain in private hands. If, for example, the marginal propensity to spend were $\frac{4}{5}$, as assumed before, a tax increase of ten billion dollars would reduce private spending by only eight billion dollars. This would be more than offset by the ten billion dollars of additional government expenditure. There would be a net addition of two billion dollars to the total spendings stream. After the multiplier effects were allowed to work themselves out, this policy would generate a ten-billion-dollar increase in national income. Since the additional income generated is just equivalent to the additional public expenditures and taxes, the "balanced-budget" multiplier is equal to one. This fact points to the difficulties of using this weapon as a major one in any fiscal-policy scheme. It requires too much change in the size of the government budget—change which in itself may be undesirable. Whereas a fifty-billion-dollar deficiency in national income might be made up by approximately a ten- or fifteen-billion-dollar deficit, the balanced budget would have to be increased by fifty billion dollars to achieve the same result. This might well require government spending in lines not traditionally held to be appropriate governmental activity. The balanced-budget multiplier does, however, serve to indicate the inflationary threat of substantial increases in the national budget, and, on the other hand, the deflationary threat of substantial decreases. If a war emergency dictates a much larger government budget, there is likely to be a threat of inflation even if extra taxes fully cover the added expenditures. Contrariwise, if a "cold war" suddenly ends, allowing a sizable reduction in defense expenditures, a deflationary impact would be present even if taxes were reduced dollar for dollar with expenditures.

It may be concluded that any over-all plan for combating depressions, especially major ones, will call for both the expansion of government expenditures and tax reduction. Antidepression fiscal policy, accordingly, carries with it the creation of a budgetary deficit, *i.e.*, government expenditures exceeding tax revenues. The next step in our discussion becomes, therefore, an examination of the problems of financing a deficit.

Ways of Financing a Deficit

If the government is to spend more than it collects in tax revenues, it must secure additional purchasing power from some source. The Federal government could simply create the money. Congress could legally authorize the issuance of paper money without limit if it chose to do so. There are, however, certain traditional beliefs and myths surrounding money which have evolved in our society. One of these appears to be that money should have some connection with gold; this was discussed in Chapter 22. It does not appear likely, therefore, that outright currency issue would be resorted to in this country as the sole means of financing a deficit.

The same results may be achieved by government borrowing from Federal Reserve Banks. The government would merely transfer instruments of debt (Treasury bills, certificates, or bonds) to the Federal Reserve Banks in exchange for a Treasury deposit account. The Treasury would then cover that portion of its expenditures not covered by taxation by drawing down these deposit accounts. Additional purchasing power in the amount of the deficit is pumped into the economy by this operation with precisely the same effects as would be the case with outright currency creation by government. The effects on bank reserves are also equivalent. The outright issue of currency would, when the money is spent by government and redeposited by individuals in commercial banks, cause bank reserves to increase by the full amount of the issue, allowing a possible multiple increase in loans and deposits. A reduction in Treasury balances at the Federal Reserve Banks is no different in this respect. As the Treasury draws down its account, individuals receiving government checks deposit them with commercial banks. Upon clearance, these checks increase member-bank reserves in the full amount of the deficit, allowing a multiple expansion in bank loans and deposits. Thus, the budget deficit may be said to generate inflationary effects in two ways. First, there is an income multiplier resulting from the increase in total spending. Second, the increase in bank reserves tends to lower interest rates and to increase the availability of bank credit to businessmen and householders. Higher investment and consumption spending would thereby be promoted. The inflationary fiscal policy would also tend to generate inflationary monetary effects.

The deficit could also be financed by government borrowing from the commercial banks. If banks hold excess reserves, this method of financing the deficit also becomes equivalent in effect to an outright creation of currency. This process was discussed in some detail in Chapter 23. The utilization of excess reserves in an initial purchase by banks of government securities allows the banking system to purchase some multiple of the excess reserves because, as the Treasury spends the proceeds, its checks are redeposited in commercial banks. Even if banks do not hold excess reserves, these can be readily created by the government's selling a small fraction of its new securities to the Federal Reserve Banks in the manner outlined in the preceding paragraph. This was the procedure followed during the deficit financing of World War II. In summary, it may be concluded that government borrowing from either Federal Reserve Banks or commercial banks is equivalent to the outright printing of paper money. The only difference is that the government interest-bearing debt is increased in the process, while in the direct issue of currency this would not be the case.

The deficit may also be financed by borrowing from individuals and nonfinancial business institutions. This method is obviously different from an issue of currency; indeed, it more closely resembles taxation. Borrowing from individuals reduces disposable incomes, and this in turn tends to reduce private spending. Borrowing does not, however, reduce private spending to the same degree as taxation. The essential difference is that lending is voluntary while taxation is compulsory. However, some of the money spent in the purchase of government securities would otherwise probably have been spent for the purchase of goods and services; not all of it would have been saved. Therefore, some of the antidepression impact of deficit financing is destroyed if the funds are borrowed from individuals. The maximum effects on total expenditures are clearly forthcoming when the deficit is financed by borrowing from banks. The sale of government securities to individuals really belongs in the realm of anti-inflation fiscal policy, and should be employed in this fashion. As we shall see later, one of the most potent antidepression weapons of monetary policy is the *purchase* of government securities from the people by the central-banking system.

FISCAL POLICY IN INFLATION

Ideally, fiscal policy during periods of inflation should be just the reverse of that followed during periods of deflation and unemployment. If the savings and spendings decisions of private individuals interact to generate a national income in excess of that necessary to maintain approximate stability in the level of prices, the budget should be adjusted so as to reduce total expenditures (the sum of private and public spending).

This may be accomplished in ways just the opposite of those cited earlier as antidepression measures. To combat inflation, either of two courses may be followed. (1) Expenditures may be lowered relative to taxes. For example, expenditures may be lowered while taxes are held constant, expenditures may be lowered while taxes are raised, etc. (2) Both expenditures and taxes may be lowered by an equal amount. The first of these courses creates a budgetary surplus (assuming that the budget was balanced before the action was taken). The second course keeps the budget balanced but at a lower level than before.

The mechanics of anti-inflation fiscal policy are also similar in reverse to those of antidepression policy. Suppose that national money income is predicted to be twenty billion dollars above that thought to be desirable and that the marginal propensity to spend is again $\frac{4}{5}$. How much should fiscal policy attempt to reduce total spending (private and public) in order to generate the twenty-billion-dollar reduction in national income? The negative multiplier also being assumed to be five, the answer is four billion. Again the method of expenditure adjustment while taxes are kept constant requires a smaller departure from budget balance than that of tax adjustment. If government expenditures are reduced by four billion dollars, and this reduction is maintained for several spending periods, income will eventually fall by twenty billion dollars. (This assumes that private investment is not directly affected.) If, however, taxes are increased and expenditures are left unchanged, a tax increase of five billion dollars will be required. For not every tax dollar would have been a spendings dollar if left in private hands. Also, as in the opposing case, the second method, that of a budget balanced at a lower level, requires a very considerable reduction in the size of the budget. This may be very difficult to effect, especially when the budget is made up largely of such items as defense expenditures, veterans' benefits, and interest on the public debt.

The most appropriate over-all scheme for anti-inflation fiscal policy should contain a combination of government-expenditure reduction and tax increases. Selectively, those expenditures having the greatest income-multiplying effects should be first reduced, and those taxes reducing spending most should be first increased.[1]

Political Problems in Anti-inflation Policy

An important distinction must be made on the political side between antidepression and anti-inflation fiscal policy. As has been pointed out, legislators find it politically popular to increase government expenditures and to reduce taxes, both of which are antidepression measures. The opposite actions, decreasing government expenditures and increasing taxation, are both unpopular politically. One conclusion is readily apparent. It will probably be harder to secure proper anti-inflation fiscal policy than anti-depression fiscal policy. The years following World War II, during which inflation threatened almost continuously, demonstrated this problem. In only three years between the end of the war and 1954 was fiscal policy clearly of the appropriate sort, and even in those years the budgetary surplus was not clearly foreseen by Congress.

Disposition of a Surplus

If appropriate anti-inflation fiscal policy is pursued via the over-balanced-budget method, there is a problem of the disposition to be made of the excess revenue collected. (Just as we have discussed the financing of the budget deficit, we must now discuss the disposition of the budget surplus.) If the government creates a surplus by collecting greater amounts in tax revenues than it spends, the full anti-inflation effects of this budget position will be present only if the surplus money does not somehow find its way back into the income or spendings stream. The simplest method of ensuring this full effect would consist in the government's "burning up the money" not needed to meet expenditures. But just as the government's rolling of the printing presses is not politically practicable in the deficit case, actual government destruction of surplus money is not practicable here. The government may accomplish the same desired result by using the surplus to build up its balance at the Federal Reserve Banks. If a larger balance is kept in the Treasury ac-

[1] Throughout the discussion in this chapter, we are concentrating upon the stabilization aspects of the fiscal policy to the neglect of effects on resource allocation and income distribution.

count, the surplus is effectively neutralized. It does not return to the spendings stream.

With a Federal debt of over 270 billion dollars, however, it would seem that any budgetary surplus of revenues over expenses should be utilized to pay off some of this enormous debt. We must then examine this possibility and inquire whether or not the government can use surplus funds to retire debt without at the same time destroying the anti-inflation effects of the surplus.

The ownership of the Federal debt may be broken down into a few major categories. These include United States government agencies and trust funds, Federal Reserve Banks, commercial banks, insurance companies and mutual savings banks, and individuals and other investors.[1] Let us trace through the effects of using a government surplus to retire government securities held by each of these major groups. First of all, the holdings of government agencies and trust funds may be neglected here. These hold special issues of debt for the most part, and there would be little reason for retiring such debt since reserves are required to be in the form of government securities.

Government repayment of debt obligations held by the Federal Reserve Banks does provide an effective way in which the surplus may be used to reduce the debt without destroying its anti-inflation effects. In any analysis of debt repayment, both the tax-collection side and the debt-repayment side must be considered. In creating the surplus, tax revenues are collected but not spent. Thus, on the tax side, the net effect is clearly deflationary. Disposable incomes are reduced; consumption spending is reduced. But the effects of taxation on bank reserves must also be considered. To pay the taxes, individuals and business firms draw down their deposit accounts. If the government spends the tax money, this tends to build these deposits up again, and there is no substantial net effect on the banking system. If, however, the government uses the funds collected in taxes to repay debt held by Federal Reserve Banks, the money will not find its way into the reserves of commercial banks, and reserves will therefore tend to be reduced by the full amount of the reduction in deposits. The net effect is that member banks' accounts with the Federal Reserve Banks are decreased and the Federal Reserve Banks' cash accounts are

---

[1] The distribution of ownership in November, 1953, was as indicated in the following table (in billions of dollars):

U.S. government agencies and trust funds	$ 48
Federal Reserve Banks	25
Commercial banks	63
Insurance companies and mutual savings banks	25
Individuals and other investors	112
Total	$273

increased. If member banks hold no excess reserves, their reserve position will be endangered, and they will be forced to curtail loans and investments. When surplus funds are used to retire Federal Reserve-held government debt, accordingly, not only is the negative income multiplier working to reduce inflationary pressures but, in addition, the deposit multiplier is set to work in a deflationary direction. Both of these effects would also be present if the surplus were used to build up Treasury balances at the Federal Reserve Banks.

If, however, the government surplus is used to retire debt owned by any of the remaining groups of security holders, the effects of the repayment itself tend to work in the opposite direction from those of the surplus creation. Consider now the repayment of debt held by the commercial banks. The initial collection of taxes reduces bank deposits, but the government in turn uses the nonexpended funds to retire bank-held securities. On the banks' balance sheets, the net effects will consist of a reduction in demand deposits on the liability side and an equivalent reduction in the government-securities item on the asset side. The reserves held by commercial banks are not finally affected, but their reserve position is strengthened. This is true because total deposits have been reduced; this means that some reserves which were previously required are now excess. This enables banks to expand loans and deposits in some multiple of the excess amount.

To illustrate this point by an arithmetical example, let us assume that the government creates a surplus of ten billion dollars and uses this to retire government securities held by commercial banks. When taxpayers pay their tax bills initially, bank deposits are reduced by approximately the amount of such payments. The surplus, we are assuming, is used to retire bonds, bills, and certificates held by the banks. The banking system's total holdings of government securities are thus reduced by ten billions. No change is effected in the actual reserves of banks, but deposits are down by ten billion dollars. So if banks are operating under a legal reserve requirement of 20 per cent, two billion dollars fewer reserves are now needed. Excess reserves appear in the amount of two billion dollars. As the deposit multiplier works itself out, this allows a potential expansion of loans and deposits of ten billions. The repayment of the government debt in this case makes possible a deposit-multiplier effect which is in the opposite direction from the original effect of the surplus. It may be concluded that the total impact of a policy of surplus financing to repay commercial-bank-held debt is probably deflationary, since the negative income-multiplier effects are probably more powerful than the positive deposit-multiplier effects. But the total impact is less deflationary than the policy of surplus financing to repay Federal Reserve-held debt or to accumulate Treasury balances.

The use of surplus revenues to repay government debt held by non-banking holders also generates opposing effects on the tax-collection and the debt-repayment sides. As taxes are collected, bank deposits are reduced. But as the government retires securities held by individuals or corporations, bank deposits are again increased. The net effect is probably deflationary, but the deflationary impact is slight relative to repayment of debt held by Federal Reserve Banks or even by commercial banks. The only deflationary effect here stems from the fact that the marginal propensity to spend is perhaps slightly greater for taxpayers in general than for bondholders.

There will be more significant effects on the pattern of spending, however. Some portion, perhaps a large portion, of tax revenues would have been spent for consumption goods if the money had been left in private hands. Public-debt repayment to individuals and corporations serves to increase their spending for outstanding government and corporate securities. This drives down interest rates and tends to increase investment spending by firms. In total, a policy of surplus financing to retire debt held by individuals and nonbank business firms tends to encourage investment relative to consumption.

SUMMARY

Perhaps the most appropriate summary of our discussion of fiscal policy consists in the statement contained in the report of Senator Douglas's subcommittee on fiscal and monetary policy:[1]

We recommend that Federal fiscal policies be such as not only to avoid aggravating economic instability but also to make a positive and important contribution to stabilization, at the same time promoting equity and incentives in taxation and economy in expenditures. A policy based on the principle of an annually balanced budget regardless of fluctuations in the national income does not meet these tests; for, if actually followed, it would require drastic increases of tax rates or drastic reductions of government expenditures during periods of deflation and unemployment, thereby aggravating the decline, and marked reductions of tax rates or increases of expenditures during periods of inflationary boom, thereby accentuating the inflation. A policy that will contribute to stability must produce a surplus of revenues over expenditures in periods of high prosperity and comparatively full employment and a surplus of expenditures over revenues in periods of deflation and abnormally high unemployment. Such a policy must, however, be based on a recognition that there are limits to the effectiveness of fiscal policy because economic forecasting is highly imperfect at present and tax and expenditure policies under present procedures are very inflexible.

[1] *Report of the Subcommittee on Monetary, Credit, and Fiscal Policies,* 81st Cong., 2d Sess., S. Doc. 129, p. 1.

CHAPTER 27

MONETARY POLICY AND THE NATIONAL DEBT

Monetary policy was defined earlier as operations by the government affecting the stock of money, its rate of turnover, and the volume of close money substitutes. In the preceding chapter we discussed monetary policy in terms of the ways of financing a budget deficit and of disposing of a budget surplus. The government debt results from fiscal policy; the government debt also provides the major weapon of monetary policy in the post-World War II economy. This is due primarily to the magnitude of the debt itself and to the problems faced in its management. The way in which the government debt is managed must influence monetary affairs to a major degree, whether this is considered desirable or not.

The mechanics of monetary policy were discussed in Chapter 23. The Federal Reserve as the central-banking authority may take action in order to combat either deflation or inflation. Politically, monetary policy is much more flexible than fiscal policy. We have traditionally allowed substantial discretionary authority to be exercised by the Federal Reserve Board in monetary matters. This should allow for a reasonably swift response to shifts in economic conditions. There is nothing to ensure that such response will be made in the proper direction, however, since the authority of the Federal Reserve Board is subject to no fixed and announced rules.[1] We shall now discuss appropriate monetary policy during depression and unemployment and then during periods of inflation.

MONETARY POLICY DURING DEPRESSION

If the level of income is falling and unemployment is anticipated, steps should be taken by the Federal Reserve Board along all its lines of action. First of all, it should lower reserve requirements of member banks; second, it should lower the rediscount or borrowing rate for member banks; and third, it should institute open-market purchases of government securities.

[1] The closest approach to a rule for policy is that contained in the Employment Act of 1946, which states that "maximum employment, production, and purchasing power" shall be promoted. This directive is obviously ambiguous and neglects even the mention of price-level stability as a goal.

These steps will have the effect of increasing excess reserves of member banks. This may not be effective, however, in checking the depression or in positively promoting recovery. Banks may be placed in a favorable reserve position, but this in itself will not increase spending on goods and services. The purchase of government securities by the Federal Reserve Banks may drive interest rates down, but the attraction of low rates and ready availability of credit may not be sufficient to encourage prospective borrowers. In a period of unfavorable expectations, business firms will not be induced merely by a lowering of interest rates to expand investment greatly. This difficulty of monetary policy in promoting recovery from a depression has given rise to the phrase "you can't push on a string." Money and credit may be made readily available at low borrowing rates, but conditions will not be much improved unless someone is willing to borrow and spend the proceeds.

For monetary policy to prove positively effective, it must directly encourage increased spending. Only the open-market purchase of securities from individuals and business firms accomplishes this purpose. Total spending will be increased to some degree by a policy of open-market purchase. For with interest rates already low, some former bondholders, now holding cash, will decide to spend more on real goods and services. Not all the money received in exchange for government securities will be reinvested in other securities.

The Treasury Department, faced with problems of debt refinancing during a depression, should pay off as much individually held debt as possible and replace this with debt held by Federal Reserve Banks and commercial banks (to the extent that the latter have excess reserves). This action on the part of the Treasury would be equivalent in result to Federal Reserve purchase of government securities from the public in the open market. This sort of Treasury policy would amount to "monetizing" a portion of the debt held by the public. And by the replacing of securities with the more liquid asset, cash, people will be encouraged to increase spending. If conditions warrant, this process of debt monetization can be accomplished without difficulty since the Treasury will constantly be faced, during the late 1950's and the 1960's, with major problems of maturing issues of the national debt. Merely by replacing maturing issues held by individuals and nonbanking institutions with securities sold to the banking system, a substantial monetization of the debt might be effected.

MONETARY POLICY IN INFLATION

During periods of inflation, the Federal Reserve should increase reserve requirements for member banks, increase the rediscount or borrowing rate, direct Federal Reserve Banks to sell securities in the open market, and perhaps impose qualitative controls on credit. The action is the reverse of that undertaken in depression. Here the phrase "you can't push on a string" must be supplemented with "but you can pull." For each of these policy steps tends to put pressure on banks' reserve positions or, in the case of qualitative controls, to restrict the demand for loans. Banks will be encouraged to restrict lending and to increase interest rates. While low interest rates are not alone sufficient to encourage expanded investment in depression, high interest rates can be sufficient to deter some investment during periods of threatening inflation.

The sale of securities in the open market by the Federal Reserve System will also have direct effects on spending apart from those generated through a contraction of bank reserves. As people are induced by higher interest rates to give up the more liquid cash for the slightly less liquid but more productive government securities, private spending will tend to be reduced.

Treasury management of the public debt can supplement Federal Reserve action in combating inflation. During such periods, the Treasury should attempt to shift debt out of the hands of the Federal Reserve Banks (and perhaps of the commercial banks) and into the hands of individuals and nonbanking institutions. By retiring debt held by the Federal Reserve Banks and refinancing this debt by sales of securities to individuals, the Treasury can create effects equivalent to Federal Reserve open-market sales of government securities to the public. If new debt is created during such periods (by deficit financing) which would, of course, represent a fiscal policy just opposite to the proper one, the new issues of government securities should obviously be sold to the nonbanking public where the total effect will be less inflationary than elsewhere. Deficit financing during an inflation is not an unusual case, as has been indicated by the Korean War experience.

THE COORDINATION OF FISCAL AND MONETARY POLICY

The discussion in this and the preceding chapter has indicated the proper lines of action in the fiscal and monetary spheres during periods of both depression and inflation. To summarize these steps: Public policy in depression should consist of increasing government expenditure and lowering taxes, thus creating a deficit. This deficit should be financed by the modern equivalent of printing money, namely, borrowing from the Federal Reserve Banks or from commercial banks. To accompany this fiscal policy, the Federal Reserve System should reduce legal reserve requirements, lower the rediscount rate, and purchase securities in the open market. The Treasury in its debt-management operations should pay off debt held by the nonbanking public and secure the funds required by sales of bonds to the Federal Reserve Banks and the commercial banks.

Public policy in inflation should consist of reducing government expenditures and increasing taxes, thus creating a surplus. This surplus should be used either to build up Treasury balances or to retire government debt held by the Federal Reserve Banks. The central-banking authorities should increase reserve requirements, increase the rediscount or borrowing rate, and sell securities in the open market. The Treasury should, if possible, refinance bank-held debt as it matures by sales of bonds to the nonbanking public.

Not all of these weapons of monetary and fiscal policy can be manipulated readily, and all are not equally effective. As mentioned earlier, it is much easier to secure political support for appropriate fiscal policy in depression than in inflation. For fiscal policy in depression involves tax reduction and expenditure expansion, both of which may secure vigorous support from separate politically powerful groups. On the other hand, proper fiscal policy during periods of inflation calls for both tax increases and expenditure reduction. Few, if any, politically powerful groups in the economy will rally to the support of this policy. It seems almost certain then that the creation of budgetary surpluses will prove much more difficult than the creation of budgetary deficits. The fiscal-policy weapon may be concluded to be more effective in combating depressions than in preventing inflation.

On the other hand, monetary policy should prove more effective in preventing inflation. This is true partly because an easy money policy, even if properly carried out, probably cannot ensure recovery from a major depression, whereas a tight money policy can ensure a check on inflation. An additional cause should be the relative freedom of the Federal Reserve Board to institute unpopular anti-inflationary policy. While political support may not be forthcoming for steps in the direction of sound anti-inflation fiscal policy, monetary policy exerting the same or similar effects may be independently initiated by the Federal Reserve Board.

The recent history of Federal Reserve action, however, seems to reverse the conclusions reached above. Actually, during the years 1946 to 1951, when inflation rather than deflation was the major threat to economic stability, monetary policy was exerted in support of inflation rather than in opposition to it. The record of fiscal policy is somewhat better, although it is not encouraging. In 1947 and 1948, significant cash surpluses were generated, but an examination of events of those years reveals that these were more or less accidental results of the inflation itself and not deliberate results of anti-inflation fiscal policy. The monetary policy of this period was discussed in some detail in Chapter 23. As a result of pressures exerted upon it by the Treasury Department, the Federal Reserve System took action to support the price of government securities. Commercial banks had been allowed to accumulate large amounts of such securities as a result of the manner in which World War II was financed. When the war was over, pressure was put on banks to extend loans to business firms and other borrowers. To meet such demands, banks desired to convert other earning assets (primarily government securities) into reserves on which a loan expansion could be initiated. Without any interference in the government-securities market, the commercial banks' attempt to sell government securities would have driven the market price down and rates of yield up. This would have caused banks to be more reluctant to sell securities, since they would have been taking a capital loss on the sale plus giving up a higher-yield asset. If this policy of noninterference had not sufficed to dampen the inflationary pressure, the Federal Reserve System could have further driven bond prices down by open-market sales.

The policy of price support did just the opposite. As banks sold government securities in order to replenish reserves, downward pressure was put on the price of such securities, and the Federal Reserve Banks were forced to buy up large amounts in order to maintain bond prices. This policy amounted to ensuring the banks that they would take no capital loss whatever on the sale of securities. So all the bank-held government securities were essentially made equivalent to excess reserves on which a multiple expansion of loans and deposits could be, and was, built. This perverse policy of the Federal Reserve System in supporting the prices of government securities must be placed as a primary causal factor in the inflation following World War II.

The sharp inflation that took place at the outset of the Korean War, from June, 1950, until April, 1951, provides us with an excellent case study of the effects of perverse monetary action. The expanded defense effort had hardly begun to take effect in terms of government expenditure during this period; actually, the government operated at a budget surplus over these nine months. Yet the level of wholesale prices rose by about 16 per cent. This price increase was brought about by the attempts of individuals to stock up on consumer goods and of business firms to accumulate inventories and to expand investment. But these attempts could only have been successful through an expansion of bank loans, and banks could only expand loans on the basis of excess reserves. Monetary actions actually created excess reserves for the banking system in this situation, rather than destroying them. The Federal Reserve Banks purchased government securities in the amount of more than four billion dollars between June 30, 1950, and March 28, 1951. Some of this potential increase in excess reserves was offset by a gold outflow, and some opposing action was finally taken in the form of an increase in reserve requirements in January, 1951, but the excess reserves already existing in June, 1950, plus those created, were sufficient to allow banks to expand loans by almost eleven billion dollars during this period.

After considerable pressure from Congressional leaders and other interested groups, as well as members of the Federal Reserve Board itself, the policy of price support for marketable government securities was abandoned in March, 1951. For a time government-security prices were allowed to find their own levels as determined by supply and demand conditions in the securities markets. Prices were allowed to drop below support levels, and yields were allowed to rise somewhat. This shift in monetary policy must be given some credit for the period of relative economic stability that followed in 1951, 1952, and 1953. Further action toward restricting the availability of credit was taken in the first half of 1953 with the change in administration. In mid-1953, however, the threat of inflation appeared to be over, and the Federal Reserve System took cautious steps toward an easing of monetary conditions. Reserve requirements were lowered, and the Federal Reserve Banks began purchasing small amounts of government securities. In early 1954 the rediscount rate was lowered as the fear of recession became more widespread.

It is not yet clear just how effective monetary policy would now be if either drastic inflation or severe depression threatened. In the case of threatened inflation, it is not certain that the Federal Reserve System would allow bond prices to fall without limit and even go beyond this to active sales if bond prices started to fall significantly, because the interests of the Treasury in refinancing maturing issues of the public debt cannot be completely overlooked. If a serious deflationary threat should arise, on the other hand, one cannot be sure that the monetary authorities would inaugurate an easy-money policy of sufficient force to prove effective. In a similar manner, Treasury officials, having seen the results of the World War II sales of bonds to the banking system rather than to the nonbanking public, may prove overly reluctant in the face of incipient recession to place new debt issues with the banking system.

It may be hoped that in either case economic stabilization is accepted as the primary goal by responsible officials of both the Federal Reserve Board and the Treasury Department. This must exist as a hope alone, however, until Congress takes effective action in laying down directions or rules of action which will ensure that economic stabilization is to be given first place in the guidance of monetary and fiscal policy.

LONG-RUN MONETARY REFORMS

The discussion of monetary policy so far has assumed that the underlying institutional structure remains unchanged. Specifically, this assumes that fractional-reserve banking subject to the central-banking controls of the Federal Reserve System remains unchanged and, further, that the Federal Reserve Board operates under no prescribed rule of policy but instead possesses wide discretionary powers.

Some students of monetary affairs recommend rather drastic and fundamental changes in this monetary structure with a view toward making monetary policy a more effective instrument of economic stabilization. First of all, they recommend the abolition of fractional-reserve banking and its replacement by 100 per cent reserve banking. This reform is designed to remove from banks the power to expand or contract the total amount of the circulating medium. Under this scheme, banks would be required to hold 100 per cent reserves behind all deposits. This requirement would prevent the operation of either a positive or a negative deposit multiplier. People's attitudes concerning the manner in which they desire to hold money, whether in the form of currency or of bank deposits, would no longer be a determining factor affecting the size of the money supply. Under a 100 per cent reserve system, the only money-creating and -destroying power would rest with government.

While this scheme would make the government solely and directly responsible for changes in the quantity of money, it would also serve to remove government interference with the lending function of banks. If banks were stripped of their money-creating and -destroying power, there would be little need for the type of control now exercised through the Federal Reserve Board. Under the 100 per cent reserve plan, banks could not lend out funds deposited with them in checking accounts. Lending banks might sell "shares" (as the building and loan associations now do) and lend out funds thus received.

The advocates of this scheme do not rely upon this reform alone to accomplish economic stabilization. By itself it would do nothing more than prevent the perverse shifts in the quantity of circulating medium in periods of depression and inflation which are made possible by the fractional-reserve system. The scheme is presented merely as one part of a total policy program. Once the government is given exclusive power to create and destroy money, then positive and definite rules must be adopted which will direct government action. One such rule, which has been supported by Professors Mints and Simons, would be the stabilization of the price level. A monetary authority would be set up and directed to operate in accordance with a rule of price-level stabilization, withdrawing money from the economy when prices tend to rise and pumping money into the economy when prices tend to fall.[1] With a national debt of such proportions as we now possess, the most important means of effectuating a price-level-stabilization policy would be provided. The monetary authority would pay off debt with newly created money when

---

[1] See L. W. Mints, *Monetary Policy for a Competitive Society* (New York: McGraw-Hill Book Company, Inc., 1950); and H. C. Simons, "Rules vs. Authority in Monetary Policy," *Economic Policy for a Free Society* (Chicago: University of Chicago Press, 1948).

the price level falls, and issue new debt in exchange for money when the price level rises.

Another plan, advanced by Professor Friedman, combines 100 per cent reserve banking with automatic, fiscally induced changes in the stock of money. This would make shifts in the quantity of money dependent only on the generation of deficits or surpluses. The government budget would be balanced at an estimated high level of income and employment. Government expenditures would be covered by tax revenues only if the estimated level of income were attained. If national income fell below this level, tax revenues would automatically be reduced, while expenditures would be increased (greater payments for unemployment compensation, etc.). This would automatically create a deficit, which would be financed by additions to the money stock. As long as income was below the desired level, deficit financing would be continued and new money created. On the other side, if an inflationary income level were generated, tax revenues would be increased, government expenditures would be decreased somewhat, and a surplus would be created. The surplus funds would be neutralized or destroyed. This surplus financing would continue until the inflationary threat had been eliminated.[1] In order to make this plan operate as effectively and as forcefully as possible, considerable built-in automaticity of response is needed. This is accomplished on the tax side by a progressive rate structure which ensures that tax revenues change more than proportionately as income changes. The same result is accomplished on the expenditure side by legal provision for such types of government expenditure as unemployment compensation, relief, old-age assistance, etc.

Neither the political practicability of securing the adoption of these rather drastic monetary reforms nor the particular problems involved in their implementation once adopted have been considered here. In this area, as in all policy areas, it is far easier to point up deficiencies in the existing institutional structure than to recommend fully acceptable alternatives. Whether or not the structural reforms mentioned here provide satisfactory long-run solutions to the problem of economic stabilization is a highly debatable question. The very severity of the reforms needed to secure full governmental control over the quantity of money does serve, however, to point up the enormity of the task of economic stabilization if the existing institutional structure remains unchanged.

[1] This plan is presented in Milton Friedman, "A Monetary and Fiscal Framework for Economic Stability," *American Economic Review*, Vol. 38, pp. 245–264 (June, 1948).

CHAPTER 28

GOVERNMENT SPENDS, TAXES, AND TRANSFERS

In Chapter 26 we discussed the fiscal policy of government in connection with its usefulness in helping to maintain desirable levels of income, employment, and prices. Government expenditure was considered primarily as a component of total demand for goods and services, and attention was focused on the inflation-preventing function of taxation. The government's budget was discussed chiefly as a tool to be used in maintaining a high level of economic activity. No attention has been given to the effects of government expenditures and taxation on the nature of economic activity, *i.e.*, on the allocation of the economic resources of the nation and on the distribution of economic rewards among the people. This chapter will discuss government expenditure and taxation in these terms.

GOVERNMENT EXPENDITURE AND RESOURCE ALLOCATION

A Limitation on Consumer Sovereignty

In the beginning of Part A, we discussed consumer sovereignty as the great organizing principle of the free-enterprise economy. Purchases by individuals in the market were considered as votes for the production of goods and services. Businessmen seeking to make the greatest possible profit are attracted by these consumer purchases to combine basic resources for necessary production of the goods and services indicated as the most desirable in a pecuniary sense. As with many of our economic constructions, however, the economy guided solely by consumer sovereignty must be recognized as an oversimplified model. There are many limitations on the operations of the guiding principle of consumer sovereignty (including monopoly in all its forms), but perhaps the most significant in the United States of today is that limitation which is due to the existence of government as a major purchaser of goods and services. In developing the principles of resource allocation in Part A, we assumed, in effect, that no government existed. This was a reasonably realistic assumption, with reference to government's economic importance, until the last half century. For this latter period, however, one of the dominant characteristics of the American economy has been the increasing amount of government activity, in both an absolute and a relative sense. The degree to which this growth has taken place may be indicated by an illustrative glance at the facts. In 1900 only one out of every twenty-five employed workers in the United States was employed by some governmental unit. In 1950, one of every eight employees in the nation worked for the government. Government now owns one dollar out of every five dollars' worth of capital assets, whereas in 1900 only one out of every fifteen dollars' worth was government owned.[1]

Total government expenditures (Federal, state, and local) in the United States amounted to approximately 12 per cent of national money income in 1929, the last year prior to the great depression. In the peak spending year of World War II, 1945, this proportion exceeded 60 per cent. Since World War II, the ratio of total government expenditures to national income has never fallen below 20 per cent. These proportions serve to make clear the significance of government in the total economy and the limitation placed on the operation of the principle of consumer sovereignty. Government demand for goods and services becomes important in determining the pattern of resource allocation. The power of individuals voting in the market to call forth goods and services, to motivate production, is reduced, and the power of individuals voting in the polling places (or their representatives) to call forth economic goods and services is correspondingly increased.[2] Voter sovereignty replaces consumer sovereignty, carrying with it all the imperfections of decision making in representative democracies, the influence of pressure groups, voter ignorance, etc. It must be recognized that one of the most difficult problems of our times concerns the proper dividing line between these two great principles of economic control.

The Government as Purchaser

In carrying out many of its functions, the government enters the market and purchases real goods and services. For example, if the service is that which is to be provided by an additional aircraft carrier, the government, via the Department of Defense, will enter into a contract with a private firm, or group of firms, for the construction of the ship. Thus,

---

[1] See S. Fabricant, *The Growth of Governmental Activity in the United States 1900–1950* (New York: National Bureau of Economic Research, Inc., 1953), for a careful presentation of these and many similar facts regarding the growth in governmental activity over the half century.

[2] For an excellent discussion of the encroachment on consumer sovereignty by government, the reader may consult George Hildebrand, "Consumer Sovereignty in Modern Times," *American Economic Review*, Vol. 41, pp. 19–33 (May, 1951).

the government's dollars "vote for" the use of resources in shipbuilding, and are as influential as are dollars of private expenditure (consumption or investment) in determining the pattern of resource use.[1]

Business firms in combining productive inputs and transforming them into final outputs will respond to government demand. As a result, a significantly different pattern of resource use arises in any economy in which government is a large purchaser from that which would arise in an economy where the government is a small purchaser. The impact of government purchases tends to affect nearly all segments of the economy in greater or lesser degree.

The input-output table introduced in Chapter 2 is useful in allowing us to trace the primary impact of expanded government purchases. In fact, this is one of the many uses to which the input-output table has been put by government economists. In order to illustrate this usage, let us assume that the government decides to construct an atomic-energy installation. Construction work will be undertaken by private firms under contract to government. The initial change imposed on the input-output table will be in the row 45, column 48, item, Government Purchases from the New Construction Industry.[2] As this item expands, the total purchases of the construction industry must expand, so the second-round effects may be traced by looking at column 45, which shows the distribution of the construction industry's purchases from other industries. By glancing over the data in column 45, it can be seen that the industries most affected will be lumber, stone, clay and glass products, iron and steel, fabricated metal products, trade, and households. The last item indicates the expansion in wages and salaries to labor. Third-round effects could now be traced by looking at the column for each of these industries. In this general way, the impact of an initial change in the pattern of government expenditure may be traced throughout the whole economic system.

The input-output table alone is both too general and too restricted to allow us to trace fully the effects of the change in government expenditure on atomic installations. First of all, the input-output table is calculated in national totals and makes no breakdown for economic regions. Clearly, one of the most important economic effects of constructing an atomic installation will be a change in the geographical pattern of economic activity. Thriving cities were created out of relatively barren countrysides at Oak Ridge, Los Alamos, and other places. An additional

[1] At times, the government may desire to influence resource allocation in other ways, *e.g.*, through the imposition of direct controls over resource use. These will be discussed in Chap. 31.

[2] We are assuming that this is a net addition to government expenditure. We are neglecting the taxation side of the government for the time being.

limitation of the input-output table is that it does not allow the effects of price changes which result from the initial expenditure to be taken into account. The atomic-energy installations near Aiken, South Carolina, for example, increased the demand for construction workers in the surrounding area. This increase in demand caused wage rates for construction workers to increase. The increase in construction workers' wages relative to wages in nearby cotton-textile mills probably served to attract workers away from the textile mills into construction. Textile-mill operators may perhaps have been forced to increase wage rates in order to hold laborers. This, had it taken place, would have tended to increase the costs of production of textile goods. This increase in cost would have shifted the supply curve of cotton-textile products to the left, which would have tended to increase price. The increase in cotton-textile prices would also have tended to reduce the quantity of cotton-textile products demanded. An increase in the price of cotton textiles might serve to increase the demand for synthetic fibers—nylon, orlon, dacron, etc. Firms producing these fibers might in this case find it profitable to expand production. Thus, the effects of the initial government expenditure can be traced throughout the economy. It should be recognized that the effects become less significant the further we trace them.

By using both the input-output table and the price-theory analysis of Part A, we have been able to indicate the manner in which government expenditure on real goods and services affects the allocation of economic resources. This type of expenditure is called "production expenditure," with the implication that something was "produced" for government in the process. The word "production" should not be thought to imply, however, that this type is more "productive" socially than "transfer" expenditure.

Indirect Effects of Government Spending

The effects of government expenditure on the allocation of economic resources are not limited to those caused directly by the government's purchases of goods and services. The provision of government services may also indirectly alter the resource-use pattern. Government provision of education is a good example here. This makes up a major portion of state and local government expenditure. Direct effects of the sort discussed above are confined to the shifting of economic resources into school-building construction and the teaching profession. The indirect effects are far more important. Public education can best be considered as an investment in human resources. This is a type of investment which appears extremely productive in a social sense yet would be much less extensive if the function were left in private hands. This is true since the benefits from education are long-run in nature and are not fully concentrated on the private individuals who would be forced to undergo the costs. Society in the next generation will benefit a great deal more from the education of children in this generation than will the parents of the children. Left alone, parents would probably tend to undervalue educational investment. As a result, we would have more investment in capital resources, less in human resources, were it not for public activity in the educational field. Similar effects result from public provision of health facilities, sanitation, and safety regulation.

Important indirect effects upon the allocation of resources can be traced from almost any major government expenditure. To provide another important example, let us consider expenditure for highways. The direct effects would be concentrated primarily in the construction, machinery, cement, and asphalt industries. The indirect effects which stem from the provision of highways and streets are concentrated, on the other hand, in the automobile and petroleum industries. By having available better highways, individuals and firms utilize far more resources in the form of automobiles, trucks, and buses than would be the case with a less adequate road system.

A significant share of government expenditure is made without the government's purchasing real goods and services at all. These are called "transfer expenditures," the implication being that funds are transferred directly to certain individuals and firms. These tend to influence economic activity by their effects on the behavior of recipients. Important categories of this type of expenditure are interest on the government debt, old-age-assistance payments, subsidies to veterans, and unemployment compensation. Some of the recipient groups are likely to exert less productive effort as a result of the government transfer payment, but this does not appear to be an important effect. Perhaps a more important type of reaction is found in the change in the saving-spending pattern. As the government assumes more and more the burden of insecurity previously borne by individuals and families, the saving by families for future rainy days is likely to be reduced and current spending for consumption increased. While this might prove a desirable reaction during times of unemployment when less saving and more spending are needed, in the long run it is likely to result in a smaller rate of real capital accumulation.

Although transfer expenditures differ basically from production expenditures in that no direct impact on resource allocation occurs as a result of government purchase of real goods and services, the distinction may easily be overemphasized. In many cases the government faces a choice between transferring funds directly to recipients and purchasing real goods for their benefit. The case of free school lunches provides an example. If the government actually purchases the lunches and gives them to the children, this outlay is considered a production expenditure.

If, however, the government gave the children the money with which they might purchase the school lunches, the outlay would be considered a transfer expenditure. For many of the welfare types of expenditures, this choice is a real one. If transfer payments are made directly to individuals, the pattern of resource allocation is modified on the spending side only to the extent that the private purchases of the recipients are shifted. If expenditure is made by government on tangible goods and services, the pattern of resource allocation is directly affected. A greater limitation is placed on the operation of the principle of consumer sovereignty in the latter case than in the former. In making decisions of this sort, great care must be exercised lest government officials begin to think that they are somehow better able to tell the people what they should want than are the people themselves.

The Real Cost of Government Services

In our discussion of costs in Chapter 5, we concentrated for the most part on money costs. This is appropriate when discussing the behavior of business firms, since business decisions are affected by money-cost considerations. However, when we discussed cost in a broader sense, we introduced the idea of alternative cost. The real cost of anything is not a money cost; money serves more or less as the unit of account in the estimation process. Real cost must be considered in the terms of sacrificed alternatives or opportunities.

This notion of alternative cost is extremely useful in considering the real costs of government services. The cost to society incurred by the government's provision of a particular public service is the amount of other goods or services which could have been produced by the economic resources that are used in the production of the public service. The cost to the United States of maintaining a large defense establishment is the goods or services which the labor and capital resources employed in the defense establishment (soldiers, workers in aircraft factories, physicists, iron, steel, etc.) might have produced alternatively, publicly or privately.

In this view, we may state that many of our post-office buildings, for example, were constructed at a very low or negligible real cost to society, even though the money costs may have been significant. This is true because many of these buildings were constructed during the great depression of the 1930's. At this time, many economic resources were unemployed and were not producing anything. Government employment of these resources allowed projects to be constructed which were essentially costless in a real sense, because little of value in the nature of alternatives was sacrificed. We may state that the real costs of government services, the production of which employs otherwise unemployed resources, consist mainly of alternative government services which might have been produced. The real costs of post-office buildings constructed in the 1930's are not represented by alternatives in the private economy but by the parks, swimming pools, etc., that could instead have been produced by government. In summary, for government services as a whole, the real costs are low in periods of depression because the private economy is not putting many resources to full use.

On the other hand, the real costs of government services in times of full employment are high. In real terms, it was much more costly for the United States to build aircraft carriers or housing projects in 1954 than it would have been in 1934, even though precisely the same amount of labor, steel, and other resources might have been used. During periods of high employment, the resource-allocation problem, or the problem of scarcity, comes into its full importance. The expansion of government services must utilize resources which would otherwise have produced something for the private economy. More tanks mean fewer private automobiles, more public housing means less private housing, etc.

TAXATION AND THE ALLOCATION OF RESOURCES

Taxation to Cover Real Costs of Government Services

Government fiscal policy alters the pattern of resource use not only on the expenditure side of the government account but on the taxation side as well. The fundamental purpose of taxation may be thought of as that of spreading the real costs of government among the people in an acceptable fashion. Thus, in a period of unemployment when real costs of government services are negligible or low, taxation need not, and indeed should not, be imposed. In such periods, the traditional function of taxation, namely, that of raising revenue, is not an appropriate one.[1] On the other hand, in periods of full or near-full employment, government services are provided only at a positive real cost in terms of alternative goods and services. In order that these real costs be spread among individuals in a reasonably fair and recognizable manner, therefore, taxes must be levied to finance government expenditures. If expenditures are not matched by taxation, government demand is merely added to private demand, and inflation is the probable result. In this sense, inflation must be looked upon as a tax levied on those persons whose incomes remain relatively fixed. As a recent example, the Korean War inflation in 1950–1951 was extremely burdensome on fixed-income groups. We may say that these groups bore a considerable share of the burden of

---

[1] This applies only to Federal-government taxation. State and local units possess no money-creating power, and therefore the traditional function of taxation for revenue only is entirely appropriate.

rearmament in this period, a share which did not appear in the allocation of the money tax burden.

Taxation and Consumer Sovereignty

The limitation on the exercise of consumer sovereignty represented by government's provision of services manifests itself also on the taxation side. Whereas government expenditures represent dollar votes calling forth production, taxation allows these government votes to be even more influential by reducing the expenditures of private individuals and firms. The power of individuals and firms to direct the flow of resources is reduced by taxation. Taxation withdraws income, thus potentially reducing both private spending and saving.

The more specific effects of taxation on the resource-use pattern depend on the way in which taxes are imposed. This involves two questions: first, who pays the taxes, and second, how the payment of the tax affects the taxpayers' economic behavior. The next step, then, is a discussion of the major types of taxes actually imposed by government, with the purpose of answering these two questions.

Personal Income Taxation

The most important single source of revenue in the fiscal system is the personal income tax. Revenues from this tax make up almost one-half of total Federal tax collections (about 33 billion dollars in fiscal 1954). This tax is perhaps the most acceptable of all taxes. First of all, it is paid directly by all individuals receiving incomes of more than a minimum amount. It is not imposed in a discriminatory fashion on a particular subgroup of individuals in the economy. The burden is general and, at the same time, recognizable. Second, it exerts perhaps a lesser effect on the organization of economic resources than any of the other major taxes. This is largely because of the generality of the tax. Since the tax is supposedly levied on all income recipients, it is difficult to escape payment by a shift of occupation or profession.

The behavior of some individuals is, of course, affected. The productive efforts of some, especially the high-income receivers, are reduced as a result of the high rates of the personal income tax. This is due to the fact that the effective marginal rates of tax are very high for those individuals who receive high incomes.

The Federal personal income tax is highly progressive in its rate structure. This means that the effective tax rate increases as income increases. Marginal rates of tax (the ratio between the additional tax liability and an additional increment of income) are higher than average rates. This tends to make the effects of the tax on productive effort more significant than would be the case if the tax rate did not increase with income.

For example, a corporation executive (or any other high-income receiver) with an annual total income of $300,000 might pay a maximum of about $200,000 in taxes (at 1953 rates); thus his average rate of tax on his whole income will be 67 per cent. However, if his income is increased from $300,000 to $320,000, with his authorized deductions remaining unchanged, his tax is increased from $200,000 to $218,400. The maximum marginal rate of tax is 92 per cent. Such high marginal rates may exert considerable influence on decisions of certain high-salaried individuals whether to play golf or to work harder, to take a Florida vacation or to stay home and work, etc. The personal income tax may also exert an influence on the rate of real-capital accumulation through its impact on savings during periods of substantially full employment. The more progressive the rates, the greater the reduction in savings that is likely to result.

The characteristic features of the personal income tax may exert, however, as much or more influence on the pattern of economic activity than the rates themselves. The tax is levied on annual incomes and contains no provision for averaging out high and low incomes over longer periods. This requires, therefore, that the individual with a fluctuating or uncertain source of income pay a higher effective rate of tax on his income over the whole earning period than the individual with a more stable and secure income. This tends to discourage persons from entering occupations with fluctuating incomes and to place an undue premium on occupations promising income stability over time.

A second characteristic of the personal income tax which exerts important economic effects is the treatment of capital-gains income. The difference between the original purchase price and the sales price of an asset held more than six months is not treated as ordinary income. Only one-half of this gain need be reported as income, and this is taxed at a preferential rate if the individual's income is high. This provides a tremendous incentive for ordinary income to be converted into capital gains in order to secure this favorable tax treatment. One of the ways in which this may be done is for a corporation to plow back its earnings into investment rather than paying such earnings out to stockholders as dividends. As the investment is expanded, capital-stock prices rise; shareholders desiring to receive income may sell off shares and pay less tax than if dividends had been paid to them directly.

A third characteristic of the personal income tax which seems to exert an indirect effect on the economy lies in the withholding features. A large proportion (about two-thirds) of Federal personal income tax collections are withheld from wages and salaries at the source of payment. This feature has the great advantage of administrative convenience to the government and the apparent advantage of easing the tax burden to the individual. This last is only an apparent advantage, however, for since individuals never "feel" the tax as such—it is removed before they look at their pay checks—they are likely to underestimate the real costs of government services. The economic effects of the withholding provision are likely to be that people will vote to have government provide more services and the private economy correspondingly less, even though, if confronted with the choice directly, they might vote the other way.

Business Taxation

The second most important source of Federal-government revenue is the corporation income tax. Over 23 billion dollars, or about 30 per cent of total Federal tax collections, was obtained from this tax in fiscal 1953. This tax is levied directly on the net incomes of corporations. Corporation net income above a $25,000 minimum amount is taxed at 52 per cent. Although it will probably remain important as a revenue producer, this tax can never be considered an equitable one, since it disregards the structure of individual ownership of corporations.

There has been much controversy over the economic effects of the corporate income tax. Businessmen contend that the tax is considered as a cost of production and that it is passed on to buyers of products through higher prices. Economists have not fully accepted this view. Their reasons for not doing so may be appreciated by a review of the analysis of the behavior of business firms. If firms (corporations) make an attempt to secure maximum profits, they will produce and sell the output for which the difference between total revenue and total costs is greatest. A necessary condition for attaining this position is that marginal revenue must equal marginal costs. This is true regardless of the market position of the firm, whether it is monopolistic or competitive. It follows that the maximum profit output would be changed only by forces changing either marginal revenue or marginal costs. If output does not change, price is not changed, since presumably price reflects buyers' willingness to demand that output.

If the tax is placed on the true net profit of corporations, this cannot affect either marginal revenue or marginal costs. This is because it is imposed as a percentage of net income. If the firm was maximizing net income or profit before the tax is imposed, then a fixed percentage tax on this net income would still leave a larger residual than would be left out of a smaller total net income before tax.

On the basis of this type of reasoning, it is concluded that a tax on true profits cannot be passed on in the form of higher prices. Therefore, the burden must rest on the owners of the corporations. Since the corporation is such an important type of business organization, the effects of the tax tend to reduce the marginal product of capital throughout the economy.

The actual effects of the corporation income tax as employed in the United States appear to be some combination of that claimed by business-men and that indicated by the use of theoretical economic analysis. There are perhaps two main explanations. First, economic analysis assumes that all business firms attempt to maximize profits. Actually, firms may be motivated by incentives other than profit maximization. This is perhaps especially true for those corporations possessing some monopoly power. A monopoly firm may decide that "reasonable profits" are a more desir-able goal, and more safe, than maximum profits. The monopoly firm may, accordingly, deliberately keep price below the profit-maximizing level in order to keep potential competitors from being too much attracted. In this situation, an increase in the corporation income tax would probably result in an increase in product price. The tax would serve to push the price up toward the profit-maximizing price.

The second reason that the corporation income tax is probably partially reflected in product prices involves a consideration of the tax base itself. If the tax were based on true net profit in an economic sense, the costs of the firm would not be affected. In actual fact, however, the corporation income tax is based on a more inclusive concept of profit. Included in profit are the total returns to the owners of the corporation, *i.e.*, the equity shareholders. Clearly, a portion of this return is cost in an economic sense. Economic profit is defined to exclude a normal rate of return (*i.e.*, what the capital could earn elsewhere) on invested capital. The inclusion of this element of cost in taxable income should not affect the short-run behavior of firms, but it may affect behavior in the long run. It serves to reduce the return to equity shareholders, and this in turn may tend to reduce the supply of equity capital for corporations relative to partner-ships and proprietorships. This reduction in supply may tend to increase the difficulty of securing equity capital for corporate investment which, in turn, may eventually result in higher product prices.[1]

Excise Taxation

The third major type of taxation consists of excises levied on the manu-facture, sale, or consumption of various commodities. This has been a relatively unimportant, although still significant, source of revenue for the Federal government. But it is the major revenue source for state governments. The two basic forms must be distinguished and considered separately because of the differences in economic impact. First, a tax may be imposed on the sale of a single commodity with other commodities and services left untaxed or taxed at much lower rates. Second, a tax

[1] For a comprehensive treatment of the corporation income tax see Richard Goode, *The Corporation Income Tax* (New York: John Wiley & Sons, Inc., 1951).

may be imposed at equivalent (or approximately equivalent) rates on the sale of all (or nearly all) commodities and services.

1. *Taxation of a Single Commodity.* The discussion of the case in which an excise tax is imposed on the sale of a single commodity allows us to utilize the analysis of Part A exceptionally well. In treating the taxes actually imposed on liquor, tobacco, and gasoline it is best to employ the single-commodity assumption. This is because these commodities are taxed at considerably higher rates than other commodities.

An excise tax on a single commodity (or the differential between this and the normal rate of tax on all commodities) will tend to be shifted in large part to the consumers of that commodity in the form of price increases. Again we must make a distinction between the competitive and the monopoly case. If the industry is fully competitive and long-run average costs are constant, the whole of the tax will be shifted to consumers in the long run. This is because firms will find that paying the tax subjects them to short-run losses; they will move out of the industry into non-taxed fields until the rate of return is again normal. This will result only when price has gone up by the full amount of the tax. This case may be shown in Figure 28.1. *D* represents the industry demand curve (which we assume to remain unchanged). S_B represents the

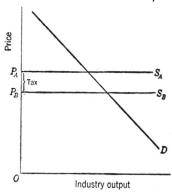

Figure 28.1. PRICE INCREASE EQUALS TAX—

In Constant Cost Industry

long-run industry supply curve before tax, S_A the corresponding long-run curve after tax.

If the competitive industry is one of increasing costs, a portion of the tax burden will be shifted backward to the sellers of productive services. As firms leave the industry as a result of the losses caused by the tax, the demands for productive services peculiarly adapted to the taxed industry are reduced. This tends to reduce prices paid to the owners of these productive services. Thus, the tax burden is borne by both consumers of the product in terms of higher prices and owners of productive services in terms of lower input prices.

When an excise tax is imposed on the product of a monopolist, this will tend to be partially borne by the monopolist and partially shifted to the buyers of the product and in some cases to the sellers of productive services. This may be illustrated in Figure 28.2.

D represents the demand curve for the monopolist's product, *MR* the marginal revenue curve, MC_b the marginal cost curve before tax. The imposition of the tax on the monopoly firm will increase marginal cost by the amount of the tax, shifting the curve to MC_a after the tax. The monopoly firm will then tend to reduce output (sales) from OB to OA and increase price from P_b to P_a. It may be noted that the price increase is not so great as the amount of the tax. The exact proportion that will be shifted forward to consumers as a price increase depends on the relative slopes of the demand curve and the marginal cost curve.

The actual effects of the taxes imposed on tobacco and liquor may be estimated by using a combination of the competitive and monopoly analyses sketched above. Both the liquor and the tobacco industries are oligopolistic; hence they contain elements of both competition and monopoly.

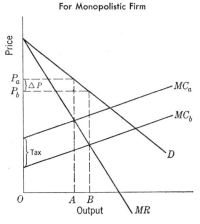

Figure 28.2. **PRICE INCREASE IS LESS THAN TAX—**

For Monopolistic Firm

The high excise taxes tend to be borne by consumers in higher prices, by firms in lower oligopoly profits, and by owners of productive services (*e.g.*, tobacco farmers) in lower prices. Another characteristic feature of the cigarette industry is the extremely low responsiveness of quantity demanded to price changes. This tends to cause a greater proportion of the tax load to be passed on in higher prices than would otherwise be the case. This fact also indicates the productivity of the cigarette tax as a revenue source and thus its political popularity.

The liquor industry provides yet another example of the workings of competitive processes. The high tax during World War II and after has tended to push consumer prices very high. This high price has provided a strong incentive for firms to produce a closely competing but slightly differentiated product, namely, untaxed liquor, or "moonshine."

2. *General Excise Taxation.* The effects of a general excise (sales) tax imposed on the manufacture or sale of most or all commodities are considerably different from those of an excise imposed on the manufacture or sale of a single commodity. If a tax is imposed generally on all commodities, a greater portion of the tax is likely to be borne by the sellers of productive services in lowered input prices than by consumers of final products in the form of higher product prices. Under given conditions of demand, the price of a product may be increased only if the quantity supplied is reduced. In the case of a particular excise tax, the egress of firms from the taxed industry does reduce quantity supplied. But if the

tax is imposed on the products of most or all industries, there can be little egress of firms or resources from taxed industries; nothing could be gained in moving from one taxed industry to another. If such shifting is not possible, the resources devoted to the production of each product remain about the same after as before the tax. Thus output remains about the same, and product prices remain about the same. But the firms affected must pay the tax out of the same total revenue as before. Therefore, the demand for productive inputs will fall. And in order for the same amount of productive inputs to be employed, input prices must fall. The major share of the burden of a general excise tax then falls upon the sellers of productive inputs. It should be recognized that the so-called general excise taxes are normally not general in the sense that they apply equally to all products and services. Most states exempt major groups of commodities and services. The effects, therefore, are likely to be some combination of the specific excise and the truly general excise tax. As the taxes become more general, a greater share of the burden tends to fall on the owners of productive services.

Property Taxation

Local units of government depend for revenue primarily on one tax, the property tax. As it is actually administered, this is nearly limited to a tax on real property. A tax on real property is the one major tax which can be effectively imposed by local levels of government, for real property is the only economic resource which is relatively immobile and therefore cannot readily be shifted across local boundary lines to escape taxation.

This relative immobility explains, in part, the peculiar difficulties that arise when we attempt to trace the economic effects of the property tax. If real property were completely immobile and also completely permanent (not subject to depreciation) and fixed in supply, a tax levied on such property would be borne exclusively by the owner of the property at the time the tax was imposed. Future owners would bear none of the burden. The tax would reduce the expected net return of the property, and, as was shown in Chapter 12, the value of a capital asset is determined by the expected net return. So future purchasers would pay less for the property than they would have paid before the tax. Current owners at the time of the imposition of the tax would bear the full burden of the tax for all time by a reduction in the capital value. This process is called the "capitalization" of the tax. Renters of the property would never pay any share of the tax under these assumptions, since the supply is not changed as a result of the tax. The tax thus has no effect on the allocation of resources; it is levied on "pure rent."

Neither land nor other forms of real property, however, fit the assumptions of absolute permanency and fixity of supply. If real property can be produced and destroyed much as other assets, then changes in supply may result from the tax, and some of the burden may be shifted both to subsequent purchasers and to renters. A high tax rate would tend to reduce the investment in the development and improvement of real property. This would reduce the supply, and this in turn would tend to increase both market value and rental charges.

THE GOVERNMENT AND REDISTRIBUTION OF INCOME

In the preceding sections, we discussed the impact of government expenditures and taxation on the allocation of economic resources. In this section, the effects of the government upon distribution of goods and services (income) will be examined. First of all, it is necessary to review in summary the analysis of income distribution contained in Part A. It was shown there that resources tend to be paid in accordance with their marginal revenue productivity to private firms. If competition prevails among buying firms, these firms will tend to purchase units of resources until the price of a resource is made equal to its marginal revenue product. If competition prevails among sellers of productive services, resources will be moved until the prices received for similar units are the same in all employments. While competition does not prevail fully in our economy, we may still say that resources tend to be paid in accordance with this productivity principle. The major virtue of this sort of payment to resources is that it is the only one which will provide incentives for owners to get resources into their most productive employments and for firms to combine inputs in the most effective fashion.

While the virtue of productivity payment to resources is a highly desirable one, the resulting distribution of income may not be acceptable. According to marginal productivity distribution, a single individual's income is determined by two things: first, the amount of resources over which he has command, and, second, the market evaluation of those resources. If the whole social income were distributed in this manner, some individuals would be extremely rich and others would starve to death. Individuals owning specialized resources upon which the market evaluation was very high (for example, a crooner or television comedian) would be paid high returns. Individuals owning no salable resources (the sick, the aged) would receive no income at all. An additional undesirable feature of the payment of resource owners in accordance with resource value productivity is the tendency toward cumulative inequality in income and wealth. An individual's income position depends in large measure on the amount of economic resources (human and nonhuman) which he inherits. A high income received by a father serves to increase the future income of the son. This is true because, first, the wealthy father is able to provide his son with favorable environmental conditions during childhood, *i.e.*, better education, health, nutrition, etc., thus making him a more productive worker later in life, and, second, the rich father may pass along to the son claims to nonhuman resources that yield income, *i.e.*, real property, stocks, bonds, cash, business connections, etc.

The undesirable features of productivity payment to resources may be largely eliminated, and yet the resource-allocation incentives of productivity retained, by a judicious use of the fiscal system. This is, in fact, accomplished to a considerable degree by the United States fiscal system. It is accomplished, however, without the redistribution of income as such being the avowed purpose; indeed, if policy makers (congressmen) were asked whether or not they approved a policy of income redistribution by the fiscal system, most of them would probably answer in the negative. Yet these same men would vote for old-age assistance, public housing, aid to the blind, grants to dependent children, etc., on the one hand and for sharply progressive income-tax rates on the other. The net result would be income redistribution.

Many government services are undertaken largely because of society's dissatisfaction with the prevailing distribution of income. At base, most of the agitation for improved housing, sanitation, nutrition, and similar services stems from a desire to improve the income position of certain groups. Public-housing projects are supported largely because slum dwellers do not have adequate incomes, not because they spend the income they do receive in what is considered a socially undesirable way.

A large share of the redistribution of income accomplished by the fiscal system arises not from the public expenditure but from the taxation side of the fiscal account. Popular ideas concerning the equitable distribution of the tax burden include the concept of progressive taxation. Even if government services were equally beneficial to all citizens, progressive taxation would ensure that real incomes—after taxes are paid and benefits from government are received—would be more nearly equal than before. Of course, not all individual taxes are progressive, but the major revenue producer, the personal income tax, clearly is progressive. Also, cumulative inequalities in income and wealth tend to be reduced by the estate, inheritance, and gift taxes. In total, considering all taxes and all government services, the fiscal system does serve to redistribute incomes substantially.[1]

---

[1] The precise amount of redistribution of real income carried out by the fiscal system is extremely difficult to determine. An estimation requires that the real burden of each tax and the real benefit of each government expenditure be imputed to individual income receivers in a specific fashion. The most complete attempt to make such a heroic estimation is that of John H. Adler, "The Fiscal System, The Distribution of Income and Public Welfare," in Kenyon E. Poole (ed.), *Fiscal Policy and the American*

It is important to realize that the fiscal system provides a way in which income redistribution may be changed without at the same time undermining the economic organization through direct interference with the price system. Individuals will continue to disagree on the amount of income redistribution actually desired. Some will want more than is now carried out; others will think we have already gone too far. The social decision will be a continuing compromise among conflicting opinions.

Although individuals may differ in their views concerning the amount of real income redistribution which it is desirable for the government to accomplish by means of the fiscal system, there should be general agreement on the desirability of public policy directed toward providing all individuals with a substantial equality of opportunity to earn income. The removal of inequalities in opportunity attacks the basic source of income inequality. Government action in the educational, health, nutrition, and sanitation areas may in many cases be best considered in this light rather than directly as income-redistribution measures. Here we find still another reason for the desirability of government action to keep markets free, *i.e.*, to encourage competition. For the maintenance of competition is one of the chief means of equalizing economic opportunity. As long as men are free to offer their services to any employer, free to enter any type of business, great pressure toward removal of severe income inequalities will be present. Monopoly, whether in the form of restrictive licensing arrangements, exclusive franchises, restrictions on entry into various occupations, or closed-shop provisos, tends always to prevent the equality of economic opportunity necessary to the smooth functioning of an enterprise system.

It was pointed out several times in Part A that the optimum allocation of resources was dependent on the assumption of a given distribution of income. A significant shift in the distribution of income will shift the allocation of resources. For example, incomes in the United States are now much more evenly distributed than they were at the turn of the century. As a result, many mansions in the old resort centers such as Newport, Tuxedo Park, and Saratoga are now tourist attractions only. Few incomes are high enough to support the lavish form of expenditure which was represented in the maintenance of such establishments. On the other hand, the leveling up of the lower incomes has increased significantly the resources devoted to the production of commodities such as meat, dairy products, and Ford and Plymouth automobiles.

Critics of the capitalistic system, especially those of the socialist and

---

Economy (New York: Prentice-Hall, Inc., 1947). Adler estimated that in 1946–1947 individuals in the lower-income brackets (under $4,000) gained from 3 to 60 per cent, while the upper-income individuals (above $4,000) lost from 4 to 23 per cent, as a result of the fiscal system (pp. 396–397).

communist varieties, pay a great deal of attention to the unequal distribution of income which arises in such a system. As pointed out here, this need not be a valid criticism at all, for we possess the means whereby the distribution can be changed within wide limits to one which is more acceptable. But another point needs to be made in rebuttal to such criticism. This concerns the distribution of rewards in any social system, whether capitalistic or not. The socialist system in which the state takes over and operates large segments of the economy is likely to generate even more severe inequalities in the distribution of rewards than is the capitalistic system. For in any system where most economic decisions are made by political groups, the inequalities of political power are likely to be more dangerous than inequalities in economic power generated by a capitalistic system.

CHAPTER 29

TWO DIFFICULT PROBLEMS: INDUSTRIAL AND LABOR MONOPOLIES

The point has been made repeatedly in this volume that monopoly is an evil. It distorts the allocation of resources and thereby diminishes the amount of goods and services which are available to consumers. In most fields, it has been contended, competitive forces should be encouraged and monopolistic tendencies should be curbed. And, although competitive elements in our economy are strong, it has been pointed out that monopoly in its various forms—single seller, oligopoly, cartel, and monopsony—is widespread. As long as we limit ourselves to broad generalizations, it is appropriate to observe that monopoly should be restrained; pure competition is the norm and the ideal. But in the real-world situation, it is clear that the ideal cannot be fully realized. Every seller who has identified his product with a trade-mark or brand name enjoys a degree of monopoly, and every entertainer attempts to develop a "style" which will differentiate his product from others. Monopoly elements of this sort are not always to be discouraged; standardization in many sectors of American life has undoubtedly already gone too far—pressures for conformity tend to wipe out all traces of individuality, to our great loss.

It should be observed, furthermore, that in a dynamic economy the evils of monopoly may be short-lived and less harmful than a strictly static analysis would indicate. The monopoly profits of innovators are likely to step up the rate of technological advance. And if freedom of entry of new firms is maintained, monopoly profits will tend to disappear in the long run as similar commodities are put on the market by other firms; even if entry is blocked, close substitutes may become available which will limit the magnitude of the monopolist's return.

This, of course, is not to deny that monopoly is an arch villain on the contemporary economic scene. If monopoly could be eliminated in all of its forms, many of the troublesome economic problems would promptly disappear. But since it is not practicable to remove all traces of monopoly from economic life and since some aspects of monopoly are relatively harmless, the question remains as to how much and what kinds of monopoly should be tolerated. This is and is likely to remain pretty largely an unsolved problem. Economic analysis can go so far, but no further, in its solution.

A REVIEW OF MONOPOLY CATEGORIES

Firms That Act Independently

Since we have discarded the idea that all monopoly in its broadest sense should be subject to government interference (because nearly every firm falls within this classification), the next step involves a reexamination of the categories of monopoly on the selling side with a view toward assessing the need for government intervention. The first of these includes those firms which disregard completely the actions of other firms and make price policy independently. This category has two subgroups. The first includes those firms which are large enough effectively to control the whole industry. The second includes those firms which disregard the actions of other firms not because they are so large but because they are so small relative to the whole industry. The first subcategory is perhaps the purest monopoly type, while the second approaches the competitive situation. For the second subcategory, the competitive solution would probably result except for the fact that each firm possesses an individual monopoly in the production and sale of its own brand-named and trademarked products. This is the area of so-called "monopolistic competition." Here monopoly power in the sense of firms' being able to secure sizable monopoly profits is severely limited. Yet the distortion of resource use may be severe because firms in this type of market situation will tend normally to undertake cost- and price-increasing activities (advertising promotion) in order to gain sales rather than cost- and price-reducing activities. The major underlying reason for the success of such sales-promotion activity is the ignorance of consumers. Again this points up a limitation of our analysis in Part A. In Chapter 3, consumer demand was discussed as if consumers knew what they were buying, when actually this is frequently not the case. In the area of "monopolistic competition," therefore, the weight of government intervention should perhaps be placed on attempts to make consumers more aware of the alternatives which are available rather than on interference with the market positions of producing and selling firms.

The first subcategory, which includes firms large enough effectively to control the market for a single commodity or service, was said above to constitute the purest monopoly type. But there another limitation of our economic analysis is immediately apparent. In Part A we discussed the pricing of products and services as if there were no problem of defining a commodity or product. Nowhere in the principles of Part A did we define a commodity clearly. For some purposes such a definition is not needed, but it is necessary here. Would a firm possessing the exclusive right to the production and sale of pearl buttons be considered a monopoly so dangerous as to warrant government prosecution? The answer depends upon whether or not we wish to define "pearl buttons" as a separate commodity category. Or would it be preferable to define "buttons" as the commodity, and say that we should consider the whole button industry? But even here, would a firm possessing effective control over the production and marketing of buttons of all types be a dangerous monopoly from a public-policy point of view? Perhaps not, unless it also controlled the market for zippers. Should the commodity grouping be widened to be "fasteners," or something of the sort? These are questions of the kind which economic analysis cannot answer satisfactorily and which nevertheless must be answered before the government can decide when public action should be taken.

A second major task facing the government, or its advisers, in dealing with this subcategory is the determination of what constitutes sufficient control over the market for a commodity, once it is defined, to warrant government intervention. If a single firm possesses exclusive control over the sale of a particular commodity or service, and the technical characteristics of the industry are such that concentrated control is not necessary, most students would agree that governmental action is appropriate to prevent such concentration of control. But if government action were limited to this type of situation, there would be little or no government action. What if a single firm controls 90 per cent of the market, with the remaining 10 per cent being made up of several small firms? Or what would be the answer if this percentage were 80, 70, 60, 50? Again, in answering this question, economic analysis gives us little to go on. The higher the degree of concentration the greater will be the power of the large concern to raise price and restrict production; economics can tell us this much. But it can do little toward telling us just *how much* concentration is socially tolerable.

Firms That Take into Account Other Firms' Actions

The same sort of difficulty in applying economic principles to public policy is found when we examine the second monopoly category, which includes firms that do take into account the actions of other firms when making price and output policies. Is the competition among oligopolists sufficient to protect the interests of the consumer and the public generally? In the extreme case, what if there are only two firms in an industry (which is called the duopoly case)? Or three, four, five, six, or ten? How many firms must be present in order that "workable competition" may be assumed to be present? Economic principles provide few answers here. Indeed, the results of oligopoly can range all the way from the purely competitive case, if the oligopolists behave in one assumed fashion, to the purely monopolistic one, if they behave in another way.

Open Agreement among Firms

The third monopoly category, that which comprises cartel agreements among firms on price and other policies, presents less of a problem. The very existence of collusion among firms indicates an unnecessary limitation on competition. It is in just this area, however, that the main governmental support for monopoly practices has been found. Economic analysis is extremely useful in pointing up the results of such perverse public policy, as the next chapter will make clear.

A SUMMARY LOOK AT THE RECORD

The Sherman Act: Our Main Antimonopoly Law

A summary examination of the history and present status of the government's attempts to regulate business monopoly reveals the scope and extent of the difficulties in this area. It has often been stated that monopoly in economics must mean one thing, and monopoly in law another. If government is to take legal action against monopolies, some precise definition of monopoly needs to be incorporated in the legal framework. Since, however, this has proved to be a difficult task, the basic antimonopoly law in this country goes to the other extreme and makes the definition as general as possible. The Sherman Antitrust Act, which was passed in 1890 and which remains today the core of all governmental action against business monopoly, declares: "Every contract, combination in the form of trust or otherwise, or conspiracy, in restraint of trade or commerce among the several states or with foreign nations, is hereby declared to be illegal." If restraint of trade is interpreted in the strict economic sense as the power to restrict supply in order to increase price, almost every industry is monopolistic and almost every firm is subject to prosecution. It is readily understandable why this literal economic interpretation has never been placed on the Sherman Act. The way was left open for the courts to determine the legal meaning of the term "restraint of trade." In 1911 the law was used to prosecute successfully two of the outstanding monopoly combinations in the country, Standard Oil and American Tobacco. In handing down the decisions in these cases, however, the Court enunciated the so-called "rule of reason" as applied to antimonopoly action. In effect, the Supreme Court rewrote the Sherman Act by stating that not all restraints of trade were illegal, but only those which were "unreasonable."

The implication of these cases seemed to be that the test of "reasonableness" was whether there was deliberate action on the part of firms to freeze out all competitors by fair means or foul. As a result, firms were encouraged to restrict their monopolistic practices after 1911 to those of the more gentlemanly types. They were encouraged to allow a few small competitors to exist as long as they remained relatively unimportant. This trend was reaffirmed in the 1920's with the decisions in the U.S. Steel and the International Harvester cases. In these cases the Supreme Court was faced with the question of determining how large a concern needs to be in order to constitute an effective monopoly. Taking an extremely conservative view, the Court held that the existence of apparently undisturbed competitors was sufficient to demonstrate the absence of unreasonable restraint of trade. The Court stated in the U.S. Steel case that "the law does not make mere size an offense." Because of the rule laid down in these cases, the Sherman Act has seldom been successfully applied in preventing or breaking up monopoly positions which were secured and maintained by large firms in areas where a substantial part of the output is accounted for by smaller companies.

On the other hand, monopoly positions secured by open agreements concerning price and output policies have often been effectively prosecuted under the Act. The application of the antitrust law in condemning price agreements among different firms was first evidenced in 1899, and it has been extended continually to date. In the famous decision upholding the prosecution of several pottery manufacturers for openly reaching a price agreement, the Court held that the "rule of reason" did not apply here. Overt price agreements have been held to be illegal per se, whether "reasonable" or not.

The Clayton and Federal Trade Commission Acts

The extremely general wording of the Sherman Act and the subsequent difficulties in its interpretation led to a demand that the government spell out specifically the business practices which were illegal. This move culminated in the passage in 1914 of the Clayton Act and the Federal Trade Commission Act. These Acts, as amended, along with the Sherman Act, remain today as the "laws" of the United States on monopoly. The Clayton Act declared certain practices to be illegal provided that the effect was to lessen competition or to create a monopoly. This proviso thus threw back upon the courts the whole question of determining when, in fact, the specified practices did tend to create a monopoly. These practices were (1) price discrimination, (2) tying contracts, (3) intercorporate stock acquisition, and (4) interlocking directorates.

The most important of these was the prohibition of price discrimination. Differences in prices due to differences in grade, quality, or quantity were specifically held to be legal and thus not covered by the Act.

The price-discrimination provision was designed primarily to prevent one form of so-called "cutthroat" competition, *i.e.*, price cutting by a firm in one segment of its market in order to drive out competition while maintaining higher prices in other less competitive segments of its market. The price-discrimination provision was extended in 1936 by the Robinson-Patman Act, an amendment to the Clayton Act, which declared that price differences based on quantity purchased were illegal unless justified by cost differences. The Act was largely supported by independent retailers and has been called the anti-chain-store bill. It was designed to eliminate the advantages that large monopsonistic buyers had been able to secure by forcing sellers to lower prices. It gives to the Federal Trade Commission the almost impossible task of deciding just what are legitimate cost differences.

The Federal Trade Commission Act, also passed in 1914, set up an independent regulatory commission, the Federal Trade Commission, designed to assist the Department of Justice in the enforcement of the Clayton Act and to act on its own initiative in preventing unfair competition. The Act stated: "Unfair methods of competition in commerce are hereby declared unlawful." As in the case of restraint of trade under the Sherman Act, however, there is no sharp dividing line between "fair" and "unfair" competition. The record of the Federal Trade Commission in encouraging over-all competitiveness in the national economy has not been a good one. It lacked adequate enforcement power prior to 1938, but the basic difficulty is the same vagueness as that which pervades the Sherman and the Clayton Acts. As a result, the Federal Trade Commission has spent much of its time in regulating petty and relatively unimportant business practices, such as deciding whether or not Airwick can really be said to eliminate cooking odors or whether Lucky Strikes are actually milder by scientific test.

Another blot on the FTC's record lies in its activities of the 1920's, when it was instrumental in promoting the formation of trade associations in various industries. Clearly, in this respect the activities of the Commission actually promoted monopoly rather than competition. Trade associations constitute one of the most effective means by which firms in the same industry can join together and agree not to compete strongly.

Some Victories over Basing-point Pricing

The rather unhappy view of the record of the Federal Trade Commission, and of antimonopoly policy in general, must be somewhat modified in the light of some successes in the late 1940's. Action initiated by the Commission has resulted in the elimination of basing-point pricing in several important industries. This step is clearly in the direction of promoting competition.

Despite its earlier efforts in this direction, the Commission made little real progress until 1945, when the courts upheld its order prohibiting basing-point pricing in the corn-products industry. But the most important step was reached in 1948, when the Supreme Court upheld the FTC's order outlawing basing-point pricing in the portland-cement industry. After this decision, the steel companies also agreed to cease the practice and reverted to an f. o. b. mill system, *i.e.*, charging freight from the actual source to the destination. But basing-point pricing is at the moment still practiced in some industries, and agitation continues for the exemption of this practice from the antitrust laws.

The Tobacco Case and the Alcoa Case

There were also some encouraging steps taken in the enforcement of the Sherman Act in the 1940's. In a case brought against the big tobacco companies the Court ruled that, even though there was no evidence of open collusion, the results were sufficient to demonstrate that collusion had been present. The evidence was found in the manner in which prices charged by the various companies had moved in relation to each other. The precedent established in the tobacco case could do much to eliminate the practice of "price leadership" in oligopolistic industries.

In a second important case, initiated in the 1930's but decided only in 1944, the government instituted antitrust proceedings against the Aluminum Company of America. In finding the company guilty of restraint of trade, the courts ruled that the mere fact that the company controlled a dominant share of the source materials for the manufacture of aluminum was sufficient evidence that the antitrust law was violated. This decision seems to modify the conclusion reached earlier in the U.S. Steel and International Harvester cases, in which the Court had said that "size alone is not an offense." But there is still no definite line, and, indeed, there cannot be one, between those firms which are large enough to be considered "monopolies" and those which are not sufficiently large to be so classed.

The shortcomings of economic analysis delineating the bounds of workable competition have been abundantly demonstrated in the enforcement of the antitrust laws. Perhaps largely for this reason, economists are prone to be too critical of the results of our antitrust policy. Clearly, the existence of the antitrust laws has served to make the economy more competitive than it otherwise would have been.

GOVERNMENT POLICY TOWARD LABOR MONOPOLIES

Public policy with reference to organized labor represents another area in which economic analysis is unable to provide satisfactory answers to all the pertinent questions. The economist's kit of tools is useful, but it leaves a number of questions unanswered.

Partly as a result of the encouragement given to organized labor by the National Labor Relations Act (Wagner Act), which was passed in 1935, the membership of labor unions in the United States increased from less than 4 million in 1935 to over 15 million in 1950. Although less than one-fourth of the total labor force is affiliated with the union movement, 80 per cent or more of workers in such industries as the following work under union agreements: coal mining, construction, railroads, men's and women's clothing, portland cement, aircraft, automobiles, and meat packing. As a result of the increasing strength of organized labor following the enactment of the Wagner Act together with the great loss of man-hours resulting from strikes (during the years from 1945 to 1947 there was an average of over 4,000 strikes per year, with an annual loss of more than 62 million man-hours of labor), there was considerable public resentment against labor unions. This led to the passage of the Labor-Management Relations Act (Taft-Hartley Act) in 1947, which attempted to "amend" the Wagner Act by defining certain "unfair labor practices" which unions were forbidden to engage in. The underlying philosophy of both the Wagner Act and the Taft-Hartley Act seems to be that it is the function of government to maintain some degree of equality in bargaining power between workers and employers.[1] An individual worker is considered to be in no position to "bargain," *i.e.*, to affect the wage rate, in negotiations with a large firm, and it was the object of the Wagner Act to improve labor's position by facilitating "collective bargaining"; what laborers could not do singly they might be able to do if they acted in concert.

As union membership increased, it began to appear to many Americans that the pendulum had swung too far in the opposite direction and that, at least in certain basic industries, organized labor had an unfair advantage in its negotiations with management. Government's "equalizing" function this time took the form of setting up a number of forbidden practices on the part of unions which were labeled "unfair" in the Taft-Hartley Act. Among these was the prohibition of the "closed shop," *i.e.*, employment cannot be restricted to union members. (Workers may, however, be forced to join the union within 30 days if a "union shop" has been voted by the employees.) The policy to which we are committed seems to require that the government make a dispassionate determination in the most passionate of all areas of economic conflict as to which side is

[1] Both Acts, in Sec. I, contain the following paragraph: "The inequality of bargaining power between employees who do not possess full freedom of association or actual liberty of contract, and employers who are organized in the corporate or other forms of ownership association substantially burdens and affects the flow of commerce, and tends to aggravate recurrent business depressions, by depressing wage rates and the purchasing power of wage earners in industry and by preventing the stabilization of competitive wage rates and working conditions within and between industries." (Sic.)

the weaker, and by strengthening the weak side and penalizing the strong to maintain as great a degree of equality of bargaining strength as possible. From a moral or ethical point of view, this program has much to commend it. If one side has the right to combine to improve its position, it may be argued that the other side has a similar right. But the economic argument for labor monopoly to bargain with an employer's monopoly is less secure. There may, indeed, be a strong presumption in favor of the view that the wage rate resulting from bilateral monopoly will more nearly approach the competitive level than the wage set by a monopsonist who hires labor in a nonunion market. But this cannot be demonstrated by economic analysis. There is no way of knowing when the opposing forces have been equalized and one monopoly has just neutralized the other.[1] The alternative policies seem to be (1) to attempt to solve the problem of monopoly by creating still more monopoly or (2) to attempt to solve the monopoly problem by eliminating monopoly. One difficulty with the first solution is that, if the two sides could be made precisely equal, conflicts might result in stalemates; if such a conflict were to be resolved, the government would have to tip the scales one way or the other, and this would mean that government would determine which side won, incurring the ill will of the side which lost. Labor, for example, hailed the Wagner Act as its "Magna Charta" but condemned the Taft-Hartley Act as a stab in the back. The second solution, on the other hand, may also be impracticable. The dissolution of monopoly, or even the reduction of monopoly power, is difficult. It is extremely unlikely that the reduction of monopoly power of labor and management could progress at the same rate, but the curtailment of labor monopoly without a corresponding reduction of employer's monopoly power would undoubtedly have significant political repercussions which might make the entire effort unworkable.

The power struggle between big business and big labor is frequently a bitter one. Often, however, there appears to be more of a conspiracy between the two than a struggle, the conspiracy being directed against the consumers. Particularly when national income is rising, employers in oligopolistic industries appear often to accede willingly to union demands for higher wages in order to be able to justify price increases. The existence of high corporate and excess-profits taxes reinforces this tendency. In other cases, there is outright collusion between employers and unions to limit the entry of new firms into a field. This occurs quite frequently in the construction industry, where workers may refuse to work for contractors who are not association members or may be willing to install only materials produced or handled by certain companies.

[1] See Fritz Machlup, *The Political Economy of Monopoly* (Baltimore: Johns Hopkins Press, 1952), p. 376.

The effects of monopoly in the sale of labor services when competition among buyers is present were pointed out in Chapter 13. Labor monopoly tends to restrict the amount of labor input in the organized sector of the market. This forces workers to seek employment in other occupations where their contribution to national real income is smaller. It also redistributes the diminished total real income in favor of the organized workers compared with the nonunion labor force. It is difficult, however, to assess the quantitative importance of these results. If a union is unable to restrict its membership and if it is unwilling to cause much unemployment among its members, it cannot raise wage rates substantially above a competitive level. If it is able to restrict membership significantly, however, it can secure wages well above competitive rates for those lucky enough to get in. The ability to restrict membership frequently exists, but it has been somewhat weakened in interstate commerce by the Taft-Hartley Act, which bans the closed shop.

In the case of monopoly in output markets, we have noted that there is little, if any, reason for antitrust action where the degree of monopoly power is small. In such cases, demand for the firm's product is likely to be so elastic that price cannot be raised very much above the competitive level. Similarly, a union which wishes to avoid unemployment among its members can raise wages only moderately if its ability to restrict membership is not substantial. If, on the other hand, the supply of labor of a particular type can be significantly restricted through union practices—which is frequently the case in the building trades—or if possible unemployment among union members is largely neglected—as is the case in the large industrial unions—there is as much reason for curbing union monopoly as there is for breaking up strong industrial monopolies.

What generalizations may be made concerning the gains and losses to the economy resulting from the imposition of higher wage rates by labor-union activity? If unions are formed in industries where firms buy labor competitively, higher wages are likely on balance to be injurious. Some laborers gain, but the gain is at the expense of others who are unemployed or whose wages are lowered, at the expense of reduced profits to management, and at the expense of higher prices to consumers. The allocation of resources is distorted, and the real income of society is reduced. If, on the other hand, unions are formed in industries in which firms enjoy monopsony profits which have been gained by paying labor less than the going rate, labor may gain by appropriating a portion of these profits with no loss to the economy as a whole. How often is this latter case met in reality? This question cannot be definitely answered, but these observations are pertinent:

1. If firms are enjoying monopsony profits, the situation would be helped by making easier the entry of new firms into the labor market.

Unless there are restrictions on such entry, monopsony profits cannot be maintained indefinitely. The entry of new firms would, of course, increase the demand for labor, causing wage rates to rise. But the existence of labor unions is likely to retard rather than encourage the entry of new firms into local areas which have an oversupply of labor.

2. If laborers in certain firms are receiving less than the competitive rate, an increase in the mobility of labor would improve the situation. In some instances the provision of information to workers concerning job opportunities and wage rates elsewhere might be enough to correct the local oversupply of labor. Labor unions, unfortunately, by making labor less rather than more mobile, tend to worsen the situation.

3. Even if some firms in an industry enjoy monopsony profits at the expense of labor, it seems unlikely that all firms in a given industry will be in such a sheltered position, and if wages are raised by union activity for the industry as a whole, some firms may be forced out of business, and, while employment in the firms which survive may be greater than before, employment in the industry as a whole may be reduced.

We may conclude that labor organizations do improve the lot of some workers, but, unfortunately, if the gains to unionized labor do not come from increased productivity, they must come at the expense of other elements of the economy. Economic analysis is unable to determine in these cases whether the gain to one group more than offsets the loss to others. About all that can be said with confidence is that, if the alternative to labor unions were perfectly competitive markets for labor as well as for products, the alternative would unquestionably be preferable.

Industry-wide Bargaining

We turn our attention finally to a consideration of the effects of industry-wide bargaining. Nationwide strikes have caused considerable public resentment toward labor in recent years, since a work stoppage in steel, coal, automobiles, or rubber has a paralyzing effect on the entire economy, and this is particularly critical in time of national emergency.[1] Whereas a local strike is usually a source of inconvenience and irritation to the local community, an industry-wide strike is likely to jeopardize the security of the entire nation. The ability of a union to declare a strike on a very broad front increases its power, and proposals to outlaw such strikes are made from time to time. The extent of multi-employer bargaining units for a recent year is indicated in Table 29.1.

It is more difficult to generalize about the economic effects of industry-wide bargaining than about the effects of wage increases granted to a small local union, because higher wages for an entire industry not only

[1] An impression of the effects of a shutdown in such a basic industry as coal and power may be gained by referring to the input-output table in Chap. 2.

affect costs of production but may have a significant effect on incomes of workers, who represent a substantial fraction of the entire economy. Three preliminary observations may, however, be made. If the workers in a basic industry such as steel obtain a wage increase, that is likely to set the pattern for wages in other industries, and the effect of the wage increase in steel is likely to be much greater than it would have been if only steelworkers had been involved. Secondly, industry-wide agreements sometimes contain an escalator clause, which ties the wage rate to the cost of living; if the living-cost index goes up a prescribed amount, the workers are automatically entitled to a wage boost which will maintain their standard of living. Even when such a clause is not included in the wage agreement, much of the effort of unions is directed toward maintaining or raising their members' living standards. Particularly in times

Table 29.1. Bargaining Arrangements in the United States in 1950

Per cent of workers in:

Single-employer bargaining units, total..........		67
Single plant..............................	28	
Multi-plant..............................	39	
Multi-employer units, total....................		33
National.................................	4	
Regional................................	6	
Local...................................	23	

Source: Carroll R. Daugherty and John B. Parrish, *The Labor Problem of American Society* (Boston: Houghton Mifflin Company, 1952), p. 512.

of emergency, when resources are being diverted to the production of military goods, prices rise because of the relative shortage of consumers' goods. Since fewer goods are available, price is performing its proper rationing function; since fewer goods are available, living standards on the average must fall. If organized labor is able, however, to maintain its standard of living by virtue of wage contracts tied to the price level, the full reduction in consumption will have to be borne by those whose money incomes do not keep pace with the rise in prices. This represents, of course, a reallocation of income from nonunion members and consumers who do not depend on labor income (*e.g.*, retired persons) to organized labor.

A third fundamental objection to industry-wide bargaining is that it imposes uniform wage rates throughout areas where conditions may not be uniform. Because of labor immobility, it is quite likely that within a given industry there may be areas of labor undersupply and other areas where labor is in oversupply. Under competitive conditions a differential in wage rates would result, but if wages must be uniform throughout the industry by virtue of a contractual agreement, some workers in labor-surplus areas will have to seek employment in other industries where they are less productive.

Let us analyze the effects of an industry-wide wage increase in a basic industry on the volume of employment during a period of business recovery. Since the marginal revenue product curve for labor in each firm slopes downward from left to right, the immediate effect of a higher wage will be a reduction of employment in each firm. This is likely, in the short run, to retard the rate of recovery for the economy as a whole. Whether the longer-run effects of the wage increase will be stimulating or depressing turns on the elasticity of demand for labor. If the market demand for labor is highly inelastic—i.e., if the firms employ nearly as many workers at the higher wage as at the lower rate—the total wage payment will be greater after the increase in wages than before. This means a greater income for labor, and this will be reflected by an increased demand for goods by laborers and, indirectly, an increased demand for labor, which may more than offset the reduction in employment resulting from the increase in wages. It should be noted, however, that in so far as labor income has increased at the expense of income recipients in other sectors of the economy, total demand will have increased only to the degree that the marginal propensity to spend is relatively higher for wage earners than for other groups.

If, however, the demand for labor is quite elastic, an increase in wages will be accompanied by a reduction of labor income as well as a reduction in employment. Those unemployed by virtue of the increase in wages will seek employment in other industries, and the increased supply of labor in those areas will cause wage rates to fall. When the demand for labor is highly elastic, accordingly, it is clear that wage increases will serve as a check on industrial recovery, since higher wages cause higher prices and a reduction in purchasing power.

Whether the demand for labor is, in fact, elastic or inelastic depends upon the expectations of management, and these are affected by many factors. When business is expanding and future prospects appear to be good, the business community is likely to be optimistic. In this atmosphere a wage increase may seem to be a relatively small deterrent to profits, and the number of workers employed at the higher wage may be virtually as great as at the lower level. Businessmen may, in fact, assume that higher labor incomes will result in greater consumer demand and that this will have a generally stimulating effect on business activity. By the same token, when the business outlook is unfavorable and expectations are poor, an increase in wages or even a refusal by the union to take a wage cut may intensify the prevailing spirit of pessimism and cause the rate of unemployment to be accelerated.

The effects of industry-wide bargaining on the volume of employment may be summarized as follows: From the point of view of the firm, an increase in wages represents an increase in costs, and this tends to cause the firm to reduce output and employment; from the point of view of labor, an increase in wages may mean either an increase in total labor income or a decrease in income, depending on the elasticity of demand for labor. If the demand for labor is highly elastic, it is clear that the volume of employment will be reduced, since both the cost factor and the income factor work in that direction; if, on the other hand, the demand for labor is highly inelastic, the income factor may make for an increased demand for labor, and this may balance or offset the adverse cost factor. It may be noted in conclusion that since the income effect may work toward an increase in employment only when the demand for labor is inelastic and the elasticity of demand for labor depends on many and varied factors, and since organized labor in any event represents only about one-fourth of the total labor force, arguments for higher wages based on "purchasing-power" effects should be viewed with considerable skepticism. Even when demands by unions for higher wages do result in an increase in employment, these gains are likely to be more than offset by the unhappy effects of the higher wages on the allocation of income between union members and the rest of the economy. If higher wages are achieved by unions without a corresponding increase in labor's productivity, such gains as organized labor may enjoy are obtained at the expense of someone else. Whether the new allocation of national income imposed by the demands of organized labor is better or worse than the old allocation depends on welfare considerations which lie outside the limits of economic analysis, but policy in the field of labor economics which ignores the contributions which economic analysis can make may jeopardize the position of labor and be injurious to the economy as a whole.

CHAPTER 30

GOVERNMENT SUPPORTS MANY PRICES

Certain limitations of economic analysis as a guide to public policy in the monopoly field were discussed in the preceding chapter, but it was pointed out that usually the public interest is served when the government encourages competition and prevents monopoly. Considerable antimonopoly action has, in fact, been taken by the Federal government. But, curiously enough, the government is also actively engaged in discouraging competition and promoting monopoly power. Local and state governments in particular appear to exert more efforts in the direction of encouraging monopoly than in maintaining competition, and it is probably true that the monopoly problem in the United States would not be a serious one if all government-supported monopoly were eliminated. Economic analysis can frequently be helpful in determining the effects of government interference with competition. This chapter considers certain government policies which have the effect of discouraging competition and which are, accordingly, from the economist's point of view suspect.

FAIR-TRADE LAWS

An outstanding example of action by both state and Federal governments which effectively discourages competition is found in the so-called "fair-trade" laws. These laws permit manufacturers of a large variety of drugstore merchandise, books, liquor, jewelry, cigars, electrical appliances, sporting goods, and many other items to specify either the exact price or the minimum price at which their products may be sold by retailers.[1] Many retailers do not wish to be bound by resale-price-fixing agreements with manufacturers and will not sign such contracts. The state laws, how-

---

[1] Forty-five states had such laws in 1953. The exceptions were Missouri, Texas, Vermont, and the District of Columbia. California was the first state to pass a resale-price-maintenance law (1931); other states followed so rapidly that even misprints in the California law were copied into the laws of ten additional states. Fortunately, a few of the laws which are on the books have been rendered inoperative by court decisions.

ever, generally contain "nonsigner clauses," which make the price agreements binding on all retailers if any retailer makes such a contract for a particular product.

Most of the important commodities in this group are traded in interstate commerce. The price-fixing agreement between manufacturer and retailer, accordingly, would normally subject the firms to prosecution under the Sherman Antitrust Law. In order to avoid such prosecution, the National Association of Druggists and others prevailed on Congress to include in the Miller-Tydings Act of 1937 a proviso which exempted such resale-price agreements from prosecution under the antitrust laws.

Price competition at the retail level for these fair-traded products was pretty much eliminated until 1951, when the United States Supreme Court decided (in the Schwegmann case) that retailers who did not sign the price agreements could not be forced to adhere to the resale prices and could, therefore, charge any price they wished. A period of much more competitive retail trade, marked by dramatic price cuts in many fair-traded items, followed this decision.

The fair-trade forces quickly devised some new Federal legislation, however, and they secured speedy passage and Presidential approval of the McGuire Act in 1952. This law, an amendment to the Federal Trade Commission Act, declares that nothing in the antitrust laws shall render it unlawful to require sellers, signers and nonsigners alike, to adhere to price-fixing agreements regarding trade-marked items where such agreements are legalized in intrastate commerce by state laws. Under this Act a private contract between a single seller and a manufacturer again becomes binding on all sellers.

The retailers' associations which promote fair-trade legislation claim that these laws are needed to protect small business from price cutting by the larger sellers. If a particular album of phonograph records, for example, is retail-priced at $6.75 by the manufacturer, no small music-store owner need worry about price competition from department stores.

The analysis of Part A points clearly to the path of proper public policy. Efficiency is secured by competition in all segments of the economy, and there appears to be no reason why a particular segment, such as retailing, should be excepted. The presumption is that retailing firms should compete among each other on a price basis just as firms at any other level should. If a firm cannot continue to exist in such an environment, it must be inefficient, and it should not be "bailed out" by government. If, for example, a drugstore is unable to sell tooth paste as cheaply as the chain food stores can, it should not expect to be able to handle this commodity in large volume. The buying public should secure the full price advantage made possible by the most efficient system of production and distribution, proper location, and effective management.

In the long run, even the individual retailing firms may not gain from resale-price agreements. New firms are usually able to enter retailing without difficulty, and they are likely to do so because of the apparent profits to be gained from the high retail markups. In addition, established firms retailing non-fair-traded items are likely to add fair-traded items. This explains, in large part, the recent adding of kitchen utensils and drugstore items to grocery-store lines.

It also seems probable that manufacturing firms may have little to gain from resale-price-maintenance contracts. It is questionable whether the psychological advantages of selling a "stable-price" trade-marked product offset the advantages of a greater sales volume which would be forthcoming from greater price competition at the retail level. An additional influence tending to reduce manufacturing firms' profits is the entry of new firms producing closely competing and non-fair-traded brands of products. Many manufacturing firms have decided to secure the benefits of resale-price maintenance by selling a highly advertised brand and, at the same time, the benefits of retail competition by selling almost the same product at a lower price under a different label.

The economic effects of the resale-price-maintenance or fair-trade laws are virtually equivalent to those of the "cartel" described in Chapter 8. The cartel case was defined as a situation in which many firms agree on price but cannot readily prevent the entry of new firms. When a price is agreed on that will result in abnormal profits, new firms will be attracted by the high rate of profits to the industry. As the new firms enter, each firm in the industry will lose sales. This will continue until enough new firms have come into the industry to eliminate all above-normal profits. But each firm will be operating in a low-sales, high-average-cost position. There will be too many firms in the industry, and each firm will be operating at less than its most efficient (lowest-cost) capacity. This is also approximately the long-run result of the fair-trade laws, which have the effect of causing whole retailing segments of the economy to be effectively cartelized.

The effects of resale-price maintenance on an individual firm are depicted geometrically in the left-hand side of Figure 30.1. The retailing industry under consideration is assumed to be purely competitive.[1] The firm is assumed to be in long-run equilibrium. The average cost curve is shown as AC, the equilibrium price is OP, the marginal cost curve is MC, and the demand curve is D. The firm sells OB units. For purposes of simplicity we assume the firm to be retailing one product only. Now suppose that a fair-

---

[1] This assumption is admittedly unrealistic, but the analysis is considerably simplified by its use. Retailing is substantially competitive in the real world, although each firm does possess some locational and service advantages for certain classes of customers, possibly including exclusive dealership for certain products.

trade retail price of OP' is imposed on the product. This appears to be fine for the firm, and it senses the nearness of abnormal profits. It now desires to sell OB' units, since this is the sales volume for which price equals marginal cost, the necessary condition for securing the greatest profit. But the firm will find this to be impossible. This is true since the total amount bought by consumers must have declined with the increase in price. This is shown for the whole retailing industry by the movement from Ob to Oa in the right side of Figure 30.1. Not only will the firm find it impossible to sell OB', but, in fact, it will find it impossible to sell as much as before unless it can take away a share of the market from another retailer. It may be able to sell only about OA units even before new firms enter the industry. But it will be happy. Abnormal profits are still being

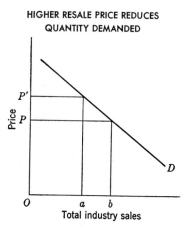

Figure 30.1. "FAIR TRADE" PROMOTES HIGH COST: LOW SALES

HIGHER RESALE PRICE REDUCES QUANTITY DEMANDED

made, and the firm considers its contribution to the campaign of the congressman who voted for the fair-trade law fully justified. Things do not bode so well for the future, however. Other firms see the greener pastures of abnormal profits, and they enter the industry as sellers of the fair-traded product or one of its close substitutes. This can only mean that the established firms' shares of the market are further reduced. This movement will be continued as long as abnormal profits are present, with the firm depicted in Figure 30.1 losing sales until it reaches a sales volume of only OX. When all firms in the industry reach this position, the industry is again in a sort of equilibrium. There is no incentive for new firms to come in, since no abnormal profits are being made. Each firm in the industry is operating in a high-cost, low-output position. The industry has more firms than are needed for efficient operation. And whereas in the cartel case we indicated that this was the spot for the price agreement to break down, here this will not happen since the agreement has the support of law.

It should be noted that the analysis above has assumed freedom of additional retailers to begin selling the commodity under consideration. The short-run gain to retailers who are licensed distributors of certain products (such as stoves and refrigerators) may be more secure, since the manufacturer or wholesaler can keep out other would-be sellers. Even here, however, the competition from other brands, from secondhand dealers, and from sellers in non-fair-trade states may make the retailer's net advantage from resale-price maintenance smaller than would be expected from a consideration of the retail markup alone.

The existence of excess capacity frequently induces the entrepreneur to begin to produce additional goods and services. This possibility was pointed out in the discussion of multiple outputs in Chapter 9. Since resale-price maintenance tends strongly to cause excess capacity in retailing by attracting new sellers and by giving a measure of protection to inefficient firms, it may also be concluded that the practice promotes an expansion of the types of goods and services offered by a retailer. It appears probable, for example, that resale-price maintenance has been a factor in causing drugstores to install book counters and to sell a tremendous variety of other articles quite outside the drug field. As more and more of our retail stores become more nearly "general" stores, there is an undesirable loss of managerial and clerical skill which might be available with greater specialization of retailing activity. For example, even the problem of *finding* items sometimes becomes difficult and may more than outweigh the convenience inherent in the carrying of a large number of items under one roof.

Once established, resale-price maintenance quite permanently burdens the economy with a wastage of resources which takes its toll in terms of national real income. Much of the value of economics is of a negative sort, in that it should guide legislators away from unwise actions which, once taken, are extremely hard to reverse. That its lessons often go unheeded will be further illustrated in the present chapter.

THE UNFAIR-PRACTICES ACTS

The same desire to curb price competition that has motivated the fair-trade laws underlies the "unfair-practices" acts which are operative in about twenty-eight states.[1] These laws have been promoted particularly by retail and wholesale trade associations, and, in general, they forbid the selling of a large variety of commodities, both branded and unbranded, "below cost." Closing-out sales, sales of damaged goods, and sales of perishable and seasonal goods are generally exempted.

[1] V. A. Mund, *Government and Business* (New York: Harper & Brothers, 1950), p. 435.

It is inherently difficult to allocate costs which are common to numerous commodities (*e.g.*, a druggist's light bill), and it is impossible to allocate joint costs (where two or more goods are produced in fixed proportions) except on an arbitrary basis. Thus the "cost" below which it is illegal to sell under the unfair-practices acts is generally not that of the individual seller but rather some "standard" cost determined roughly by means of a survey of sellers' opinions. Since it is to the sellers' advantage to overstate cost in such surveys, an upward bias is inevitable. The trade associations or other interested groups which conduct the surveys, furthermore, have an incentive to establish uniform markups sufficiently high to cover the costs of the less efficient firms rather than just those of the more efficient sellers.

The difficulties in correctly estimating costs do not, however, represent the primary reason that these "unfair" trade-practices laws discourage rather than encourage competition. If competition is to prevail, there must be no legally fixed relationship between prices and average cost, even if the latter could be accurately estimated. Prices may be above, below, or equal to average costs of production at any given time, depending on the demand and supply conditions in the industry. Firms should not be concerned about covering average costs in the short run; rather short-run supply will be governed by marginal costs if the firms are to maximize profits. If unfair-practices laws prevent firms from reducing prices below average costs, a rational adjustment to a decline in demand for the firm's product is prevented. A firm will be forced to reduce output more than it would otherwise do, and its fixed plant and equipment will tend to be utilized at less than profit-maximizing output.

The only way in which the long-run tendency toward equality between price and average costs in a competitive industry can be brought about quickly is by a divergence between price and average costs in the short run. If there are too many firms in an industry as a result of a declining demand, a drop in price below average cost levels will tend to drive out the less efficient firms. If this normal adjustment is prevented, these inefficient firms tend to remain in the industry, and the declining demand is likely to be met by increasing selling costs (*e.g.*, advertising) rather than by engaging in price competition. And, as Chapter 7 pointed out, competition among firms by the selling-cost method does little to benefit consumers. The price rigidities imposed upon the economy by both the resale-price-maintenance laws and the unfair-practices acts are among the many such rigidities mentioned in Part B which contribute to the decline in real income when money income falls. Fluctuations downward in money demand tend to be reflected in reduced output, and ultimately in diminished employment, rather than in price reductions.

PARITY PRICES FOR FARM COMMODITIES

One of the most striking of government activities to support prices is found in Federal agricultural policy, particularly in the parity-price program. There is perhaps some greater justification for governmental interference on behalf of producers in agriculture than elsewhere since fluctuations in prices and incomes tend to be more severe in the agricultural sector than in other parts of the economy. This is primarily explained by the highly competitive nature of agriculture due to the large number of firms. Since no one farmer is able to influence through his own individual actions the price of the product which he sells, agricultural output tends to remain high in times of low aggregate demand. In order for this output to be sold, prices must fall to extremely low levels, and this is accompanied by falling farm incomes. On the other hand, there is little or no unemployment in the farming sector during depressions. The farm groups argue that if the government is to take action to relieve unemployment in the sectors where depressions are characterized by reduced production and employment, the government should likewise take action to keep the prices of farm products from falling so low during such periods, *i.e.*, they argue that price relief is as justifiable as unemployment relief. This has provided much of the rationale for the government's program of supporting the prices of agricultural commodities.

The support levels below which farm prices are to be prevented from falling are determined by an elaborate formula which compares the prices of products which farmers sell with the prices that farmers must pay for products which they buy. The ratio of farm prices to the prices farmers must pay is related to the corresponding ratio prevailing during the base period, 1910 to 1914. The parity price for any commodity is that price which will provide a unit of the commodity the same purchasing power in terms of the things the farmer buys that it had in the base period. One of the difficulties with the parity concept is that the pattern of things which the farmer buys changes through time; the typical farm family today spends a significant part of the family budget on goods which were unknown in 1910. Modifications of the parity formula have been made in an effort to take into account major changes in prices of farm commodities relative to one another. The new formula would have the effect of raising some parity prices and lowering others, and on the whole, if parity pricing is to be used, the new version appears to be superior to the old. But the law directs the Department of Agriculture to use either the old formula or the new, depending upon which results in the higher price, so the effect of the formula revision is to support farm prices at still higher levels.

Prices may be supported to keep them in a required relation to parity (*e.g.*, 90 per cent of parity) in several ways. The Commodity Credit Corporation may make direct purchases by entering the market for the particular commodity. For storable commodities, the more common practice is the making of "nonrecourse" loans to farmers. These are loans secured by the expected crop, but in the event that the price of the commodity turns out to be so low that the value of the crop is less than the amount of the loan, it is understood that the farmer may simply default on the loan, and the government will take title to the crop in full payment of the loan. The farmer will, of course, sell the crop and repay the loan if the market value of the crop is greater than the amount borrowed.

In either case, the total effect is to establish a floor below which the prices of agricultural products can fall only slightly. The Commodity Credit Corporation acquires inventories of storable products in the process. Huge quantities of dried eggs, for example, have been stored in caves in Kansas. The potato situation of several years ago became so ridiculous that it finally resulted in the removal of potatoes from the support list of commodities. The very fact that the program has resulted in the government's being forced to purchase stocks of agricultural commodities indicates that support prices have, on the average, exceeded what would have been equilibrium market prices, *i.e.*, those prices which would have equated quantity demanded with quantity supplied.

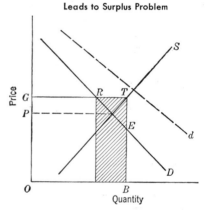

Figure 30.2. SUPPORT PRICE ABOVE EQUILIB-
RIUM—

Leads to Surplus Problem

The parity-price program provides us with our best practical illustration of the statement made in Chapter 4 that if price is set above equilibrium levels a problem of surplus disposal tends to arise. The program lends itself to simple analysis through the use of supply and demand curves. In Figure 30.2, the curve D represents the total private demand for a particular agricultural commodity at all possible prices; S represents the short-run industry supply curve. If there were no interference with the market, the price would tend to be established at OP. This is the equilibrium or free market price. The support price is, however, OG. At this price, private buyers will demand only the quantity GR. Farmers will desire to put an amount GT on the market. The government will be required to buy up the amount of the difference between the quantity people want to buy and the quantity farmers want to sell, or RT. The shaded area represents the total costs to government; the total income of farmers is shown by the rectangle $OGTB$.

The government is severely restricted in its disposition of the surplus commodities purchased. Obviously, it cannot sell the surplus on the domestic market, for this would drive the price down (to BE, in Figure 30.2). It cannot readily give the surplus away to domestic consumers, since this would also tend to affect prices (by shifting the market demand curve downward). It could give the surplus commodities away only to users who would not otherwise purchase them. Some attempts are made in this direction by making the surpluses available for free-school-lunch programs and to certain nonprofit institutional users. Another manner of disposition is to sell the surplus commodities for a completely different use at greatly reduced prices. The sale of "blue" potatoes for fertilizer was an example. Outright destruction of the surplus commodities is also a practice which has, at times, been followed.   Another way in which government may dispose of the surplus agricultural commodities without at the same time affecting domestic prices is by selling them in foreign markets at prices below domestic prices. This is called "dumping," a practice not conducive to friendly international economic relations. But having large stocks of surplus commodities on hand, governmental agencies are under strong pressure to institute some sort of dumping program, and this has been legally authorized. The Commodity Credit Corporation may sell surplus commodities in foreign markets, and the Economic Cooperation Act of 1948 allowed the Secretary of Agriculture to sell agricultural products in foreign markets at prices well below domestic prices.[1]

Still another way in which the surplus commodities might be disposed of is by storing them until equilibrium prices rise above support levels and then reselling them on the normal domestic markets. Should demand rise to d (Figure 30.2), the government would be able to sell previously accumulated surpluses. The peculiar manner in which parity prices are calculated, however, makes this possibility somewhat remote, since a general increase in money income, increasing the demand for all goods and services, would also make parity prices increase. In any event, the sale of the accumulated surpluses would reduce prices and would be opposed by domestic producers.

If support prices are set permanently above equilibrium or market-clearing prices, it appears probable that problems of surplus storage and/or disposal will become more and more acute. This is likely to lead to measures designed to accompany the support programs with limitations

---

[1] The same results are achieved without the government's ever acquiring title to the commodities through the use of export subsidies which the Secretary of Agriculture may place on any agricultural commodity. This also allows products to be marketed in foreign countries at a price below that prevailing in domestic markets. For an excellent discussion of export subsidies and dumping see D. Gale Johnson, *Trade and Agriculture* (New York: John Wiley & Sons, Inc., 1950), pp. 13–18.

on agricultural output. The surplus-disposal problem could be eliminated if agricultural output were limited to GR (in Figure 30.2). But if output were thus limited, no support policy would be needed, since OG would then be the normal demand price. The incomes of farmers would, of course, be lower, by the full amount of the shaded rectangle, than under a policy of no output limitation but with full price support. But they would still get higher incomes than they would have if free market prices were allowed to prevail, provided that the demand curve for the agricultural commodity under consideration is inelastic over the significant price range, which is normally the case for most agricultural commodities.

Historically, attempts to limit the supply of agricultural commodities have been almost as much a part of the government's agricultural program as has the use of parity support prices. Marketing quotas and acreage allotments are used to restrict the production of certain agricultural commodities. Tobacco is currently the most important commodity of this group. Difficulties in a program of this sort arise because a restriction of acreage does not necessarily accomplish the desired restriction in production; farmers may take out of cultivation the least productive land and cultivate the rest more intensively.

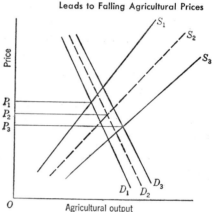

Figure 30.3. SUPPLY INCREASING FASTER THAN DEMAND—

Leads to Falling Agricultural Prices

What effects does the government's agricultural program have on the allocation of the nation's economic resources? As mentioned earlier, one of the justifications for the price-support program was held to be the severe fluctuations in agricultural prices. A second justification claimed by supporters of the farm program is that agricultural production is chronically in surplus and that consequently farm prices tend permanently to be driven down relative to nonfarm prices. Although this is true, it provides no reason for the type of support program we have been using. Chronic overproduction of farm commodities arises because improved technology in agriculture has been increasing production more rapidly than the demand for agricultural products has increased. As a result, agriculture tends to be a declining segment of the economy in terms of employment. Figure 30.3 illustrates the problem. Demand for farm products has increased over time from D_1 to D_2 to D_3, but this increase in demand is more than offset by the increase in supply, from S_1 to

S_2 to S_3. As a result, farm prices tend to fall from P_1 to P_2 to P_3 if free market forces prevail.

The normal free market adjustment would be for farm prices to fall relative to nonfarm prices; farm incomes would therefore fall relative to nonfarm incomes; resources (mainly labor) would be induced to leave farms for employment in nonfarm opportunities. It can easily be seen that the price-support program tends to stop this normal resource adjustment. It diverts income from the nonfarm to the farm population. This tends to encourage farmers to remain in agriculture, and the net economic effect is to keep more resources in agriculture than the demands of consumers (consumer sovereignty) indicate to be desirable.

MARKETING AGREEMENTS AND ORDERS

Closely related to the Federal price-support program are "marketing agreements" and "marketing orders" covering a number of commodities, often perishable in nature, which do not receive direct support through loans and purchases. Marketing agreements are based on the Agricultural Marketing Agreement Act of 1937, which permits the Secretary of Agriculture to enter into contracts with handlers of any agricultural commodity, exempting such agreements from the antitrust laws. Marketing agreements are of most importance for milk but have also been made for such commodities as cauliflower, citrus fruit, grapes, pears, plums, peaches, potatoes, and peas.

Under terms of marketing agreements, processors or other handlers agree to pay no less than designated minimum prices to farmers. In other cases, farm prices are indirectly supported by means of controlling supply through a "control board" established under terms of an agreement or by direct (involuntary) order of the Department of Agriculture. Marketing agreements require approval of handlers of not less than 50 per cent of the commodity and of at least two-thirds of the growers. Like the fair-trade laws, however, agreements are binding on nonsigners as well as on signers.

Marketing agreements eliminate sharp price fluctuations, price uncertainty, and monopsonistic price pressure on farmers, which are frequent sources of complaint in the absence of such agreements. As in the case of direct price support, however, the benefits of the scheme seem to be heavily outweighed by its demerits. Marketing agreements were introduced during the depression of the 1930's as a relief measure, but they were continued through periods of farm prosperity. Like direct price supports, they give most relief to the wealthiest farmers. Quantities which cannot be sold at the minimum prices are diverted to inferior uses. For example, surplus-milk production is often diverted to the production of ice cream, which in part accounts for the relatively low prices at which this product is frequently retailed. Fluid milk itself, a basic food of infants and the aged, is kept artificially high in price.

Where abundant pasture is available and feeds are cheap, the farmers themselves are apt to be disappointed with the results of minimum milk prices. Like resale-price maintenance and prohibition of sale below cost, minimum-price agreements tend to attract additional producers. The result may be that, despite higher prices paid by consumers, the typical farmer may enjoy only ordinary returns for his labor and capital since new sellers will encroach on his sales volume. He cannot cut price in order to move unsold supplies except for secondary uses. Once the excess capacity has been attracted, it is extremely difficult to remove minimum prices or discontinue supply limitations, since the short-run effect of such action would be precipitation of price warfare and the elimination of weaker competitors. Farmers are likely to vote against removal of marketing agreements for this reason. Consequently, the main hope for consumer relief lies with legislative bodies, which have shown few signs of willingness to risk the displeasure of agricultural interests.

MINIMUM-WAGE LEGISLATION

Like many other prices, wage rates paid to workers engaged in interstate commerce are subject to a floor, or legal minimum. The Fair Labor Standards Act of 1938, as amended, provides for a minimum wage of 75 cents per hour and for overtime payment above 40 hours per week at one and a half times the regular rate. Since most workers in covered employments earn more than this amount, the minimum-wage provision does not affect so large a portion of units sold as do the laws which have been examined heretofore. Nevertheless, it has important repercussions on the economic status of individuals in the lower-wage occupations and on industries employing such workers.

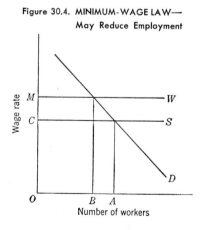

Figure 30.4. MINIMUM-WAGE LAW—
May Reduce Employment

These effects can usefully be viewed in supply-demand terms relating to an individual firm's demand for unskilled labor. In Figure 30.4, curve D is the firm's demand for such workers (which, it should be remembered from Part A, is the marginal revenue product of labor as successive units of labor are conceived as being applied to a given amount of capital). If the firm is assumed to hire workers in a perfectly competitive labor market, the supply of labor will be perfectly elastic (since the firm's purchases are an insignificant part of the total demand for labor). Curve S is assumed to be the supply of labor to the firm at the competitive wage rate.

If a minimum wage OM (which is higher than OC) is authoritatively imposed, the firm will find it desirable to cut back employment from OA to OB, since otherwise it would be paying BA workers more than they add to the firm's revenue. The reduction in employment may be insignificant or it may be large, depending on the slope of the demand curve and on the difference between the minimum wage and the wage rate previously paid. Some firms may be forced out of business entirely. For example, some companies in the South which used unskilled part-time workers to shell pecans were forced to discontinue operations when the Fair Labor Standards Act was passed. The shelled pecans were sold competitively, and the marginal revenue product of labor was nearly horizontal over a wide range of inputs—that is, each additional worker, needing very little capital equipment, could add about as much to the firm's revenue as the previous one. The minimum-wage law put the supply curve above the demand curve at all input quantities, necessitating discontinuance of operations or, in some cases, conversion to pecan-shelling machinery.

Workers who continue to be employed after having their wages raised by the Fair Labor Standards Act are, of course, better off than before. Those deprived of jobs, however, are apt to be poorer than before, since they are often forced into jobs in intrastate commerce (not covered by Federal law) at lower wage rates than they received previously. This means that resources are no longer allocated so efficiently as before. Employers and workers in the high-wage areas of the country are generally not affected at all by the minimum-wage law. Industrialization of the low-wage areas, however, is impeded because their wage advantage is lost, at least in part. Since capital must move into low-wage areas (or labor must move out) in order to raise real wages significantly, the minimum-wage law works to the disadvantage of the poorer areas of the country.

The adverse effects of minimum-wage legislation have been stressed so far, and these probably outweigh the beneficial results. On the other side, minimum-wage legislation undoubtedly prevents some employers from paying workers less than their marginal revenue product. This is especially apt to happen when workers do not "shop around" enough to be aware of alternative employment opportunities or if these alternatives are few or nonexistent. This is the monopsony case, discussed in Chapter 13. Under this sort of situation it is possible that the imposition of a minimum wage will make the firm hire more rather than fewer workers. For this effect to follow, however, the legal minimum wage would have to be placed between the wage rate actually being paid by the firm and the marginal revenue product of the labor employed (between OW and OW' in Figure 13.3). This gap will vary from firm to firm. This makes it extremely unlikely that the imposition of a uniform legal minimum wage (affecting all firms) has the over-all effect of increasing rather than decreasing employment. The minimum wage affects only relatively unskilled labor which usually has a more substantial number of employment alternatives than does higher-paid, but also more highly specialized, labor. Unskilled workers, on the other hand, are often more ignorant of alternative employment opportunities.

Minimum-wage legislation has been supported largely for humanitarian reasons and has been proposed to improve the income position of certain low-paid wage workers. Economic analysis reveals that it probably does not accomplish this purpose. It tends to reduce total real income by causing some workers (who simply cannot produce enough to warrant the minimum-wage payment) to become unemployed or to find employment in less productive jobs not covered by the Fair Labor Standards Act. The geographical allocation of resources is distorted, since capital investment in low-wage, low-income areas is discouraged. This tends to preserve the low-wage, low-income regions that are established and to prevent the normal economic adjustments which would tend to equalize resource returns through the economy.

BUILDING CODES

Space limitation permits only brief mention of one of several other important ways in which government action serves to interfere with free market determination of prices. Most of these, like the fair-trade laws and the agricultural program, tend to serve politically influential seller interests at the expense of consumers. Building codes as they exist in many communities are an outstanding example. They exemplify a familiar pattern in which certain restrictions are actually needed in order to ensure safety and other legitimate ends, but many additional and unnecessary restrictions are imposed to benefit sellers by curbing competition. The restrictions contained in the building codes are imposed by local governmental bodies, and they are usually supported by labor unions, contractors, and established material suppliers. Sometimes the restrictions are embodied in union agreements with employers instead of being legislated explicitly in the form of building codes. Licensing provisions for particular occupations frequently also contribute to the web of monopolistic restrictions in the construction industry.

For example, the use of "ready-mix" concrete (which is mixed in the truck on the way to the job) has been prohibited in some instances. Lathers have at times secured a prohibition of the use of factory-cut lathing, while in other cases the installation of doors which are not glazed on the job has been forbidden.[1] The width of the paintbrush has been limited in some cases, and in others the use of paint-spraying equipment has been banned. In a well-known instance it was necessary for a contractor to employ an electrician for a full day so that he could plug in an electric pump in the morning and unplug it in the afternoon. The last hour of "work" was paid at the overtime rate because the standard day for electricians was shorter than for other workers.[2]

All such restrictions and make-work provisions tend to increase costs and thus restrict supply. This is accomplished not only by preventing established firms from reaching least-cost input combinations but also by preventing entry of new firms producing close substitute products. The building codes have in one instance proved to be a major obstacle to the development of an entirely new industry—the prefabricated production of residential homes.

The effects on resource allocation are clear. The supply price of housing tends to be increased; this causes a reduction in the quantity of housing units demanded. As a result, fewer resources are devoted to housing than the principle of consumer sovereignty would dictate. Total real income is reduced through artificial restrictions and limitations on cost-reducing methods of production. Real income is diverted from consumers to sellers of construction services and materials.

SUMMARY

In this chapter we have discussed in some detail a few of the many governmental programs which tend to interfere with rather than promote the workings of the competitive market mechanism. A complete list would indeed be lengthy, and it would include many regulations which appear necessary and desirable for non-economic reasons. Among these are sanitary regulations, quarantine rules, licensing requirements, fire regulations, etc., all of which may involve economic effects which are detrimental to the consumer and beneficial to producer groups. The economic effects need not be decisive in determining the appropriateness of such public policies, but they should at least be taken fully into account. The discussion of this chapter should reveal the usefulness of economic analysis in understanding more fully the total impact of many governmental policies.

[1] Stephen P. Sobotka, "Union Influence on Wages: The Construction Industry," *Journal of Political Economy*, Vol. 61, p. 131 (April, 1953).

[2] Miles L. Colean and Robinson Newcomb, *Stabilizing Construction: The Record and Potential* (New York: McGraw-Hill Book Company, Inc., 1952), p. 121.

CHAPTER 31

DIRECT CONTROL OF PRICES AND PRODUCTION

Price has two vital functions in a private-enterprise economy, which were designated in Part A as the rationing and the production-motivating functions. The rationing function is being properly performed when existing consumers' goods are distributed among buyers in conformity with their willingness and ability to pay for them. Price usually serves effectively also in rationing (or allocating) productive resources of all sorts— labor, land, machines, industrial materials—among alternative employments, eliminating those which use these inputs inefficiently. We have seen repeatedly that resource allocation is worsened by private and public price-increasing practices on either the selling or the buying side of the market.

The production-motivating function of price consists of encouraging the production of goods for which price is relatively high in relation to cost, since this reflects an insufficiency of supply in relation to demand. This is closely related to the rationing of productive inputs, because those firms which are producing or wish to produce goods which are in strong demand relative to supply are the ones which can afford to outbid other firms in the competition for factors of production. The more detailed explanation of these normal functions of price occupied most of Part A.

Various types of government interference with prices have been described in Part C (and to a lesser extent in Part B). Public-utility rates are regulated by publicly appointed commissions, and, as will be pointed out in the next chapter, this practice appears justifiable when there is actually real danger of monopoly pricing in the absence of regulation. On the other hand, such government interference with price as is involved in resale-price-maintenance laws, unfair-practices acts, parity-price support for farm commodities, and United States bond-price support has been cited as being ill-advised from an economic point of view and often not permanently helpful even to the sellers concerned.

A different sort of government interference with prices and their functions is exemplified by price and production controls imposed by the Federal government during the two world wars (especially the second), during the period of postwar adjustment (1945 and 1946), and again during the Korean War emergency. These are often called "direct controls," in contrast to monetary and fiscal measures, which are termed "indirect controls." Anyone who understands the tremendous role played by market-determined prices in our economy tends to view direct controls with skepticism. Some economists oppose price control even in periods of all-out war because they feel that prices will adequately perform their usual functions even under extreme emergency. Probably the majority of economists believe that the price and wage controls which were reimposed in the United States in 1950 were both unnecessary and ineffective.

DIRECT CONTROL OF PRICE

Under conditions short of all-out war, it appears better to rely exclusively on monetary and fiscal measures as a means of curbing demand to whatever extent is necessary to prevent general inflation of prices. Within a framework of restrained over-all demand, relative prices of goods can rise or fall in such a way as to encourage the production of some goods (including munitions and the capital equipment and other resources needed in their manufacture) and to discourage the production of other goods.

The nature of the inflationary forces which exist in such a period may be illustrated in terms of the national-income analysis set forth in Part B. Government spending on munitions, labor services, and other items increases sharply. Private investment, especially in munitions plants, also increases, and the individual propensity to consume tends to be high to the extent that civilian goods are available. Unless monetary and fiscal policy is such as to reduce consumption and investment drastically, a serious "inflationary gap" will exist. This gap may be thought of geometrically as the difference between the spending which would take place at a full-employment-without-inflation level of national income and the volume of spending which would just support such a level of national income. This is illustrated in Figure 31.1.

The level of national money income which is just sufficient to employ resources fully at a constant general level of prices is assumed to be OF. In order to support this level of income, spending of the same amount, i.e., FH, would be required. But actual spending at this income level would be FR, leaving an excess of HR as the inflationary gap. Under conditions pictured, actual national income would be ON, but the entire amount FN would be accounted for by price inflation rather than by an increase in real income.

If general inflation is to be prevented, the problem is to keep national money income from rising above OF, that is, the $C + I + G$ curve must be made to intersect the 45-degree line at point *H*. Appropriate policy calls for the elimination of all unnecessary expenditures by consumers, firms, and governments. Since the emergency requires large-scale spending by the government and a large amount of new investment by firms, the major reduction in spending must be at the consumption level. Ideally this reduction in consumption spending should be primarily effected through an increase in taxation. In practice, politicians are unlikely to increase taxes sufficiently, and instead of generating the required surplus they will probably engage heavily in deficit financing. As indicated in Chapter 26, if deficits are incurred in such periods, they should be financed

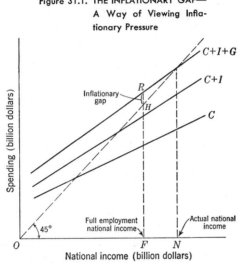

Figure 31.1. THE INFLATIONARY GAP—
A Way of Viewing Inflationary Pressure

as far as possible by sales of bonds to individuals. Judging from past experience, an inflationary gap is likely to be present, especially if the emergency is an all-out war, and some resort to direct controls over prices may be made in an attempt to forestall the threatened general rise in prices and, consequently, national income. Even if during an all-out war strong anti-inflationary policies were adopted at the monetary and fiscal level, as they should be, it is unlikely that individual prices could perform their supply-motivating and rationing functions in a satisfactory manner.

Supply Motivation Undependable

When a nation is at war it is, of course, imperative that production of all sorts of munitions and their components and raw materials be quickly and tremendously increased in conformity with military plans (which, in part, must be made to conform with munitions-production possibilities). Government planning to a greater than normal degree replaces consumer sovereignty as the organizing principle for the economy. Important supporting products such as housing, food, and transportation must also be turned out in adequate quantities. Expansion of plant capacity for munitions, for their components and raw materials, and for important civilian goods must often take place before the end products can be secured in adequate volume.

Favorable contractual and market prices can do much to stimulate privately owned firms to undertake the production of war-supporting goods. The motivating power of favorable prices, however, is reduced by several considerations:

1. Enterprisers are reluctant to undertake plant expansion and other costly expenditures which can be recouped only over a long period of time when they are highly uncertain as to how long the war-stimulated demand will last. The supply-motivating power of high prices is diminished by uncertainty as to their duration. For example, even the prospect of large short-run returns may not stimulate the private financing and building of apartments near army camps, since long-run rental prospects are unclear.

2. Technological change is especially rapid with respect to munitions in wartime. Changes in the fortunes of war can cause sudden cancellation of contracts for some items and create an urgent need to switch quickly to others.

3. Producers of civilian goods are often reluctant to convert to munitions production, even when lucrative contracts or subcontracts are offered, because long-time customers for civilian goods may be permanently lost, and supply and distribution channels may be disrupted to the detriment of peacetime prospects.

Rationing Function Weakened

The rationing function of price, like its supply-motivating function, is also carried out less successfully under wartime conditions than in normal times. Since the proper rationing or allocation of materials among producers is essential to the motivation of supply of end products, the reasons for this conclusion coincide in part with those just given.

Even if strong anti-inflationary fiscal and monetary policy is followed (which was not the case during World War II, when borrowing financed over one-half of Federal expenditures), the most that can be hoped for is stability in the *general* level of prices. Particular commodities, especially those for which demand or supply is inelastic, will rise in price. Some of the most important items in the cost of living of lower-income families, however, are subject to relatively inelastic and stable demands. Many types of food—beef, potatoes, milk, bread, etc.—are of such basic importance that consumption is not highly responsive to price. These are likely in the absence of price control to increase substantially in price (as some resources are withdrawn from their production) even if over-all purchasing power is kept in check. The supply of rental housing is very inelastic in the short run. As a consequence, sudden migrations of workers or servicemen to particular areas would occasion extreme increases in rents in the absence of rent control.

The drastic price increases for consumers' goods would serve to equate the amount demanded and the amount supplied. This mode of rationing would work a particular hardship on low-income groups, however, and provide windfall profits to those fortunate enough to own such resources as apartment buildings in boom towns, inventories of appliances, food-processing plants, etc. Such hardship and such windfall gains, being occasioned by the calamity of war, can scarcely be justified as consistent with the ordinary spinning of the wheel of fortune in a private-enterprise economy.

Certain materials such as steel, copper, aluminum, tin, tungsten, and many others are vital to the success of a war-production effort. It is dangerous to rely on price to allocate these materials in an all-out war. While munitions producers and their numerous suppliers and subcontractors are in a good position to obtain materials by making attractive price offers (at the taxpayers' expense), many makers of luxury civilian goods (*e.g.*, Cadillac convertibles) are also in a strong position to compete for critical materials. Their bids are supported by the demand of wealthy customers, and the producers are apt to have well-established supply channels. Frequently basic materials are produced by the same companies that turn out civilian goods; such "integration" makes it particularly likely that critical material allocations, guided by price alone, would not be sufficiently favorable to munitions output and other war-supporting production. The speculative holding of inventories in anticipation of further price increases would also deprive vital production, at least temporarily, of raw materials if price were allowed to do the entire rationing job in wartime.

Since price is undependable in wartime as an allocator of materials and as a motivator of the kinds of production deemed necessary, and since the rationing of consumers' goods by price would work a hardship on low-income consumers and provide windfalls to owners of certain resources, it appears wise to impose Federal price control during a large-scale war. This makes it necessary to use other means for guiding production, allocating resources, and distributing consumers' goods.

Price Control Necessitates Rationing

As was pointed out in Chapter 4, if price is set below the market level, a rationing problem is created. During the early 1950's price control was imposed but no rationing system was employed. The lack of need for such authoritative rationing was in itself evidence of the ineffectiveness of price control during the period. This can easily be demonstrated with a simple supply-demand diagram.

If a commodity is produced under competitive conditions, its equilibrium price is determined by the intersection of supply and demand curves. In Figure 31.2, OP is the equilibrium price. If the government authorities consider this price to be too high, they may place a ceiling price at a lower level, e.g., OC. The ceiling price may be established *before* the price rises to a level such as OP, or it may represent a "rollback" from a price which has already been charged. In the latter case, demand prior to the emergency may have been represented by the broken line d, and the pre-emergency free market price by OC.

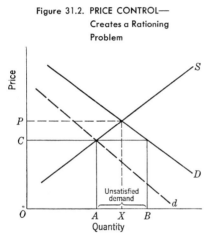

Figure 31.2. PRICE CONTROL—Creates a Rationing Problem

In the absence of the price ceiling, the quantity supplied and quantity demanded would both be OX. Price would have served to ration the commodity to those able and willing to pay an amount just sufficient to induce sellers to supply quantity OX. With the price ceiling OC in effect, sellers will wish to supply only OA, while buyers will wish to purchase OB. Unsatisfied demand will be the quantity AB.

A new type of rationing problem is faced, which is never present when free markets are allowed to set price. Sellers may distribute available supplies among potential demanders on a first-come-first-served (queue) basis, on the basis of personal preference (butchers bask in the sunshine of housewives' smiles when meat supplies are short), on the basis of reciprocal favor (I'll sell you a load of brick if you sell me a new car), or to those willing to pay black-market (above-ceiling) prices.

In order to distribute consumers' goods more equitably in such situations, the government is likely to, and should, install a rationing system, usually involving the use of tickets of some sort which must be given to the seller along with the appropriate sum of money. The problem of distributing the proper number of ration points is itself a difficult one.

Referring to Figure 31.2, the rationing authority should attempt to distribute enough tickets so that the amount OA will be demanded. This may require issuance of more than enough ration points to buy OA, since some will go to persons who will not use them unless price is below OC. This problem may be substantially eliminated, however, if a free market in points is allowed to exist, and resale and repurchase of points permitted. In this case, those point owners who cannot afford to purchase the commodity (*e.g.*, beef) can augment their income by selling their unused points to those individuals desiring to purchase more of the commodity than their own ration points would permit.[1] Unfortunately, thousands of persons are required to work exclusively at the job of administering a rationing system and hence cannot directly contribute to war production.

Subsidies and Price Control

Since price control may have the effect of reducing output of certain critical materials, the governmental authorities may attempt to offset these supply-limiting effects by paying subsidies to their producers. A subsidy is a negative tax—that is, a producer is paid a certain amount per unit by the government to the extent that he meets specified requirements. During World War II, production-motivating subsidies were paid on copper, lead, zinc, petroleum, and some other urgently needed items. After the war, subsidies were paid to producers of eleven critical building materials in an effort to stimulate the building of veterans' housing.

The government's objective in paying a subsidy (usually denoted by the gentler term "premium payment" because no seller likes to admit that he is subsidized) is to encourage more production than firms are will-

---

[1] The combined results of direct price controls and rationing of specific consumer goods may be achieved by a system of rationing total expenditures among consumers. Under this plan specific prices would not be fixed, but each consumer would be allowed a maximum amount of dollar expenditure per week or per month. The total allowed expenditure would be adjusted so as to take into account available supplies, and the objective would be to prevent the general price level, rather than specific prices, from rising. Specific prices would be left free to fluctuate as determined by supply and demand forces.

This scheme is essentially a compromise between the indirect fiscal and monetary controls and the direct control of specific prices. Fiscal and monetary controls can keep the general price level from increasing, but, in periods of war emergency, they can do little to ensure an equitable distribution of relatively scarce consumers' goods. They cannot prevent the wealthy consumers from bidding up prices of scarce and essential items. General expenditure rationing, which would effectively prevent such consumers from spending more than a maximum total amount, may, therefore, prove to be an appropriate supplement to the broader fiscal and monetary controls. The major advantage of general expenditure rationing over direct price controls coupled with specific rationing lies in the greater freedom of choice left to individuals and in the greater use made of supply and demand forces in establishing prices for specific commodities.

ing to turn out at the ceiling price. Alternatively, it would be possible to motivate additional output by raising the ceiling price, but a well-administered subsidy is "cheaper," in that the sum paid by the government to producers is less than the additional amount which consumers would pay. It places the added cost on the taxpayers, rather than on buyers, which is sometimes more feasible politically. This was the case in connection with the postwar Veterans' Emergency Housing Program, when there was public sympathy with returning veterans engaged in the difficult search for housing.

Generally subsidies are paid only to firms which succeed in producing in excess of "quotas" which are computed by the Federal authorities. If properly calculated, these quotas for each participating firm are approximately equal to the output which would be provided in the absence of the subsidy incentive. In that case the government pays the premium only on units which would not otherwise have been produced. This sort of subsidy for above-quota production is illustrated in Figure 31.3.

Figure 31.3. SUBSIDY TO INCREASE OUTPUT— May Be "Cheaper" than Raising Price Ceiling

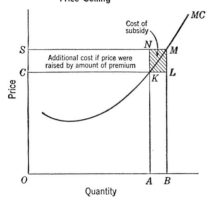

Curve MC represents a firm's marginal cost of producing the commodity (e.g., zinc) the output of which the government wishes to stimulate. If OC is the ceiling price imposed by the price-control authorities, the firm will maximize net returns by producing at a rate OA. It would be possible to induce the firm to expand output to OB by raising the ceiling price to OS. The same effect can probably be achieved, however, by paying a subsidy of CS per unit only on units produced above the quota OA. It is only the output AB which the firm considers unprofitable at the ceiling price. The total price to the firm is OS on the last AB units—OC coming from consumers and CS from the government. These additional AB units are now worth producing because their marginal cost is covered by the price plus subsidy per unit. The cost of the subsidy to the government is represented by the shaded area $KLMN$, which is the product of the subsidy per unit and the added output AB. If the administrative authorities had granted a ceiling price increase equal to CS, the same production stimulus would have been provided, but monetary returns to the firm would have been greater by the rectangle $CKNS$. This difference in income explains why the government often has difficulty in "selling" firms on the desirability of a subsidy.[1] They would prefer a price increase, since this would apply to *all* units sold, and because once a subsidy is in effect the control authorities are unlikely to raise ceiling prices.

A further advantage of the subsidy, from the point of view of the government's twin objectives of holding down prices and stimulating production, is that the shape of marginal cost curves can only be guessed at on the basis of information furnished by firms. When a ceiling-price increase is granted there may be *no* resultant increase in output. This would occur if the marginal cost curve were vertical at the existing rate of output, as a result, for example, of inability to obtain raw materials needed for a larger output. (Shortage of an essential material for which no substitute is possible places an absolute limit on the rate of output which can be achieved.) In this situation the results of the price increase would be disappointing to the government, but if a subsidy were offered for added output, no payments would be made. On the other hand, the ceiling-price increase is simpler administratively. Unnecessary subsidy payments are more likely to be made than are unnecessary price increases, because the government agencies are apt to be actively seeking spots for the spending of available subsidy money whereas the price-control authorities generally let industry take the initiative in seeking price relief.

PRODUCTION CONTROLS

In the normal workings of a private-enterprise economy, private firms make much use of production scheduling relating to their own output. A tractor manufacturer, for example, is likely to schedule output by months for a year or more into the future, subject, of course, to revision at any time. This permits him to arrange for the arrival of materials and parts and for employment of labor so as to make it possible to meet the output schedule. In his scheduling of both outputs and inputs the manufacturer will be guided by his estimate of marginal revenue and marginal cost and by the prices and marginal physical products of input factors.

In wartime, manufacturers continue to schedule outputs and inputs, but many are guided not by the usual array of private forces but by broad production plans formulated by the Federal government. Thus a great deal of the production motivation in wartime comes directly from the government. In the case of civilian goods, however, reliance is usually placed primarily on private demand and profit seeking to provide needed goods and services even in wartime.

In order to assist prime contractors and subcontractors who supply

---

[1] That it may be difficult to spend available subsidy money was illustrated in the postwar housing program. Of $400 million appropriated by Congress less than $28 million was paid out to building-material manufacturers as premium payments.

military goods and producers of especially important civilian goods, the Federal government in wartime may build up a complicated structure of regulations designed to channel materials into preferred uses. The principal regulations of this sort can be classified as priorities, allocations, and limitation orders. These will be examined briefly in an effort to evaluate their economic roles.

Priorities: One Rationing Device

Priority or preference ratings issued by the Federal production authorities may be applied to contracts in order to secure earlier delivery of critical materials. If a machine-tool company has on hand orders bearing different preference ratings, it can be legally required to fill orders rated A (or designated by some other symbol) before those rated B, which in turn are to be filled before those with C ratings, etc. If a new jet fighter, for example, is wanted urgently by the Air Force, it may be given top-priority rating, and this rating would also apply to all critical components—at least where there was a possibility of their going into other uses in such a way as to delay completion of the fighter plane.

Like money, priority ratings diminish in value when issued in excessive quantities. This is frequently a problem in the administration of such a system. To use an extreme example, suppose that *all* prospective buyers were able to obtain A ratings. Then the situation would be the same as if no ratings had been issued. The rating would be only a "hunting license," and many Nimrods would come home empty-handed. It should be recognized that the priority ratings are actually one method of solving the general rationing problem created when excess demand is present. As they have been used, priorities have applied to industrial goods and other rationing schemes to consumer goods.

Allocations and Limitations

Another way in which the rationing problem may be met for industrial materials is through the use of a system of "allocations." This is a more powerful and more complicated method than priorities for centrally directing materials; it is, consequently, likely to be used only for the more important materials such as steel, copper, and aluminum. When an allocations scheme is employed for a material, it is necessary that the government authorities calculate as well as they can the schedule according to which important manufacturers will require the material. The government authorities may then direct sellers to deliver the material to particular plants at designated times. Plants which would like to use the material to produce civilian items which the government considers nonessential may be unable to secure any allocation whatsoever.

An indirect and supplementary approach to the rationing problem, which was employed both during and after World War II and again during the Korean War, consists of the limitation of some economic activities as a way of conserving resources for uses deemed more important. For example, almost all construction was halted in 1942, except where specific permission was obtained. Automobile output was virtually halted in order to conserve steel, labor, and other resources. In addition, the substitution of less critical materials (such as plastics) was enforced for many products. The accumulation of inventories of many critical materials beyond designated amounts was also prohibited in an effort to secure their immediate use as productive inputs. This indirect approach to the rationing problem is a particularly risky one, since it is virtually impossible to know how much some activities should be curtailed in order to free resources for other uses. Unless the positive rationing actions—priorities and allocations—are effective, the materials conserved by limitation orders may still not be used as the government wishes.

Whatever devices are used under emergency conditions to perform the materials-rationing function which normally is left to uncontrolled prices, their use involves a whole complex of problems. A private-enterprise system normally relies on a high degree of decentralization of decisions and economic actions. This permits firms to utilize the expert opinions of specialists regarding types of materials needed, time schedules according to which they are needed, sources of supply, and a host of other details. The attempt to substitute centralized direction of resources, even in only a limited sphere of the economy, leads to a fuller admiration for the way in which resources are normally directed by the price mechanism.

SUMMARY

Knowledge of the detailed workings of price and production controls is much less important to the student of economics than is the ability to evaluate their economic effects and to determine their consistency with other types of interference with prices and the allocation of resources.

First, it should be noted that price control is aimed at keeping prices *down* rather than up, as is the case with so many types of government interference with particular prices. Thus, price controls are imposed, rightly or wrongly, with the purpose of protecting the consumers' interests rather than the interests of particular producer groups.

It is important to see that price control is not an effective *substitute* for anti-inflationary monetary and fiscal measures. Fundamentally, inflation should be attacked indirectly, by attempts to reduce total spending, rather than directly, by attempts to impose legal price ceilings. If fiscal and monetary measures are adequate, price control will normally not be needed except in cases of all-out war emergency. In full emergencies the supplies of certain essential cost-of-living items (*e.g.*, shoes, meat, gasoline) available for civilian use are likely to be sharply reduced. If free market pricing is allowed to continue, wealthy consumers will be able to bid up the price of these scarce commodities, and lower-income consumers will be unable to purchase them at all. Selling firms will also reap unwarranted "war profits" as a result of these price increases. In situations like this, direct controls over prices of such scarce commodities (accompanied by an equitable rationing scheme) may be justified as a supplement to the over-all monetary and fiscal policy. The price controls would be depended upon not to fight inflation but rather to ensure that the available real goods and services be equitably shared among different classes of consumers and that real income be more equitably shared between consumers and producers.

Similarly, price control in wartime helps prevent a substantial diversion of real income from taxpayers to owners of resources which would occur if prices of such industrial materials as copper, aluminum, and steel were determined by market forces alone. The sudden expansion in demand for such materials occasioned by huge war-production programs would cause sharp rises in their prices even if a strong anti-inflationary monetary and fiscal policy were in force. Oligopoly is common in the production of many industrial materials, and taxpayers can be heavily exploited in wartime through price agreements unless effective price control is enforced.

A leading danger in connection with price control is that it will be used to persuade the public that a genuine attempt is being made to curb inflation when actually such an effort is not being made. This political abuse of price control was evident in the years immediately following the invasion of South Korea. Price control was a smoke screen to hide the strongly inflationary policies adopted at the same time. These were mainly of three types:

1. Inflationary monetary and fiscal measures which were, in large degree, followed by the Federal government despite some success on the part of the Federal Reserve Board in securing conditions which led to a moderate rise in interest rates.

2. The weakness of the price-control law itself, which required that the Office of Price Stabilization rubber-stamp most price increases desired by sellers. (The same was especially true of wage and salary "stabilization.")

3. Price-supporting measures such as the fair-trade laws, parity-price program, and import quotas and tariffs which were advocated just as vigorously by congressmen as if the threat of inflation were nonexistent.

Under emergency conditions short of all-out war it appears better not to control individual prices administratively but to rely on the curtailment of over-all demand through such measures as reduction of the money supply, higher interest rates, and budgetary surpluses. Antitrust laws should be more vigorously enforced and government price-supporting actions curtailed in any genuine anti-inflation effort.

CHAPTER 32

GOVERNMENT MUST REGULATE
THE NATURAL MONOPOLIES

The public-utility industries, particularly in the areas of transportation, communication, and power, have traditionally been considered in the United States as representing a unique industrial category in which competition is unworkable. Even those who have advocated vigorous anti-monopoly policies in general have felt that monopoly in the public utilities is necessary, and it has often been argued that in many respects monopoly in the public-utility fields is desirable. Public utilities are, it has often been said, "natural" monopolies. Utility companies often, for example, utilize the streets for street railway tracks, electric-light cables, or gas lines. Even if a city had very wide streets, probably not more than two streetcar companies could lay their tracks down the principal avenues. If several gas companies had their mains buried under the streets, repairs to the lines would probably keep the streets torn up much of the time. Overhead power and telephone lines are unsightly at best, and if a community were served by several companies, the aesthetic offense would be unnecessarily magnified.

In addition to the practical and aesthetic arguments advanced against the maintenance of competition in the public-utilities area, it has been maintained that there are significant economic reasons for setting up monopolies in this field. First, it is pointed out that frequently public-utility firms have very high fixed costs and relatively low variable costs. It follows, accordingly, that as the firm's output increases over a wide range the cost of producing a unit of service is likely to fall. In railroading, for example, the firm has a tremendous investment in land, tracks, bridges, tunnels, rolling stock, freight and passenger stations, repair shops, and so on. The expense of maintaining these properties goes on largely independently of the amount of traffic hauled by the railroad. The marginal or "out-of-pocket" cost of hauling an additional barrel of flour, for example, may be pretty nearly zero, and even the shipment of an entire trainload of wheat may add relatively little to the company's total cost.

As a consequence, within very broad limits, the more traffic the railroad hauls, the smaller will be the average cost (per ton-mile) of the service rendered. In similar fashion it may be argued that if four or five electric-power companies served the same community there would be an unnecessary duplication of expensive specialized capital equipment, and it is likely that no firm would be able to use its facilities at the minimum-cost output.

Furthermore, it has been observed that in many public-utility areas the economies of large-scale production are so great that, within limits, the larger the plant the lower are average costs of production. Because of increasing returns to scale, a firm using a small plant would not be able to compete with a firm using a large plant. It is concluded, therefore, that in the nature of things public utilities must be monopolies; public utilities are "natural" monopolies.

Second in significance to the monopolistic character of public utilities is the fact that they render services which are economically important. Modern economic life could not continue without fundamental change if an urban area were deprived of the services of electric, gas, water, railroad, telephone, or telegraph companies. For most of these services only unsatisfactory substitutes are available. Society has, accordingly, found itself in the dilemma of depending on private monopolies for certain important services. Unwilling, at least without a struggle, to pay monopoly profits to private concerns for rendering these services, policy makers have usually resorted to the device of issuing exclusive franchises to public-utility companies and then subjecting the firms to regulation, usually by a public-utility commission. In this way it is hoped that the public can gain the advantages of large-scale production while avoiding the risk of exploitation at the hands of the private monopolies. It is with the strengths and shortcomings of this system that we are concerned in this chapter.

THE NATURE OF PUBLIC UTILITIES

That public-utility companies are unlike department stores or the corner grocery store in certain fundamental respects is undeniable. It seems clear that because of certain practical and economic considerations some public utilities must be operated as local monopolies, and, if they are monopolies, the public interest requires either that they be owned outright and operated by the government—Federal, state, or local—or that they be subjected to public regulation. But it does not follow simply because public utilities are monopolies that there cannot be problems of excessive monopoly even in this area; and there is a hazard that industries which are not in fact "natural" monopolies will seek public-utility status in order to be rendered legal monopolies and thus escape the rigors of competition. If regulation were completely effective, *i.e.*, if utility companies were in fact deprived of all monopoly profits, this last point would be of little economic consequence. But, as we shall see, the regulation of privately owned public utilities poses real practical problems even when the theoretical issues are clearly understood by those charged with the responsibility of regulating rates and service in the public interest. And in numerous instances utility regulation in practice seems designed to protect the utility company rather than the general public.

It should be recognized that governments have not, in fact, limited their regulatory activities to the public-utility industries. The Federal and state governments have at various times and places imposed direct regulations on almost every type of industry, usually under the guise of claiming that the industry in question was "affected with a public interest." Whether or not a business was "affected with a public interest" has been the center of many a stormy legal controversy. Since 1934 court decisions have, however, made it clear that government regulation may be extended to almost any industry in the economy.

The regulation of industries which do not fit the public-utility category will not be discussed here. The dividing line between what is and what is not a public utility is legally obscure, but we shall confine our attention here to firms in the areas of communication, transportation, water, and power, where perhaps the only genuine cases of natural monopoly may be found. These public utilities are characterized as follows:

1. A public utility usually operates under an exclusive franchise granted by a governmental unit. An electric-power company, for example, receives from the city government the exclusive right to provide electric power to all buyers within the municipality. The power company is then not only a natural monopoly but a legal monopoly as well; there can be no competition from another power company for the life of the franchise.

2. A public-utility company usually has the power of eminent domain, *i.e.*, the power to take private property for public use after fair compensation. This is a power normally reserved for the government alone.

3. A public-utility company is subject to government regulation, usually by a public-utility commission, but it is entitled to reasonable compensation—a "fair" return.

4. A utility company is required to render adequate service to all comers.

5. A utility company is required to charge "reasonable" rates, and it is prohibited from discriminating among customers of the same class. "Reasonable" rates are presumed to be those which will provide the company with a "fair" return.

ECONOMICS OF PUBLIC UTILITIES

Let us apply techniques of economic analysis to the problems of public-utility regulation in an effort to evaluate policies in this area. We shall first investigate the implications of the fact that utility companies enjoy increasing returns to scale of plant. It will be assumed in what follows that the firm has only a single plant and that no distinction need be made between economies of scale for plant and firm.

Because of certain technical factors many utility companies, particularly those in the fields of gas and electric power, are characterized by decreasing costs as the size of the plant increases. In most market areas

Figure 32.1. INCREASING RETURNS TO SCALE—
May Create Natural Monopolies

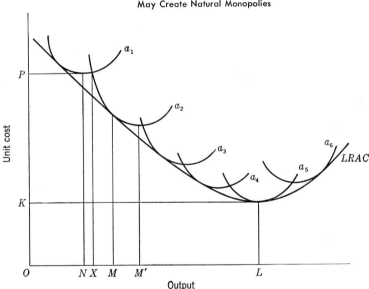

the demand for electric power is insufficient to justify the construction of the optimum-sized production and distribution system. As was pointed out in Chapter 5, a company contemplating the building of a new plant is confronted with a choice as to scale. A relatively small plant, as, for example, a_1 in Figure 32.1, would have higher average costs than a larger plant, e.g., a_2. The optimum-sized plant would be a_5, which could produce an output of OL at an average cost per unit of OK. If the market is too small to justify a plant of this size, a smaller one will be constructed. If it is anticipated that less than OX units will be sold per time period, plant a_1 will be preferred to a_2. If the anticipated output is OM, that output can be produced by plant a_2 at a lower average cost than by any other sized plant.

Suppose that the market is currently being served by a firm with a plant of the a_1 size. If demand is sufficient and a new company builds a plant of a_2 size, it will be able to undersell the first plant; at any price below OP the first plant will be selling below cost while the larger plant will be able to sell at a price somewhat below OP and enjoy considerable profit. If competition is allowed to operate without restriction in this situation, either the first company will be forced out of business or the two companies will get together and agree on a price which will provide monopoly profits to one or both concerns. In neither case will the consumers' interest be protected by the competitive forces of the market.

Figure 32.2 represents the cost and revenue data for firm a_2 of Figure 32.1. $LRAC$ is the long-run average cost curve. The firm's short-run

Figure 32.2. DECREASING SHORT-RUN COSTS—
Characterize Long-run Equilibrium

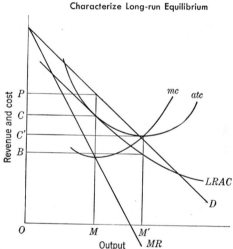

average cost curve is atc, and its short-run marginal cost curve is mc. D is the market demand curve, and MR is the firm's marginal revenue curve. In the long-run equilibrium position the firm will operate to the point where $MR = mc$ and $atc = LRAC$. At this output the price would be OP, the average cost would be OC, and the profit per unit of output would be CP. The following points should be noted:

1. This firm can produce the output OM at a lower cost than it could with a plant of any other size. This follows from the fact that the $LRAC$ curve indicates the lowest cost at which any output can be produced, and, at output OM, $LRAC = atc$.

2. Although this plant can produce an output of OM at a lower cost than any other larger or smaller plant, it can produce the larger output OM' at even lower cost, i.e.. OC'' is less than OC.

3. Although this plant can produce OM' units at a lower cost than it can produce OM units, a larger plant could produce OM' units of output at a lower cost per unit than this firm can; OB is less than OC'.

Two conclusions follow from this analysis: (1) In an industry characterized by decreasing long-run costs each firm in the industry will, if it is in long-run equilibrium and is maximizing profits, operate under conditions of short-run decreasing costs, *i.e.*, to the left of the lowest point on the short-run average cost curve. (2) In an industry characterized by decreasing costs competition tends to become "cutthroat" or "ruinous," with monopoly finally emerging.

To the extent that the assumptions made in this analysis correspond with reality in the public-utility field, the conclusion is that rates and services cannot be regulated by competition, but monopoly is the inevitable and "natural" state for these industries. The pressures for increasing output and thereby reducing costs, both in the short run and in the long run, will be so great that every effort will be made by firms to undersell competitors until all competition has finally disappeared. It is clear, however, that the advantages of increasing size are not without limit, and in recent years there seems to have been some tendency for plants of smaller size to be substituted for larger plants in the production and distribution of electric power.

As was pointed out in Chapter 7, the desire to hold some degree of monopoly power is universal among sellers, and managers of public-utility companies are no exception. It has been insisted by some writers, in fact, that the concept of a natural monopoly is largely a fiction invented to justify exclusive markets for public-utility companies.[1] On two points we can be reasonably sure: (1) Even if local monopolies of public utilities are necessary, and it seems that they are, it does not necessarily follow that public utilities should be national or regional monopolies. Except where hydroelectric resources can best be exploited by very large plants, for example, it does not appear that an electric generating and distributing system large enough to supply power to fifty communities has a significant cost advantage over a plant designed to serve a much smaller market. (2) Although we have assumed that when competition cannot be relied upon to maintain "fair" prices it becomes necessary for the state to regulate public utilities to protect the general interest, a number of industries have been regulated as public utilities for reasons other than the protection of consumers. Some firms, such as taxicab companies, have sought public-utility status because they have felt that the gains from exclusive markets outweigh the disadvantages of public regulation. In other cases, such as interstate motor trucks and vans, regulation was imposed not to

[1] See Horace M. Gray, "The Passing of the Public Utility Concept," *The Journal of Land and Public Utility Economics*, Vol. 16, pp. 8–20 (February, 1940).

protect consumers but to protect the railroads with which trucks and vans compete. There is, of course, no simple formula for determining whether a firm should be treated as a natural monopoly, but the public interest requires that legal monopolies be no more numerous or extensive than is necessary. Since, as will be demonstrated later in this chapter, public regulation of monopolies is at best a poor substitute for competition, its scope should be restricted to those areas where competition is clearly unworkable.

Rate Regulation in Principle

In regulating public-utility monopolies the courts have laid down the principle that the utility is entitled to a "fair return on a fair value." To allow more than a fair return would be to permit the firm to enjoy monopoly profits; to allow less than a fair return would be to deprive the firm of property without due process of law, and such a rate would be declared unconstitutional.

Let us suppose that Figure 32.3 represents the short-run cost and revenue data for a local utility firm. If the firm were allowed to operate as a private monopoly and attempted to maximize profits, it would produce OM units of output and sell them at a price of MP per unit. A "fair" rate would be represented by OR, since this is the rate at which price equals average total cost, on the assumption that the average total cost includes a "normal" or "fair" rate of return on capital investment. The output under such regulation would be MN units greater than under unrestrained

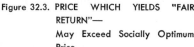

Figure 32.3. PRICE   WHICH   YIELDS   "FAIR RETURN"—

May Exceed Socially Optimum Price

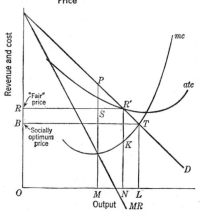

monopoly, and the price would be lower by PS. It should be noted, however, that while this regulated price, OR or NR', is equal to average total cost, it is greater than marginal cost. Marginal cost at output ON is only NK. This indicates that output is still too low in terms of the ideal allocation of resources. This is true because marginal cost represents the amount of additional resources required to put an additional unit of the service on the market; price represents the amount consumers are willing to give up in order to secure the additional unit. As long as price exceeds marginal cost, more resources should be devoted to the production of the service. The ideal price from the resource-allocation point of view would therefore be LT, and the ideal output OL.

It should be recalled from the analysis in Part A that under purely competitive conditions price equals marginal cost, and the optimum allocation of economic resources is thereby achieved. But under conditions of perfect competition, price is also equal to average cost, so that in long-run equilibrium firms neither make abnormal profits nor incur losses. Rate regulation for public-utility companies poses, therefore, a policy dilemma. If prices are set at average cost levels (OR in our example), the output of the utility may be restricted below that which is socially most desirable in terms of consumer sovereignty. On the other hand, if price is set at marginal cost levels, the utility company may be unable to cover average costs and thus suffer losses or may make abnormal or monopoly profits. In our geometrical example, marginal cost pricing would cause the utility company to incur losses, since price falls below average cost. If, however, the demand curve were to intersect the marginal cost curve somewhere to the right of the lowest point on the average cost curve, marginal cost pricing would allow the company to secure an abnormal return.

In actual practice, utility commissions have followed the rule of "fair" return, and have made an attempt to keep prices at average cost levels. As a result, output in the utility industries may be below or above that which is socially most desirable. A simple example may be cited to illustrate the point. Suppose that a toll bridge is constructed. It is estimated that the annual cost of interest plus amortization charges on the original cost of construction is $100,000. It is further estimated that 100,000 vehicles will travel over the bridge each year. Average cost pricing of the bridge would require, therefore, that toll charges be $1 per vehicle. (The fact that this bridge normally would be owned by government rather than a private company makes no difference in our analysis.) But the actual cost of resources "used up" in moving an additional vehicle across the bridge may be very slight, perhaps 10 cents. Let us suppose that there are several ferryboats operating near this bridge, and a reasonably competitive price of 50 cents per vehicle is established. Now this 50-cent price pretty well reflects the additional cost of moving a vehicle across the river by ferry. Many motorists will travel by ferry and pay 50 cents rather than pay $1 to go across the bridge. But if they travel by ferry, they will actually use up 50 cents' worth of economic resources, while if they had traveled by the bridge they would have used only 10 cents' worth. This shows that the practice of setting toll rates at average cost ($1) results in restricting unduly the use of the bridge and promoting a socially undesirable utilization of the ferryboats. But unless average cost prices are charged, how should the bridge be paid for?

Presumably an all-wise socialist state could set prices at marginal cost levels, subsidizing some industries and taxing others, but a further problem is raised when long-run considerations are taken into account. If marginal cost pricing were adopted, the optimum allocation of resources would be achieved once the bridge was constructed. But how could the decision ever be made whether to build a bridge in the first place? About the only criterion available for such decisions is "will it pay?" And to make a project pay, average cost pricing is almost necessary.

We must conclude that the setting of utility rates by commission, no matter how wise and objective the rate-setting body happens to be, can rarely achieve socially optimum results. Such rate setting does serve the interests of the consumer better than unrestrained private monopoly, but at best commission regulation fails to utilize resources in full accordance with consumer preferences.

Our theoretical model suggests one more shortcoming of commission regulation of public utilities. Since the company is legally entitled to a fair return, *i.e.*, a normal profit above costs, there is little incentive for the firm to attempt to cut costs. If by improving efficiency and curtailing all unnecessary expenses the firm is able to reduce average costs, the old rates will then provide a surplus above costs, and the firm will be enjoying monopoly profits. Since the company will be making more than a fair return, the logic of utility regulation would require that rates be lowered. Since, in fact, rates are not adjusted frequently, an increase in efficiency may for a time increase the profits of the firm, and this may be sufficient inducement for the introduction of cost-reducing innovations. But clearly the same incentives for cost cutting do not exist in a regulated monopoly that operate in a highly competitive industry, and in some instances it appears that there is a premium on inefficiency in the regulated utilities. The difference between the strength of the incentive for greater efficiency in privately owned public utilities and those operated by a governmental unit probably is not great.

Rate Regulation in Practice

We have so far examined some of the theoretical difficulties involved in the setting of utility rates by public authorities. There are, in addition, some extremely troublesome practical problems in utility-rate determination which deserve brief attention here. In the famous case of *Smyth v. Ames* (1898), the Supreme Court stated that railroads and other public utilities are entitled to a "fair return on the fair value" of property being used for the convenience of the public. The courts have always had great difficulty in determining what is fair in both regards.

"Fairness" of a rate of return on capital depends in large measure on the riskiness of the investment. Thus a return of $2\frac{1}{2}$ or 3 per cent may be appropriate on a United States government bond while 20 per cent might be consistent with the risk of investing in a Central American oil property where the authorities might decide suddenly to expropriate all foreign-owned oil wells. In general, the riskiness of investment in the utility fields is low—at least where the industry is properly a regulated public utility because close competition is, and should be, absent. On this account a relatively low rate of return should make it possible for utilities to attract capital in competition with more competitive fields in which uncertainty is greater. Utility investors and officials are, of course, anxious to receive the highest possible rate of return on the investment. Administrative commissions and courts have no clear-cut criteria to follow in arriving at a fair rate of return and must resort to largely arbitrary judgment which is often influenced by the amount of pressure brought to bear by interested groups. Generally the courts have held that a return of 6 to 8 per cent was "fair," and in recent years a return of 5 per cent or less has sometimes been considered adequate. But if 5 per cent is a fair return, it is to be 5 per cent of what?

This raises the question of how to compute the "fair value" of utility property. The Supreme Court in *Smyth v. Ames* set forth a confused array of considerations to be taken into account by regulatory commissions, including: (1) original cost of construction, (2) the amount expended in permanent improvements, (3) the amount and market value of its bonds and stocks, and (4) the present as compared with the original cost of construction.

Of these several considerations which the Court said must be taken into account in determining the value of utility property, the market value of the company's securities is clearly the most inappropriate. The value of the company's securities might be helpful in determining the valuation of a firm's property for some purposes, *e.g.*, a valuation for tax purposes. But the market value of the company's stocks cannot properly be used to determine appropriate rates, since the value of the stocks depends upon the rates charged. Virtually any rates could be justified if the market value of the company's stocks were used to determine "fair value." If, for example, the commission has set very low rates, the company's earnings will be low, and the value of its securities will be correspondingly low; the low income represents a fair return on the low valuation. If, on the other hand, the commission has set very high rates and the firm's income as a result is high, the company's securities will have a high market value; the high income represents a fair return on the high valuation. Since the value of the securities depends on the rates charged, it is circular reasoning of the most vicious sort to argue that the fair rate should be determined by the value of the securities.

Original cost (including improvements) and reproduction cost have both been frequently accepted by commissions and courts as appropriate capital values for rate-making purposes. The former has often been modified by the "prudent-investment" concept, according to which clearly improper expenditures—on poorly engineered projects, bribes, and unscrupulous promoters—are disallowed. Utility companies themselves have usually favored the reproduction-cost basis, since the long-term upward trend in prices generally makes reproduction cost higher than actual cost.

The concept of reproduction cost is inherently a vague one. If an existing railroad were actually reproduced at the present time, it would be necessary to provide plant facilities for turning out types of locomotives and cars no longer being produced. How can one reasonably estimate what such equipment would cost today? Further, what is to be assumed regarding obstacles to construction? It may have been necessary a hundred years ago to cut down a forest where none exists today. Should the area be mentally reforested? Land values have risen greatly since the railroad-building era of the nineteenth century. Public land grants of tremendous size were made to the railroads by the United States government. Should the railroads now be considered to buy the land at today's high values (which in part are due to the existence and influence of the railroads themselves)? The same perplexing problems exist with respect to the notion of reproduction costs of electric-power companies, gas companies, etc., although they are generally less striking than in the case of the railroads.

Recent years have seen a new approach to the fair-return-fair-value problem. In 1944 the Supreme Court handed down the Hope decision, which, at least for the moment, ranks with *Smyth v. Ames* in importance in the public-utilities field. The Federal Power Commission had valued the property of a natural-gas company at 33 million dollars after depreciation and allowed a return of 6½ per cent. The company insisted on a valuation of 66 million dollars and a return of 8 per cent. In deciding against the company, the Court did not take a stand in favor of any rate base. It was the view of the Court that if the end result is rates which enable the company to operate successfully, to attract capital, and to compensate its investors for risks assumed, those rates are sufficiently high.

The effect of the Hope decision is to relieve the commissions of the necessity of setting rates which provide a fair return on the present fair value of the utility property, as required by the *Smyth v. Ames* decision. Instead, the fairness of the rates is judged primarily by their effects on the ability of the utility to furnish adequate service and secure needed financing. This judicial guidance is so vague that there is probably even more room than before for differences in opinion as to what rates are appropriate.

SUMMARY

We have seen in this chapter that the public utilities, because of both economic and non-economic reasons, often must be operated as monopolies. In some instances the geographic extent of the monopoly has probably been greater than optimum, and in other cases firms have been made legal monopolies when actually a workable degree of competition could have been maintained. It has been clearly established, however, that competition is not workable in some areas.

Unwilling to depend upon unrestrained private monopoly for the provision of important services, the American public has insisted that the utility firms be subjected to regulation, usually by public commissions. This has given rise to numerous theoretical and practical problems. The courts have for many years insisted that the utility companies are entitled to a fair return on a fair investment. What constitutes a fair return must be determined more or less arbitrarily, and the establishment of fair value has given rise to the rate-base controversy. The Hope decision seems to indicate that the Court has abandoned the rate-base approach to the valuation problem and substituted the idea of the "end result." It is clear that no satisfactory solution to the valuation problem has yet been devised, and it is doubtful that there is any real solution.

There is no way for a commission to provide a "fair return on a fair investment" and at the same time to allocate resources strictly in accord with consumer preferences. Commission regulation and consumer sovereignty are not completely compatible. Commissions, in fact, are not likely to concern themselves with the problem of efficiency of resource allocation even though their decisions have an important bearing upon how the economy's resources will be utilized.

Other practical problems harass utility commissions in their efforts to regulate rates and service. Commissioners are frequently poorly paid by the states, and in competition with the highly paid lawyers and engineers representing the utility companies they are often at a serious disadvantage. In addition it is frequently difficult to prevent a "community of interest" from arising between regulatory-commission employees and the companies regulated, especially since such employees often are either obtained from or likely to move into the industry regulated. If the commissioners lack insight into the problems of the companies which they regulate, they may inadvertently handicap them in their efforts to provide good service at reasonable rates. The great difference in financial resources of the companies being regulated and the commissions has frequently worked out to the disadvantage of the public.

This has been a case study of an area where competition cannot be relied upon to protect the public interest. We have tried to contrast the complexities of regulation with the relative simplicity of the operation of the free market place. In spite of the difficulties, regulation has in many instances worked out rather satisfactorily to all concerned; during the last two decades, electric power, for example, has been one of the few commodities steadily to decline in price. But regulation of private monopoly is inherently more complicated than competition, and the extension of the legal monopoly status to additional firms should be undertaken only when it is clear that competition cannot be entrusted with the responsibility of maintaining reasonable prices and adequate service. Some industries, such as trucking and taxicab service, now treated as utilities, might well be returned to a fully competitive status. The advantages of large scale in these industries are not so great as to make them appropriate fields for regulated monopoly.

CHAPTER 33

INTERNATIONAL COMMERCIAL POLICY

Two points which are basic to a consideration of international commercial policy were made in earlier chapters dealing with international economics. It was pointed out in Chapter 15 that, although all countries gain from foreign trade as a long-run matter, any change in a country's pattern of international trading may generate extremely difficult short-run readjustments in the domestic economy. Substantial liberalization in international-trade policy would tend to revamp the entire organization of the economy, increasing the demand for some products and some factors and reducing the demand for others, increasing the output of some goods and reducing the output of others, raising some incomes and lowering others. This suggests that while from the point of view of the consumer free international trade is clearly beneficial, contributing as it does to higher living standards, there may be producer groups in the economy which are adversely affected by extensions of foreign trade. Those whose sales will be reduced by the foreign competition and those whose incomes will be reduced if foreign goods are made available to domestic consumers will look upon imports as an evil, and they are likely to foster restrictive policies which will make it difficult or perhaps even impossible for certain foreign products to compete with domestic products in the domestic market. The first fact to be kept in mind in evaluating international commercial policy is that any change generates a conflict among economic groups within the country. A policy of expanding trade with foreigners will help some but hurt others; a policy of restrictionism will benefit some at the expense of others. Policy in this area, as in most, consists in large part of determining what groups are to be helped at the expense of other groups. Since producer groups are likely to be more vocal and more powerful politically, the interests of domestic producers are likely in practice to be protected against the interests of domestic consumers.[1]

[1] If one accepts Adam Smith's view that the interests of consumers and the general welfare are identical, the case against trade restrictions appears to be conclusive. Smith said: "Consumption is the sole end and purpose of all production; and the

A second point of significance in evaluating international commercial policy was made in Chapter 14. Here it was pointed out that the balance of payments must balance. A policy which calls for payment by foreigners to Americans of old debts and interest on the old debt is inconsistent with a policy which provides a net export balance for goods and services items. Both policies cannot be carried out at the same time. Either Americans must import more than they export under such conditions, or foreigners will be forced to default on their obligations to Americans. Policy makers in the field of international trade must, therefore, first determine what groups are to be helped at the expense of other groups, and, second, they must determine whether a given policy which they are proposing will make impossible the carrying out of another policy to which they are also committed.

The determination of appropriate policy in situations in which one group stands to gain at the expense of other groups poses some of the most difficult problems in political economy. Policies of this sort in the field of international economics would include the following:

1. Proposals which would benefit the world as a whole but might help some nations and injure others

2. Proposals which would benefit the nation as a whole but might help some groups and injure others

3. Proposals which would benefit some groups but would injure the nation as a whole

Those who advocate restrictions on international trade seldom claim that their policies fall in category 1. Trade restrictionism is usually advocated as a frankly nationalistic policy. American tariffs are supported because it is alleged that they benefit American business. Argentine exchange control was imposed in the belief that it helped the Argentine economy. British cartels are given government support because it is thought that they help British industry. Arguments which suggest that the aggregate world production would be greatest under free trade usually make little impression on those who advocate restrictionism; their objective is not world welfare but national well-being. Whether this is a proper objective for public policy is a matter which need not concern us

---

interest of the producer ought to be attended to, only so far as it may be necessary for promoting that of the consumer. The maxim is so perfectly self-evident that it would be absurd to attempt to prove it." Adam Smith, *The Wealth of Nations* (New York: Modern Library, Inc., 1937), p. 625. A similar view was expressed by Professor Simons: "All the grosser mistakes in economic policy, if not most manifestations of democratic corruption, arise from focusing upon the interests of people as producers rather than upon their interests as consumers. One gets the right answers usually by regarding simply the interests of the consumers, since we are all consumers. . . . " Henry C. Simons, "Some Reflections on Syndicalism," *Economic Policy for a Free Society* (Chicago: University of Chicago Press, 1948), p. 123.

here, but whether trade restrictionism is injurious or beneficial to the nation is a matter upon which economic analysis can throw some light.

PROTECTIVE TARIFFS

The device resorted to most frequently by American policy makers in an effort to restrict the free flow of goods into the country is the protective tariff. By levying a tax on goods coming into the country, the government can make imported goods more expensive than comparable domestic goods, which, of course, are not subject to the tax. If the tariff is sufficiently high, American consumers will find the imported goods too expensive to buy; if they consume the commodity at all they must buy the domestic good.

The most obvious effect of the protective tariff is that it raises the prices of commodities protected by it; if it did not raise prices, it would afford no protection. The increase in prices represents a gain to domestic producers, at least in the short run, and a loss to consumers. The higher price for the product is likely to mean greater income for producers and a reduction in living standards for consumers. The reduction or perhaps elimination of foreign competition secures the domestic market for domestic producers and tends to make them look with favor upon the protection of a tariff when the threat of competition from foreign sellers is significant.

Under conditions of full employment, if the price of a commodity is increased as a result of the enactment of a tariff, domestic producers of that commodity are likely to expand production, drawing labor and other resources from other industries, some of which will come from export industries. This results in a reallocation of resources, taking them from industries where the country has a greater comparative advantage and adding them where comparative advantage is smaller or, perhaps, nonexistent. As in the case of all monopolistic malallocations of resources, the real value of the aggregate output of all industry is less than if resources were allocated by the competitive forces of the free market, and the productivity of factors of production, e.g., labor, is less than if employed in industries where comparative advantage is greater, with the result that the compensation to factors, e.g., wages, is reduced.

The kinds of adjustments which restrictions on the free flow of goods in international trade bring into being depend upon the particular circumstances obtaining in a given case. Since no thoroughly satisfactory generalization is available to explain the repercussions which will follow from any possible interference with the normal currents of world trade, we shall analyze three different models, each making different assumptions with reference to the basic facts of the case.

Case I. Tariff Excludes Some Imports but Not All: Constant World Supply Price

Let us consider first a situation in which a part of the domestic supply of a commodity is produced domestically and a part is imported. The wool industry in the United States typifies this case; some sections of the country are well adapted to wool producing, but the amount of wool which can be produced in these areas is insufficient to meet the total domestic demand. In Figure 33.1, S_d represents the domestic short-run supply schedule for the industry, which we assume sells competitively, and D_d the domestic demand. In the world market the commodity is also sold under conditions of perfect competition, and the world price is assumed to be OW, which is un-affected by changes in the volume of American imports.

Figure 33.1. **PRICE INCREASES BY AMOUNT OF TARIFF—**

When World Supply Price Is Constant

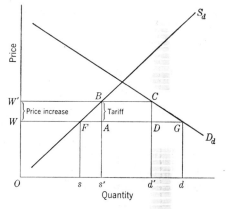

With a world price of OW, do-mestic producers will be willing to supply Os units, and domestic demand will be Od units. The dif-ference between the quantity de-manded by domestic consumers and the quantity supplied by do-mestic producers will be imported; in Figure 33.1 this is sd units.

Suppose now that a tariff equal to WW' is levied on all imports of this commodity. The price to do-mestic consumers will rise by the full amount of the tariff to OW'. At the higher price, resources which were more productive in other employments before the enactment of the tariff will now be attracted to the wool indus-try, and the total quantity supplied by domestic producers will be Os', an increase of ss'. At the higher price, however, domestic consumers will take fewer units of the commodity, the total quantity demanded at price OW' being Od', a reduction of $d'd$ units. Imports will accordingly be reduced from sd to $s'd'$.

What is the nature of the short-run gains and losses resulting from the tariff? Domestic-producer income has clearly increased. Before the enact-ment of the tariff, domestic wool producers received $OWFs$ for the Os units produced; now they receive $OW'Bs'$ for Os' units, an increase equal to $WW'BA + sFAs'$. On the presumption that the additional inputs could earn an amount equal to $sFBs'$ in alternative employments, the net gain to domestic producers in the short run would be $WW'BF$. This is sufficient incentive for producer groups to favor the tariff. If price OW' is high enough to provide short-run abnormal profits, these would tend in the long run to be eliminated through entry of new wool producers and encouragement of substitute products, *e.g.*, synthetic fibers.

Consumers are injured by the tariff, especially in the short run. The price has gone up by the full amount of the tariff, from OW to OW'. Since in the particular case represented by Figure 33.1 the elasticity of the domestic demand between prices OW' and OW is less than 1, the total expenditure at the higher price, $OW'Cd'$, is greater than that at the lower price, $OWGd$; that is, after the tariff, consumers actually spend more for the smaller number of units than they previously spent for the greater number.

Since imports after the tariff are equal to $s'd'$ and the central government collects a tariff of WW' on each unit imported, the total amount collected by the government as a tariff is equal to $ABCD$. This may be considered as a gain to the tariff-levying country, but it should be noted that consumers pay an amount equal to $WW'CD$ more for the Od' units than those units would have cost in the absence of the tariff, and this exceeds the amount collected by the government by $WW'BA$.

The income of foreign producers from sales in this market has been reduced by the tariff from $sFGd$ to $s'ADd'$, a reduction equal to $sFAs' + d'DGd$. This will cause a loss of export sales to the country levying the tariff. If the tariff-levying country were the United States, the dollar balances of foreigners would be smaller and the foreign demand for American goods would be reduced. This means that export industries will decline, and the long-run effect of the tariff will be to shift resources out of export industries, where the nation has a comparative advantage, to import industries, where resources can be utilized relatively ineffectively.

Case II. Imports Available under Conditions of Increasing Costs

Let us consider as our second model the case in which imports are available to the tariff-levying country under conditions of short-run increasing costs. Suppose, for example, that the United States produces a part of its supply of a given commodity and imports a part, but that all of the commodity imported comes from Canada. That part of Canada's output which she would be willing to sell to the United States would be represented by a positively sloping curve. In Figure 33.2, S_a is the United States domestic short-run supply curve, D_a is the domestic demand curve, and S_{a+c} is the domestic supply plus the quantity available from Canada.

In the absence of restrictions on international trade, the price OP will be established, and Americans will buy Od units, Os from domestic producers plus sd from Canadian sellers. Suppose now that a tariff equal to HC is levied on imports from Canada. This will have the effect of shifting the S_{a+c} curve to S'_{a+c}, and price will rise to OP'. At this price American consumption will fall from Od to Od', domestic production will increase from Os to Os', and imports will decline from sd to $s'd'$.

Let us assess the short-run gains and losses in this case. Again the incomes of domestic producers have increased. Before the tariff was enacted, the total income received by American suppliers was $OPFs$; after the tariff it rose to $OP'Bs'$, an increase equal to $PP'BA + sFAs'$. On the presumption that alternative employment of resources would have provided domestic producers with an income equal to $sFBs'$, their net gain resulting from the tariff is $PP'BF$.

Figure 33.2. PRICE INCREASES BY LESS THAN TARIFF—
With Rising Supply Price

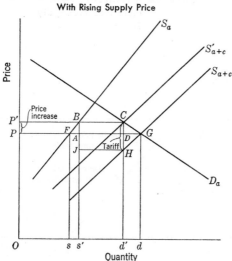

The price paid by American consumers has gone up from OP to OP', but the increase in price PP' is less than the amount of the tariff HC. This results from the fact that a part of the tariff is shifted backward to the foreign producers. The total amount which American consumers pay for imports is equal to the area $s'BCd'$. Of this amount, the area $JBCH$ is collected by the American government as a tariff. The net income to foreign producers is accordingly $s'JHd'$, and the price per unit realized by Canadian producers is equal to $d'H$, which is less by the full amount of the tariff than the price received by American sellers.

The income received by Canadian sellers in the American market after the tariff is less than that received by them before the tariff by an amount equal to $sFAs' + d'DGd + JADH$. Again, this means that Canadians will have fewer American dollars with which to buy American goods, and there will be a shifting of resources in the United States out of the export industries, where resources can be utilized more effectively, into import industries, where resources can be utilized less efficiently, with the result that total product and real income in the United States will be reduced.

Case III. Tariff Strengthens Domestic Monopoly

In Figure 33.3, d and mr represent a monopoly firm's demand and marginal revenue curves; mc is the firm's marginal cost curve. If we assume that the firm sells only in the domestic market and that there is no competition from foreign sellers, it will maximize profits by producing to

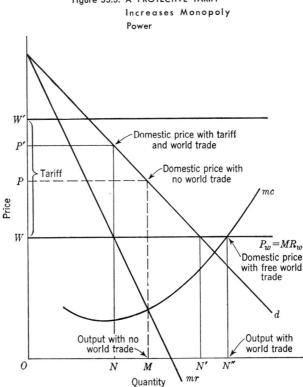

Figure 33.3. A PROTECTIVE TARIFF—
Increases Monopoly
Power

the point where marginal cost equals marginal revenue. Monopoly price will be OP, and output will be OM.

If we now assume that this firm's product is sold in the world market under competitive conditions and that the world price OW is not affected by this firm's actions, the domestic firm, in the absence of a protective tariff, will have to sell at price OW instead of price OP. At the lower price, ON' units will be demanded in the domestic market. The total output of the firm will now be ON'' since at this point marginal cost equals marginal revenue in the world market (MR_w) which is equal to world price; $N'N''$ units will, accordingly, be sold abroad. Whereas the firm would be a monopolist in a closed economy, it is placed in a competitive position under free international trade. This model shows clearly that one of the most effective ways of preventing domestic monopoly and encouraging competition is the adoption of free trade.

Now suppose that a high tariff, *e.g.*, a 100 per cent duty, is enacted. The tariff WW' is equal to OW, the world price. The effect of the tariff is to keep foreign competition out of the domestic market while retaining the world market for that part of the firm's output which can be sold abroad to better advantage than it can be sold at home. Under these conditions the firm will sell no more than ON units in the domestic market; for any output greater than ON, the marginal revenue resulting from sales in the world market will be greater than if they were sold in the domestic market; (*mr* lies below MR_w). The firm will, therefore, sell ON units at price OP' in the domestic market, and NN'' units at price OW in the world market. But OP' is an even higher price than the monopoly price OP which would prevail in a closed economy, and the monopolist enjoying the protection of a tariff will restrict domestic sales to ON. We may generalize by saying that a monopolist operating behind a high tariff wall is able not only to sell at a higher price than if there were no tariff but perhaps to restrict sales and maintain high prices to a degree which would not be possible for a firm operating in a closed economy. The tariff in such cases not only maintains monopoly but may cause domestic monopoly price to be higher by making it possible for the monopolist to discriminate between domestic and foreign buyers. Even in this extreme case it should be noted that monopoly price does not rise by the full amount of the tariff.

Evaluation of Tariff

In each of the three models analyzed, the conclusion was that certain domestic-producer groups made short-run gains at the expense of the nation as a whole. These cases may be taken to be representative though not exhaustive. It is possible, in fact, if (1) other nations do not retaliate with tariffs of their own and (2) the demand of foreign countries for the products of the tariff-levying country are sufficiently inelastic, that the tariff may improve the country's terms of trade, *i.e.*, the amount of imports received in exchange for a given amount of exports. In periods of less than full employment, a protective tariff may increase total spending on domestically produced goods and services. The tariff serves to shift domestic demand from foreign to local goods and services and, by reducing the supply of foreign exchange available to foreigners, to shift foreign demand from domestic to foreign markets. Whether or not total spending on domestic goods will be increased or decreased by such a policy depends upon the respective elasticity of demand of Americans for foreign goods and of foreigners for American goods. Spending, and hence employment, will be increased only if Americans will, as a result of the tariff, shift more aggregate demand from foreign to the domestic market than foreigners will shift away from the domestic market. Conversely, if the respective elasticities are in the proper relation to each other, a protective tariff may serve to reduce inflationary pressures in domestic markets. Despite the possible favorable effects which a tariff might have on income and employment if imposed unilaterally, it is not to be recommended as appropriate policy. The fact is that other nations can and will retaliate, and, if all countries follow a tariff-raising policy, the volume of world trade will decline and every nation will suffer.

The economist's chief charge against the tariff is that it brings about a misallocation of resources. In the long run, even domestic producers may not gain. If the tariff results in abnormal profits and if competition prevails in the domestic market, new firms will enter the protected industries until profits disappear. This effect is similar to that observed in connection with such other government interferences with price as the fair-trade laws, marketing agreements, and unfair-trade-practices acts. This represents a shift of resources from areas where resources can be utilized more efficiently to areas where they can be used less efficiently. But when the tariff is up for revision, Congress unfortunately is not likely to have the problem of efficient allocation in mind at all. Instead, each congressman is apt to be thinking of what will happen to certain firms, owned by and employing constituents of his, if the protection of the tariff is reduced.

In spite of the understandable pressures for higher and higher tariffs in this country, the last decades have seen considerable progress in the lowering of trade barriers, and it seems that the business community understands more clearly than ever before in our history the necessity of reducing restrictions on international trade. The Smoot-Hawley Act of 1930 provided the highest average rates of any tariff in our history, and this remains the basic tariff law of the land. But in 1934, largely as a result of the efforts of Secretary of State Cordell Hull,[1] Congress passed the Reciprocal Trade Act which permitted, among other things, the reduction of tariff rates up to 50 per cent. By the end of the first decade, about half of the duty reductions had been for the full 50 per cent. In 1945, the President was authorized to reduce the rates prevailing at that

[1] See William R. Allen, "The Trade Philosophy of Cordell Hull, 1907–1933," *American Economic Review*, Vol. 43, pp. 101–116 (March, 1953).

time up to 50 per cent, so the rates on commodities which had taken the first full 50 per cent reduction could now be reduced to 25 per cent of the 1934 level. Since that time, multilateral trade agreements have been worked out with several countries with the result that the average tariff rates imposed by the United States are now lower than they have been in several decades.

Big business concerns which have become large importers as well as exporters have to an increasing extent seen the difficulties which tariffs and other trade restrictions have been responsible for, and some of them have taken a firm position in favor of tariff reductions.[1] Many local and regional groups of businessmen have in recent years announced that they favor a policy of tariff reduction. Although the tariff on many commodities remains so high that the volume in which they are imported is low, the situation has shown marked improvement in recent years, and the prospects for the future appear to be better than most economists thought possible a short time ago.

INTERNATIONAL CARTELS

Although high tariffs have been the chief device employed by the United States to restrict imports, other measures which have similar restrictive effects have been employed from time to time. Other countries whose record on the tariff is better than that of the United States have worse records than ours with respect to other forms of restrictionism. The ideal of free multilateral trade requires that all barriers to the movement of goods between countries be removed. We shall briefly consider a number of these restrictive devices, beginning with international cartels.

An international cartel is an agreement, formal or informal, entered into by firms situated in different countries and doing business across international boundaries when the purpose of the agreement is to increase profits by reducing competition. The term "cartel" has been used in this book to denote sellers who surrender their price-setting and related powers to a central association. These sellers may be numerous or relatively few. For the most part, our previous discussions of cartels have assumed that a large number of sellers are associated. International cartels, however, are typically combinations of oligopolistic sellers situated in different countries and doing business both domestically and beyond national boundaries. The cartel arrangements make possible extremely effective oligopolistic collusion to the benefit of the producers and the detriment

---

[1] See, for example, "General Motors Overseas," *Fortune*, November, 1945, pp. 125*ff.*, and "Import and Prosper," *ibid.*, pp. 113–114. In an Associated Press dispatch for Feb. 17, 1953, Henry Ford was quoted as favoring immediate repeal of the 10 per cent tariff on automobiles and "the most rapid possible elimination of all tariffs."

of consumers. Cartel-determined prices are likely to approach closely those which would be charged by a single firm operating in international markets. Like domestic cartel arrangements, international cartels frequently have the outright support of government.

Numerous devices are employed by cartels. The members may enter into a single agreement to maintain prices. They may allocate markets geographically among the members of the cartel, or they may assign sales to an international trade association which maintains a joint sales agency for the members of the cartel. They may exchange patents and secret processes. Or the member firms in the cartel may be owned by the same group of men through an exchange of stock, a holding company, or other monopolistic devices. Since American antitrust laws prevent the kind of price agreements which firms in other countries may freely enter into, those cartels which include American firms usually attempt to utilize the patent in the hope that their actions will not be held illegal.[1]

Frequently cartel agreements are sponsored by governments. During the 1930's, government schemes to control the international output and price of wheat, sugar, coffee, tea, tin, and rubber were entered into by the leading exporting countries. The first international wheat agreement, which became effective in 1933, may be taken as representative. The governments of Argentina, Australia, Canada, and the United States, the principal wheat exporters, agreed as an antidepression measure to restrict the export of wheat during the next two crop years and to allocate exports in accordance with an assigned quota arrangement. Other wheat-exporting countries, including Russia, also agreed to reduce their exports, and thirteen wheat-importing countries, including France, Germany, and England, attempted to prevent an expansion of domestic production. Upon the expiration of the first international wheat agreement, new agreements were entered into, and by 1949 an International Wheat Council was established to administer a plan whereby the importing nations agreed to purchase guaranteed quantities of wheat over a five-year period and exporters agreed to sell those quantities, totaling 500 million bushels, at a fixed schedule of prices.[2]

---

[1] A list of international cartel agreements in effect in 1939, which was prepared by the U.S. Department of Justice, showed that 109 of the 179 agreements included American firms. Corwin D. Edwards, "International Cartels as Obstacles to International Trade," *American Economic Review*, Supplement, Vol. 34, p. 330 (March, 1944).

[2] J. B. Condliffe, commenting on this agreement, says: "It was made clear by this action that although the negotiation of such an agreement contravened the spirit if not the letter of the International Trade Charter, there was enough political influence in the hands of organized farm groups to put through a series of international commodity agreements if agricultural prices should decline at all sharply." J. B. Condliffe, *The Commerce of Nations* (New York: W. W. Norton & Company, 1950), p. 788.

Even older than intergovernmental arrangements to control commodity prices and output are the unilateral governmental control schemes designed to restrict exports in order to maintain high monopoly prices. In 1910, the German government established a compulsory cartel to regulate domestic and foreign sales of potash, of which Germany had a virtual world monopoly. Before the development of synthetic nitrogen, the Chilean government sponsored cartel arrangements for the sale of sodium nitrate, of which Chile was the world's sole producer. Since 1918, the Japanese government has had a world monopoly of natural camphor. The Dutch East Indies government for many years restricted the sale of cinchona bark, the source of quinine. In 1928, the Italian and Spanish governments established a bilateral cartel to regulate the sale of mercury throughout the world. The cartel allotted 40 per cent of the world market to Italy and 60 per cent to Spain.[1]

More important than government monopolies or intergovernmental commodity agreements have been voluntary cartel arrangements entered into by enterprisers from different countries. The potential power of a cartel to raise prices is indicated in the case of tungsten carbide. A cartel arrangement between General Electric and Krupp, a German firm, raised the United States price from $50 per pound to more than $450.[2] Cartels are usually less interested in quality than in price, but the formation of a cartel agreement is likely to reduce a firm's interest in quality improvement, and sometimes the cartel permits a firm to dispose of inferior goods which otherwise could be sold, if at all, only at a price discount. Under a cartel arrangement between du Pont and Nobel, a British firm, a market was maintained for a relatively unsatisfactory military powder produced by Nobel, since du Pont was required by the cartel arrangement to refuse the business of Nobel's dissatisfied customers.[3] Cartels not only restrict output of existing plant but also sometimes attempt to limit construction of new capacity. Edwards reports: "In the case of magnesium, American productive capacity was limited by agreements between the Aluminum Company of America, Dow Chemical Company, and I. G. Farbenindustrie, which provided for the closure of the Aluminum Company's plant in the United States in order to give Dow a monopoly, the exclusion of new competitors, a maximum limit upon Dow's production, and prices so high that even this maximum could not be attained."

[1] George W. Stocking and Myron W. Watkins, *Cartels or Competition?* (New York: The Twentieth Century Fund, Inc., 1948), pp. 69–76.

[2] Edwards, *op. cit.*, p. 332.

[3] *Ibid.*

EXCHANGE CONTROL

A third device which has been used frequently in recent years to control the amount and direction of international trade is exchange control. Like international cartels, exchange controls have assumed a variety of forms and have been used to accomplish several purposes. During periods of war, most nations have made some use of exchange controls, and totalitarian nations have made elaborate exchange-control systems a permanent part of their programs.

Under conditions of free world markets in both commodities and currencies, an exporter sells his goods in a foreign market and usually receives a foreign currency in payment. He is free to use the foreign money in any way he chooses; he may invest his funds in the foreign country, he may buy goods for import, or he may exchange his foreign balances for the currency of his own or another country. An importer, in the absence of controls, may buy foreign currencies with his own money and buy goods or services in any part of the world he chooses. The prices of one currency in terms of others are established in a highly competitive free market, and consumers are able in this way to get the best quality and the lowest prices which the markets of the world provide. The effect of the imposition of exchange controls is to substitute the decisions of a government agency as to what and how much will be imported and exported for those of firms and individuals trading in free markets. When exchange controls have been invoked, a seller in foreign markets is required to turn his foreign balances over to a government bureau, and he will receive from them the "equivalent" in terms of his own currency. An importer will have to buy foreign exchange from the government agency at the legal rate. The government reserves the right to refuse to sell foreign currencies to domestic importers except to pay for imports of goods which it has determined should be imported, and it may require a license before goods can be exported.

The nature of exchange controls may be illustrated by the elaborate system set up by Argentina. Three export rates of exchange have been established. The lowest rate (5 pesos to the dollar) is used to redeem dollars acquired by Argentine exporters of commodities in which Argentina has a great comparative advantage and for which the land has poor alternative uses. Although the return to the exporters is relatively small, they have little choice but to export. A higher rate (7.5 pesos to the dollar) is applied to specific commodities which have alternative (nonexport) uses. The higher rate makes export of these commodities more attractive than it would otherwise be and increases the amount of foreign exchange acquired by the central government. The highest rate, the so-called free market rate, applies to commodities which would not be exported at all at the lower rates.

There are also in Argentina three rates of exchange on the import side. The lowest rate applies to basic commodities which must be imported, such as coal, coke, and petroleum. The effect of this rate is to obtain these goods as cheaply as possible in terms of the domestic currency. The bulk of Argentina's imports come in under a somewhat higher rate. All nontrade transactions (*e.g.*, the purchase of foreign currencies by those who plan to travel abroad) are subject to the highest ("free market") rate. Through the use of multiple rates of exchange and by requiring permits to import and export, the central government is able to replace in large measure the principle of consumer sovereignty with deliberate decisions of a governmental bureau.

IMPORT QUOTAS

The last of the restrictive devices to be considered in this chapter is the import quota. Introduced in France in the 1930's as an antidepression measure, it became a significant part of the international commercial policy of most European nations until the outbreak of World War II, affecting in some instances a major portion of a country's imports. In some respects the effects of import quotas are similar to those of a protective tariff, but in general it may be argued that import quotas introduce rigidities in the price structure and isolate the economy from changes in the rest of the world to a degree which makes quotas even more offensive, from the point of view of the optimum allocation of resources, than protective tariffs.

The points of similarity and difference between quota restrictions on imports and a protective tariff may be observed in Figure 33.4. D_d and S_d represent the domestic demand and supply for a commodity. OW is assumed to be the world price of the commodity, and conditions are assumed to be the same as in the first tariff case discussed earlier in the chapter. If there are no restrictions on imports, Os units will be produced domestically, Od units will be demanded, and sd units will be imported. Suppose now that an import quota equal to BC is imposed. The domestic price will rise to OP, and at this price Os' units will be produced domestically, Od' units will be demanded, and imports will be $s'd' = BC$. The quota has resulted in an increase in domestic producers' income equal to $WPBF$, assuming that resources have been shifted from uses in which they earned $sFBs'$. Price to consumers has increased by WP; foreign producers' income from sales in this country has decreased by an amount equal to $sFAs' + d'DGd$; and importers will make an additional profit of AB per unit on the smaller number of units imported.

If, instead of an import quota, the government had levied a tariff equal to WP, the effect on price, quantity of imports, exports, production, and consumption would have been the same. The only difference would have been that the $ABCD$ additional profits received by importers under the quota arrangement would have been paid to the government under the tariff (compare Figures 33.1 and 33.4). But now suppose that the domestic demand increases from D_d to D'_d without any change in the quota. Price would now rise to OP', domestic production would increase to Om, and imports would be mn, which is equal to $s'd'$. Consumers are now injured to a greater extent than they would be with a tariff. Price cannot be forced by a tariff to rise by more than the amount of the tariff (except

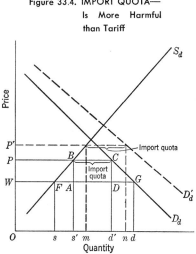

Figure 33.4. IMPORT QUOTA—
Is   More   Harmful
than Tariff

in the rare case of decreasing cost), but there is no upper limit to the price increase which can result from a quota. The increase in demand under the quota arrangement has resulted in an increase in domestic production with no change in imports; under a tariff the increase in domestic demand would call forth a greater quantity of imports with no change in domestic production, which makes the quota arrangement more protective than a protective tariff. A decline in the world price, moreover, would not help domestic consumers if a quota system had been established, whereas, under the assumptions of the model, any fall in world price would be reflected in a reduction in domestic price under a tariff.

SUMMARY

In conclusion we may observe that international-trade restrictions reduce the amount of world trade and, consequently, the gains which would result from the free movement of goods throughout the world. From the point of view of a single country, it is possible that restrictive legislation may benefit the nation at the expense of the rest of the world to a limited degree and for a short time. But since other nations can, and in practice do, retaliate, gains to the country as a whole resulting from restricting trade are not permanent. Both as between nations and within a single country, trade restrictions benefit some and injure others. The United States has traditionally followed a high-tariff policy designed to help certain domestic producers at the expense of consumers. In recent years, however, tariff rates have been significantly lowered in this country, and there seems to be hope that the downward revision will be continued. With respect to other forms of trade restrictionism, *e.g.*, international cartels, exchange controls, and import quotas, American policy has been less objectionable than that of many countries, but the ideal of free multilateral trade requires that all restrictions be eliminated in order that resources may be allocated in accordance with the principle of consumer sovereignty.

There are, of course, considerations which may in certain situations outweigh the strictly economic factors, and an economy may rationally pursue policies which would result in a reduction in living standards. Adam Smith observed, for example, that defense is of much more importance than opulence. Is it not true in these days of international insecurity menaced by the constant threat of atomic warfare that certain materials should be produced domestically whether we have a great comparative advantage in their production or not and, if necessary, that domestic producers be provided the protection of a high tariff? The answer to this question is that a high tariff has not, in fact, made us independent of other countries for war materials. During World War II, in spite of many years of high-tariff policy, a long list of critical materials had to be imported. A tariff cannot make us militarily or economically independent of the rest of the world. Furthermore, if there are industries which are so vital to national defense that they should be maintained without regard to efficiency considerations, it should be observed that a tariff is not the only, and certainly not necessarily the best, method of maintaining such industries. A direct subsidy from the public treasury might well be less expensive to the taxpayer and less detrimental to the interests of consumers than a tariff. In addition, government stock-piling of a critical imported material will sometimes serve as a satisfactory substitute for domestic production of the material under tariff or direct subsidy protection. Finally, if we deliberately reduce our living standards by imposing trade restrictions, for whatever purpose, we should understand that we are in fact lowering standards of living, and that should be reckoned as a part of the cost of the policy being undertaken.

CHAPTER 34

FREE MARKETS AND FREE MEN

A few generations ago, it was customary for fiction writers occasionally to digress from the main theme of the story and to address a few words to the "gentle reader." We have for the most part resisted the urge to chat with the reader. But we have come a long way together as we have explored the mysterious realm of economic analysis, and, as is often true of distant travels, perhaps the happiest part of the trip is its ending. As we complete the expedition, a few words to those who are still with us seem appropriate. Let us discuss where we have been and what we have seen, with perhaps a word about where we go from here.

The first chapter really gave us a forecast of what the book attempts to accomplish. This purpose is to show the way in which our economy, organized on the free-enterprise, or competitive, principle, solves those fundamental economic problems which must somehow be solved by any economic system. We have attempted to answer such questions as the following: How does this system of organization allow consumers' choices as to what is to be produced to make themselves meaningful? How does it get the proper goods and services produced if men are permitted freely to choose among occupations and among different lines of business? How are the various inputs combined to produce the desired outputs? How is the distribution of the fruits of all the economic effort carried out? We know that all these things are done; we knew this before we began to study economics. It is hoped, however, that the reader now possesses a fuller understanding of the leading role which prices play in the solution of the fundamental economic problem of scarcity, and how they organize the extremely complex and interdependent economy which is reflected, for example, in the input-output table.

This book has been designed in large part to show how the competitive economy does allow this miracle—for it is no less than a miracle—to take place. In order to demonstrate the efficacy of the cooperative process which is generated by free markets, it was necessary for us to concentrate on the efficiency aspects of the allocation of resources. We have shown that a system of free markets not only will get goods produced but will do so in a highly efficient manner. The real income of society will be maximized by a system of purely competitive markets.

But this suggests the first complicating problem which we encountered. What do we mean by "maximizing real income"? Heterogeneous goods and services cannot be added together except in value terms. But the prices which enter into values are affected by consumers' effective demand for goods, and these demands are largely determined by the distribution of income. So when we say that the social real income would be maximized under pure competition, we must be understood to be taking the distribution of income as given. Wants are satisfied by the competitive system in proportion to the purchasing power of individuals and families.

This raises an ethical question. Is the distribution of income which arises in a competitive economy a desirable one? We have shown that the distribution of income is determined in the input markets. The forces of competition tend to reward the owners of the most productive inputs. This sort of input pricing does serve to channel productive services into the spots where they are most efficient, to the advantage of both the individual and society. But is the resulting distribution of rewards equitable? On this question we may disagree. To the extent that the productivity of one's labor depends upon personal effort both in acquiring the necessary training and in performing the job well and faithfully, a certain appropriateness seems to attach to distribution according to marginal revenue productivity. To the extent that a high value of the labor and capital services over which one has command are due to luck, health, or inherited characteristics or wealth, the appropriateness of income distribution according to productivity is much more questionable. Most people will agree that some departure from competitively determined incomes is desirable. If we did not admit this, we would be contending that those individuals who are completely unproductive should receive no income at all; this would include many of the aged, the ill, and the disabled. Unless one is willing to embrace a Spartan philosophy of liquidation of the least useful members of society, one is forced to concede that the free market distribution of income must be modified somewhat in the direction of greater equality. But if we admit this, do we not also have to admit that we do not desire free markets? Not at all. For we may without difficulty separate the problem of income distribution from that of resource allocation. We may agree to modify the distribution of income and wealth as we will, but once we have done so, we may still allow free markets to secure an optimum allocation of resources within the accomplished distribution.

While examining the allocative efficiency of the economy, we encountered a second problem of major proportions. This is the problem of monopoly. Upon investigating the way in which our system actually operates, we found that the pure competition of our theoretical model is a rather imaginary conception. Competition is actually a tremendous force in our economy, but sellers of both outputs and inputs are constantly striving for, and in some measure securing, monopoly power. Our analysis demonstrated that departures from competition generally serve to distort the allocation of resources and thereby to make the economy less efficient. Monopolists tend to restrict the flow of economic resources into certain areas of production. In this way they prevent the equalization of returns at the margin, that is, the equalization of the value of the marginal product of like resource units in different employments, and thereby lower the social product.

As we finished Part A, we were forced to admit that yet another ugly problem exists in the real world—a problem which we were temporarily obliged to ignore in order to concentrate adequately on resource allocation. This is the problem of stabilization of the general level of economic activity. If large-scale unemployment of labor and capital exists, we cannot so easily acclaim the efficiency with which the employed resources have been allocated among alternative uses. Or if full employment is accompanied by inflation with its attendant impact on the distribution of income, our economy is not functioning in a wholly admirable fashion. It was necessary, therefore, for us to examine in some detail the determination of national income and aggregate employment of resources. Fluctuations in national money income were shown to be dependent on the spending decisions of individuals, firms, and government. The instability of the total stock of money, due particularly to our system of fractional-reserve banking, was cited as a factor which amplifies economic fluctuations in both directions. And it was pointed out that the existence of all sorts of rigidities in the structure of prices generally means that real national income will fall when there is a decline in national income measured in dollars. This spells unemployment, the most severe of all varieties of economic waste.

In our analysis of the economy in Parts A and B, we found, therefore, that there are three major problems connected with the working of the free-enterprise economy. First there is the problem of income distribution; second, the ubiquitous problem of monopoly; and third, the problem of general economic instability. These clearly suggested our third step, which was to examine the way in which these problems may best be faced. This involved us in a consideration of the government's role in the economy—a matter which we had largely neglected earlier. Government, particularly the Federal government, is the only agency equipped to deal with the problems of distribution, monopoly, and stabilization. Part C was devoted, therefore, to certain aspects of "political economy," a study of the economic impact of government.

The question of the role of government in combating general economic instability was first considered. We observed that there is reason to believe that proper monetary and fiscal policy can do a great deal to prevent both drastic deflation and inflation. There are difficult problems relating to the amount and timing of government action, however, and "politics" plays a part which students of economics should not overlook.

When we came to the monopoly problem, the conclusions as to what the Federal government both should do and can do were not so clear. The vexatious problem is just "how much" competition constitutes workable competition or, obversely, "how much" monopoly we can put up with. Government has not been very successful in its attempts to prevent monopoly in output markets, but neither can its attempts be written off as a complete failure. The main protector of the public interest is the good old force of competition itself. Monopoly, including labor unionism, would not be nearly so troublesome if it did not so often receive a helping hand from government. This is so serious a threat to our economy that we devoted considerable space to a discussion of some of the many ways in which government action has established and encouraged monopoly rather than restricting or prohibiting it. Thus we discussed such measures as resale-price maintenance, farm subsidies, building codes, and tariffs. We must admit, of course, that there are some segments of the economy where competition can never be expected to work. These are the "natural" monopolies, where government ownership or private ownership and government regulation must be resorted to. We outlined some of the pricing principles which are involved in this area.

It should not be overlooked that our whole analysis has been conducted within a static framework—wants, resources, and technology were held constant in order to keep the analysis manageable. This is an especially important reminder in connection with the monopoly problem. Ours is a dynamic, growing economy, and this reduces considerably the threat imposed by monopoly. Technological change, especially, is apt to bring into existence new productive methods and new products which can, at least in part, be substituted for inputs and outputs which are monopolistically priced.

We spent little time on the problem of income redistribution. We emphasized only the essential fact that the fiscal system provides us with a way in which income may be redistributed without disturbing too greatly the operation of the market mechanism. Some of the economic effects of taxes and public expenditures were analyzed, but we did not go into the extremely difficult problem of determining the most desirable distribution of income, which is essentially a matter of ethics rather than of economics.

Where have all this analysis and examination led us? Have we described the way in which the United States economy works at mid-twentieth century? Clearly the answer is no. But this has not been our purpose. Had it been, we would have found it necessary to present several hundred more pages loaded with figures, tables, charts (and even pictures), plus an overwhelming amount of historical and factual comment. And still we should have failed. An adequate description of the economy simply cannot be accomplished within the confines of two hard covers. If not to describe, what has been our purpose? It has been to provide a framework of analysis with which one may make sense out of the descriptions he meets elsewhere. As a businessman, you will face problems of the XYZ industry; you will know from experience the factual background of that industry much better than anyone could tell you in a textbook. So this book, instead of providing factual data concerning many industries, is designed to provide you with a systematic *way of thinking* about the problems of the XYZ industry and its relationship to the total economy. As a congressman, you will know from experience the industrial potential of your district much better than a textbook in economic geography could tell you. So this book is designed to provide you with a systematic *way of thinking* about the problems of your district in its relation to the total economy. As an ordinary citizen, you know the particular background of your job better than any college professor knows it. So this volume is designed to provide you with a systematic *way of thinking* about problems beyond those of your particular job—a way of thinking, for example, about national, state, and local governmental policies which are, and must continue to be, concerns of everyone.

An unlimited number of problems are certain to arise in the years ahead; we have no way of knowing when these will arise, where they will arise, or what will be their nature. The analysis has been designed to provide a rather simple kit of tools which may be applicable to any of many problems. The student who has learned economic analysis may be likened to the mechanic who leaves the garage to repair a broken-down automobile without knowing in advance exactly what is wrong with it. He carries a set of tools which may fit several possible situations. So with economic analysis. The mastery of it should enable you to predict the results of a proposed unfair-trade-practices act in your state, a merger of the main department stores in your town, the closing down of an established plant, an increase in the general wage level, an increase in the interest rate, a decrease in the price of pickles, and a multitude of other possible changes that may occur in the economy, any or all of which may affect you directly or indirectly.

This has been one purpose of this book. But it has not been the only one. Perhaps a more important, albeit less direct, purpose has been that of providing the reader with an appreciation of the free-enterprise, or competitive, system as a means of solving society's economic problem. We believe that the best approach to a genuine appreciation of the free-enterprise system is through an understanding of the manner in which it operates. This book has indicated that the free-enterprise system can operate efficiently and effectively if government is careful to fulfill its proper role, which involves positive action in some areas and deliberate refusal to act in others. And the private-enterprise system operates without restricting individual economic freedom. Free enterprise means essentially the freedom of anyone to set up any enterprise. People freely choose in the market place among goods and services; people choose the work they do; firms choose what, how, and how much to produce.

This broader aspect of the free-enterprise system now requires our attention. It is conceivable that a completely socialist state, in which all or most economic decisions would be centrally made, could prove as "efficient" in practice as the free-enterprise system. (We do not think this would be the case, but let us assume that it might be.) The case for a private-enterprise system would still be strong. The socialist state or other type of centrally planned economy (*e.g.*, the fascist states of Hitler and Mussolini) secures such efficiency as it achieves only at the cost of freedom of the individual. Freedom to change occupations, move from one area to another, and establish new firms is certain to be restricted in a socialist or fascist state. The free-enterprise system is the only one that guarantees a maximum degree of freedom for the individual along with a high degree of productivity efficiency.

Ultimately, therefore, the essential defense of the competitive system lies in its political as well as its economic aspects. It solves the economic problem without undue governmental direction of individuals or firms. It largely removes the whole area of economic decisions from government, allowing such decisions to be made instead by millions of individuals, families, and business units. The competitive system is a scheme of decentralization, a means of removing from the hands of government officials the multifarious economic decisions relating to what, how, and for whom goods are to be produced. As a means of decentralizing economic control, the competitive system can be considered one of the major bulwarks of political democracy. Democracy in the sense of participation in the governing process by the whole body politic can function effectively only if the area of governmental decision is severely restricted. A government that is required to make most of the economic decisions cannot long remain effectively democratic in any meaningful sense. As government becomes more powerful in economic affairs, legislators and administrators are increasingly subjected to pressure by organized groups seeking economic gain. Democratically chosen officials who wield great economic power are especially unlikely to be champions of the rights of the people as a whole. In a fundamental sense, therefore, the competitive economy may be considered a necessary condition for the maintenance of political democracy.

This is so important a point that it should make one highly skeptical of efforts to impose authoritative price, wage, and production controls except under conditions of all-out war. Whenever indirect governmental controls are adequate to the task at hand they should be employed in preference to direct controls over prices, inputs, and outputs. Monetary and fiscal measures have the great advantage of interfering to a minimum extent with the market mechanism, allowing the shifting forces of supply and demand for particular commodities to be reflected in appropriate price adjustments.

There is meaning in the principle of gradualism as applied to government intervention in economic affairs as well as to other spheres of government activity. By pursuing short-run will-o'-the-wisp policies indicated to be desirable by considerations of expediency while neglecting the longer-run effects, we may act to jeopardize the fundamental values of our society. Many ill-conceived economic experiments have a way of leaving quite permanent flaws in our social fabric.

APPENDIXES

APPENDIX A

BASIC ACCOUNTING CONCEPTS

Although an understanding of basic accounting concepts is not entirely necessary to an understanding of economic principles, it is often helpful to use changes in hypothetical accounts as illustrative material—for example, in connection with the expansion of loans and deposits by the banking system. Furthermore, present-day economists are increasingly interested in national accounting. The beginning student is more likely to understand the underlying economic analysis if he is familiar with some fundamentals of accounting.

The simplest form of accounting is the maintenance of a chronological account of financial events as they occur. Another such device is the maintenance of a cash ledger showing all income and outgo of cash but nothing more. Neither device is satisfactory unless the business is an extremely simple one such as that of the newspaper-delivery boy or the individual household. For more complex types of enterprise, "double-entry" bookkeeping is almost universal. This system facilitates the summarization of data, provides internal checks on accuracy, and provides fuller information useful in the determination of policy.

The principle of double-entry bookkeeping is simple; each transaction is recorded in two different accounts. For example, if cash is spent on raw materials, it is not enough merely to record the diminution of the cash balance, but it is also necessary to show the gain in the raw-material inventory. If the raw materials are purchased on credit instead of for cash, there will be an increase in a liability account corresponding to the build-up in the raw-material inventory. If cash is spent for labor, the offsetting gain is actually in the form of labor services received, but the accountant views these services in a negative way as "labor expense." He picks up the value of labor services when he records income from the sale of goods, since the value of goods sold will normally be enhanced by the expenditure on labor employed in their manufacture or distribution.

The two most important accounting statements are the balance sheet and the profit and loss statement. The balance sheet is a "snapshot" picture of the value of the enterprise and its ownership at a particular date, often the last day of the calendar year. Underlying the balance sheet is the simple idea that all valuable things (assets) in the firm must be owned by someone. The "liabilities" of the firm are claims to these assets possessed by persons outside the company who have made loans to the firm (in cash, materials, or other forms); the "net worth" of the owners is the value of assets minus these liabilities. The balance sheet must always balance, since the following equation is always true:

$$\text{Assets} = \text{liabilities} + \text{net worth}$$

Suppose the consolidated balance sheet of a manufacturer on December 31, 1954, is as follows:

3-D TV Corporation
Consolidated Balance Sheet

Assets		*Liabilities and net worth*	
Current Assets:		Current Liabilities:	
Cash	$ 10,000	Accounts payable	$ 30,000
Accounts receivable	40,000	Notes payable	20,000
Raw-material inventory	75,000	Fixed Liabilities:	
Finished-goods inventory	25,000	Mortgage debt	80,000
Fixed Assets:		Bonds payable	20,000
Land	100,000		
Buildings and equipment	250,000	Net worth:	
		Preferred stock	100,000
		Common stock	200,000
		Surplus	50,000
		Total Liabilities and Net	
Total Assets	$500,000	Worth	$500,000

Total assets are valued at $500,000 while liabilities are $150,000. This leaves $350,000 as the net worth, or equity, of stockholders (who are the owners of the corporation). The "capital accounts" of $100,000 in preferred stock and $200,000 in common stock represent the original amounts raised by the sale of these types of securities to the public—they have nothing to do with the current value of the stocks in the security markets. Dividends on common stock depend entirely on profits earned and dividends declared by the directors. Preferred stock carries a fixed dividend rate which, however, has to be paid only when earnings are adequate. Preferred-stock holders usually have no vote at the stockholders' annual meetings. Bond holders are not owners at all, but creditors of the corporation.

As of the date of our balance sheet, the equity of the common-stock holders is not the $200,000 which they originally paid in, but $250,000. This is found by adding the $50,000 "surplus" to their $200,000 original investment. How did this gain in equity arise?

Normally, the additional equity of the common-stock holders, designated by the term "surplus," is built up through the retention ("plowing back") of earnings in the company. The $50,000 surplus on December 31, 1954, does not mean that $50,000 of earnings were retained during the year 1954 but rather that this net amount of profits has been retained in the company over its entire history. It is even possible that 1954 itself was not a profitable year for the corporation.

The other accounts shown in the highly consolidated balance sheet are easier to understand. Assets which are in the form of cash or in a form normally converted into cash within a short period of time are called "current assets." Those less easily converted into cash are designated "fixed assets." It should be noted that only cash can be exactly measured. All other assets are entered at values which are really only educated estimates, although they are usually made on a consistent basis from one balance sheet to the next. Even "accounts receivable," which at first thought seems to be an exactly measurable asset, must be partly estimated, since the extent to which debtors will default on payments is unknown.

There is substantial leeway in the accountant's estimate of the value of a major fixed asset such as "buildings and equipment." A common practice is to carry such assets on the books at original cost and to deduct estimated accumulated depreciation up to the date of the balance sheet. (The $250,000 shown represents value after deduction of depreciation to date.) The accumulated loss of value is usually called "reserve for depreciation"—a rather misleading term, since it suggests but in fact is not a fund of cash or other liquid assets set aside as a "sinking fund" to replace these fixed assets at some future date.

As indicated earlier, the liability accounts represent debts owed by the corporation, both short-term and long-term. These are exactly measurable, since the company does not expect to default on its obligations.

Suppose now that the corporation earns a net profit of $100,000 in the year 1955, the twelve months following the point of time for which the balance sheet just examined was prepared. This profit would appear on the profit and loss statement for 1955 which, in highly condensed form, might look as follows:

3-D TV Corporation
Statement of Profit and Loss, Year 1955

Income from sales		$307,000
Less: cost of goods sold:		
Raw materials and supplies	$70,000	
Wages	80,000	
Depreciation	10,000	
Repairs	5,000	
Less: other costs:		
Salaries	20,000	
Interest paid	12,000	
Insurance	10,000	
Total cost		207,000
Net profit		$100,000

Interpretation of the accounts in the profit and loss statement presents little difficulty except for "depreciation." This may be considered to be an estimate of the amount of service capacity lost by the fixed assets during the year. It would be highly misleading to charge the entire cost of fixed assets to the year in which they happen to be purchased. Consequently, accountants use some rather arbitrary formulas for allocating the cost of durable assets to each year of their estimated usefulness. Frequently they simply divide the original cost of an asset by its expected life in years in order to secure an estimated yearly depreciation to enter in the profit and loss statement. (This is called straight-line depreciation.)

How will the $100,000 net profit earned in 1955 affect the balance sheet when it is drawn up on December 31, 1955? This relationship between the two statements is one of the most important things to learn in acquiring a basic understanding of accounting.

First of all, the net assets of the corporation will be $100,000 greater at the end of 1955 than at the end of 1954. "Net assets" are defined as total assets minus total liabilities. The $100,000 profit must appear in precisely this increase in net assets because the balance sheet is assumed to be drawn up prior to any payments of corporation income taxes or dividends. Since the profit has been earned and is still in the company, it must be reflected in the asset and liability accounts. A large number of different sorts of changes can occur in these accounts which would have the effect of bringing about the $100,000 increase in the difference between total assets and total liabilities. Most frequently, perhaps, assets would be increased (say $80,000) and liabilities decreased ($20,000). If liabilities remained the same, total assets would have to increase $100,000; if assets stayed the same, total liabilities would have to decrease $100,000. Both accounts may go up or both may go down, so long as the end-of-year result is a $100,000 increase in their difference.

Since the $100,000 net profit earned in 1955 has increased the difference between assets and liabilities, the balance sheet will no longer balance unless "surplus," one of the net worth accounts on the right-hand side, is also increased by $100,000. (Like other changes, this increase in surplus would come into the balance sheet through the normal double-entry accounting processes rather than by being entered at the end just to "balance" the statement.) It is, of course, appropriate that the surplus account be increased by $100,000 (to a level of $150,000), since that account reflects the additional equity which common-stock holders have obtained in the corporation over a period of years by virtue of profits which have been earned but retained. The most common error made by those entirely unfamiliar with accounting is the identification of "surplus" with a stock of cash or other liquid wealth in a corporation. It should be clear by now that a company might have a large surplus but very little cash if the managers had found it preferable to hold assets in other forms. Consequently, a corporation with a large surplus account is not necessarily in a position to pay dividends; it may be highly inconvenient to turn other assets into cash, and it will be costly to borrow.

Unfortunately for the common-stock holders, a substantial income tax will be due to the Federal government. Preferred-stock holders must, in addition, receive their dividends before the common-stock dividend, if any, is declared. Suppose Federal taxes of $40,000 are paid and preferred-stock-dividend payments amount to $7,000. The surplus account would then be $103,000. (Original $50,000 + $100,000 − $40,000 − $7,000.) If the board of directors decided to pay no common-stock dividend, the net result of the year's operations from the viewpoint of the common-stock holders would be a $53,000 gain in the net worth of the company which they own. It should not make much difference to the common-stock holders whether dividends are paid or not. In one case they receive the cash payment, but in the other they should benefit about equally by the higher value of their securities in whatever market these prices are quoted. The common-stock holders may, in fact, be better off *not* to receive cash dividends. A stockholder who realizes a profit on the sale of shares may pay a smaller Federal income tax on the gain than he would have paid on a cash dividend, because of the preferential tax treatment given to capital gains (see Chapter 28).

The economist defines profit and cost somewhat differently than does the accountant. Not all of the $100,000 which was earned by the 3-D TV Corporation is economic profit, because the figure includes a certain amount which could, alternatively, have been earned elsewhere on the capital owned by the company. The net worth accounts show that the stockholders owned $350,000 worth of capital in the corporation as of December 31, 1954. Suppose that they could have earned $35,000 in interest on this amount of capital if they had invested it in some other field of comparable riskiness. Then the economic profit for 1955 was $65,000. Above-normal returns would have been earned, and, if this was the case for other firms as well and if there were no restrictions on entry, new firms would be attracted into the production of three-dimension television receivers. The long-run competitive-equilibrium situation would be reached when a sufficient number of new firms had entered to bring economic profit down to zero. At this equilibrium, accounting profit would still exist, however, since corporations would still receive a normal return on equity (ownership) capital.

In the case of small, nonincorporated businesses, the proprietors are likely not to include their own salaries as bookkeeping costs. Accounting profit must then be reduced also by an amount which represents alternative earnings of proprietors if they did not work for themselves. For example, the profit shown on the books of a small filling station might be $4,000 for a particular year. If, however, the owner could have earned $5,000 a year by working for someone else and if the capital which he had invested in the business could, alternatively, have earned $1,000, economic profit would be a negative $2,000. This means that the labor and capital used in the enterprise earned less than normal wage and interest income, and suggests that there is overcapacity in the field.

APPENDIX B

FUNDAMENTAL QUANTITATIVE RELATIONSHIPS

Much of economics is concerned with quantities and their relationships. In many instances these relationships can best be understood if they are treated mathematically. Simple geometry and algebra have been used in the body of this book in an effort to clarify numerous problems. Even this much mathematics could have been avoided, but in many instances that would have required lengthy and cumbrous explanations which would have made the text more difficult (unless the book were deliberately kept simple by the omission of all the difficult problems). By a greater use of mathematics, some of the points discussed in the text may be made more precisely, and, for those who have some knowledge of mathematics beyond algebra and geometry, these matters can more readily be understood if the relationships are expressed in mathematical terms. The purpose of Appendix B is to provide simple mathematical formulations of topics which either were developed in the text in non-mathematical language or were not treated in detail at all. Students with an interest in mathematics and a knack for quantitative analysis should find these notes of considerable help. Even those whose experience with grade-school arithmetic and high-school algebra has (unfortunately and foolishly) convinced them that they do not have "mathematical minds," if they apply themselves to the task with the same determination and energy with which they might approach, say, the learning of a new dance step, may discover that the mathematics required for an understanding of the economic principles developed here is well within the grasp of normal garden-variety human beings.

1. FUNCTIONAL RELATIONSHIPS

Frequently in analyzing economic data it is discovered that one magnitude depends upon another. The total cost of producing automobiles, for example, depends upon the number of automobiles to be produced: the greater the output, the greater the total cost. The two magnitudes—output and cost—are referred to as "variables." As one magnitude varies, the other also varies. It is often convenient to consider one variable as *independent* and the other as *dependent*. We may assume that the output of automobiles is the independent variable and that the cost is the dependent variable. If the output is 1,000 units, the total cost will be, say, $2,000,000; if the output is 10,000 units, the total cost might be $17,000,-000. For every output there is a corresponding total cost.

When magnitudes are related in this way, it is said that one variable is a "function" of the other. The total cost of producing automobiles, for example, is a function of output. If we let C stand for total cost and O stand for output, the statement that total cost is a function of output may be written in this form:

$$C = f(O)$$

The symbol f simply stands for function. The equation does not mean that O is multiplied by f; it is read simply that C is a function of O. The equation does not even tell us whether C and O move in the same or opposite directions. It merely says that for every value of O there is a corresponding value for C.

While it is true that the total cost of producing automobiles is a function of the number of units produced, it is also true that total cost depends upon numerous other factors. A change in the wages paid to laborers in the automobile plant or a change in the price of steel would affect the total cost of automobiles at each output level. We may, accordingly, say that the total cost of automobiles is a function of the wages paid to the plant's employees, and this may be written in symbols as follows:

$$C = g(W)$$

where W represents the wage rate. The symbol g is here used for function instead of f to indicate that the functional relationship between cost and wages is different from that between cost and output.

The fact that total cost is a function of the price of steel may be represented as

$$C = h(P_s)$$

where P_s represents the price of steel. The h symbol indicates that this functional relationship is different from that between either cost and output or cost and wages.

The dependence of cost on all three variables—output, wages, and the price of steel—may be expressed as follows:

$$C = F(O, W, P_s)$$

and this is read: "Cost is a function of output, wages, and the price of steel." If we concentrate on just one functional relationship, *e.g.*, $C = f(O)$, we assume that all other variables, *e.g.*, W and P_s, remain constant. The device of assuming other things unchanged is referred to as the *ceteris paribus* (abbreviated *cet. par.*) assumption. Since in reality the "other things" often do not remain the same, this kind of assumption introduces an element of unreality into the picture. One advantage of the application of mathematics to economic problems is that frequently several variables can be treated simultaneously, whereas without the use of mathematics keeping track of more than two or three variables at a time requires an intellectual endowment that is denied most of us.

Demand as a Functional Relationship between Price and Quantity

We may say that the quantity of commodity X demanded is a function of the price of X. This may be expressed in symbols as $D_x = f(P_x)$. But we know that the amount of commodity X which consumers will take at any price is affected by factors other than its price. Changes in the prices of substitute and complementary goods will affect the consumer's demand for commodity X. Changes in the consumer's income or tastes will also affect his demand for X. All this may be put in the equation:

$$D_x = f(P_x, P_a, P_b, \ldots P_n, Y, T)$$

where P_a, P_b, $\ldots$ P_n represent the prices of other goods, Y is income, and T represents tastes.

When we say that $D_x = f(P_x)$, we are making the *ceteris paribus* assumption that everything else remains the same. But, clearly, if the price of X falls, *everything* cannot remain the same. If the prices of other commodities and the consumer's money income have remained the same, his real income has increased as a result of the decline in the price of X, or, if his real income is held constant, his money income must have fallen or other prices must have increased.

This is not, of course, to argue that, since all other things cannot remain constant as the price of X varies, it is useless to look upon the amount of X demanded as a function of the price of X. But it is important to keep in mind that a change, for example, in money income will change the functional relationship between price and quantity; for each level of assumed income there may be a different quantity demanded at each assumed price.

Particular functional relationships between two variables can be represented graphically. If three variables are used, the graph becomes quite complex, and for more than three variables the graphic technique breaks down completely. Geometry serves us, accordingly, only when the number of variables is restricted and "other things" are assumed to remain constant. More complex problems require the use of the calculus and other more powerful mathematical tools.

Fortunately, many problems in economics can be solved with the use of two variables and the *ceteris paribus* assumption, and they therefore lend themselves to graphic treatment. Let us suppose that the demand of a consumer for commodity X is indicated in the "demand schedule" given in Table B.1.

Table B.1. Demand Schedule

Price	Quantity demanded
$12	0
10	1
8	2
6	3
4	4
2	5
0	6

The demand schedule indicates that for each price listed there is a specific quantity which the consumer would buy during a particular time period. Each set of price and quantity represents alternative combinations.

The data of Table B.1 are plotted graphically in Figure B.1. The quantity demanded is measured on the horizontal or x axis, and the price is measured on the vertical or y axis.

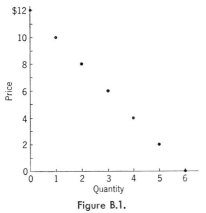

Figure B.1.

Each price-quantity combination in Table B.1 is represented by a dot on Figure B.1. To indicate that if the price of the commodity were $6 the consumer would buy 3 units, we move from the *origin* (the point of intersection of the two axes) to the right (*i.e.*, in the x direction) 3 units and then up 6 units. That locates the point $P = \$6$ and $Q = 3$. Each of the other points representing combinations of price and quantity is similarly plotted.

From the data given in Table B.1, this is all we can do. There is a temptation to draw a smooth curve through the several points and in this way present the "demand curve." But this would assume that, since the consumer would take one unit at a price of $10 and 2 units at a price of $8, he would take $1\frac{1}{2}$ units at a price of $9. This may seem to be a reasonable assumption. But the table does not tell us that it is true. The data in the table are given in *discrete* units, and the graphic representation of the table must, therefore, also be in discrete units.

But suppose that in place of Table B.1 we are given the information that the consumer will buy commodity X on the basis of the equation

$$D_x = 6 - y/2$$

where y = price and D_x = quantity demanded. We can then draw up a demand schedule for any value of y with the corresponding value for x. By assuming various values for y we may derive the demand schedule shown in Table B.2.

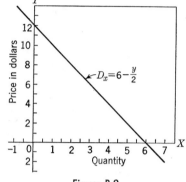

Figure B.2.

Table B.2. Demand Schedule
$D = 6 - y/2$

Price	Quantity demanded
$12	0
10	1
8	2
6	3
4	4
2	5
0	6

It will be noted that this demand schedule is identical with that of Table B.1. The difference is that the second schedule represents points on a continuous curve. By substituting $9 for y in the equation, we see that the quantity demanded is $1\frac{1}{2}$. By making the appropriate substitution we could determine the quantity demanded at any price, e.g., at $8.98. All of the points representing combinations of price and quantity would lie on the straight-line demand curve which has an *intercept* at $12 on the y axis and an intercept of 6 on the x axis. This is shown in Figure B.2.

If we assume a value of $14 for y in our demand function, we find that x has a value of -1. Or, if price is assumed to be $-$2, the quantity demanded would be 7. But since it is unrealistic to assume either that the consumer will buy less than zero units or that the price will be less than zero, we ignore as irrelevant all portions of the demand curve except those lying in the quadrant in which both x and y values are positive.

2. AVERAGE, TOTAL, AND MARGINAL RELATIONSHIPS

We have seen that the equation

$$x = 6 - y/2$$

may be viewed as a demand function if x is the quantity demanded and y is price. By multiplying both sides of the equation by 2, we get

$$2x = 12 - y$$

This may be written

$$y = 12 - 2x$$

In this form we are saying that $y = f(x)$, whereas in the original equation we had expressed x as a function of y. Table B.2 and Figure B.2 represent the data for the new expression as well as for the old. When we say that y is a function of x, we are saying that the price which the seller can get for the commodity depends upon the number of units he sells per time period. The price per unit sold represents to the seller his *average revenue;* if he sells three units at $6 each, his revenue per unit is $6. If we measure average revenue on the y axis, we may write the equation for average revenue as follows:

$$AR = y = 12 - 2x$$

where AR is average revenue. When plotted, the average revenue curve is seen to be the same as the demand curve in Figure B.2. Demand and average revenue, then, are the same thing from slightly different points of view.

Suppose that we are interested in knowing what the total revenue would be at any price. If we know the revenue per unit (price) and the number of units that can be sold at each price, we can determine the total revenue by multiplying average revenue by the quantity sold. In this way the total revenue column of Table B.3 is determined.

Table B.3. Average and Total Revenue

Average revenue	Quantity demanded	Total revenue
$12	0	$ 0
10	1	10
8	2	16
6	3	18
4	4	16
2	5	10
0	6	0

It will be noted that the total revenue starts at zero, increases for a time as average revenue (price) decreases, reaches a maximum of $18 when price is $6, and then decreases as price decreases.

Since total revenue is average revenue multiplied by quantity sold, and since the quantity sold is x in the equation, total revenue is x times average revenue. Since average revenue is $12 - 2x$, total revenue is given by the equation

$$TR = x(12 - 2x)$$
$$= 12x - 2x^2$$

where TR is total revenue. By substituting values from zero to 6 for x in this equation, it will be seen that the total revenue will be that indicated in Table B.3. The total revenue and average revenue functions are plotted in Figure B.3.

The determination of marginal revenue introduces a complexity which we have not previously met with in this section. Marginal revenue has been defined in the text as the additional revenue resulting from the production of an additional unit of output. If, for example, we are currently selling two units of commodity X per time period, the average revenue function tells us that each unit can be sold for $8, and our total revenue will, accordingly, be $16. If we now wish to increase sales to three units,

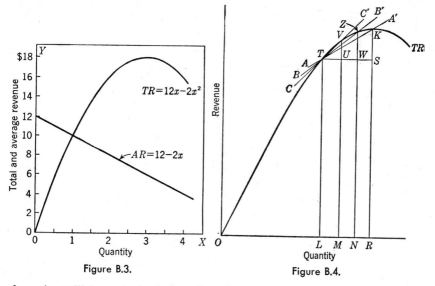

Figure B.3.

Figure B.4.

the price will have to be lowered to $6, total revenue will be $18, and marginal revenue will be $2. But marginal revenue might just as well have been defined as the reduction in total revenue resulting from selling one less unit per time period. If sales were reduced from two to one, price would be $10, total revenue would be $10, and marginal revenue computed in this way would be $6. Either method is only an approximation which may be close enough for most purposes, but it is possible to measure marginal revenue precisely at any output, as will be demonstrated below.

In Figure B.4, TR is the total revenue curve. If the quantity sold is OL, total revenue is LT. Suppose that sales are now increased to OR; total revenue will be RK. The increase in sales LR has resulted in an increase in revenue of SK. The marginal revenue, then, is $SK \div TS$ ($TS = LR$). If the increase in total revenue is represented by ΔR (the symbol Δ—pronounced *delta*—means simply a change, an increase if positive and a decrease if negative), and if the increase in total quantity sold is represented by ΔQ, marginal revenue is represented by $\Delta R/\Delta Q$. The line AA' is drawn through the points T and K. This means that the slope of AA' (slope is defined as $\Delta y/\Delta x$—in this case, SK/TS) is equal to marginal revenue as output increases from OL to OR.

Suppose now that output is increased by a smaller amount, from OL to ON. Marginal revenue would then be WZ/TW = slope of BB', which is drawn through points T and Z. Similarly, if output is assumed to increase from OL to OM, the marginal revenue is equal to the slope of CC'. It will be noted that as the increase in sales (ΔQ) is assumed to be smaller

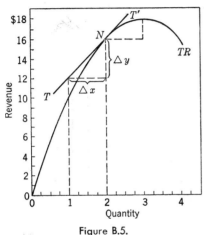

Figure B.5.

and smaller, marginal revenue is equal to the slope of a line which approaches nearer and nearer the tangent to the TR curve at point T. We may say, therefore, that the marginal revenue at any output is equal to the slope of the tangent to the total revenue curve at that output. In Figure B.5, the marginal revenue at output 2 is the slope of TT', which is tangent to the TR curve at N. The slope of $TT' = \Delta y/\Delta x = \frac{4}{1} = 4$. The difference between this measure of marginal revenue and that which would result if marginal revenue were measured between discrete units may be indicated by noting that if output were assumed to increase from one to two, total revenue would increase from 10 to 16, *i.e.*, marginal revenue would be indicated as 6.

The general relationship between marginal, total, and average revenue can be indicated by the use of the calculus. Marginal revenue represents the *rate of change* of the total revenue as x increases, and the marginal revenue function is called the *first derivative* of the total revenue function. If the total revenue function is

$$TR = 12x - 2x^2$$

the rules of the calculus tell us that the marginal revenue function is

$$MR = 12 - 4x$$

Total, average, and marginal revenue are plotted in Figure B.6. It will be noted that at any output marginal revenue is less than average revenue. This must always be true when average revenue is decreasing; in order to "bring the average down," marginal must be less than average. Marginal revenue is equal to zero at the output where total revenue is at a maximum; when marginal revenue is positive, total revenue is increasing, and, when marginal revenue is negative, total revenue is decreasing.

The relationship between average revenue and marginal revenue can also be demonstrated with the use of elementary geometry. In Figure B.7, DD' may be viewed either as the average revenue (demand) curve and TT' as the tangent to the average revenue curve at S or TT' may be assumed to be a linear (straight-line) demand curve. If TT' is the demand

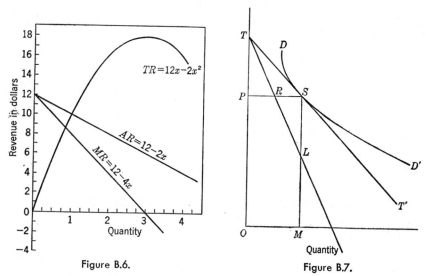

Figure B.6.   Figure B.7.

curve, it may be demonstrated that the line TL drawn through T and bisecting any horizontal line drawn from the y axis to the demand curve is the corresponding marginal revenue curve. If output is OM, price will be OP, and total revenue will be indicated by the equation

$$TR = OP \cdot OM = OPSM$$

But total revenue is also equal to the area under the marginal revenue curve (the sum of the revenues added by all the units sold will equal total revenue). Total revenue is, therefore, equal to

$$TR = OTLM$$
$$\therefore OPSM = OTLM$$

But

$$OPSM = OPRLM + RSL$$

and

$$OTLM = OPRLM + PTR$$
$$\therefore RSL = PTR \text{ in area}$$

But
$$\angle TPR = \angle RSL$$
and
$$\angle PRT = \angle SRL$$
$$\therefore \angle PTR = \angle RLS$$
and
$$RSL \cong PTR$$
$$\therefore PR = RS$$

We may generalize by saying that if the average revenue curve is linear, the marginal revenue curve will also be a straight line beginning at the intercept of the average revenue curve on the y axis and bisecting any horizontal line drawn from the y axis to the average revenue curve. If the average revenue curve is nonlinear (*e.g.*, DD'), the marginal revenue *at any output* can be determined by drawing a tangent to the curve at that output and treating the tangent as if it were the average revenue curve. In Figure B.7, the marginal revenue at output OM is ML. To determine the marginal revenue at any other output (assuming that DD' is the average revenue curve), a tangent to the curve would have to be drawn at that output and the process repeated.

3. PRICE ELASTICITY OF DEMAND AND SUPPLY

By the elasticity of demand is meant the percentage change in quantity demanded divided by the percentage change in price. If, for example, a 1 per cent drop in price is followed by a 1 per cent increase in the quantity demanded, elasticity of demand is equal to 1; if a 1 per cent drop in price is followed by more than a 1 per cent increase in the quantity demanded, elasticity is greater than 1; and if a 1 per cent drop in price is followed by a less than 1 per cent increase in the quantity demanded, elasticity is less than 1.

The elasticity formula for a linear demand function may be put in the form of the following equation:

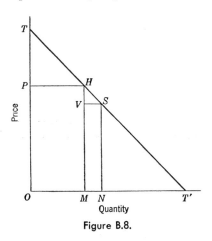

Figure B.8.

$$E_d = \frac{\Delta x/x}{\Delta y/y}$$

where E_d is elasticity of demand, x is quantity demanded, and y is price. Through the use of Figure B.8 the formula may be simplified as follows:

$$E_d = \frac{\Delta x/x}{\Delta y/y} = \frac{MN/OM}{VH/MH} = \frac{MN}{OM} \cdot \frac{MH}{VH} = \frac{VS}{OM} \cdot \frac{MH}{VH} = \frac{VS}{VH} \cdot \frac{MH}{OM}$$

$$= \frac{PH}{PT} \cdot \frac{MH}{OM} = \frac{OM}{PT} \cdot \frac{OP}{OM}$$

$$= \frac{OP}{PT}$$

$$= \frac{T'H}{HT}$$

$$= \frac{MT'}{OM}$$

The elasticity of demand at any price is indicated by OP/PT; the elasticity of demand at any output is indicated by MT'/OM. If P falls midway between O and T, $E_d = 1$; at any higher price elasticity is greater than 1, and at any lower price elasticity is less than 1. It will be noted that a straight-line demand curve, such as TT', will have a different elasticity at every price. And any straight-line demand curve with an intercept at T on the y axis will have the same elasticity as TT' at any given price regardless of the relative slopes of the two curves. By referring to Figure B.6, it can be seen that, when $E_d = 1$, marginal revenue is zero and total revenue is at a maximum.

A general formula for elasticity, which applies to nonlinear as well as linear demand curves, substitutes the symbol d for $\Delta : \frac{dx/x}{dy/y}$. The symbol d represents a change which is infinitesimally small.

The formula for elasticity of supply (E_s) may be developed with the use of Figure B.9.

$$E_s = \frac{\Delta x/x}{\Delta y/y} = \frac{MN/OM}{VR/MW} = \frac{MN}{OM} \cdot \frac{MW}{VR} = \frac{WR}{OM} \cdot \frac{MW}{VR}$$

$$= \frac{WR}{VR} \cdot \frac{MW}{OM} = \frac{PW}{PT} \cdot \frac{MW}{OM} = \frac{OM}{PT} \cdot \frac{OP}{OM}$$

$$= \frac{OP}{PT}$$

$$= \frac{AW}{TW}$$

$$= \frac{AM}{OM}$$

If the supply curve has a positive intercept on the y axis, as in Figure B.9, E_s will be greater than 1. If the supply curve has a positive intercept on the x axis, as in Figure B.10, E_s will be less than 1. If a straight-line supply curve passes through the origin, as in Figure B.11, E_s will be equal to 1 at any price. If either the demand curve or the supply curve is nonlinear, elasticity at any price can be determined by drawing a tangent to the curve at that price, extending the tangent to the y axis at T, and measuring elasticity at that price as OP/PT. If the curve has a negative slope, *e.g.*, a demand curve, elasticity will be negative, and if the curve has a positive slope, *e.g.*, a supply curve, the elasticity will be positive.

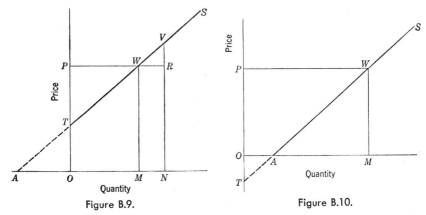

Figure B.9.   Figure B.10.

For most purposes, however, the algebraic sign of the coefficient of elasticity of a curve is ignored; *e.g.*, an elasticity of demand of -4 is considered to be greater than an elasticity of -3.

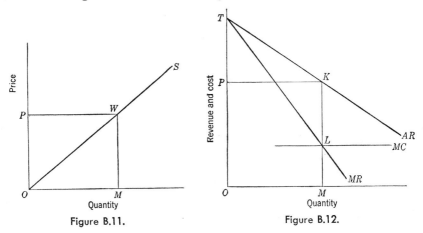

Figure B.11.   Figure B.12.

The relationship between elasticity of demand and the retailer's markup can be shown with the use of Figure B.12. If we let e stand for elasticity of demand, then

$$e = \frac{OP}{PT} = \frac{MK}{KL} = \frac{MK}{MK - ML}$$

Let p = optimum (profit-maximizing) price (MK)
and m = marginal cost at optimum output (ML).

Then

$$e = \frac{p}{p - m}$$
$$e(p - m) = p$$
$$ep - em = p$$
$$ep - p = em$$
$$p(e - 1) = em$$
$$p = \frac{em}{e - 1}$$
$$p = m \left(\frac{e}{e - 1} \right)$$

If elasticity of demand is 2 in the relevant range, profit maximizing price is

$$p = m \left(\frac{2}{2 - 1} \right) = 2m$$

That is to say, if the retailer's rule of thumb says to apply a 100 per cent markup to his cost price, the rule assumes that elasticity of demand is 2; if elasticity of demand is not 2, a 100 per cent markup is not the appropriate markup to maximize profits. In this way merchants who know nothing about the concept of elasticity implicitly make use of it nonetheless.

Figure B.12 may also be used to show that a firm with positive marginal costs will always sell at a price at which elasticity of demand is greater than 1. Let m this time represent marginal revenue (mr and mc are equal when profit is maximized).

Then

$$e = \frac{p}{p - m}$$
$$e(p - m) = p$$
$$ep - em = p$$
$$-em = p - ep$$
$$m = \frac{ep - p}{e}$$
$$m = p \left(1 - \frac{1}{e} \right)$$

If $e = 1$, marginal revenue (and therefore marginal cost) at profit-maximizing price is zero. If $e < 1$, marginal revenue (and marginal cost) is less than zero. These relationships may be confirmed by reference to Figure B.6. If a firm sells at a price at which elasticity of demand is less than 1, it could increase profits simply by reducing output and thereby increasing total revenue.

4. PROFIT-MAXIMIZING OUTPUT

Suppose that a given firm has the total revenue function given by the following equation:

$$TR = 12x - 2x^2$$

and the total cost function indicated by

$$TC = x^3 - 4x^2 + 8x + 4$$

where x is output. It will be noted that the firm's total cost at output zero would be 4; this is the total fixed cost. The rest of the cost function, $x^3 - 4x^2 + 8x$, represents total variable cost; it assumes a different value for each value of x. The total revenue and total cost functions are plotted in Figure B.13.

If the firm's object is to maximize profits, it will operate at the output where the difference between total revenue and total cost is a maximum,

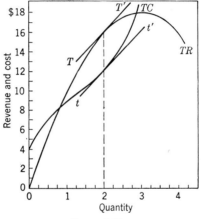

Figure B.13.

i.e., where the vertical distance between the TR and TC curves is a maximum. This appears from inspection to be at output 2. It will be noted that the tangent to the TR curve at output 2, TT', has the same slope as the tangent to the TC curve at that output, tt'. But the slope of the tangent to the total revenue curve is equal to marginal revenue, and the slope of the tangent to the total cost curve is equal to marginal cost. Since the slope of TT' equals the slope of tt', marginal revenue equals marginal cost, and profits are therefore maximized at an output of 2.

The same result follows if we analyze the problem in terms of average and marginal functions. We have seen that if total revenue is equal to

$12x - 2x^2$ the equations for marginal revenue and average revenue will be given by the following:

$$AR = 12 - 2x$$
$$MR = 12 - 4x$$

Similarly, if the total cost function is $x^3 - 4x^2 + 8x + 4$, average total cost and marginal cost will be

$$ATC = x^2 - 4x + 8 + \frac{4}{x}$$
$$MC = 3x^2 - 8x + 8$$

The average revenue, marginal revenue, average total cost, and marginal cost curves are plotted in Figure B.14. It will be noted that the most profitable output, *i.e.*, where $MC = MR$, is 2 units. The average cost per unit at this output is $6 and the selling price is $8, which provides a total profit of $4. This confirms the conclusion reached in connection with

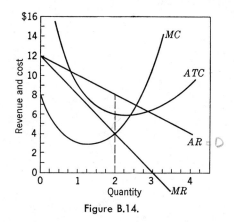

Figure B.14.

Figure B.13, where, with an output of 2 units, total revenue was $16 and total cost was $12.

A third, and still more general, solution of the problem of determining the output providing maximum profit may be indicated algebraically. We know the marginal revenue function and the marginal cost function, and at the maximum profit output these two will be equal. We may then set these equations equal to each other and solve for x:

$$MR = MC$$
$$12 - 4x = 3x^2 - 8x + 8$$
$$3x^2 - 4x - 4 = 0$$
$$(3x + 1)(x - 2) = 0$$
$$x = -\tfrac{1}{3}$$
$$x = 2$$

Since output cannot be less than zero, profits will be maximized when output is 2.

5. NATIONAL-INCOME CONCEPTS

National income may be considered from either of two points of view. If we are interested in the source of national income, we may say that it is the result of expenditures on consumer goods and expenditures on investment goods. Since all goods are classified either as consumer goods or investment goods, we may write

$$Y = C + I$$

where Y is national income, C is expenditure on consumption goods, and I is expenditure on investment goods. We may, on the other hand, wish to indicate how income recipients dispose of their incomes. Since saving means not spending, the consumer has the choice of spending or not spending, *i.e.*, saving, and we may write

$$Y = C + S$$

where S represents saving. But since

$$Y = C + I$$

and

$$Y = C + S$$

it follows that $S = I$, *i.e.*, the amount actually saved must equal the amount actually invested.

When a consumer receives additional income, he will spend a part and save a part of the additional income. We may write

$$\Delta Y = \Delta C + \Delta S$$

where the Δ sign indicates the amount of the increment of each magnitude. The ratio of additional consumption to the additional income is called the marginal propensity to consume, and it may be written

$$MPC = \frac{\Delta C}{\Delta Y}$$

Similarly, the marginal propensity to save may be written

$$MPS = \frac{\Delta S}{\Delta Y}$$

Since $\Delta Y = \Delta C + \Delta S$, it follows that

$$\frac{\Delta C}{\Delta Y} + \frac{\Delta S}{\Delta Y} = MPC + MPS = 1$$

When a new investment is made, the investment expenditure generates additional income. The ratio of the additional income to the additional investment is called the income multiplier. If we let M represent the multiplier, we may write

$$M = \frac{\Delta Y}{\Delta I}$$

If we assume that the change in income generates no secondary repercussions on investment, this equation may be simplified as follows:

$$M = \frac{\Delta Y}{\Delta I} = \frac{\Delta Y}{\Delta Y - \Delta C} = \frac{\Delta Y/\Delta Y}{\Delta Y/\Delta Y - \Delta C/\Delta Y} = \frac{1}{1 - MPC} = \frac{1}{MPS}$$

If, for example, $MPC = \frac{9}{10}$, $M = \frac{1}{1 - \frac{9}{10}} = 10$; *i.e.*, for each dollar of new investment national income would be increased by $10.

A more general formulation which takes into account possible income-induced changes in investment may be shown as follows. If ΔI_p represents the primary or initial change in investment and ΔI_i the induced change in investment,

$$M = \frac{\Delta Y}{\Delta I_p}$$

$$= \frac{\Delta Y}{\Delta Y - \Delta C - \Delta I_i}$$

$$= \frac{1}{1 - [(\Delta C + \Delta I_i)/\Delta Y]}$$

$$= \frac{1}{1 - MPX}$$

where MPX represents the marginal propensity to spend. If ΔI_i is zero, this formulation is identical with that given above.

APPENDIX C

THE FIRM AS A BUYER OF INPUTS
AND A SELLER OF OUTPUTS

In Part A we were concerned with the pricing of outputs (products) and inputs (factors of production) in output and input markets. The forces affecting prices were analyzed in some detail, and it was discovered that either type of market might be either competitive or monopolistic on either the buying or the selling side. That is to say, both input and output markets might be characterized by (1) competitive buyers and competitive sellers, (2) competitive buyers and monopolistic sellers, (3) monopsonistic buyers and competitive sellers, or, finally, (4) monopsonistic buyers and monopolistic sellers.

Whether a particular market is an input market or an output market is frequently simply a matter of point of view, since the output of some firms is the input of others. Sheet steel, as was pointed out in an early chapter, is an output of the steel industry but an input of the automobile industry; flour is an output of a milling firm but an input to the bakery. This is made abundantly clear in the input-output table of Chapter 2.

All ambiguity as to whether a given market is an input market or an output market is removed if we assume the point of view of a particular firm. In this appendix we are looking upon the firm as a buyer of inputs and a seller of outputs. Firms, like input and output markets, may be classified under four headings. They may (1) buy inputs competitively and sell outputs competitively, (2) buy inputs competitively and sell outputs monopolistically, (3) buy inputs monopsonistically and sell outputs competitively, or (4) buy inputs monopsonistically and sell outputs monopolistically. Each of these cases will be examined in turn.

The point was made repeatedly in Part A that a firm must, if it is to maximize profits, equate marginal cost and marginal revenue. If we are concerned with determining the output which will maximize profits, the rule is that a firm should produce to the point at which

$$MC_o = MR_o$$

where the subscripts refer to output. But since each output decision implies an input decision, the rule may also be stated in terms of inputs: To maximize profits, the firm must employ all factors to the point at which

$$MC_i = MRP$$

where the subscript refers to input and MRP represents marginal revenue product. If the firm is producing to the point where $MC_o = MR_o$, it will be employing inputs to the point where $MC_i = MRP$. Since in the text the analysis has run sometimes in terms of output and sometimes in terms of input, we shall here bring together the two views of the firm to indicate that either approach leads to the same conclusion.

BUYING AND SELLING IN PURELY COMPETITIVE MARKETS

If a firm sells outputs in a purely competitive market, its average revenue (demand) curve will be a horizontal line, and, accordingly, its marginal revenue will be represented by the same horizontal line. The intersection of the marginal revenue and marginal cost curves will determine

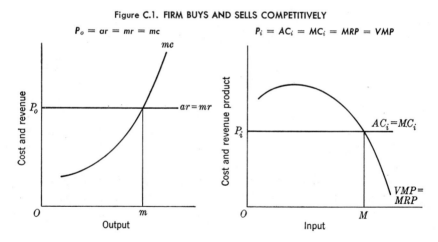

Figure C.1. FIRM BUYS AND SELLS COMPETITIVELY

the most profitable output, Om in Figure C.1. Price, of course, is determined in the market and must be accepted as a datum by the firm.

The right-hand side of Figure C.1 indicates the most profitable number of inputs to be hired by the firm which buys and sells competitively. Since the firm is assumed to be buying competitively, it can buy as many inputs as it needs at the going rate, OP_i; its average input cost and marginal input cost are represented by a single horizontal line. And since the firm is selling in a purely competitive market, it can increase its sales of output without affecting the selling price; marginal revenue product and the value of the marginal product are, therefore, equal at all inputs. If the firm maximizes profits, it will hire inputs until marginal input cost and marginal revenue product are equal; OM is optimum input in Figure C.1. This implies that in order to produce Om units of output the firm must employ OM units of input. The profit-maximizing condition is that $mr = mc$ or that $MRP = MC_i$; if marginal cost equals marginal revenue, marginal revenue product must equal marginal input cost.[1]

BUYING COMPETITIVELY AND SELLING MONOPOLISTICALLY

Next we consider the firm which buys competitively and sells monopolistically. Since the firm sells monopolistically, its average revenue (demand) curve is negatively inclined, and the marginal revenue curve lies

Figure C.2. FIRM BUYS COMPETITIVELY AND SELLS MONOPOLISTICALLY

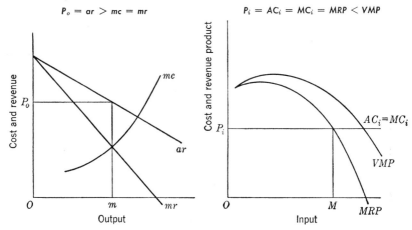

$P_o = ar > mc = mr$

$P_i = AC_i = MC_i = MRP < VMP$

below average revenue (price). The most profitable output is determined by the intersection of the marginal revenue and marginal cost curves, which in terms of Figure C.2 is Om with a price of OP_o. Or, alternately,

---

[1] This may be demonstrated as follows:
Let MP = marginal physical product

$$MC_o = \frac{MC_i}{MP} \quad \text{and} \quad MR_o = \frac{MRP}{MP}$$

Then if $MC_o = MR_o$

$$\frac{MC_i}{MP} = \frac{MRP}{MP}$$

and

$$MC_i = MRP$$

These relations hold whether the firm is buying competitively or monopsonistically and selling competitively or monopolistically.

the firm's most profitable rate of operations can be determined in input terms. Since the firm buys competitively, its average input cost and marginal input cost curves will have the same form as those in the first case. But since the firm sells monopolistically, it will have to lower price in order to increase its volume of sales; this means that the sale of additional units of output will add less to the firm's total revenue than the value of the additional output sold, since the revenue on the original output will be reduced by virtue of the lowered price at which all units now sell. In graphic terms this is represented by a marginal revenue product curve which lies below the value of the marginal product curve.[1] In Figure C.2, the firm should employ OM units of input, since at this input marginal input cost equals marginal revenue product.

BUYING MONOPSONISTICALLY AND SELLING COMPETITIVELY

Our third model assumes that the firm buys monopsonistically and sells competitively. Since the firm sells in a competitive market, its average revenue and marginal revenue curves are represented as a single horizontal line. But since the firm buys monopsonistically, it will have to increase the payment to input units as more of them are hired. This has the effect of causing the marginal cost curve to slope upward more steeply. In Figure C.3, the most profitable output is Om, which is determined by the intersection of the marginal revenue curve and the monopsony marginal cost curve (mc_m).

If we are interested in analyzing the most profitable scale of operations for the firm in input terms, we will note that since the firm is buying monopsonistically its average input cost curve is positively inclined and its marginal input cost curve, accordingly, lies above the average input cost curve. Since the firm sells competitively, marginal revenue product and value of the marginal product are equal. The most profitable input is

---

[1] The relationship between marginal revenue product and the value of the marginal prouct may be demonstrated as follows:

Let P = the original price of output, X = the original output, P' = the new lower price, X' = the new larger output, ΔP = the change in price, and ΔX = the change in output.

$$\begin{aligned} MRP &= P'X' - PX \\ &= P'(X + \Delta X) - X(P' + \Delta P) \\ &= P'X + P'\Delta X - P'X - \Delta PX \\ &= P'\Delta X - \Delta PX \end{aligned}$$

$P'\Delta X$ is the value of the marginal product. If the firm sells competitively, $\Delta P = O$; marginal revenue product and the value of the marginal product are therefore equal. If, however, the firm sells monopolistically, marginal revenue product is less than the value of the marginal product by the amount of ΔPX.

OM, where $MRP = MC_i$. The price of each input unit will be OP_i as determined by the point on the AC_i curve just above M.

Figures C.3 and C.4 are not to be interpreted as implying that the marginal output cost of a firm which buys monopsonistically is greater than the marginal cost of another firm which buys competitively. The mc_m curve indicates that in addition to the normal factors which would

Figure C.3. FIRM BUYS MONOPSONISTICALLY AND SELLS COMPETITIVELY

$P_o = ar = mr = mc_m > mc_c$ $\qquad\qquad$ $P_i = AC_i < MC_i = MRP = VMP$

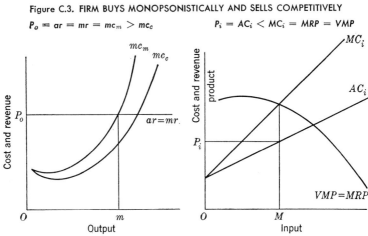

cause marginal costs to rise as output increases, which are reflected in the mc_c curve, marginal costs also rise because of the necessity of taking into account the payment of higher and higher prices as more units of input are employed. For this reason the monopsonistic firm's output will be restricted to a greater extent than it would be if the production of additional output did not require the payment of higher prices to all input units.

BUYING MONOPSONISTICALLY AND SELLING MONOPOLISTICALLY

Our final model assumes that the firm both buys and sells in monopolistic markets. Its revenue curves will therefore be the same as those in the second model, and its cost curves will be like those in the third case. The average revenue curve in Figure C.4 slopes downward, and the marginal revenue curve lies below it. Monopsony marginal cost lies above competitive marginal cost. The most profitable output is Om, where $mr = mc_m$. In output terms, the monopsonistic control of the buying firm over input price causes its marginal cost curve to slope upward more rapidly than would be the case if inputs were purchased at uniform prices. In Figure C.4, mc_m represents the marginal cost curve of the monopsonist, and profit-maximizing output is Om.

On the input side, marginal input cost lies above average input cost, and the marginal revenue product lies below the value of the marginal product. The most profitable input for this firm is OM, which is determined by the intersection of the MC_i and the MRP curves. The price of the input factor is OP_i, which is determined by the point on the AC_i curve above point M.

Figure C.4. FIRM BUYS MONOPSONISTICALLY AND SELLS MONOPOLISTICALLY

$P_o = ar > mr = mc_m > mc_c$ $P_i = AC_i < MC_i = MRP < VMP$

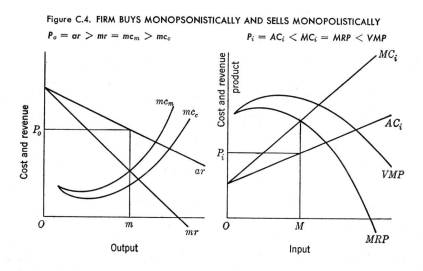

INPUT EQUILIBRIUM

We have considered the manner in which a firm in all possible market situations determines its optimum input of a particular type of factor, using the assumption that all other inputs are given. The firm actually has the problem, especially in the long run, of securing simultaneously the optimal (least-cost) combination of *all* types of inputs. This is achieved when the ratio of marginal physical product to marginal input cost is equated for each type of input. Algebraically, this can be stated as follows:

$$\frac{MP_a}{MC_a} = \frac{MP_b}{MC_b} = \frac{MP_c}{MC_c} \cdot \cdot \cdot = \frac{MP_n}{MC_n}$$

the subscripts designating the particular types of inputs.

It may be seen that when the firm has purchased *each* input to the point where marginal revenue product equals marginal input cost, as developed in the four models, the least-cost combination of inputs is attained. This may be shown as follows:

$$MRP = MC_i$$

Substituting $MR_o \cdot MP_i$ for MRP, we obtain

$$MR_o \cdot MP_i = MC_i$$

$$MR_o = \frac{MC_i}{MP_i}$$

$$\frac{MP_i}{MC_i} = \frac{1}{MR_o}$$

If

$$\frac{MP_a}{MC_a} = \frac{1}{MR_o} \quad \text{and} \quad \frac{MP_b}{MC_b} = \frac{1}{MR_o}$$

then it follows that

$$\frac{MP_a}{MC_a} = \frac{MP_b}{MC_b}$$

If inputs are hired competitively, marginal input cost and price are equal and the least-cost combination has been attained when

$$\frac{MP_a}{P_a} = \frac{MP_b}{P_b} = \frac{MP_c}{P_c} \cdots = \frac{MP_n}{P_n}$$

SUMMARY

The four models considered in this appendix are useful in analyzing the effects of monopoly, whether on the buying or on the selling side, on the allocation of resources. The ideal, or normative, case may be taken to be the situation in which the firm both buys and sells competitively. In this case the average input cost curve represents the firm's supply of inputs curve, and the value of the marginal product is the firm's demand for inputs curve. The number of units employed is determined by the intersection of the supply and demand curves, and the input factors receive the full value of their marginal product. By employing inputs to the point where $MC_i = MRP$, the firm not only maximizes its profits but also employs just enough inputs to make the average input cost equal to the value of the marginal product; that is to say, resources are allocated in accordance with consumer preferences, since the value which consumers have attached to the marginal product of the factor employed is just equal to the marginal cost of the firm producing those units of output.

When monopoly elements appear on either the buying or the selling side, however, resources are not allocated optimally. The allocation of resources in accordance with consumer preferences requires that the firm employ input factors as long as the average input cost to the firm is less than the value attached by consumers to the marginal product of the input factors; *i.e.*, the firm should employ inputs to the point where $AC_i = VMP$. It will be noted in Figures C.2 and C.3 that the firm which is buying or selling monopolistically will maximize profits by using less than the socially optimum number of inputs. And if the firm is both buying and selling monopolistically, the number of inputs employed, and consequently the number of output units sold, will be restricted from both causes. It is for this reason that the economist takes the perfectly competitive case as the normative case and views monopoly in much the same way that the preacher contemplates sin. As was pointed out in Part C, public policy in areas where pure competition is impracticable, *e.g.*, the public utilities, should be directed toward attaining in so far as possible the results which would obtain if the industry were competitive.

INDEX